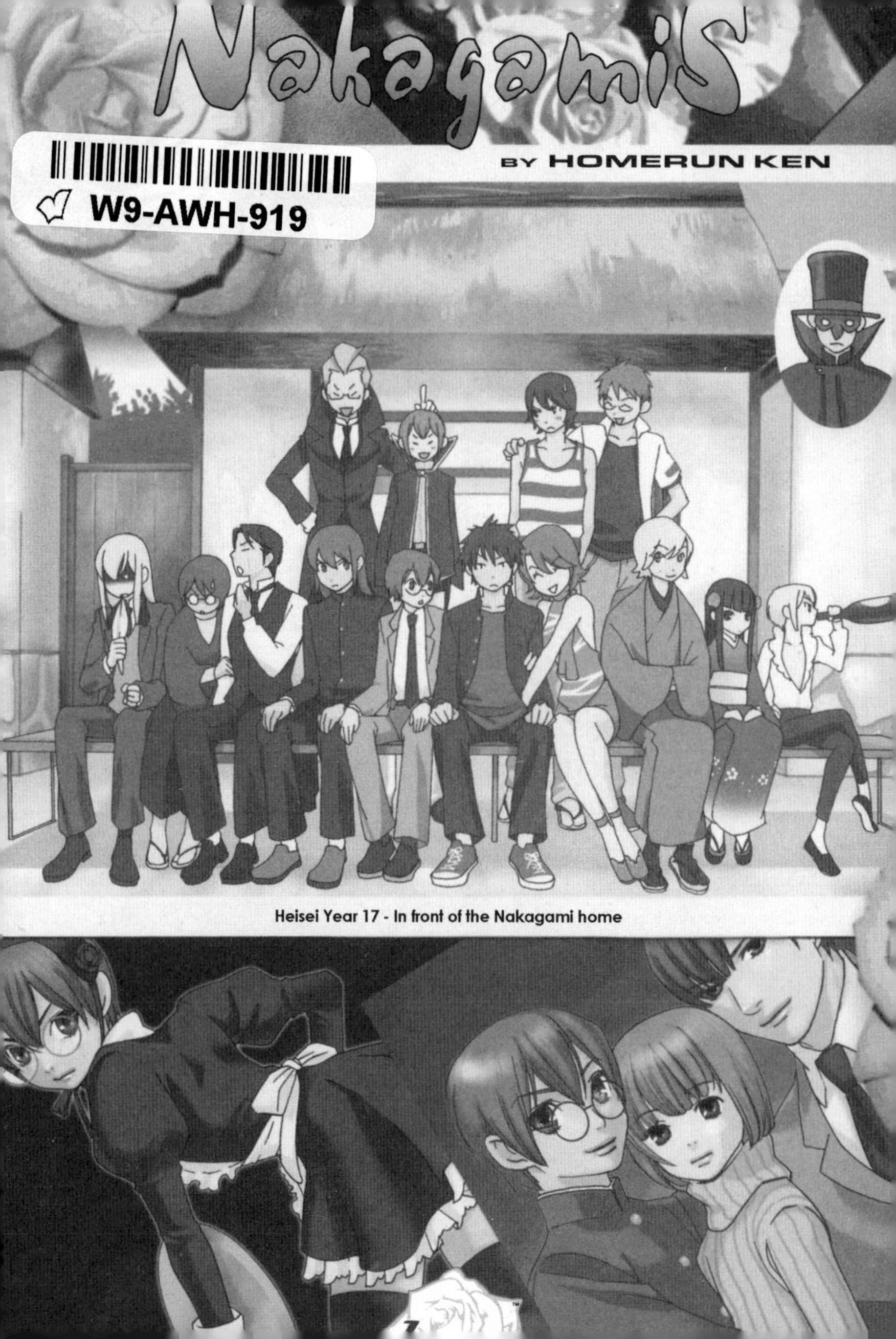
Nakagamis
BY HOMERUN KEN
Heisei Year 17 - In front of the Nakagami home

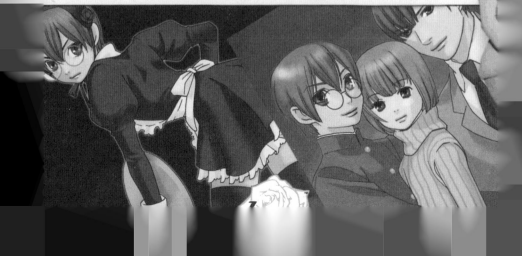

Clan of the Nakagamis

CONTENTS

Translation — Sachiko Sato

Graphic Design — Fred Lui/Eric Rosenberger

Lettering — Pat Duke

Will Allison

Editing — Elin Winkler

Editor in Chief — Fred Lui

Publisher — Hikaru Sasahara

English Edition Published by
DIGITAL MANGA PUBLISHING
A division of DIGITAL MANGA, Inc.
1487 W 178th Street, Suite 300
Gardena, CA 90248

www.dmpbooks.com

First Edition: May 2006
ISBN: 1-56970-896-7

10 9 8 7 6 5 4 3 2 1

Printed in China

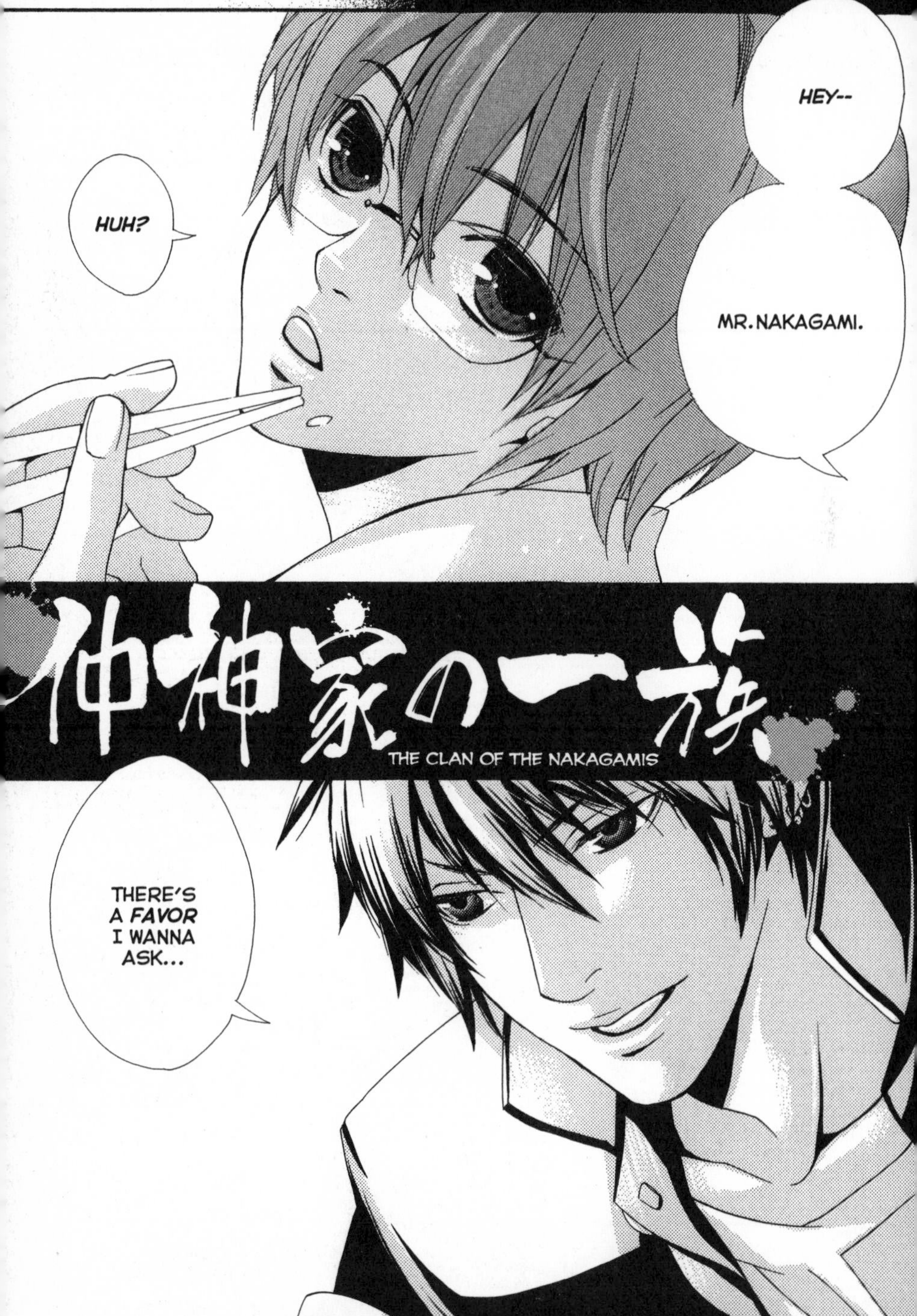
HEY--
MR.NAKAGAMI.
HUH?
仲神家の一族
THE CLAN OF THE NAKAGAMIS
THERE'S A FAVOR I WANNA ASK...

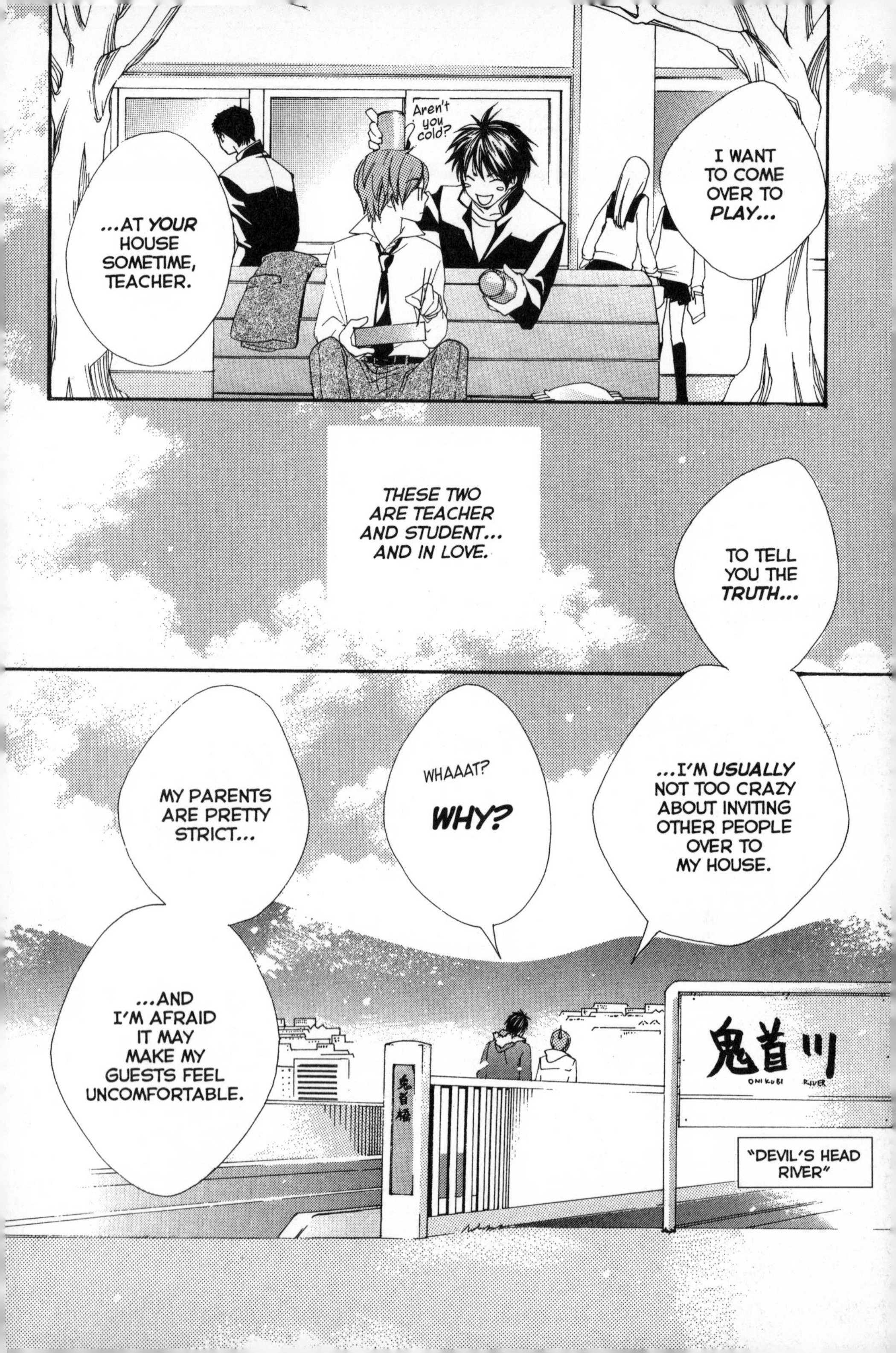
I WANT TO COME OVER TO *PLAY*...
Aren't you cold?
...AT *YOUR* HOUSE SOMETIME, TEACHER.
THESE TWO ARE TEACHER AND STUDENT... AND IN LOVE.
TO TELL YOU THE *TRUTH*...
...I'M *USUALLY* NOT TOO CRAZY ABOUT INVITING OTHER PEOPLE OVER TO MY HOUSE.
WHAAAT?
WHY?
MY PARENTS ARE PRETTY STRICT...
...AND I'M AFRAID IT MAY MAKE MY GUESTS FEEL UNCOMFORTABLE.
鬼首川
ONIKUBI RIVER
"DEVIL'S HEAD RIVER"

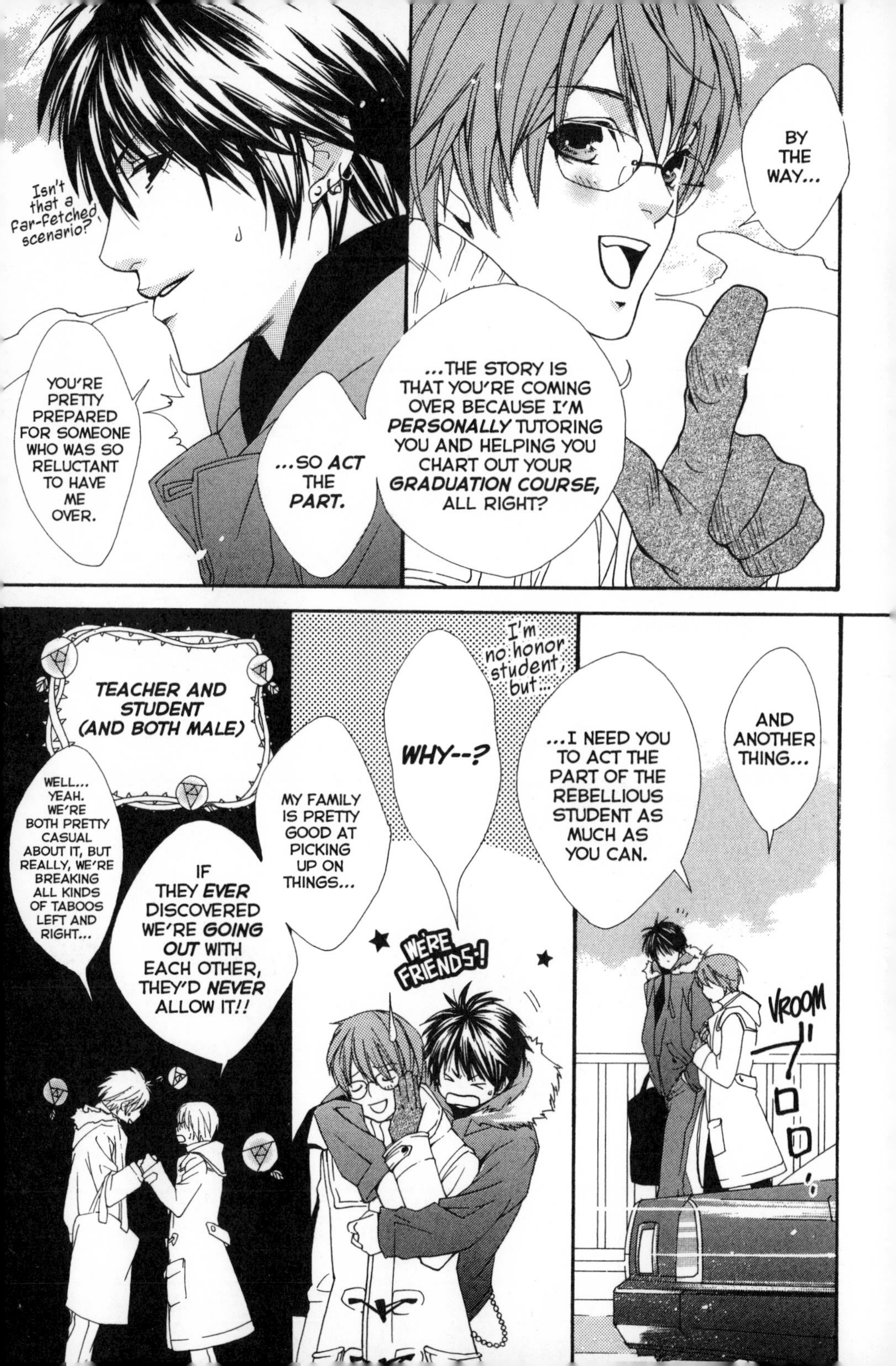
BY THE WAY...
...THE STORY IS THAT YOU'RE COMING OVER BECAUSE I'M *PERSONALLY* TUTORING YOU AND HELPING YOU CHART OUT YOUR *GRADUATION COURSE,* ALL RIGHT?
...SO *ACT* THE *PART.*
Isn't that a far-fetched scenario?
YOU'RE PRETTY PREPARED FOR SOMEONE WHO WAS SO RELUCTANT TO HAVE ME OVER.
AND ANOTHER THING...
...I NEED YOU TO ACT THE PART OF THE REBELLIOUS STUDENT AS MUCH AS YOU CAN.
VROOM
I'm no honor student, but...
WHY--?
MY FAMILY IS PRETTY GOOD AT PICKING UP ON THINGS...
WE'RE FRIENDS-!
TEACHER AND STUDENT (AND BOTH MALE)
WELL... YEAH. WE'RE BOTH PRETTY CASUAL ABOUT IT, BUT REALLY, WE'RE BREAKING ALL KINDS OF TABOOS LEFT AND RIGHT...
IF THEY *EVER* DISCOVERED WE'RE *GOING OUT* WITH EACH OTHER, THEY'D *NEVER* ALLOW IT!!

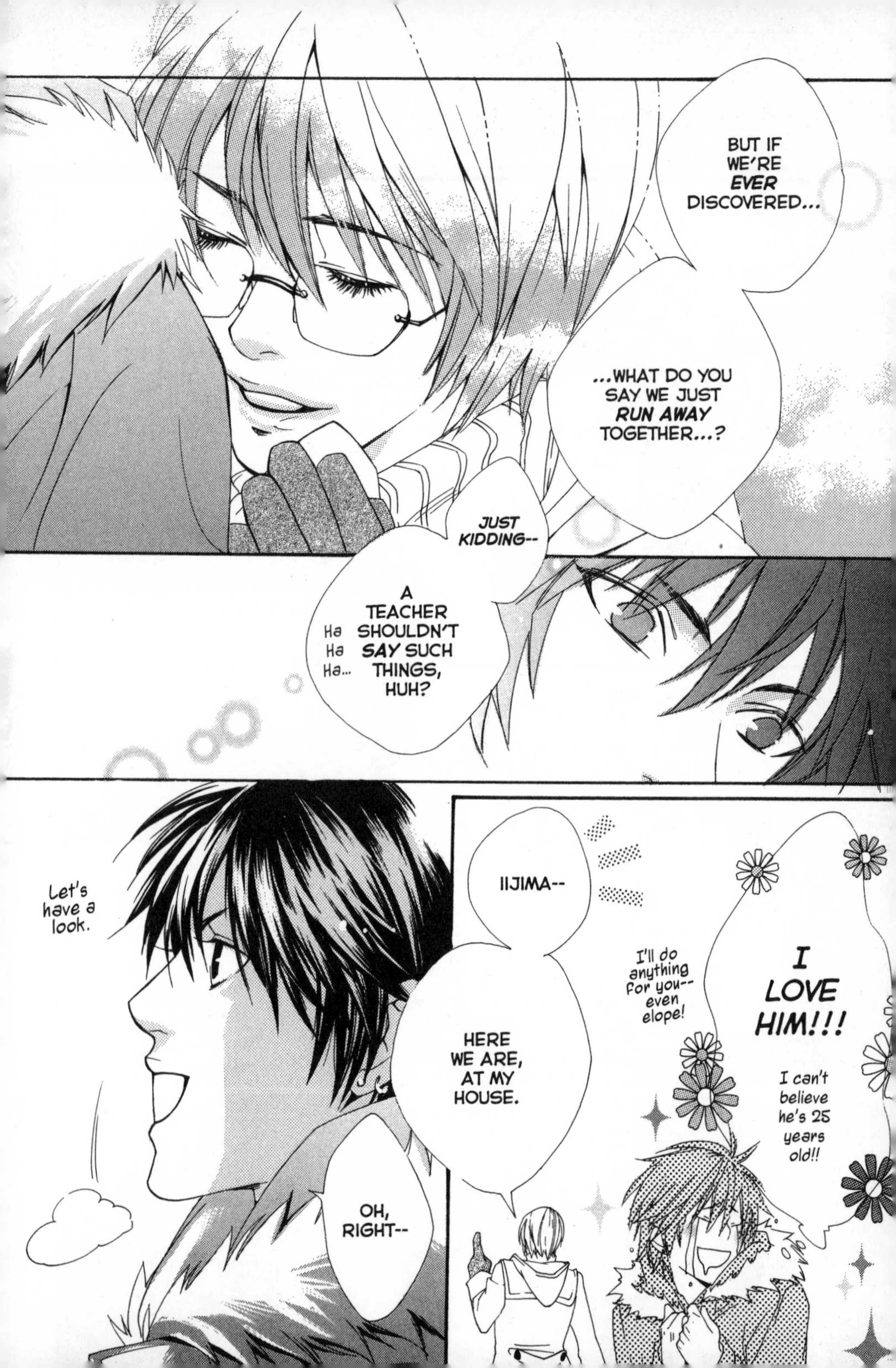
BUT IF WE'RE EVER DISCOVERED...
...WHAT DO YOU SAY WE JUST RUN AWAY TOGETHER...?
JUST KIDDING--
A TEACHER SHOULDN'T SAY SUCH THINGS, HUH?
Ha Ha Ha...
I LOVE HIM!!!
I'll do anything for you--even elope!
I can't believe he's 25 years old!!
IIJIMA--
HERE WE ARE, AT MY HOUSE.
OH, RIGHT--
Let's have a look.

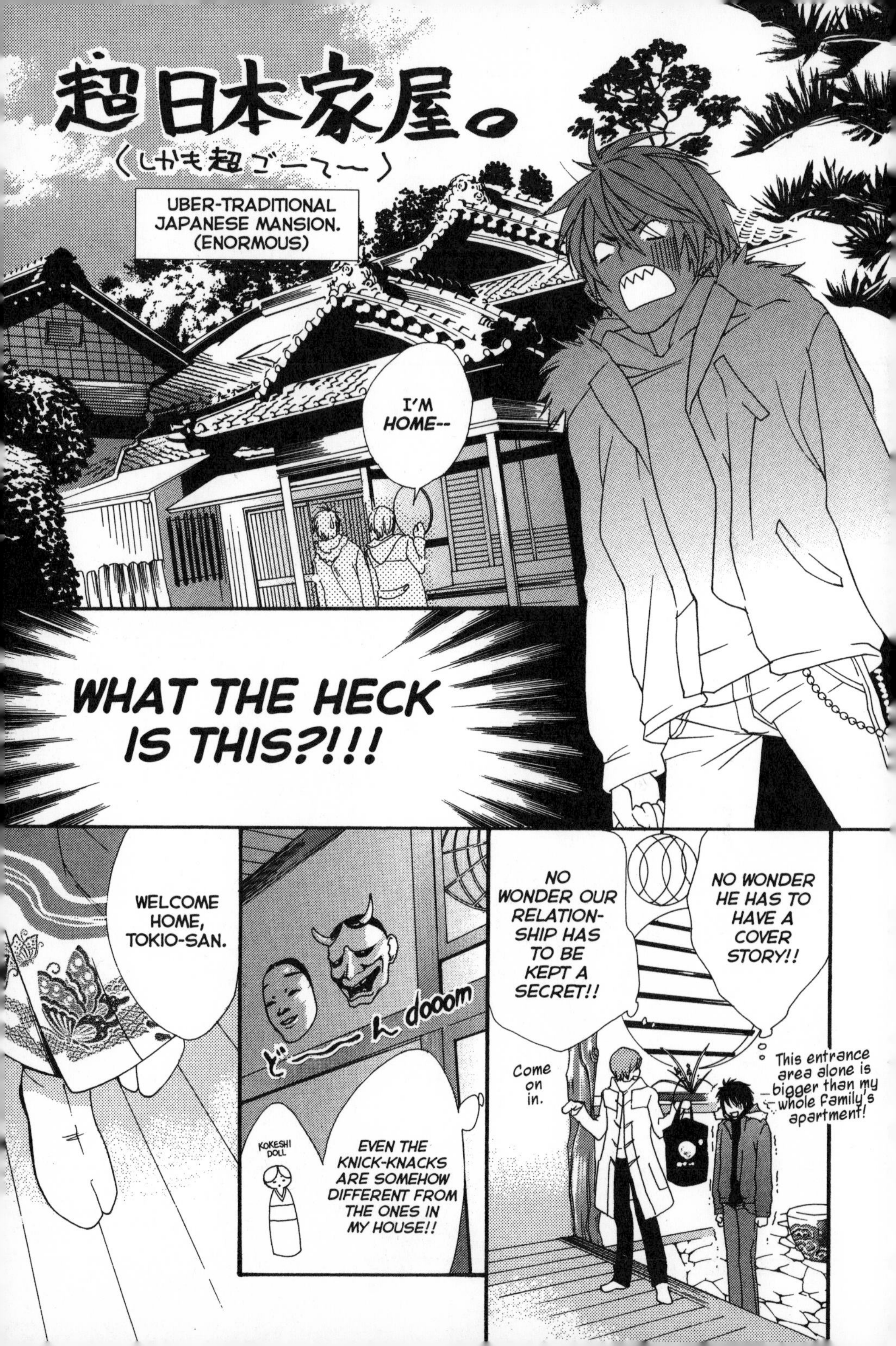

超日本家屋。
〈しかも超ごーて〜〉
UBER-TRADITIONAL JAPANESE MANSION. (ENORMOUS)
I'M HOME--
WHAT THE HECK IS THIS?!!!
NO WONDER HE HAS TO HAVE A COVER STORY!!
NO WONDER OUR RELATION-SHIP HAS TO BE KEPT A SECRET!!
This entrance area alone is bigger than my whole family's apartment!
Come on in.
どーーん dooom
EVEN THE KNICK-KNACKS ARE SOMEHOW DIFFERENT FROM THE ONES IN MY HOUSE!!
KOKESHI DOLL
WELCOME HOME, TOKIO-SAN.

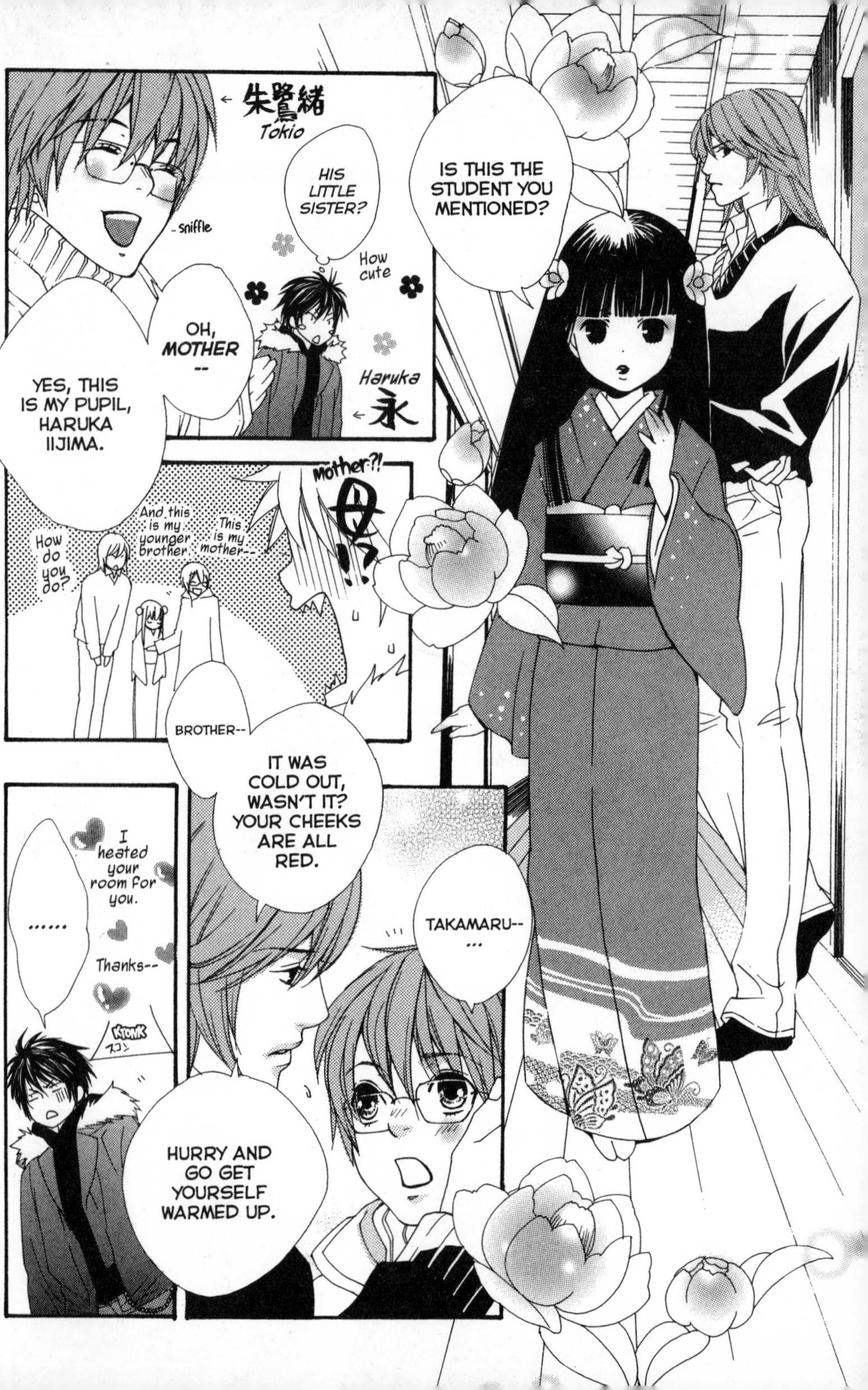
IS THIS THE STUDENT YOU MENTIONED?
朱鷺緒
Tokio
HIS LITTLE SISTER?
How cute
Haruka
永
-Sniffle
OH, MOTHER --
YES, THIS IS MY PUPIL, HARUKA IIJIMA.
mother?!
母
This is my mother--
And this is my younger brother
How do you do?
BROTHER--
IT WAS COLD OUT, WASN'T IT? YOUR CHEEKS ARE ALL RED.
TAKAMARU-- ...
I heated your room for you.
......
Thanks--
KTONK
HURRY AND GO GET YOURSELF WARMED UP.

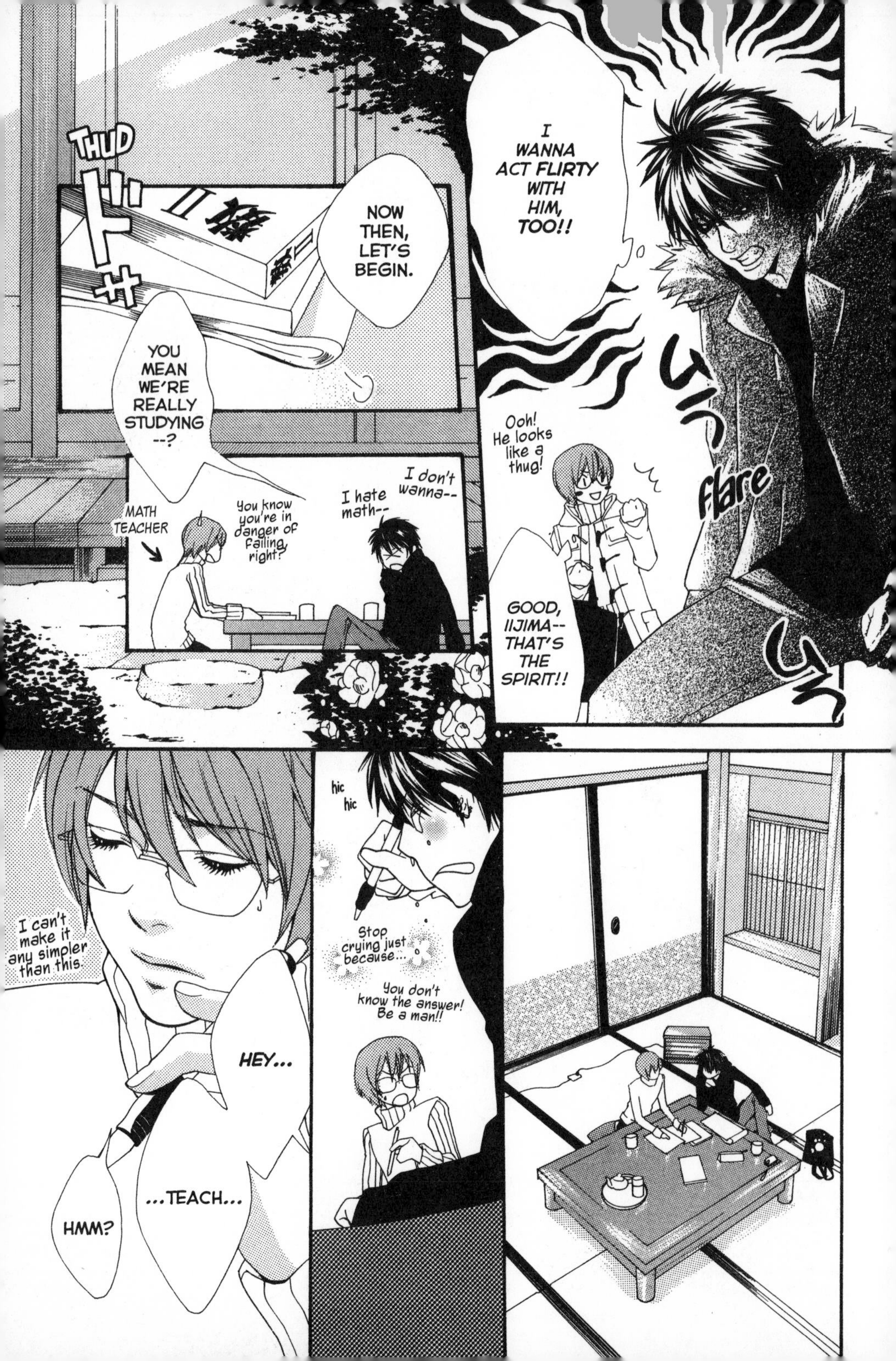
I WANNA ACT FLIRTY WITH HIM, TOO!!
Ooh! He looks like a thug!
flare
GOOD, IIJIMA--THAT'S THE SPIRIT!!
THUD
NOW THEN, LET'S BEGIN.
YOU MEAN WE'RE REALLY STUDYING--?
I don't wanna--
I hate math--
You know you're in danger of failing, right?
MATH TEACHER
hic
hic
Stop crying just because...
You don't know the answer! Be a man!!
I can't make it any simpler than this.
HEY...
...TEACH...
HMM?

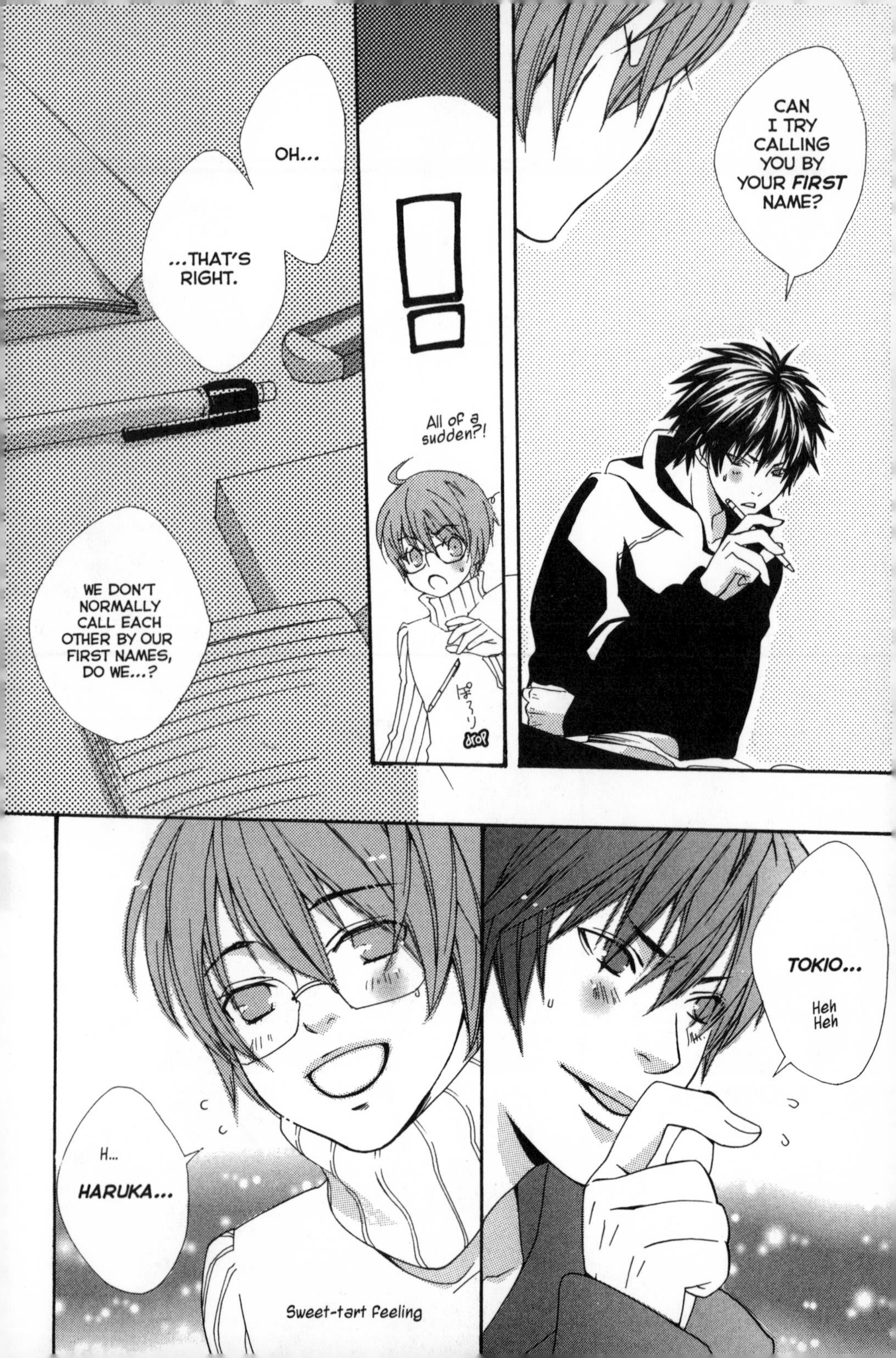
CAN I TRY CALLING YOU BY YOUR *FIRST* NAME?
!
All of a sudden?!
ぽろり
drop
OH...
...THAT'S RIGHT.
WE DON'T NORMALLY CALL EACH OTHER BY OUR FIRST NAMES, DO WE...?
TOKIO...
Heh Heh
H...
HARUKA...
Sweet-tart feeling

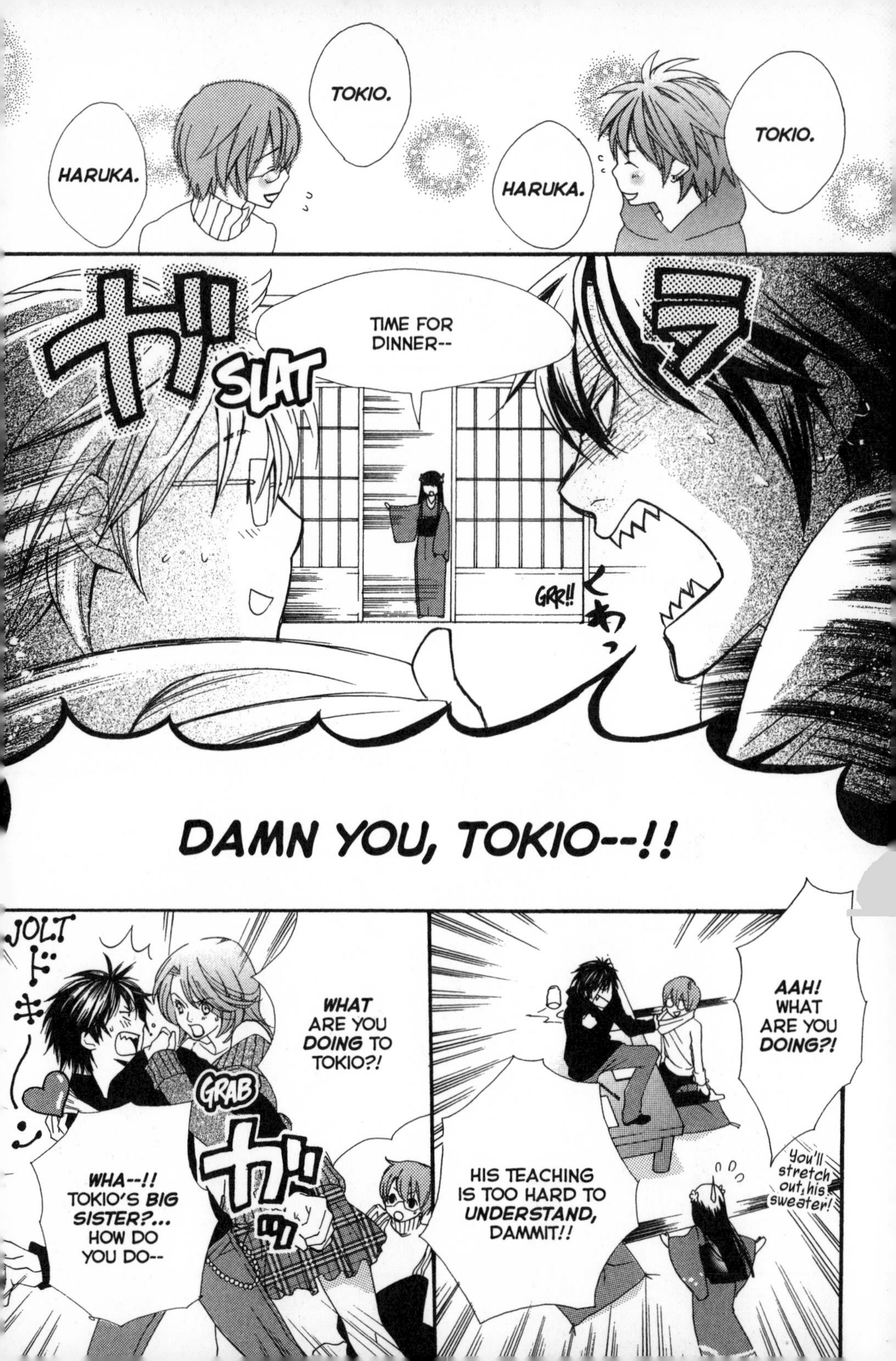
TOKIO.
HARUKA.
TOKIO.
HARUKA.
SLAT
TIME FOR DINNER--
GRR!!
DAMN YOU, TOKIO--!!
AAH! WHAT ARE YOU DOING?!
You'll stretch out his sweater!
HIS TEACHING IS TOO HARD TO UNDERSTAND, DAMMIT!!
WHAT ARE YOU DOING TO TOKIO?!
GRAB
WHA--!! TOKIO'S BIG SISTER?... HOW DO YOU DO--
JOLT

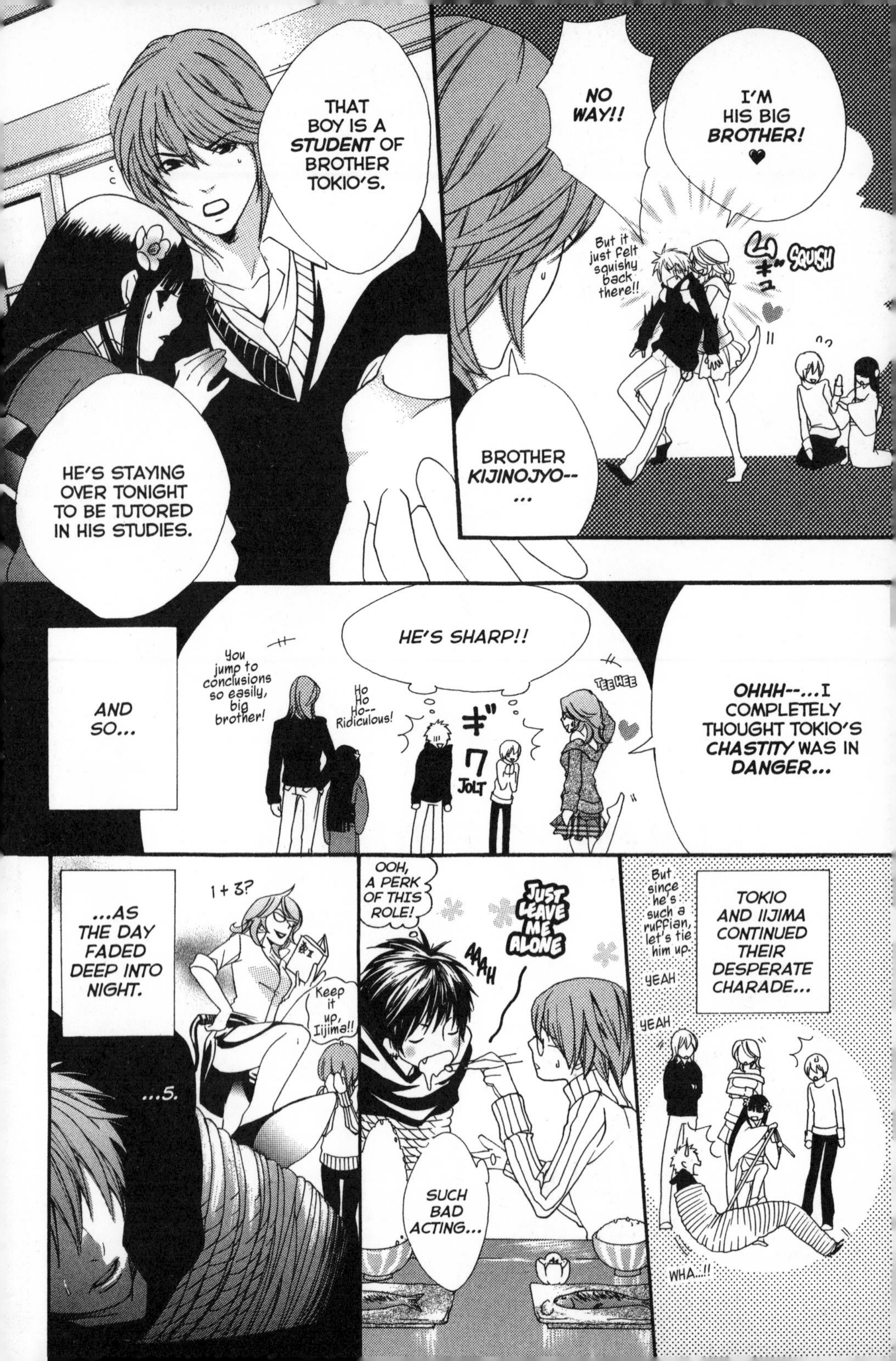
I'M HIS BIG BROTHER! ♥
NO WAY!!
SQUISH
But it just felt squishy back there!!
BROTHER KIJINOJYO-- ...
THAT BOY IS A STUDENT OF BROTHER TOKIO'S.
HE'S STAYING OVER TONIGHT TO BE TUTORED IN HIS STUDIES.
OHHH--...I COMPLETELY THOUGHT TOKIO'S CHASTITY WAS IN DANGER...
TEE HEE
HE'S SHARP!!
JOLT
Ho Ho Ho-- Ridiculous!
You jump to conclusions so easily, big brother!
AND SO...
TOKIO AND IIJIMA CONTINUED THEIR DESPERATE CHARADE...
But since he's such a ruffian, let's tie him up.
YEAH
YEAH
WHA...!!
JUST LEAVE ME ALONE
OOH, A PERK OF THIS ROLE!
AAAAH
SUCH BAD ACTING...
...AS THE DAY FADED DEEP INTO NIGHT.
1 + 3?
Keep it up, Iijima!!
...5.

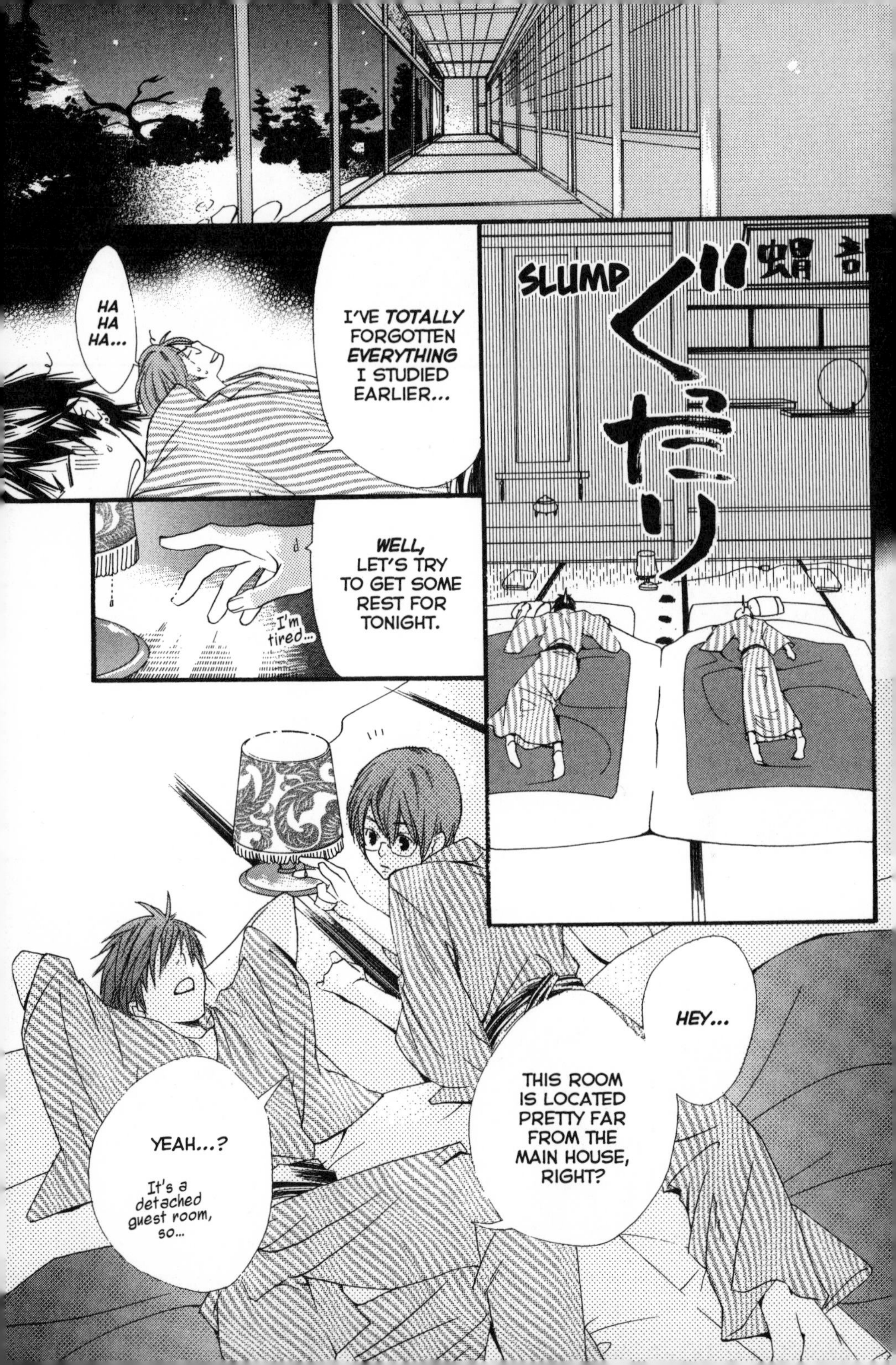

SLUMP
ぐったり
I'VE *TOTALLY* FORGOTTEN *EVERYTHING* I STUDIED EARLIER...
HA HA HA...
WELL, LET'S TRY TO GET SOME REST FOR TONIGHT.
I'm tired...
HEY...
THIS ROOM IS LOCATED PRETTY FAR FROM THE MAIN HOUSE, RIGHT?
YEAH...?
It's a detached guest room, so...

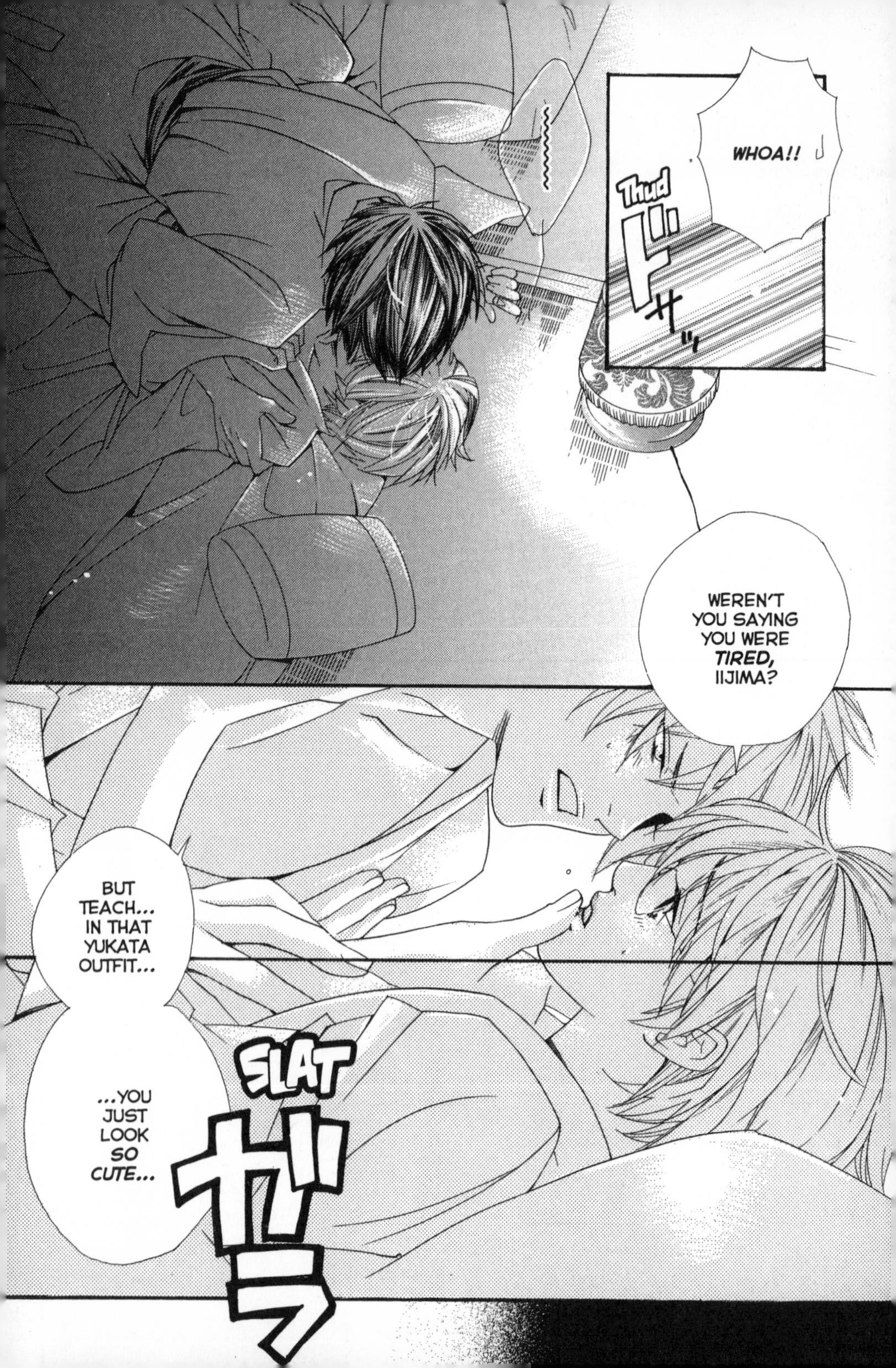
WHOA!!
Thud
WEREN'T YOU SAYING YOU WERE *TIRED,* IIJIMA?
BUT TEACH... IN THAT YUKATA OUTFIT...
...YOU JUST LOOK *SO CUTE...*
SLAT

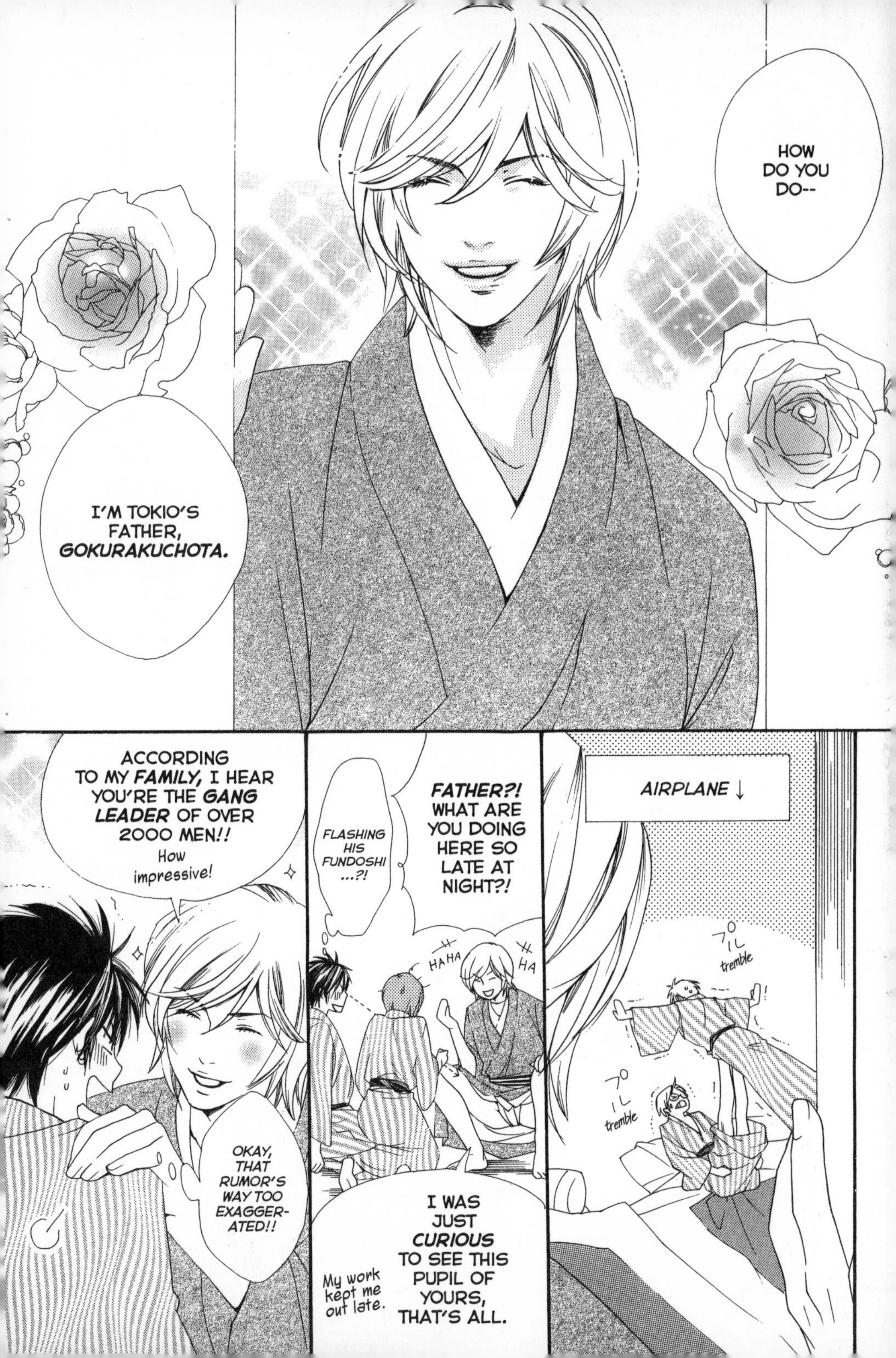
HOW DO YOU DO--
I'M TOKIO'S FATHER, GOKURAKUCHOTA.
AIRPLANE ↓
プル tremble
プル tremble
FATHER?! WHAT ARE YOU DOING HERE SO LATE AT NIGHT?!
FLASHING HIS FUNDOSHI ...?!
HA HA
I WAS JUST CURIOUS TO SEE THIS PUPIL OF YOURS, THAT'S ALL.
My work kept me out late.
ACCORDING TO MY FAMILY, I HEAR YOU'RE THE GANG LEADER OF OVER 2000 MEN!!
How impressive!
OKAY, THAT RUMOR'S WAY TOO EXAGGERATED!!

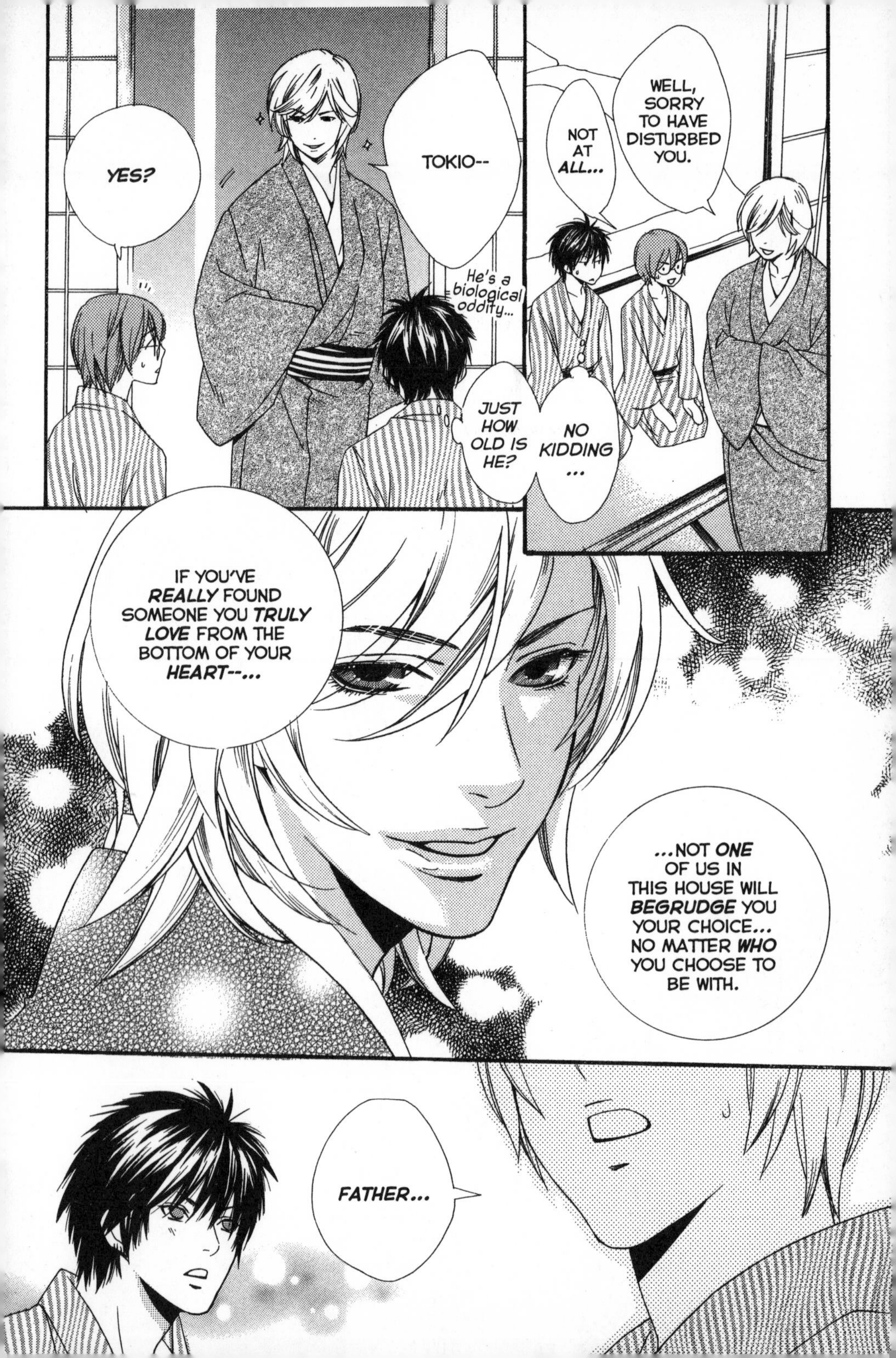
WELL, SORRY TO HAVE DISTURBED YOU.
NOT AT ALL...
TOKIO--
YES?
He's a biological oddity...
JUST HOW OLD IS HE?
NO KIDDING...
IF YOU'VE REALLY FOUND SOMEONE YOU TRULY LOVE FROM THE BOTTOM OF YOUR HEART--...
...NOT ONE OF US IN THIS HOUSE WILL BEGRUDGE YOU YOUR CHOICE... NO MATTER WHO YOU CHOOSE TO BE WITH.
FATHER...

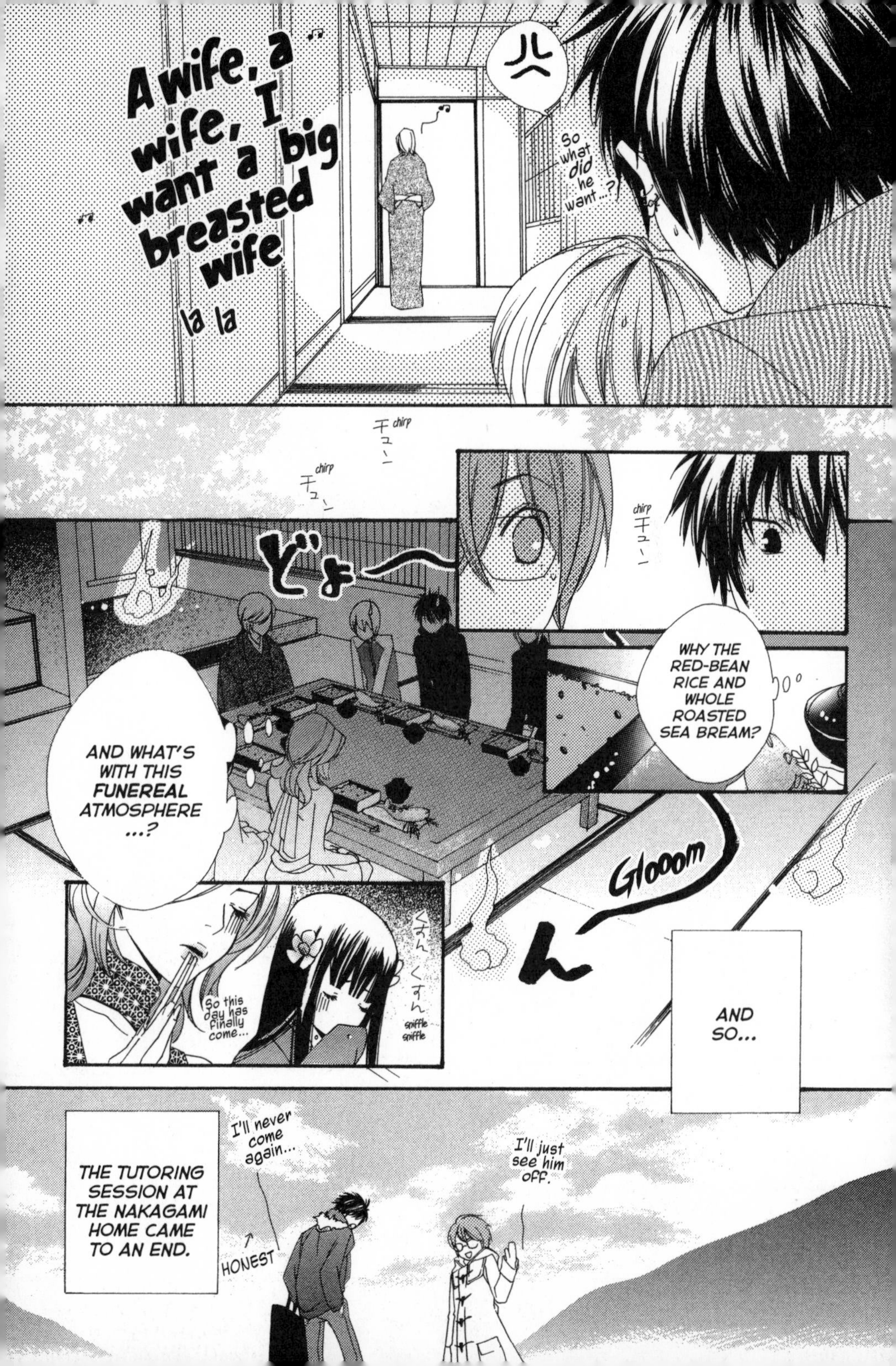

So what did he want...?
A wife, a wife, I want a big breasted wife
la la
チュン chirp
チュン chirp
chirp チュン
WHY THE RED-BEAN RICE AND WHOLE ROASTED SEA BREAM?
どよ～ん
Glooom
AND WHAT'S WITH THIS FUNEREAL ATMOSPHERE ...?
くすん くすん spiffle sniffle
So this day has finally come...
AND SO...
I'll just see him off.
I'll never come again...
HONEST
THE TUTORING SESSION AT THE NAKAGAMI HOME CAME TO AN END.

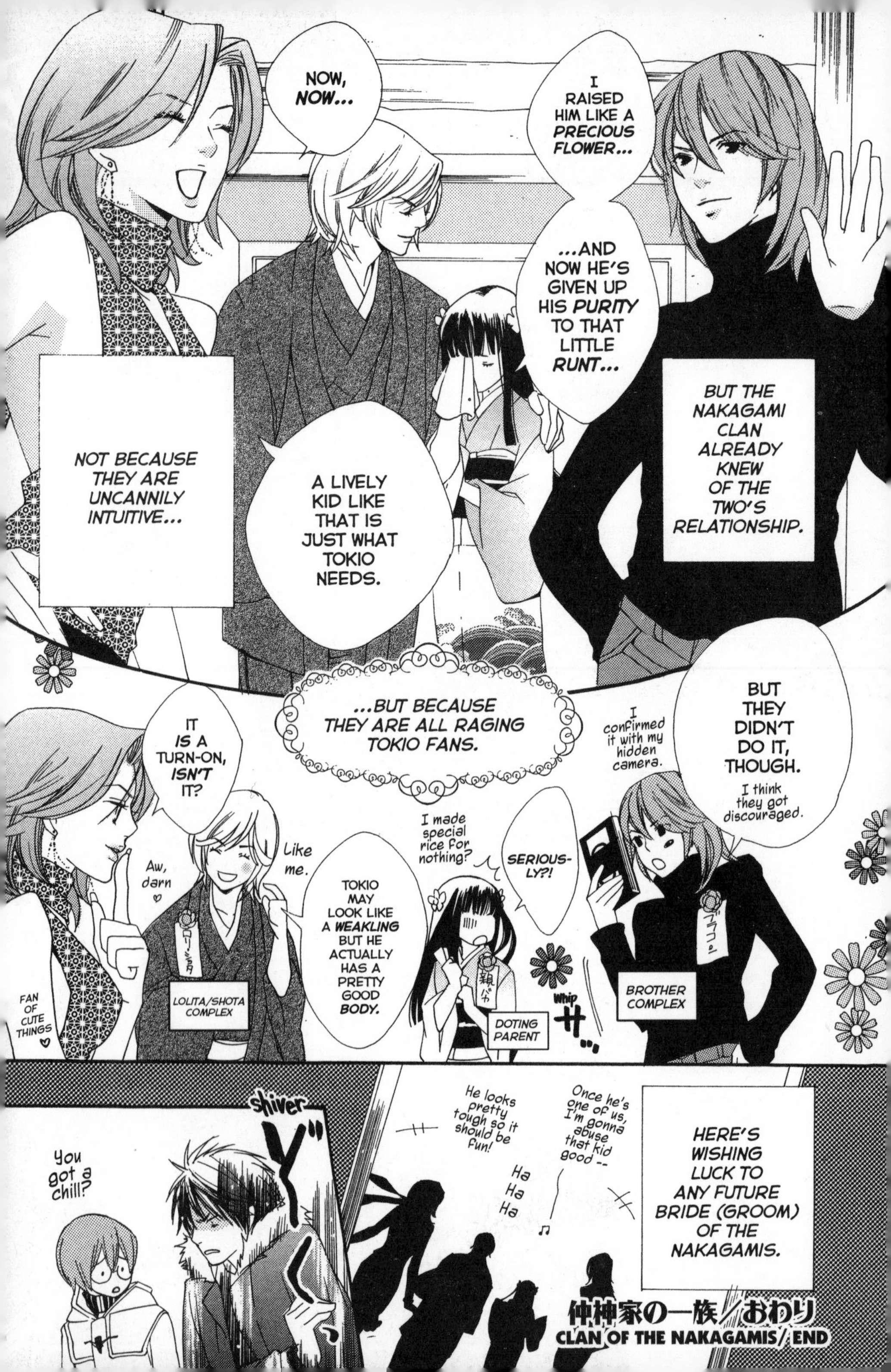

I RAISED HIM LIKE A PRECIOUS FLOWER...
...AND NOW HE'S GIVEN UP HIS PURITY TO THAT LITTLE RUNT...
BUT THE NAKAGAMI CLAN ALREADY KNEW OF THE TWO'S RELATIONSHIP.
NOW, NOW...
A LIVELY KID LIKE THAT IS JUST WHAT TOKIO NEEDS.
NOT BECAUSE THEY ARE UNCANNILY INTUITIVE...
...BUT BECAUSE THEY ARE ALL RAGING TOKIO FANS.
BUT THEY DIDN'T DO IT, THOUGH.
I confirmed it with my hidden camera.
I think they got discouraged.
BROTHER COMPLEX
SERIOUS-LY?!
I made special rice for nothing?
Whip
DOTING PARENT
TOKIO MAY LOOK LIKE A WEAKLING BUT HE ACTUALLY HAS A PRETTY GOOD BODY.
Like me.
IT IS A TURN-ON, ISN'T IT?
Aw, darn
LOLITA/SHOTA COMPLEX
FAN OF CUTE THINGS
HERE'S WISHING LUCK TO ANY FUTURE BRIDE (GROOM) OF THE NAKAGAMIS.
Once he's one of us, I'm gonna abuse that kid good --
He looks pretty tough so it should be fun!
Ha Ha Ha
shiver
You got a chill?
仲神家の一族／おわり
CLAN OF THE NAKAGAMIS/ END

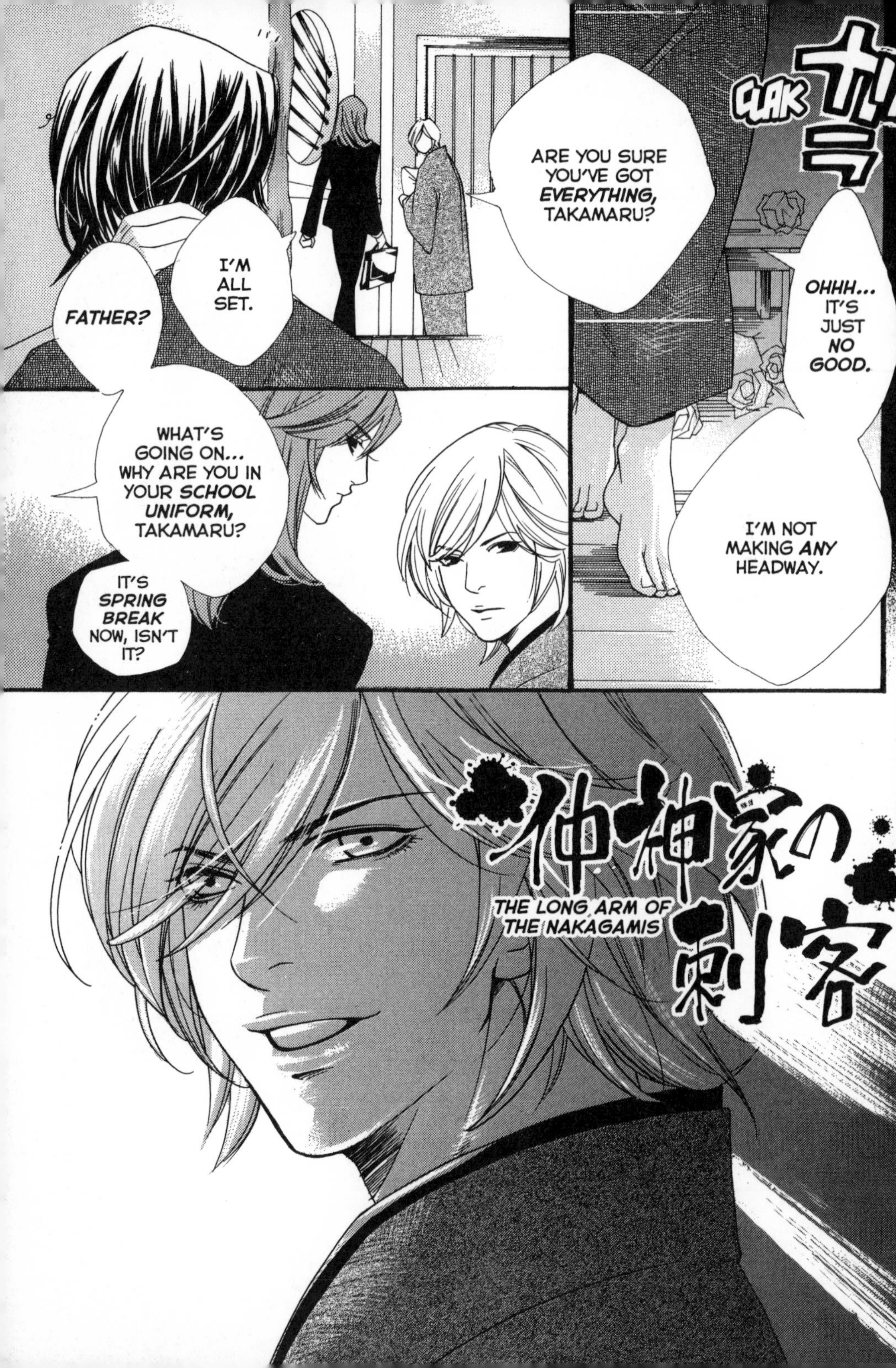
CLAK
OHHH... IT'S JUST NO GOOD.
I'M NOT MAKING ANY HEADWAY.
ARE YOU SURE YOU'VE GOT EVERYTHING, TAKAMARU?
I'M ALL SET.
FATHER?
WHAT'S GOING ON... WHY ARE YOU IN YOUR SCHOOL UNIFORM, TAKAMARU?
IT'S SPRING BREAK NOW, ISN'T IT?
仲神家の刺客
THE LONG ARM OF THE NAKAGAMIS

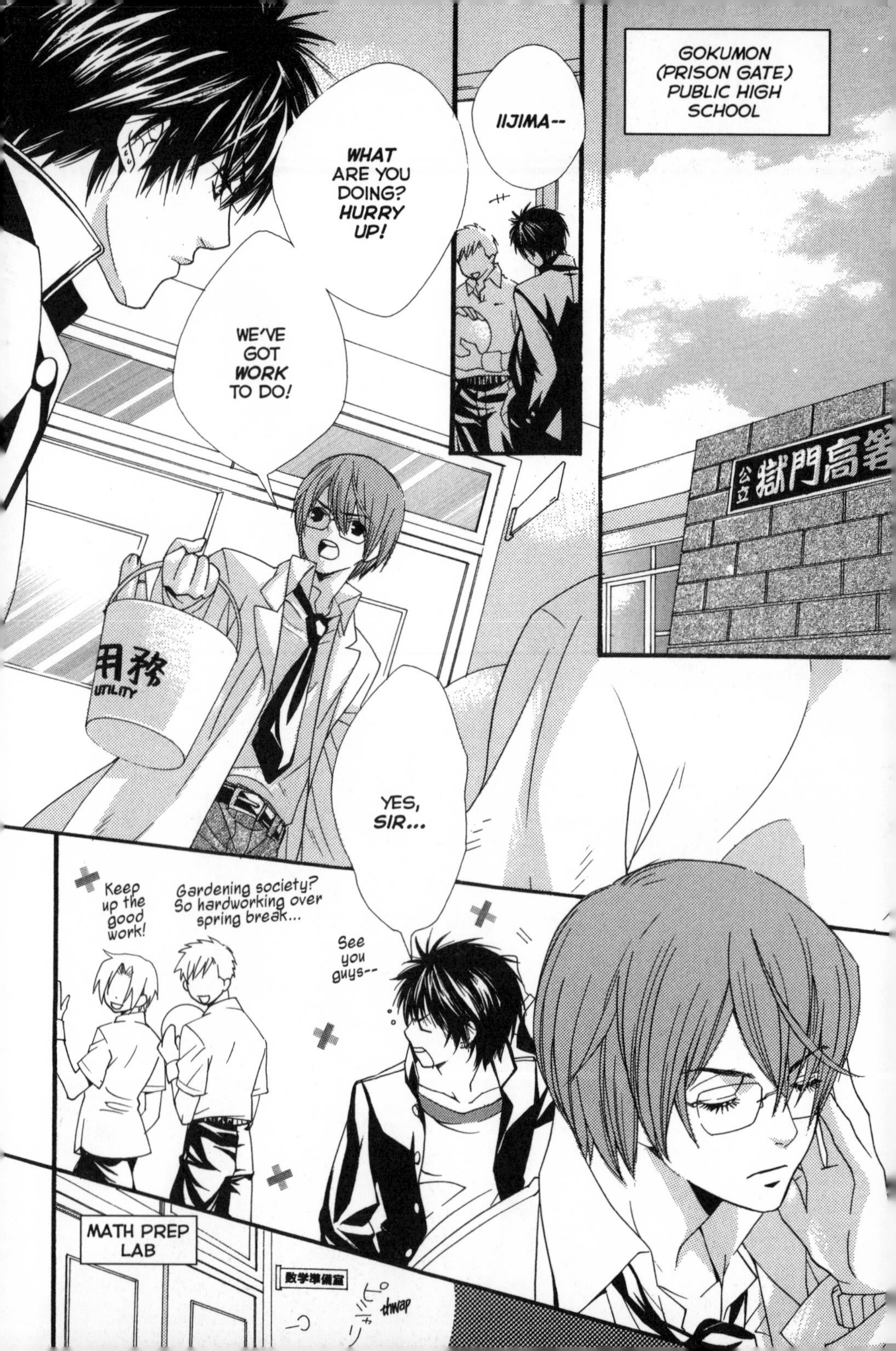
GOKUMON (PRISON GATE) PUBLIC HIGH SCHOOL
公立 獄門高
IIJIMA--
WHAT ARE YOU DOING? HURRY UP!
WE'VE GOT WORK TO DO!
用務
UTILITY
YES, SIR...
See you guys--
Gardening society? So hardworking over spring break...
Keep up the good work!
MATH PREP LAB
数学準備室
thwap
ピシャ

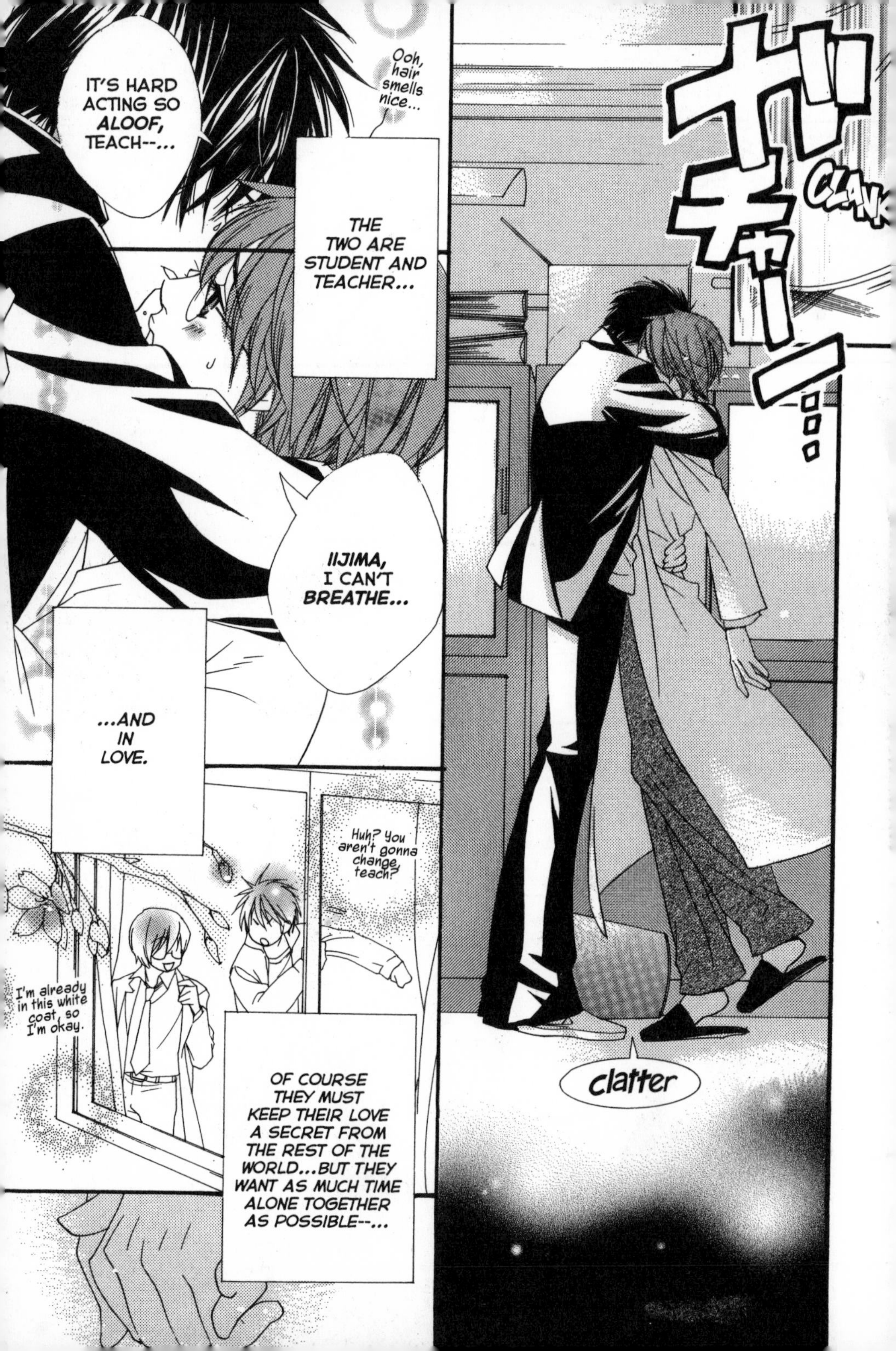
ガチャーン
CLANK
clatter
Ooh, hair smells nice...
IT'S HARD ACTING SO *ALOOF*, TEACH--...
THE TWO ARE STUDENT AND TEACHER...
IIJIMA, I CAN'T *BREATHE*...
...AND IN LOVE.
Huh? You aren't gonna change, teach?
I'm already in this white coat, so I'm okay.
OF COURSE THEY MUST KEEP THEIR LOVE A SECRET FROM THE REST OF THE WORLD...BUT THEY WANT AS MUCH TIME ALONE TOGETHER AS POSSIBLE--...

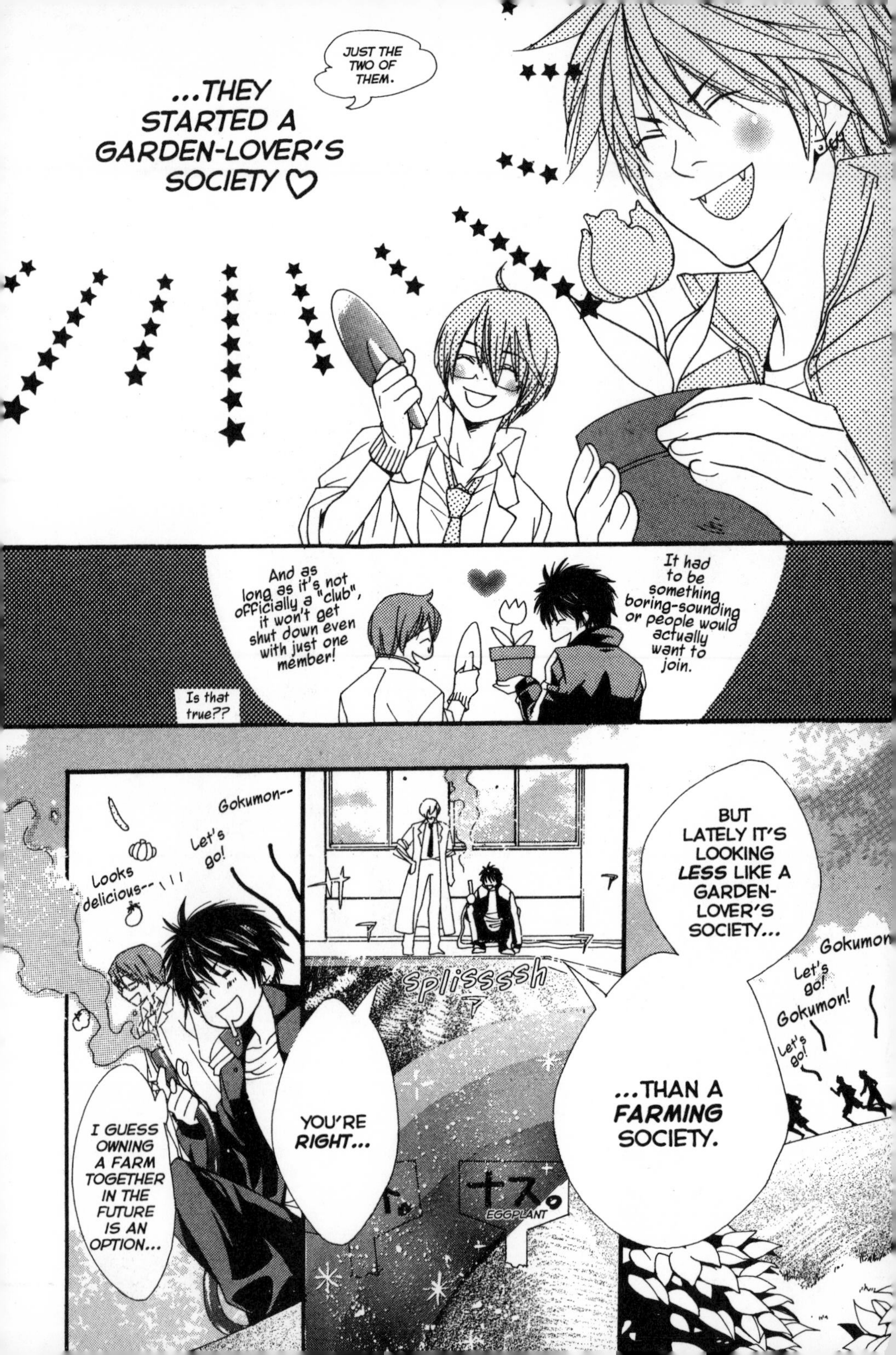
...THEY STARTED A GARDEN-LOVER'S SOCIETY ♡
JUST THE TWO OF THEM.
It had to be something boring-sounding or people would actually want to join.
And as long as it's not officially a "club", it won't get shut down even with just one member!
Is that true??
BUT LATELY IT'S LOOKING LESS LIKE A GARDEN-LOVER'S SOCIETY...
...THAN A FARMING SOCIETY.
Gokumon
Let's go!
Gokumon!
Let's go!
Splisssssh
Gokumon--
Let's go!
Looks delicious--
YOU'RE RIGHT...
I GUESS OWNING A FARM TOGETHER IN THE FUTURE IS AN OPTION...
ナス。
EGGPLANT

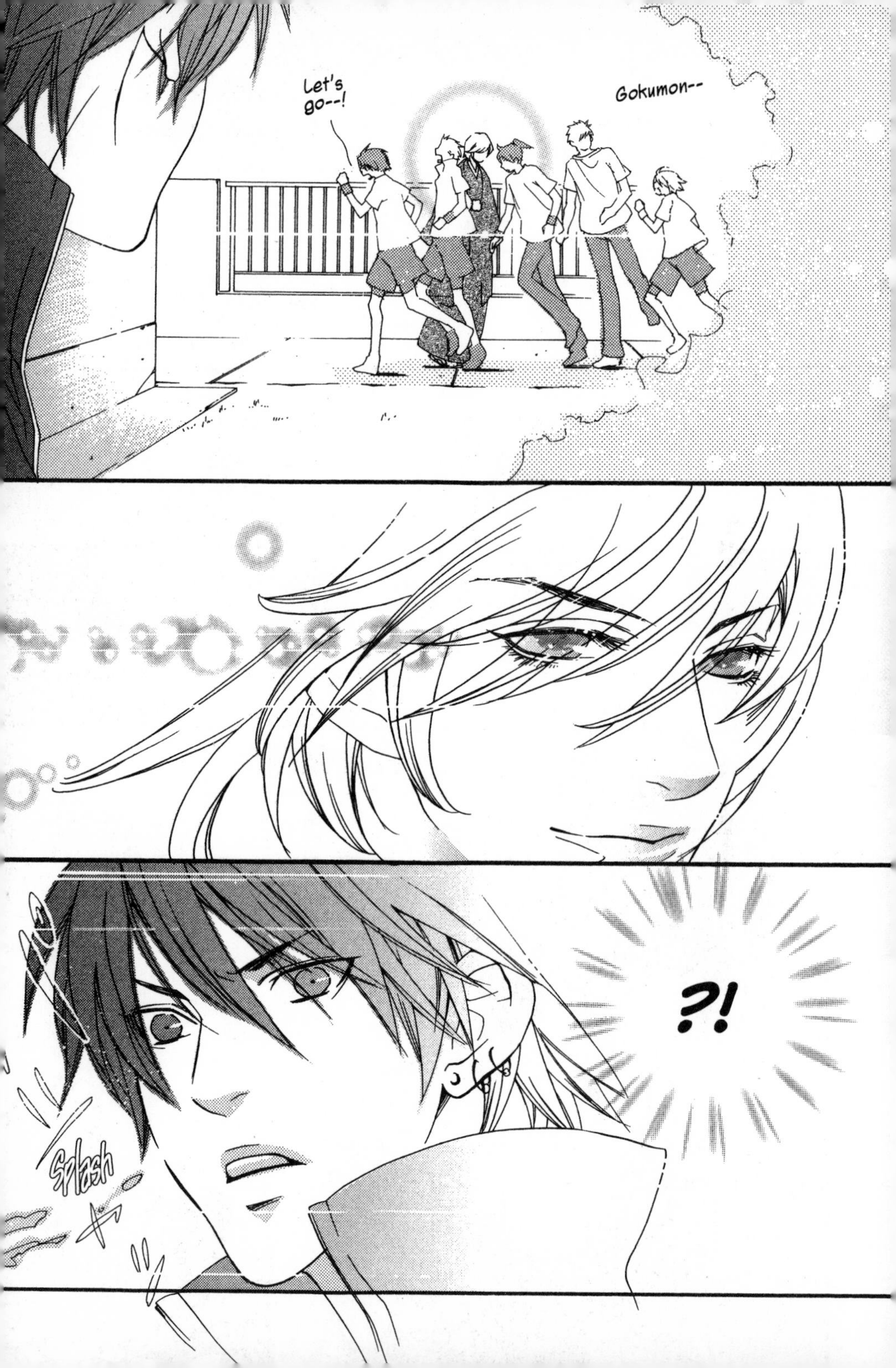
Gokumon--
Let's go--!
?!
Splash

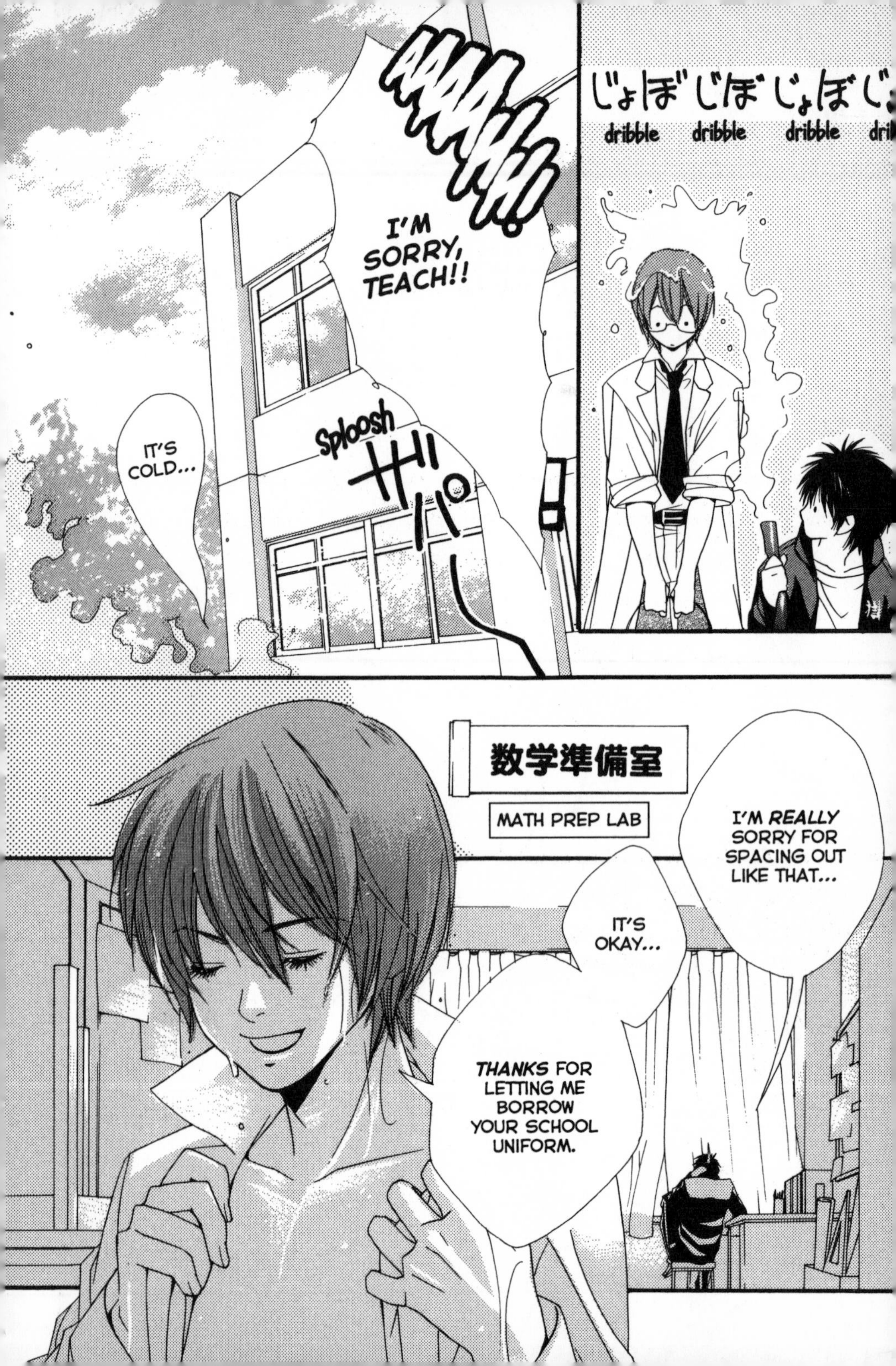
じょぼじぼじょぼじ
dribble dribble dribble dri
AAAAHH!
I'M SORRY, TEACH!!
Sploosh
ザパー
IT'S COLD...
数学準備室
MATH PREP LAB
I'M *REALLY* SORRY FOR SPACING OUT LIKE THAT...
IT'S OKAY...
THANKS FOR LETTING ME BORROW YOUR SCHOOL UNIFORM.

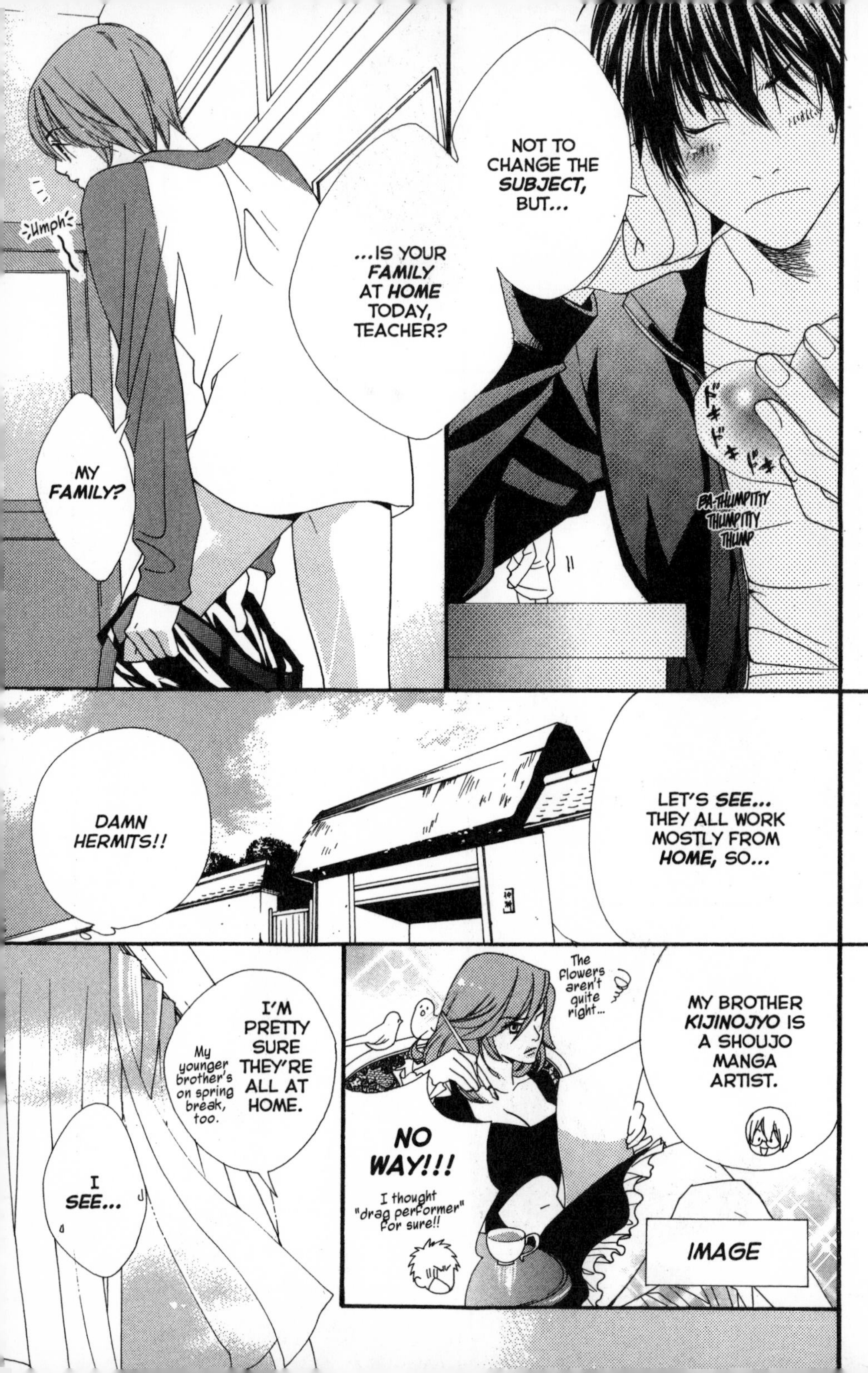
NOT TO CHANGE THE SUBJECT, BUT...
...IS YOUR FAMILY AT HOME TODAY, TEACHER?
BA-THUMPITTY THUMPITTY THUMP
Umph
MY FAMILY?
LET'S SEE... THEY ALL WORK MOSTLY FROM HOME, SO...
DAMN HERMITS!!
MY BROTHER KIJINOJYO IS A SHOUJO MANGA ARTIST.
The flowers aren't quite right...
IMAGE
NO WAY!!!
I thought "drag performer" for sure!!
I'M PRETTY SURE THEY'RE ALL AT HOME.
My younger brother's on spring break, too.
I SEE...

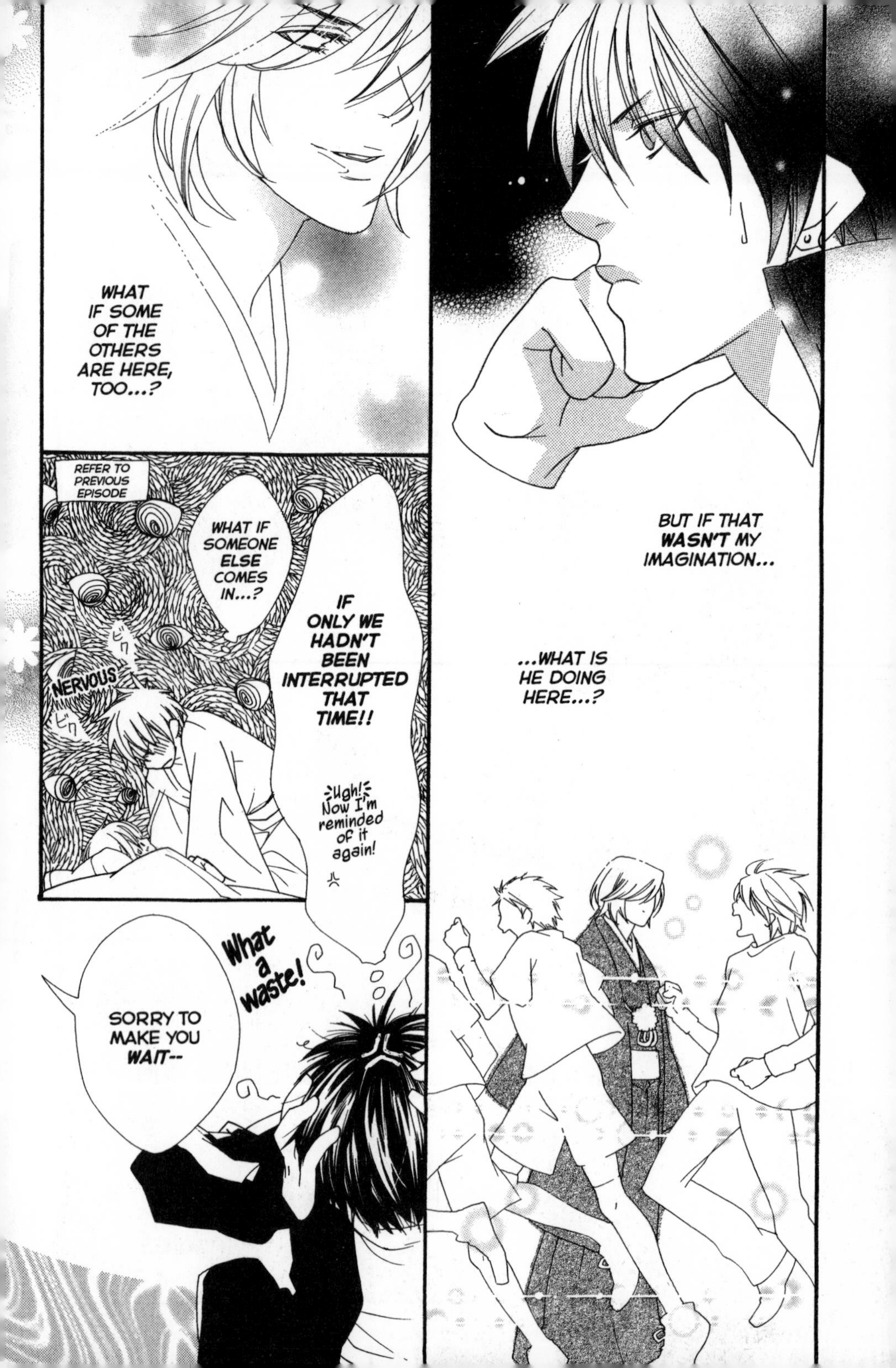
BUT IF THAT WASN'T MY IMAGINATION...
...WHAT IS HE DOING HERE...?
WHAT IF SOME OF THE OTHERS ARE HERE, TOO...?
REFER TO PREVIOUS EPISODE
WHAT IF SOMEONE ELSE COMES IN...?
IF ONLY WE HADN'T BEEN INTERRUPTED THAT TIME!!
ビク
NERVOUS
ビク
Ugh! Now I'm reminded of it again!
What a waste!
SORRY TO MAKE YOU WAIT--

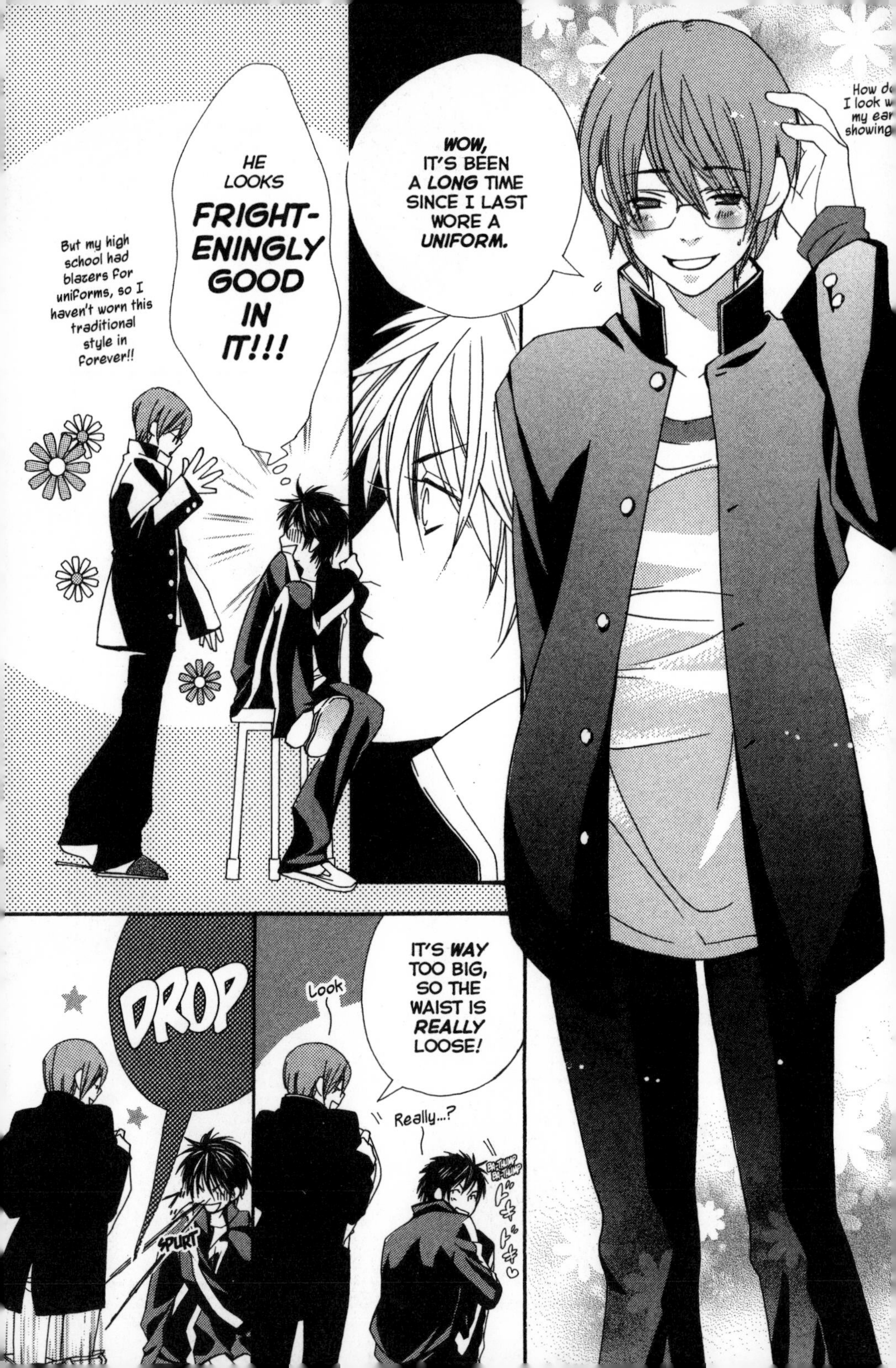
How d
I look w
my ear
showing
WOW, IT'S BEEN A LONG TIME SINCE I LAST WORE A UNIFORM.
HE LOOKS FRIGHT-ENINGLY GOOD IN IT!!!
But my high school had blazers for uniforms, so I haven't worn this traditional style in forever!!
IT'S WAY TOO BIG, SO THE WAIST IS REALLY LOOSE!
Look
Really...?
BA-THUMP BA-THUMP
DROP
SPURT

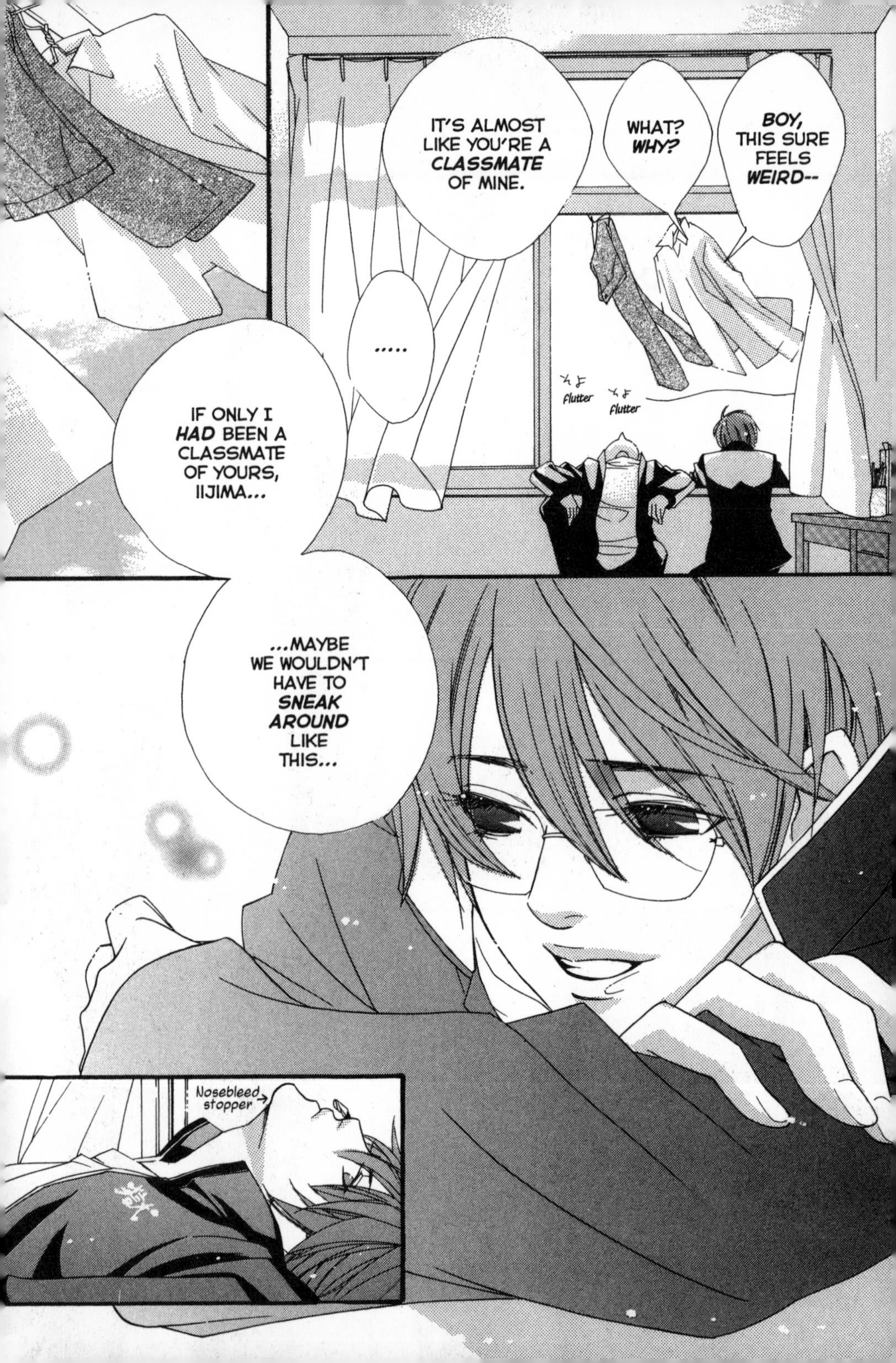
BOY, THIS SURE FEELS WEIRD--
WHAT? WHY?
IT'S ALMOST LIKE YOU'RE A CLASSMATE OF MINE.
.....
flutter
flutter
IF ONLY I HAD BEEN A CLASSMATE OF YOURS, IIJIMA...
...MAYBE WE WOULDN'T HAVE TO SNEAK AROUND LIKE THIS...
Nosebleed stopper

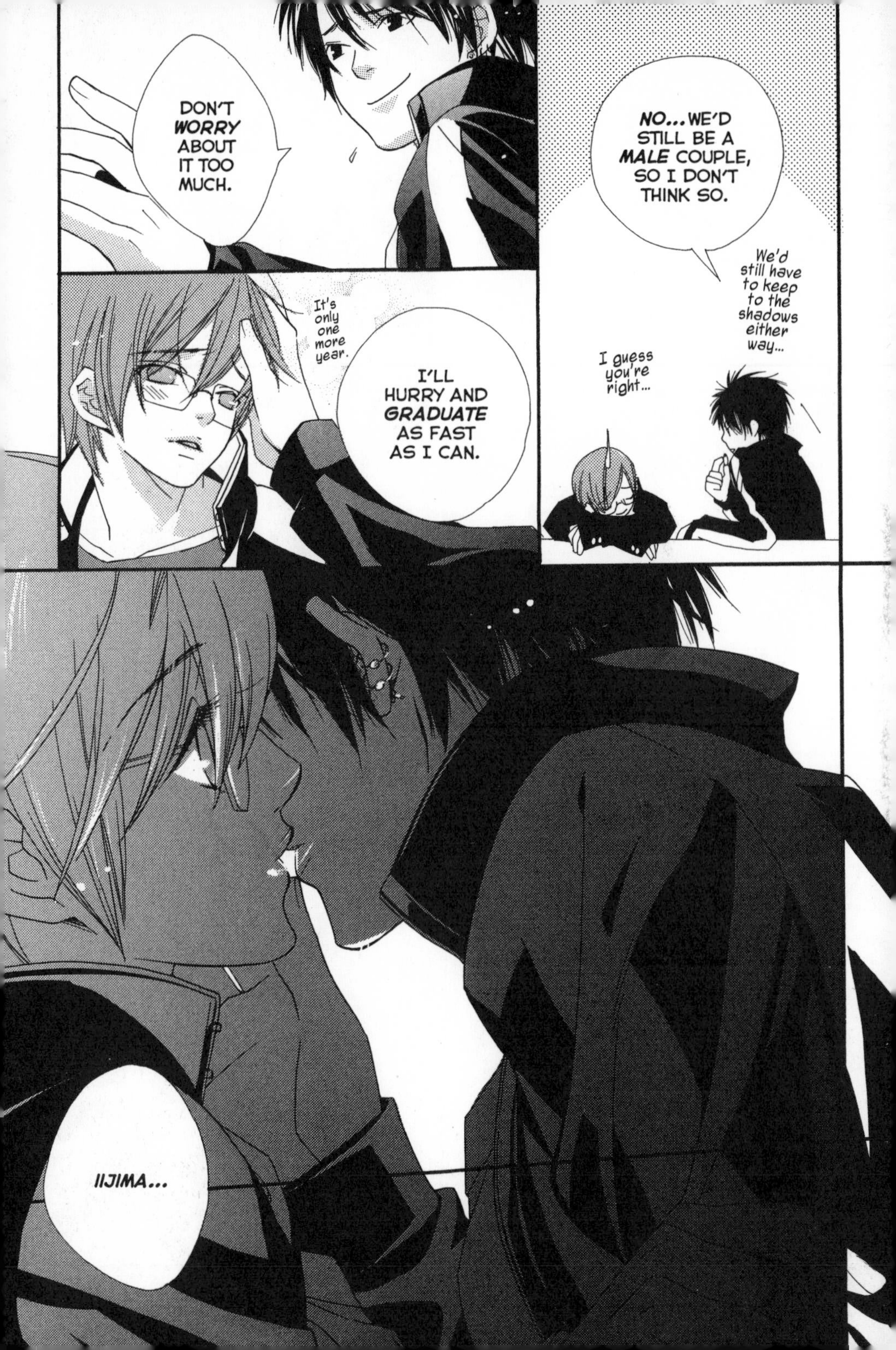
NO... WE'D STILL BE A MALE COUPLE, SO I DON'T THINK SO.
We'd still have to keep to the shadows either way...
I guess you're right...
DON'T WORRY ABOUT IT TOO MUCH.
It's only one more year.
I'LL HURRY AND GRADUATE AS FAST AS I CAN.
IIJIMA...

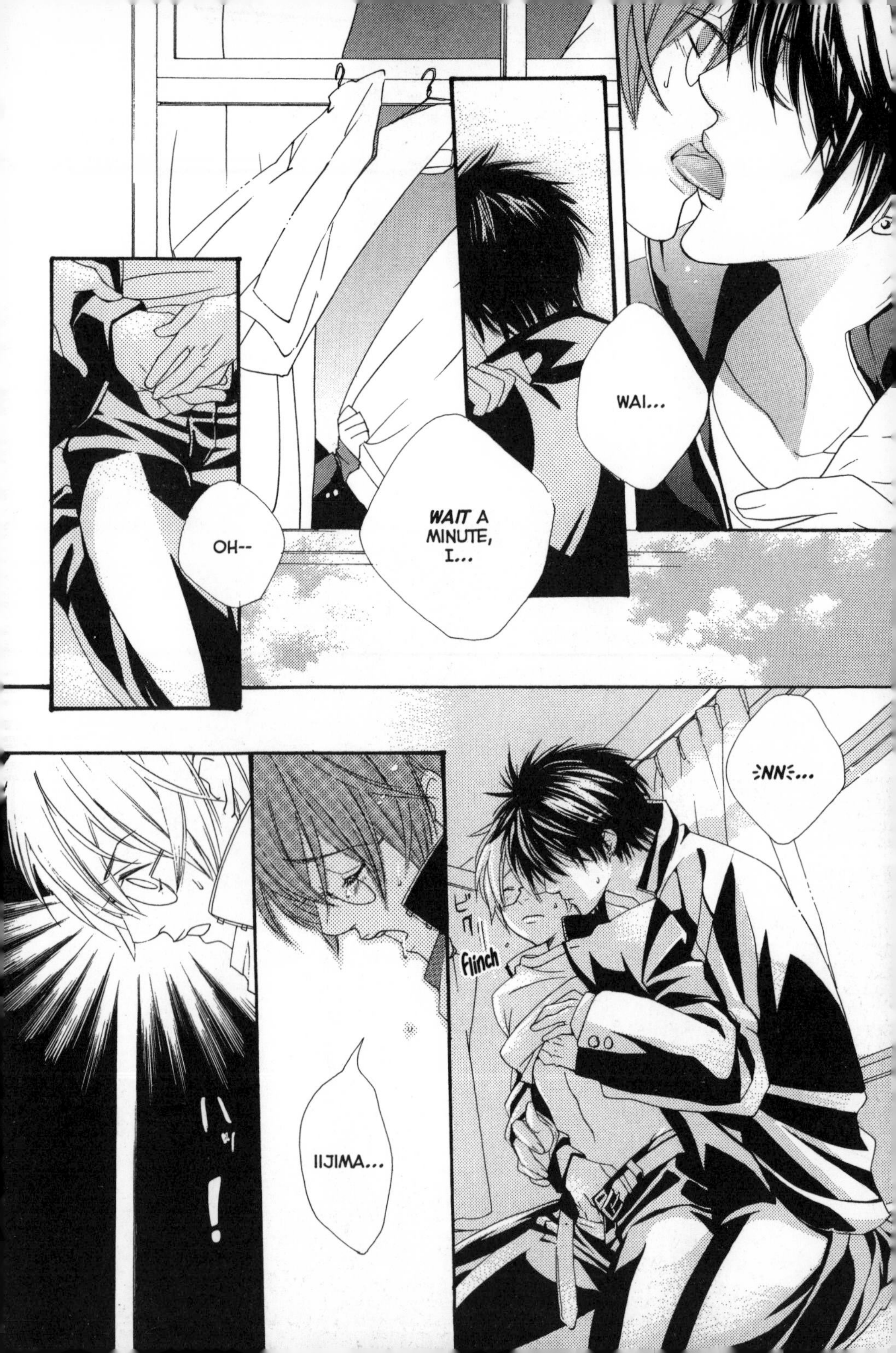
WAI...
WAIT A MINUTE, I...
OH--
NN...
Flinch
IIJIMA...

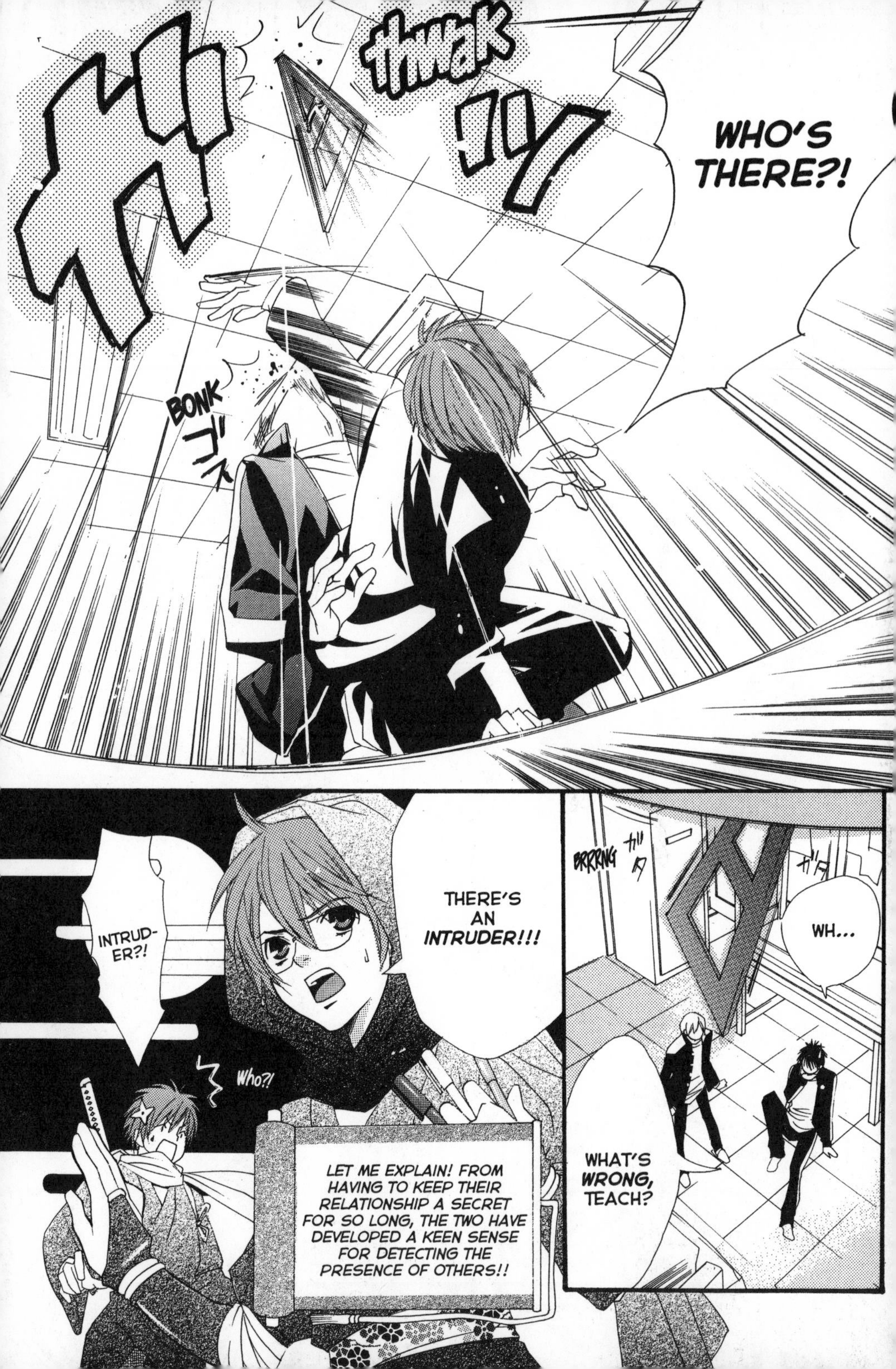
WHO'S THERE?!
thwak
BONK
BRRRNG
WH...
WHAT'S WRONG, TEACH?
THERE'S AN INTRUDER!!!
INTRUDER?!
Who?!
LET ME EXPLAIN! FROM HAVING TO KEEP THEIR RELATIONSHIP A SECRET FOR SO LONG, THE TWO HAVE DEVELOPED A KEEN SENSE FOR DETECTING THE PRESENCE OF OTHERS!!

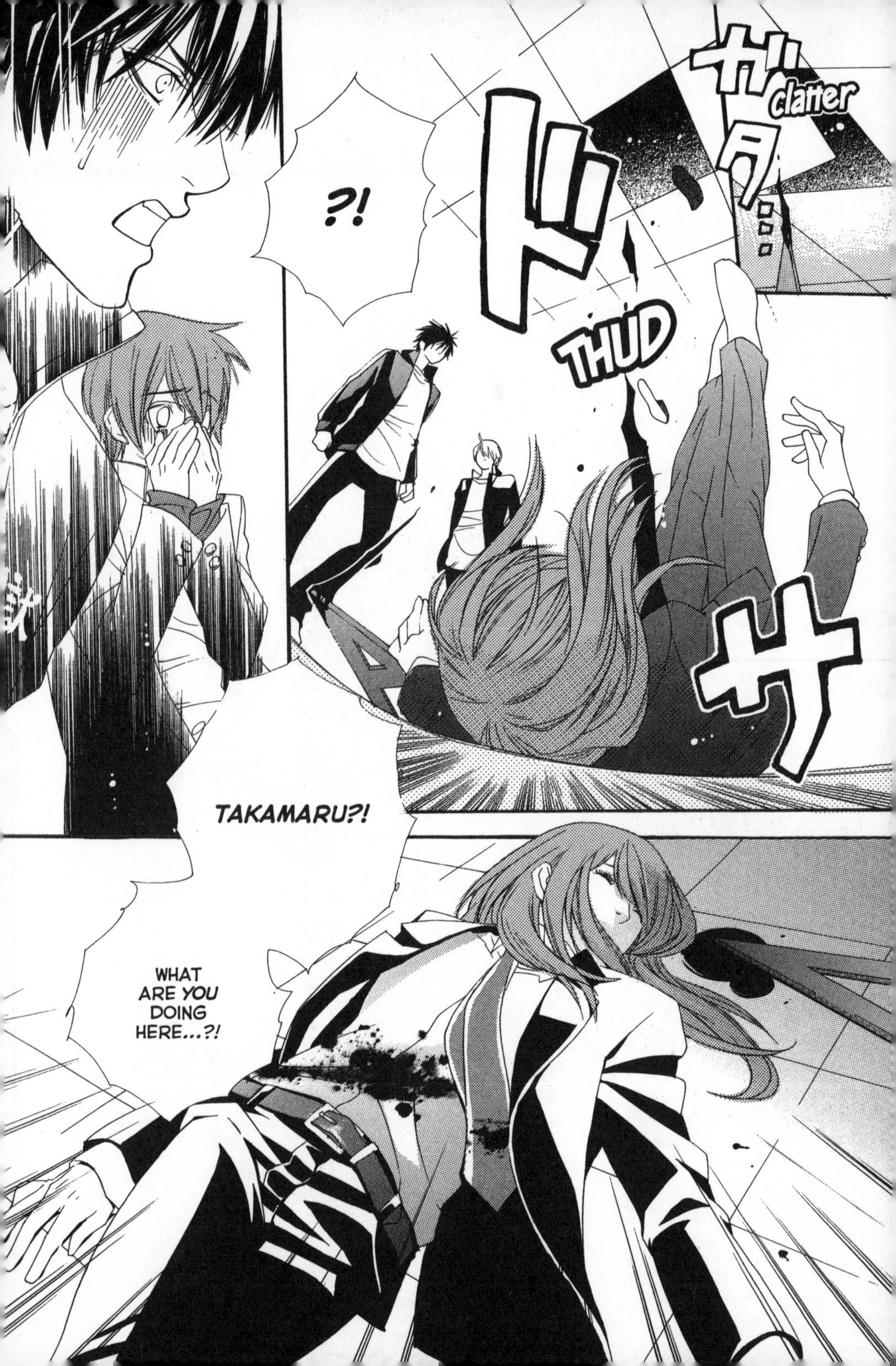

ガタ…
clatter
ドッ
THUD
?!
サ
TAKAMARU?!
WHAT ARE *YOU* DOING HERE...?!

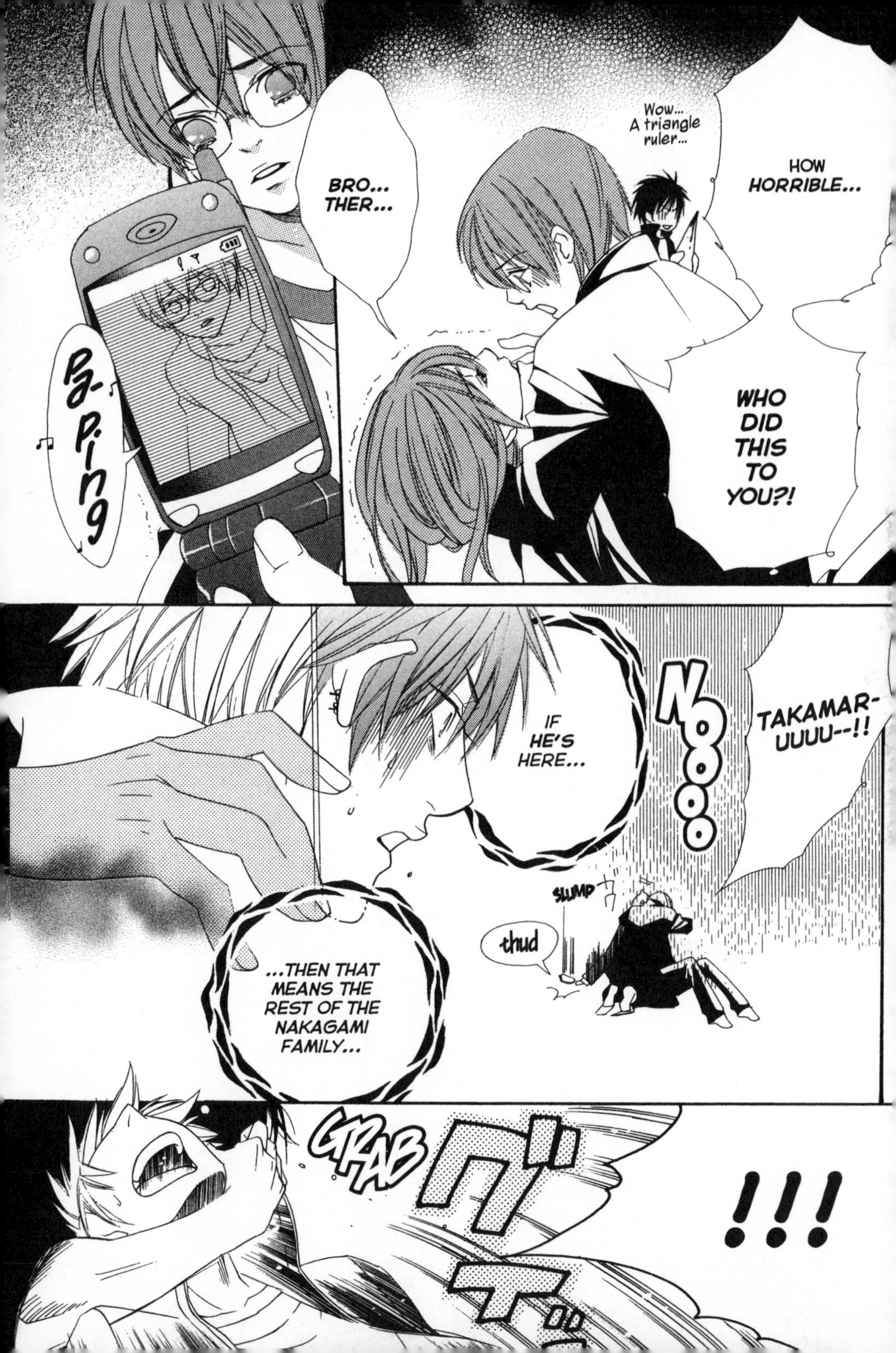
HOW HORRIBLE...
Wow... A triangle ruler...
WHO DID THIS TO YOU?!
BRO... THER...
pa-ping
TAKAMAR-UUUU--!!
NOOOO
SLUMP
thud
IF HE'S HERE...
...THEN THAT MEANS THE REST OF THE NAKAGAMI FAMILY...
!!!
GRAB

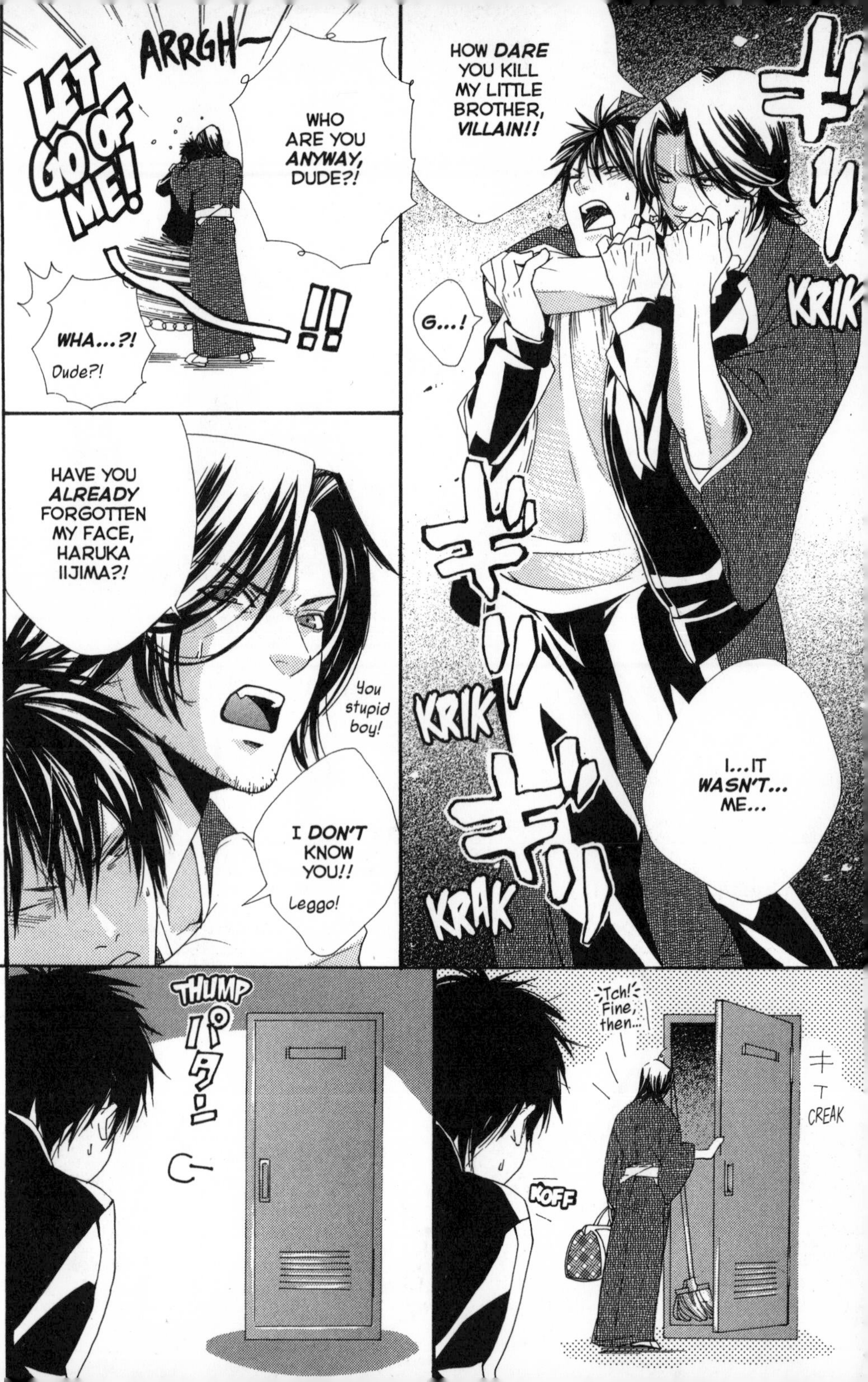
HOW DARE YOU KILL MY LITTLE BROTHER, VILLAIN!!
KRIK
G...!
KRIK
I...IT WASN'T... ME...
KRAK
ARRGH—
LET GO OF ME!
WHO ARE YOU ANYWAY, DUDE?!
WHA...?!
Dude?!
!!
HAVE YOU ALREADY FORGOTTEN MY FACE, HARUKA IIJIMA?!
You stupid boy!
I DON'T KNOW YOU!!
Leggo!
Tch! Fine, then...
CREAK
KOFF
THUMP

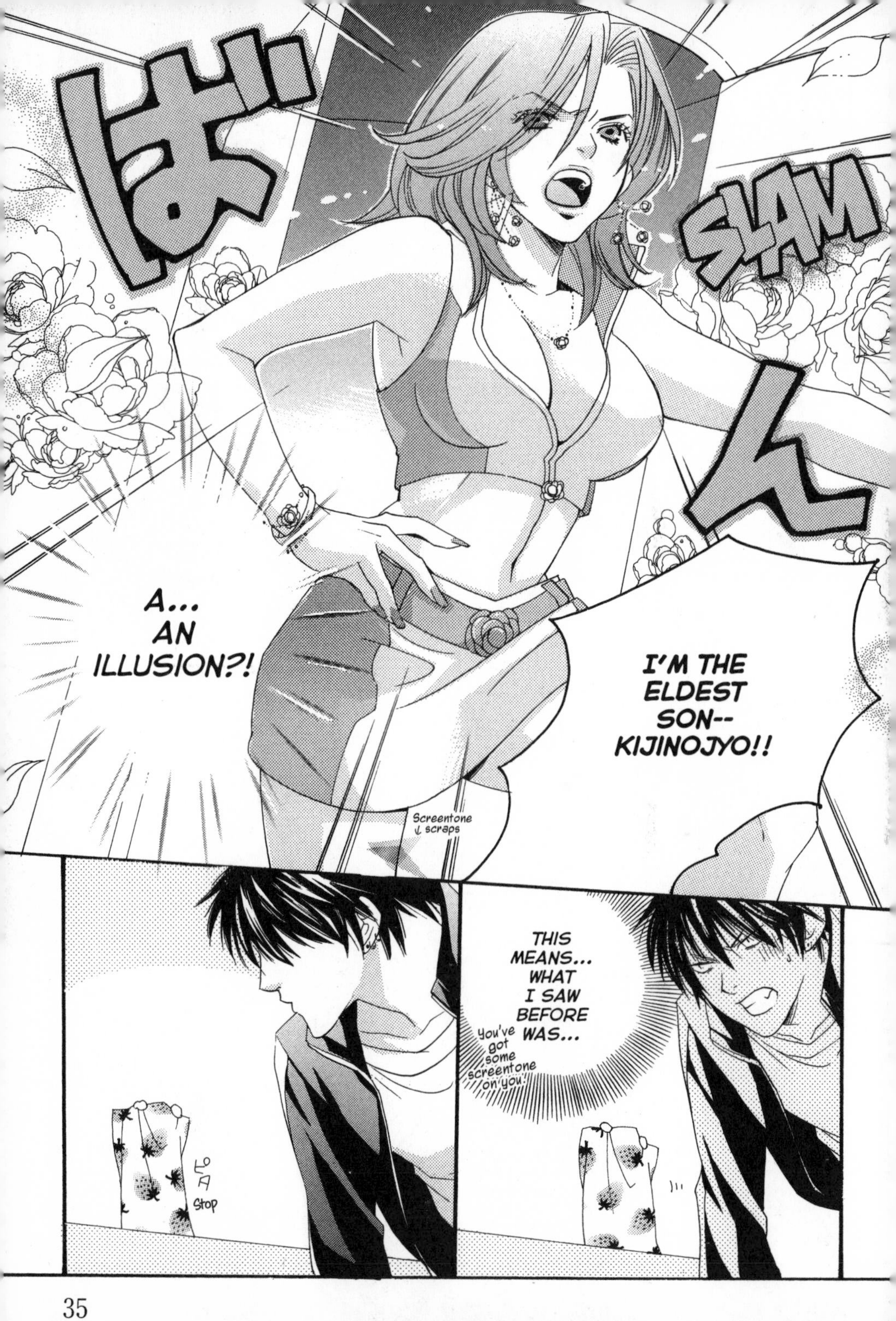
ばん
SLAM
I'M THE ELDEST SON-- KIJINOJYO!!
A... AN ILLUSION?!
Screentone scraps
THIS MEANS... WHAT I SAW BEFORE WAS...
You've got some screentone on you!
ピタ
Stop

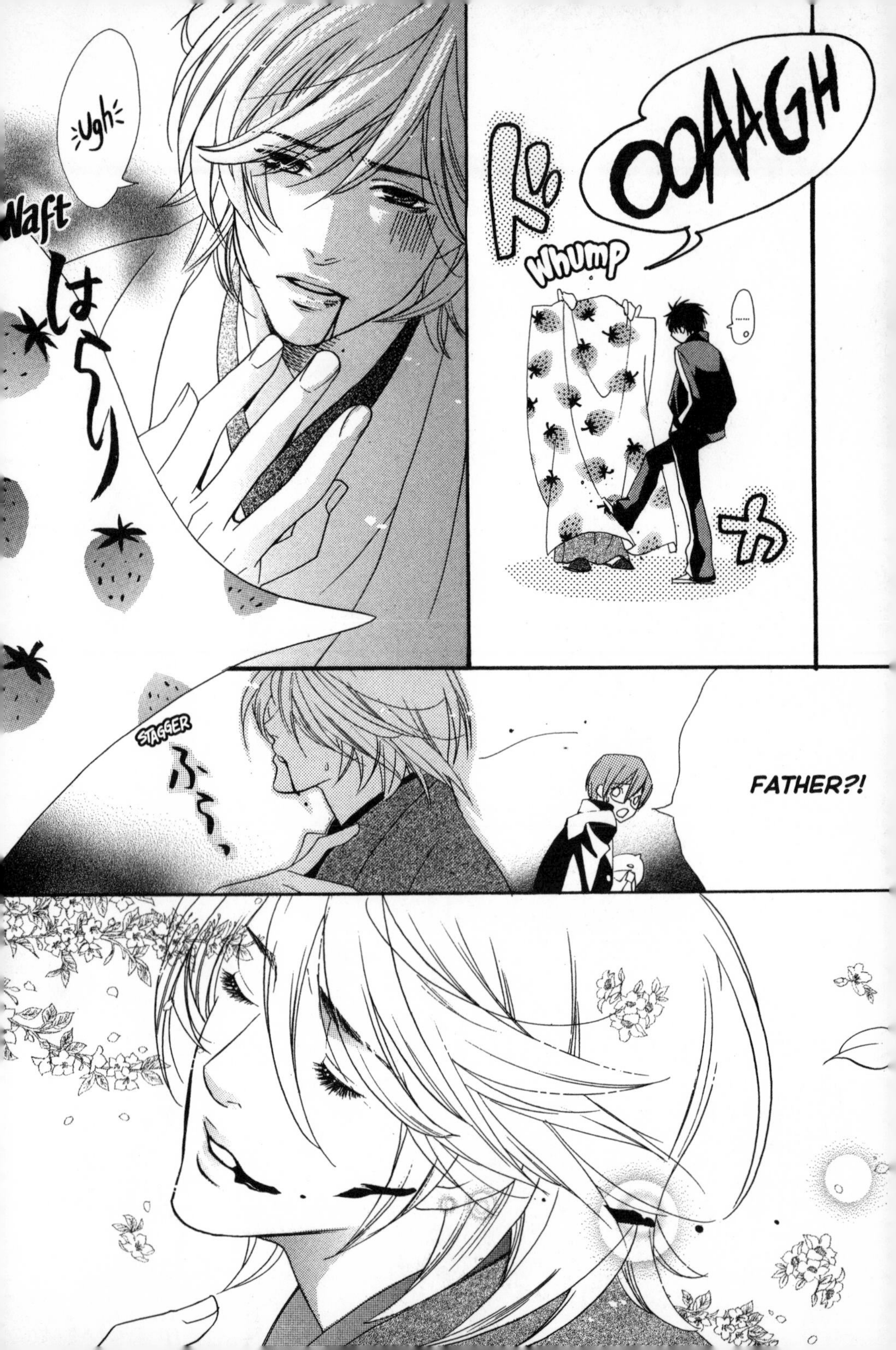
OOAAGH
Whump
......
Ugh
Waft
はらり
FATHER?!
Stagger
ふら

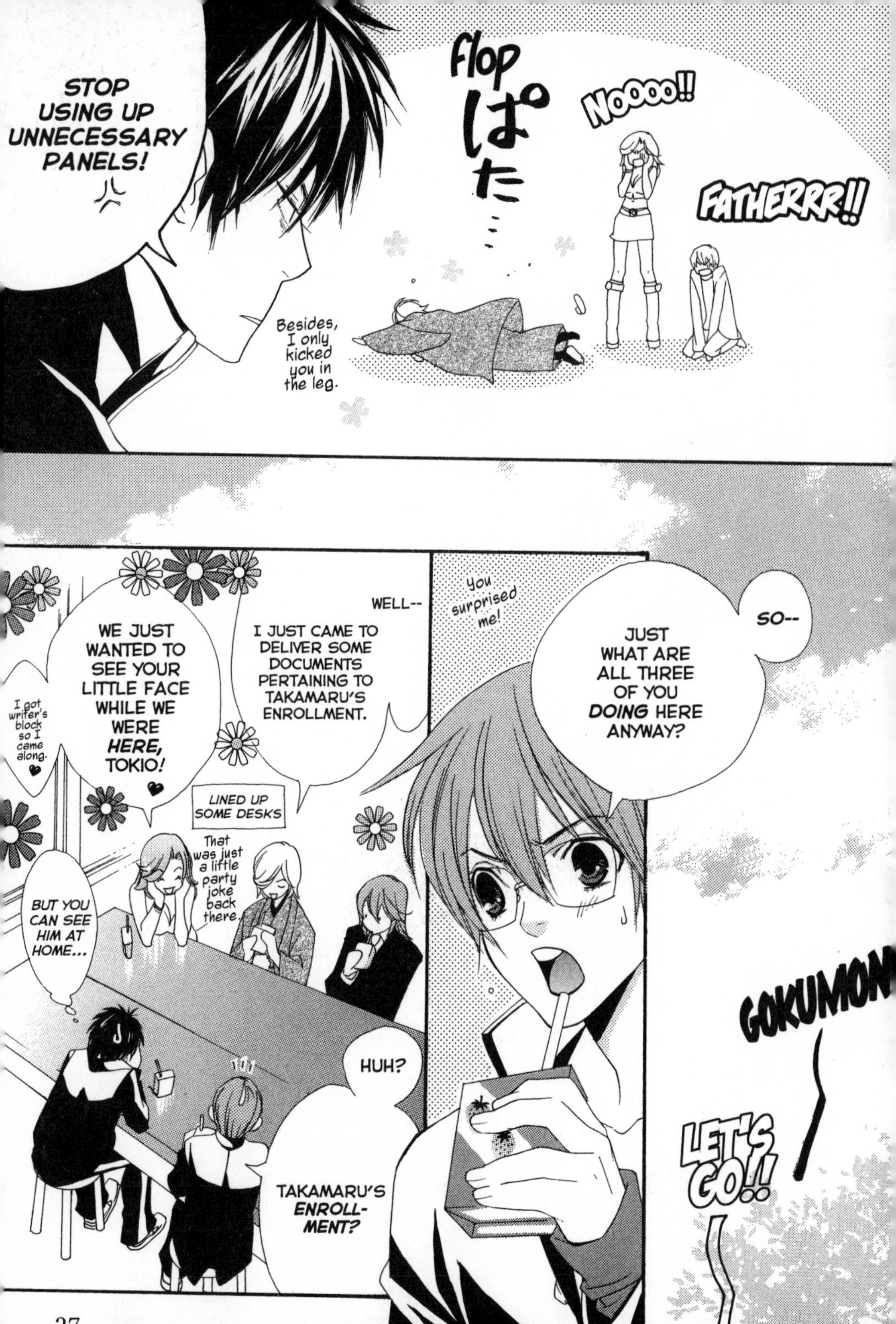
Noooo!!
FATHERRR!!
flop
ぱた…
STOP USING UP UNNECESSARY PANELS!
Besides, I only kicked you in the leg.
GOKUMON
LET'S GO!!
SO--
JUST WHAT ARE ALL THREE OF YOU DOING HERE ANYWAY?
You surprised me!
WELL--
I JUST CAME TO DELIVER SOME DOCUMENTS PERTAINING TO TAKAMARU'S ENROLLMENT.
WE JUST WANTED TO SEE YOUR LITTLE FACE WHILE WE WERE HERE, TOKIO!
I got writer's block so I came along.
LINED UP SOME DESKS
That was just a little party joke back there.
BUT YOU CAN SEE HIM AT HOME...
HUH?
TAKAMARU'S ENROLLMENT?

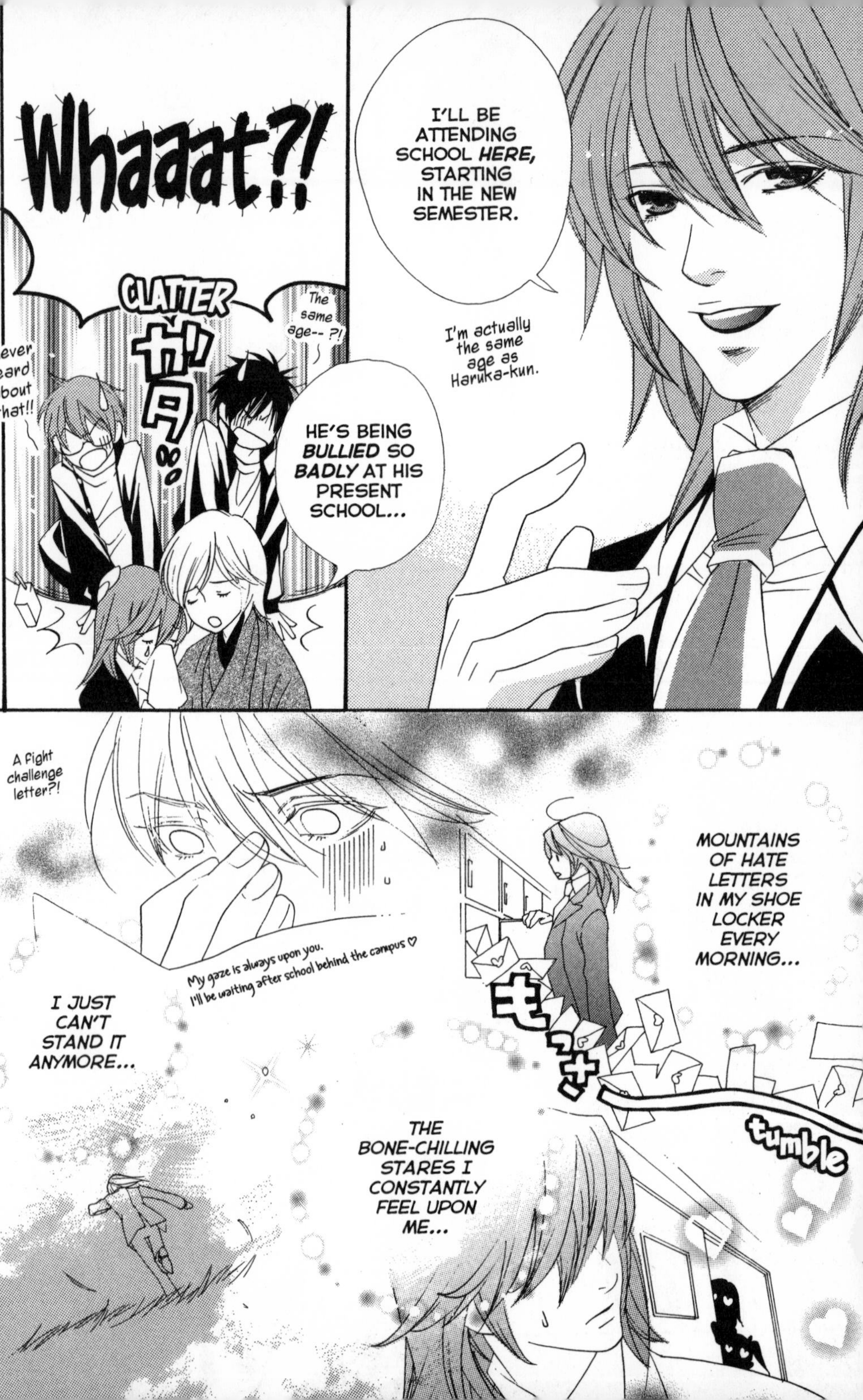
I'LL BE ATTENDING SCHOOL HERE, STARTING IN THE NEW SEMESTER.
I'm actually the same age as Haruka-kun.
Whaaat?!
The same age-- ?!
CLATTER
I never heard about that!!
HE'S BEING BULLIED SO BADLY AT HIS PRESENT SCHOOL...
MOUNTAINS OF HATE LETTERS IN MY SHOE LOCKER EVERY MORNING...
tumble
THE BONE-CHILLING STARES I CONSTANTLY FEEL UPON ME...
A fight challenge letter?!
My gaze is always upon you.
I'll be waiting after school behind the campus ♡
I JUST CAN'T STAND IT ANYMORE...

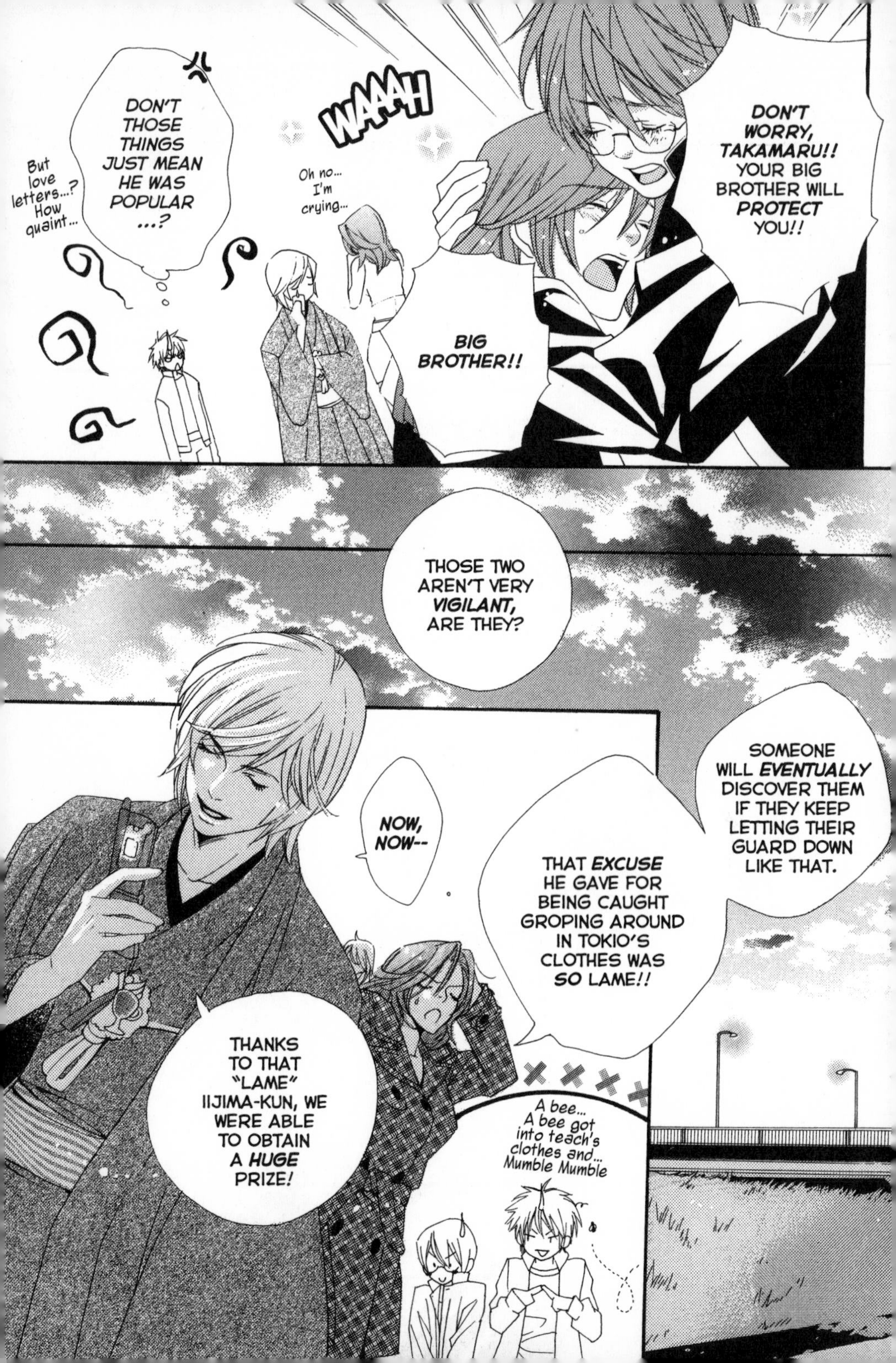
DON'T WORRY, TAKAMARU!! YOUR BIG BROTHER WILL PROTECT YOU!!
BIG BROTHER!!
WAAAH
Oh no... I'm crying...
DON'T THOSE THINGS JUST MEAN HE WAS POPULAR ...?
But love letters...? How quaint...
THOSE TWO AREN'T VERY VIGILANT, ARE THEY?
SOMEONE WILL EVENTUALLY DISCOVER THEM IF THEY KEEP LETTING THEIR GUARD DOWN LIKE THAT.
THAT EXCUSE HE GAVE FOR BEING CAUGHT GROPING AROUND IN TOKIO'S CLOTHES WAS SO LAME!!
NOW, NOW--
THANKS TO THAT "LAME" IIJIMA-KUN, WE WERE ABLE TO OBTAIN A HUGE PRIZE!
A bee... A bee got into teach's clothes and... Mumble Mumble

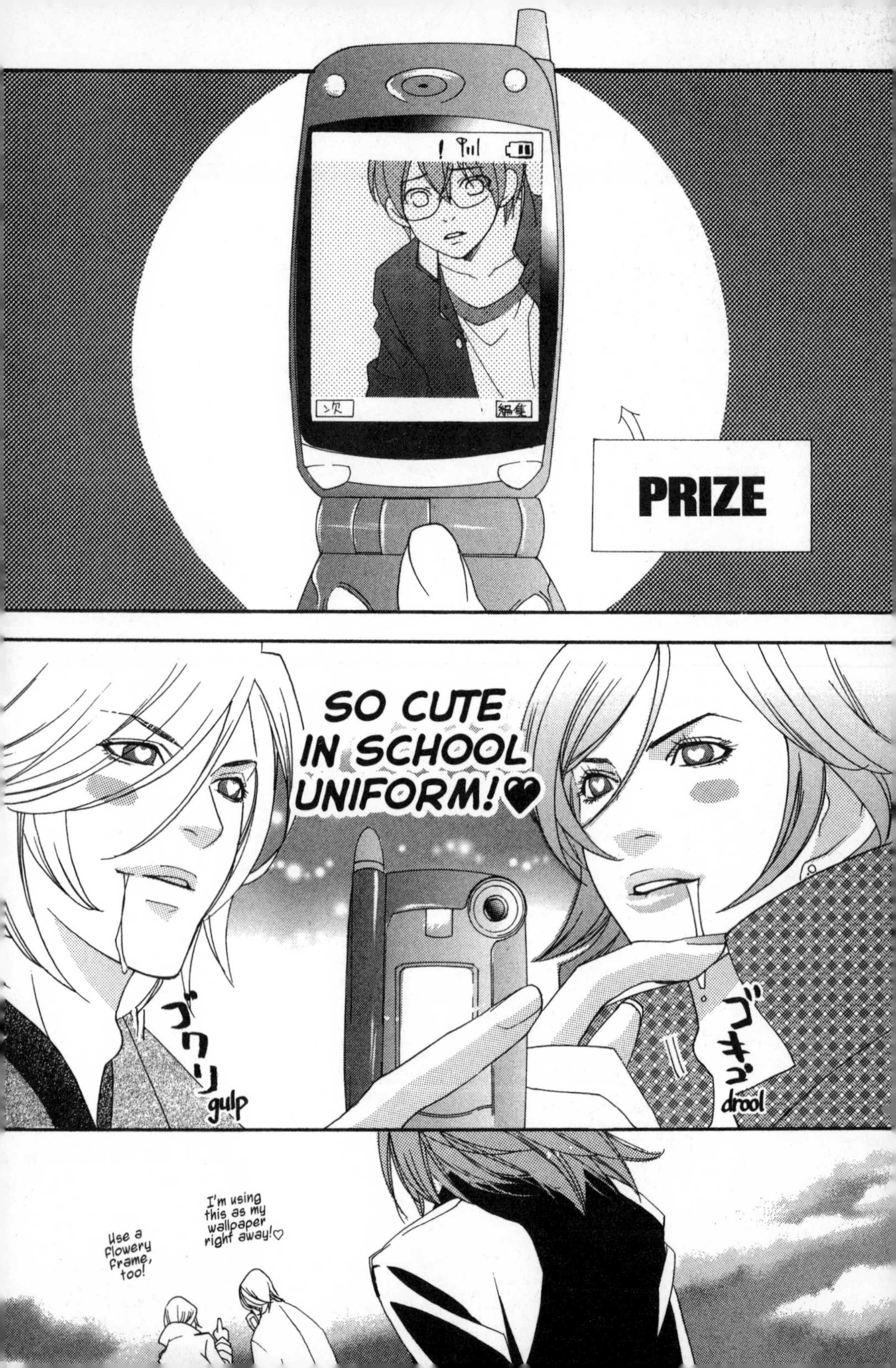

次
編集
PRIZE
SO CUTE IN SCHOOL UNIFORM!♥
drool
ゴクリ
gulp
I'm using this as my wallpaper right away!♡
Use a flowery frame, too!

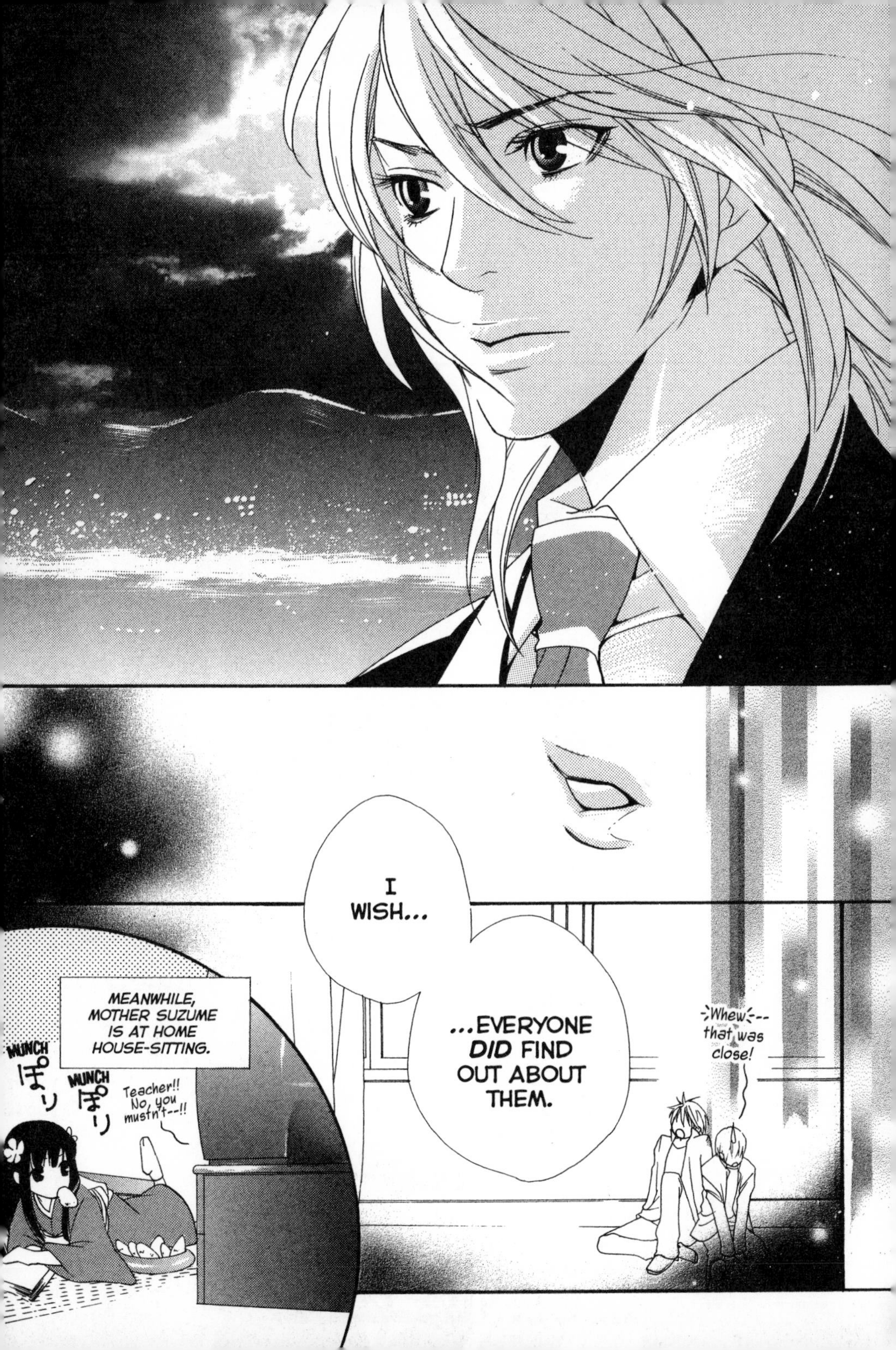
I WISH...
...EVERYONE DID FIND OUT ABOUT THEM.
Whew--that was close!
MEANWHILE, MOTHER SUZUME IS AT HOME HOUSE-SITTING.
MUNCH ぽり
MUNCH ぽり
Teacher!! No, you mustn't--!!

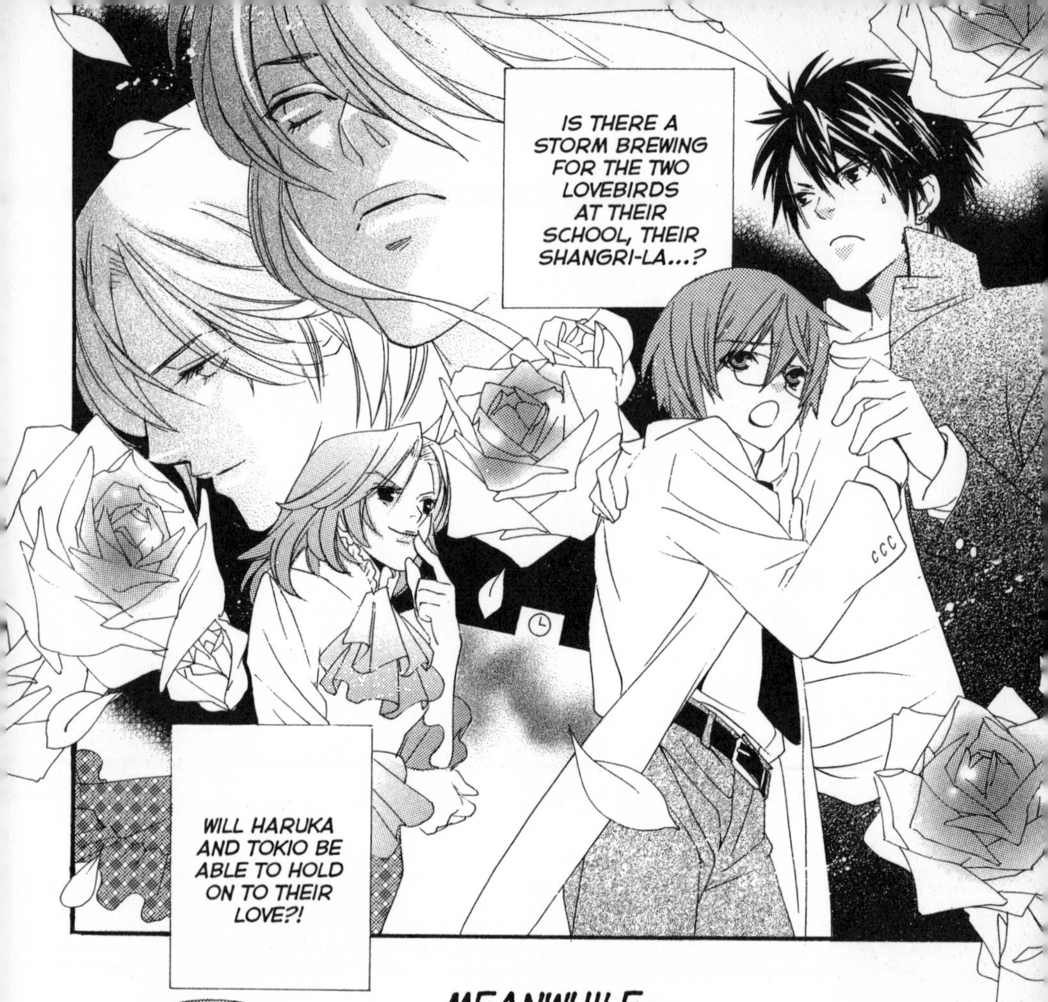
IS THERE A STORM BREWING FOR THE TWO LOVEBIRDS AT THEIR SCHOOL, THEIR SHANGRI-LA...?
WILL HARUKA AND TOKIO BE ABLE TO HOLD ON TO THEIR LOVE?!

MEANWHILE--

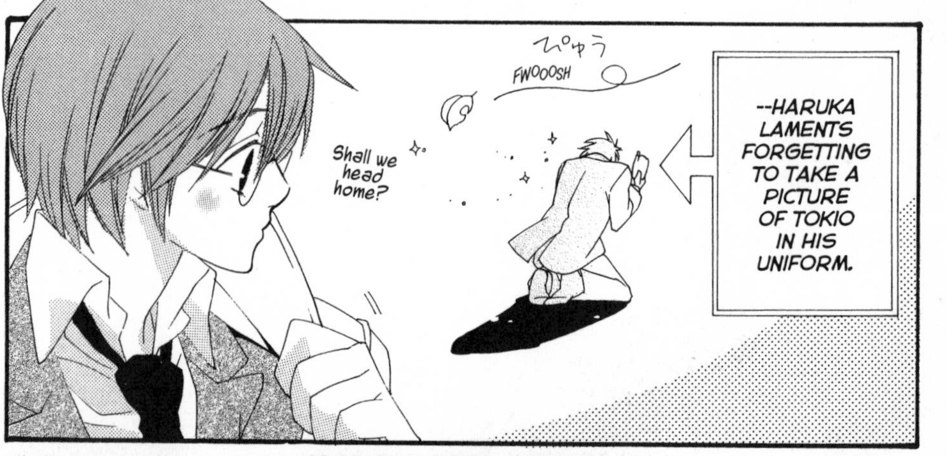
--HARUKA LAMENTS FORGETTING TO TAKE A PICTURE OF TOKIO IN HIS UNIFORM.
ぴゅう
FWOOOSH
Shall we head home?

仲神家の刺客／おわり

THE LONG ARM OF THE NAKAGAMIS / END

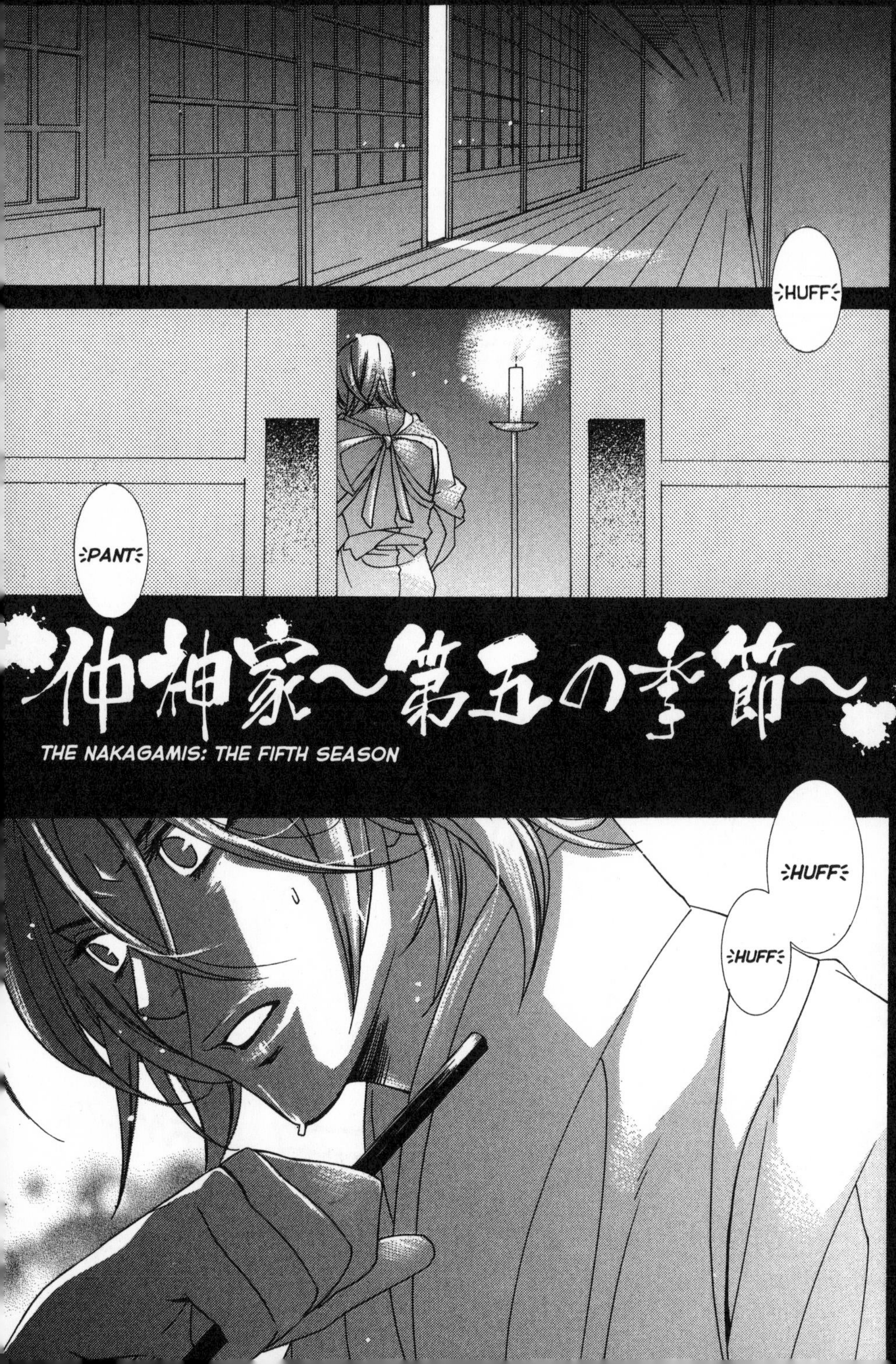
HUFF
PANT
仲神家～第五の季節～
THE NAKAGAMIS: THE FIFTH SEASON
HUFF
HUFF

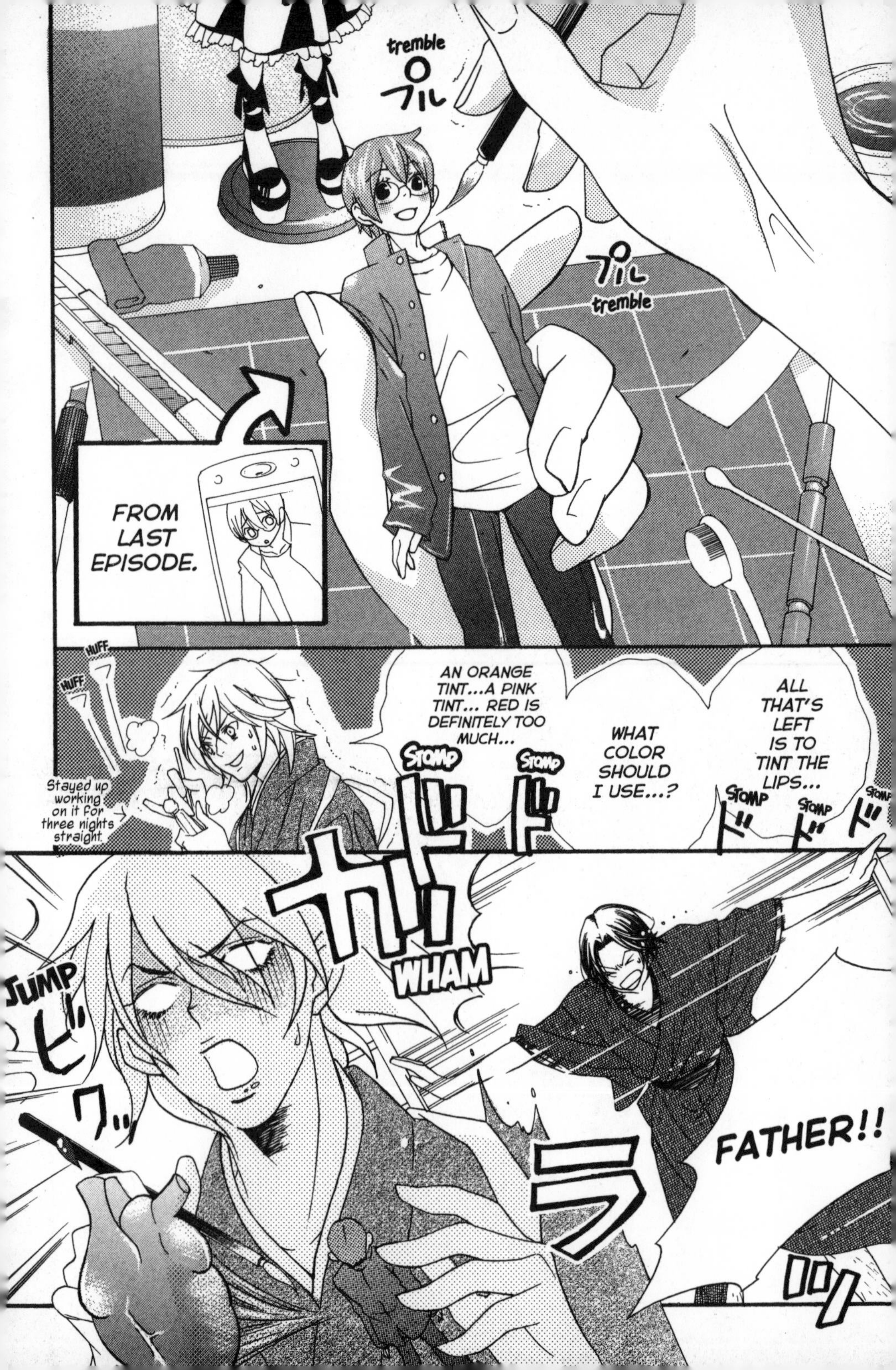

tremble
プル
プル
tremble
FROM LAST EPISODE.
ALL THAT'S LEFT IS TO TINT THE LIPS...
STOMP
STOMP
STOMP
WHAT COLOR SHOULD I USE...?
AN ORANGE TINT...A PINK TINT... RED IS DEFINITELY TOO MUCH...
STOMP
STOMP
HUFF
HUFF
Stayed up working on it for three nights straight.
FATHER!!
WHAM
JUMP

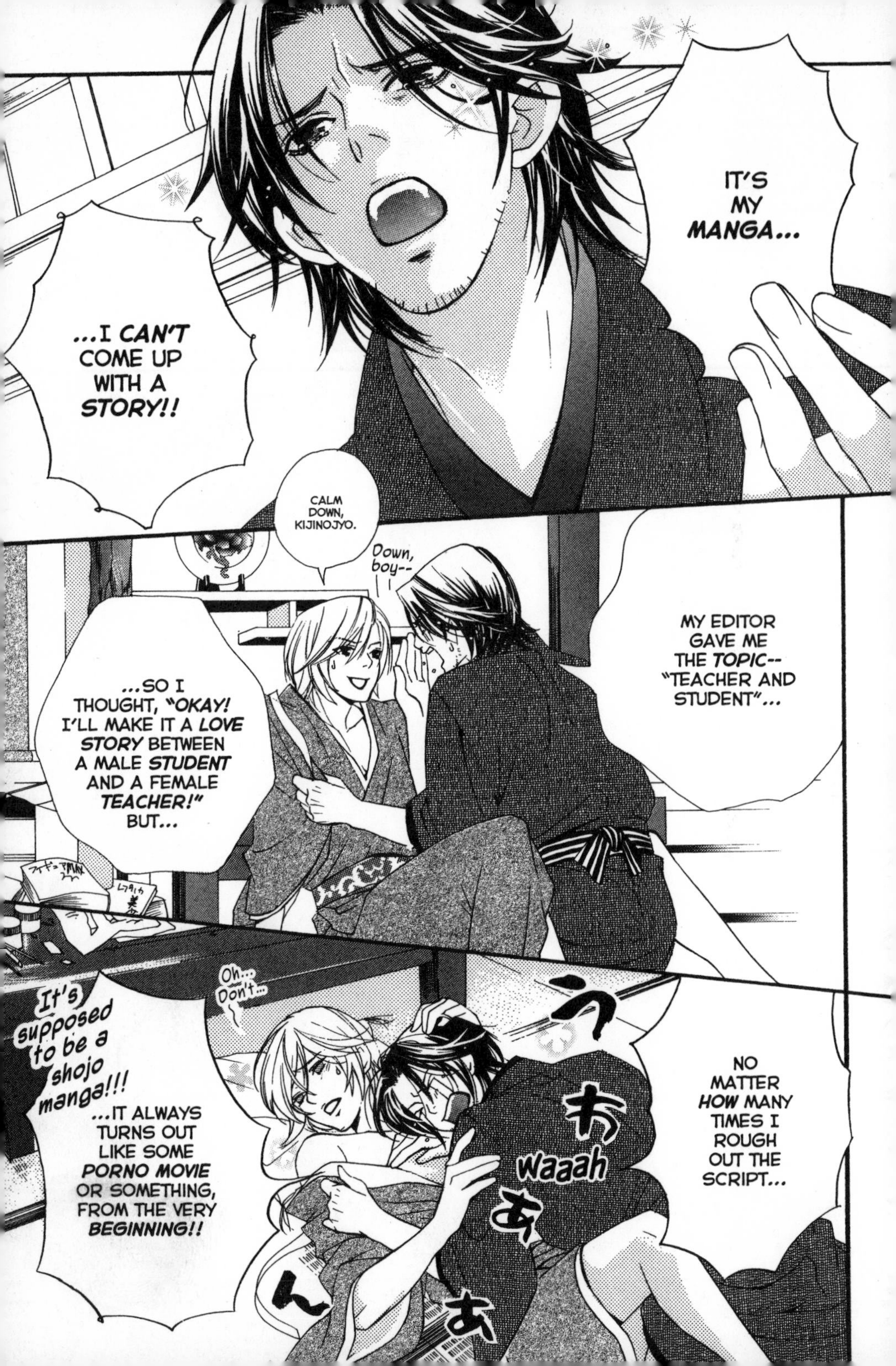
IT'S MY MANGA...
...I CAN'T COME UP WITH A STORY!!
MY EDITOR GAVE ME THE TOPIC-- "TEACHER AND STUDENT"...
CALM DOWN, KIJINOJYO.
Down, boy--
...SO I THOUGHT, "OKAY! I'LL MAKE IT A LOVE STORY BETWEEN A MALE STUDENT AND A FEMALE TEACHER!" BUT...
NO MATTER HOW MANY TIMES I ROUGH OUT THE SCRIPT...
waaah
Oh... Don't...
It's supposed to be a shojo manga!!!
...IT ALWAYS TURNS OUT LIKE SOME PORNO MOVIE OR SOMETHING, FROM THE VERY BEGINNING!!

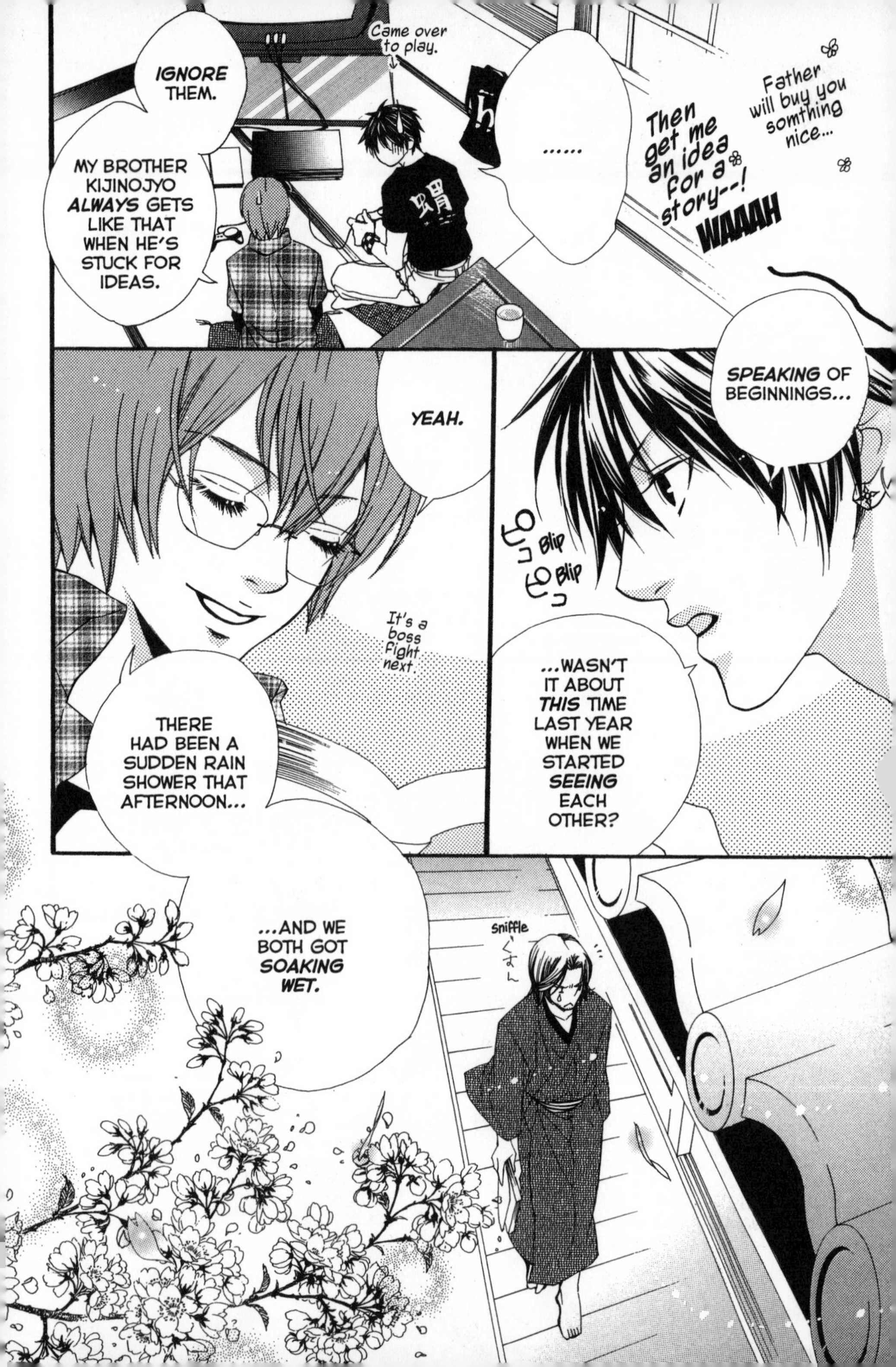
Father will buy you somthing nice...
Then get me an idea for a story--!
WAAAH
......
Came over to play.
IGNORE THEM.
MY BROTHER KIJINOJYO ALWAYS GETS LIKE THAT WHEN HE'S STUCK FOR IDEAS.
SPEAKING OF BEGINNINGS...
Blip Blip
...WASN'T IT ABOUT THIS TIME LAST YEAR WHEN WE STARTED SEEING EACH OTHER?
YEAH.
It's a boss fight next.
THERE HAD BEEN A SUDDEN RAIN SHOWER THAT AFTERNOON...
Sniffle
ぐすん
...AND WE BOTH GOT SOAKING WET.

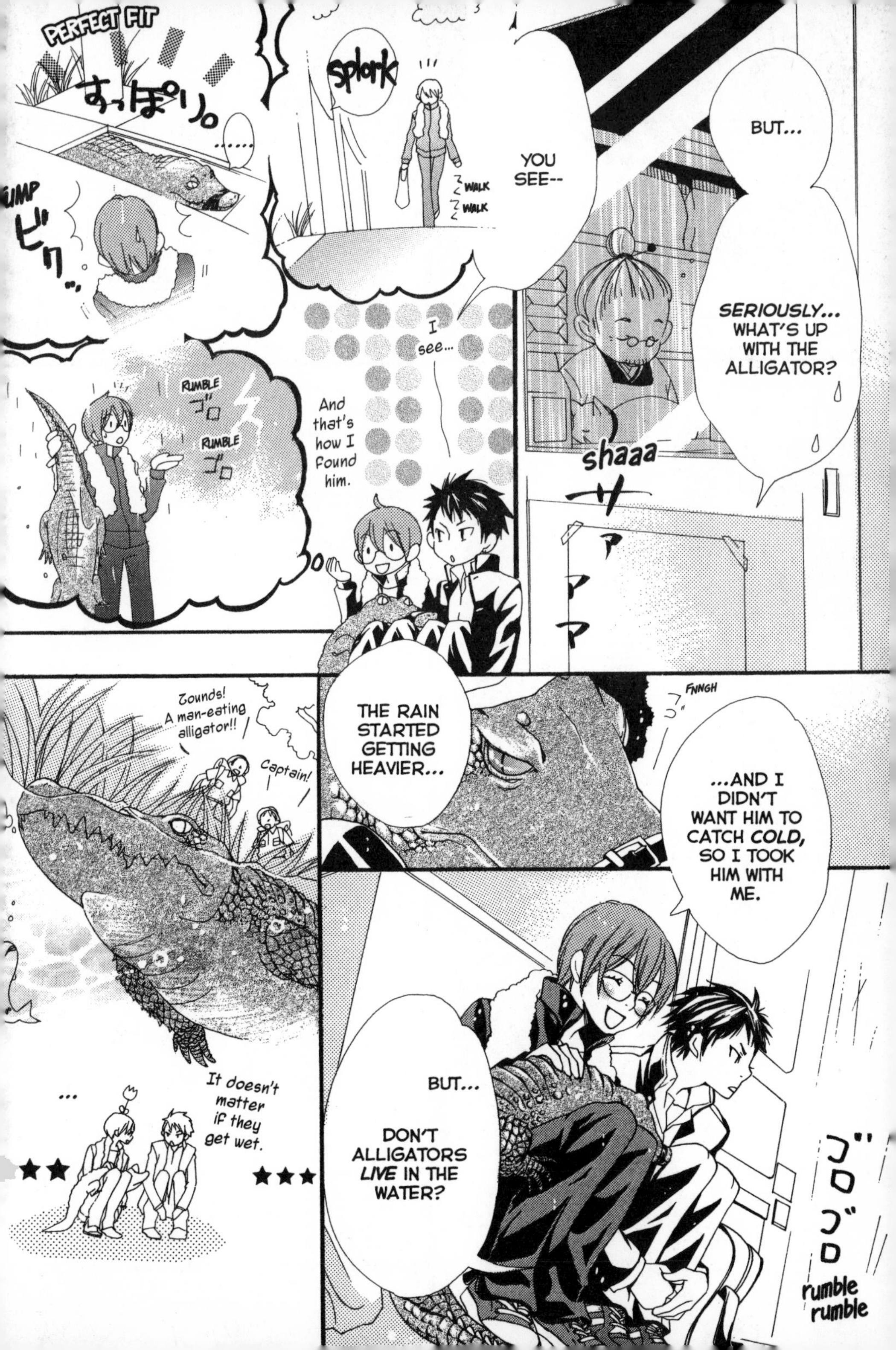
BUT...
SERIOUSLY... WHAT'S UP WITH THE ALLIGATOR?
shaaa
サァァァ
YOU SEE--
splork
WALK
WALK
PERFECT FIT
すっぽり。
......
JUMP
ビクッ
RUMBLE
ゴロ
RUMBLE
ゴロ
I see...
And that's how I found him.
THE RAIN STARTED GETTING HEAVIER...
FNNGH
...AND I DIDN'T WANT HIM TO CATCH *COLD,* SO I TOOK HIM WITH ME.
BUT...
DON'T ALLIGATORS *LIVE* IN THE WATER?
ゴロゴロ
rumble rumble
Zounds! A man-eating alligator!!
Captain!
...
It doesn't matter if they get wet.

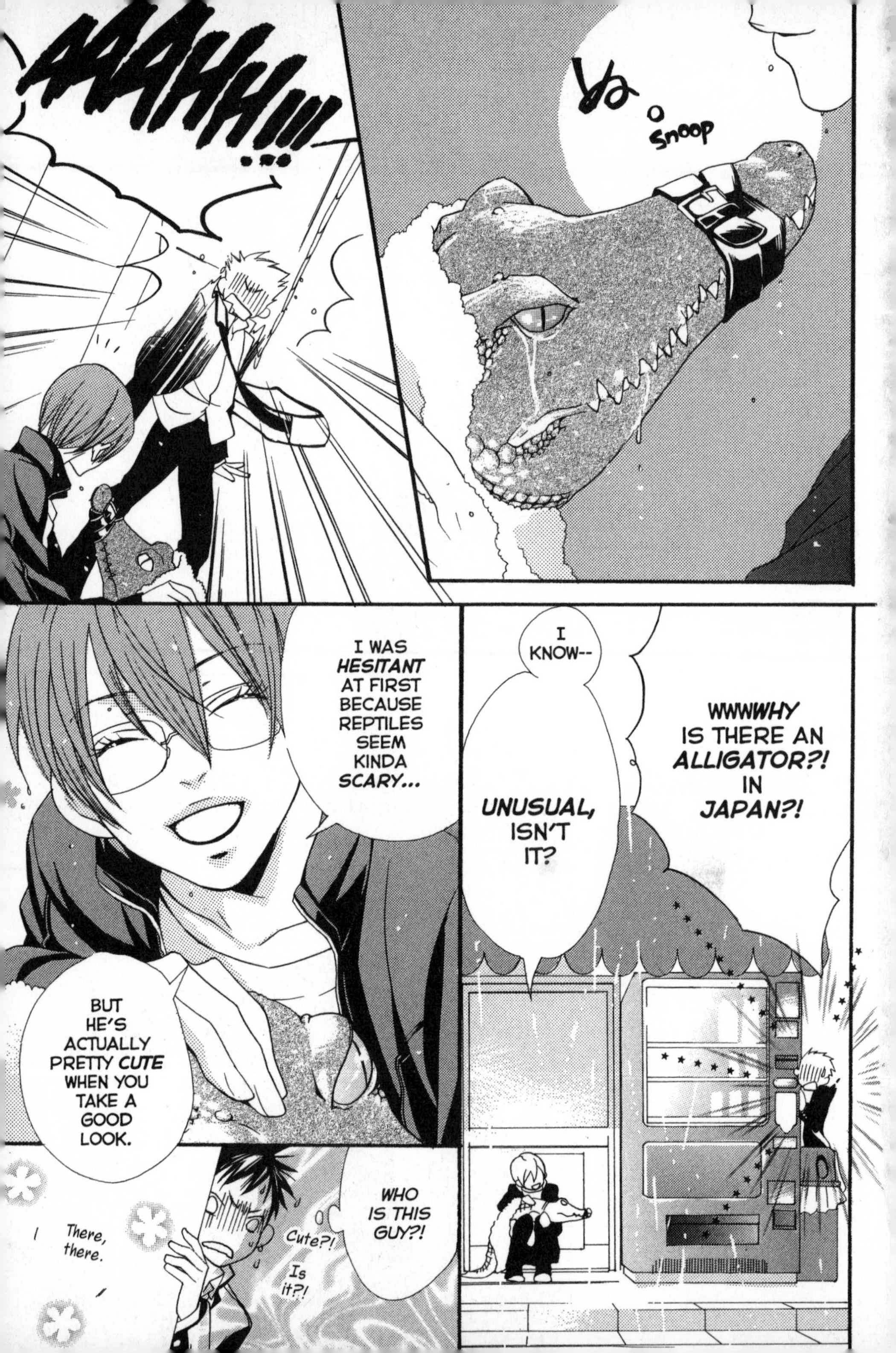

ぬ
Snoop
AAAHH!!!
WWWWHY IS THERE AN ALLIGATOR?! IN JAPAN?!
I KNOW--
UNUSUAL, ISN'T IT?
I WAS HESITANT AT FIRST BECAUSE REPTILES SEEM KINDA SCARY...
BUT HE'S ACTUALLY PRETTY CUTE WHEN YOU TAKE A GOOD LOOK.
WHO IS THIS GUY?!
Cute?!
Is it?!
There, there.

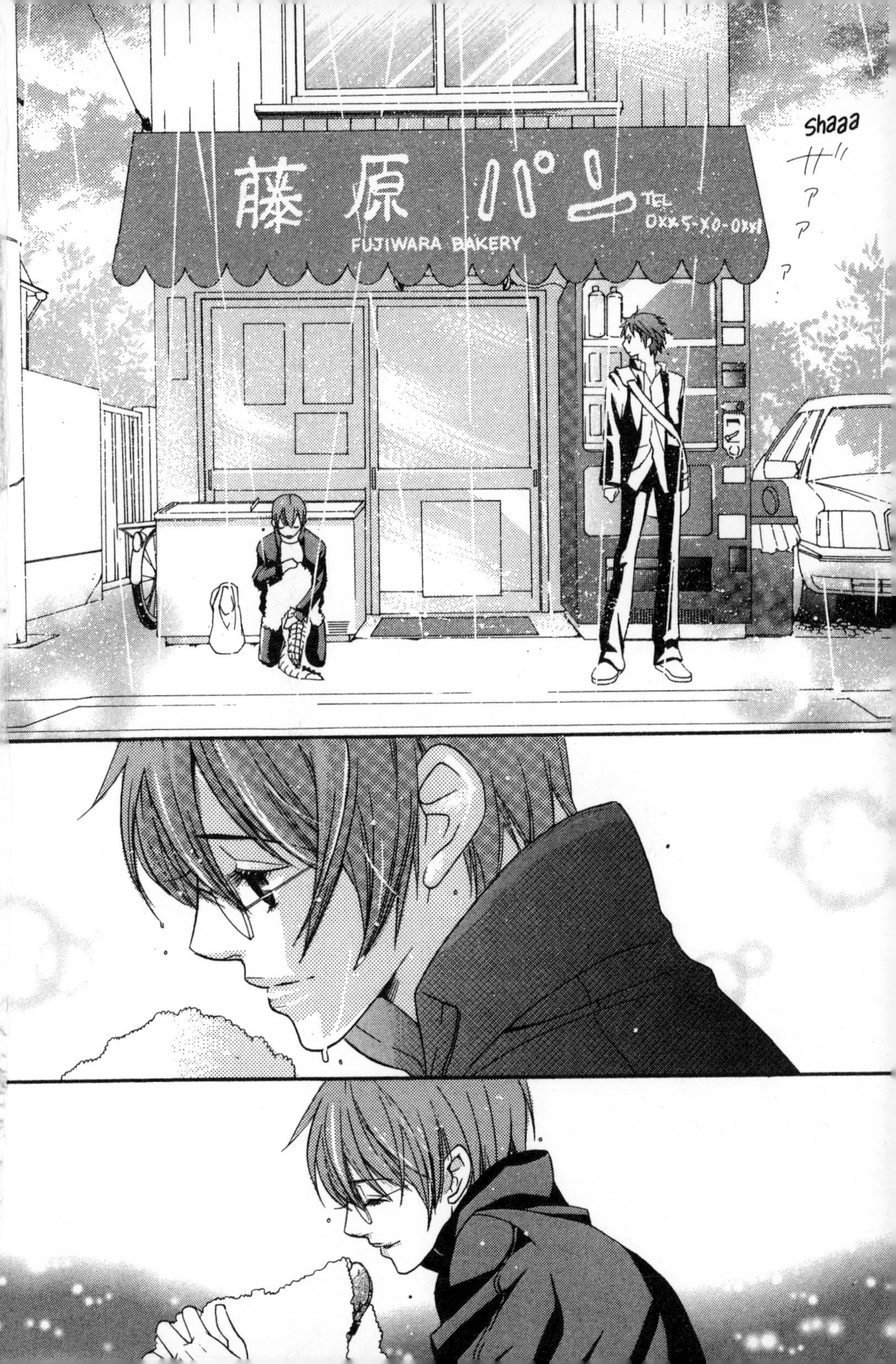
Shaaa
ザァァァ
藤原パン
FUJIWARA BAKERY
TEL
0××5-×0-0××1

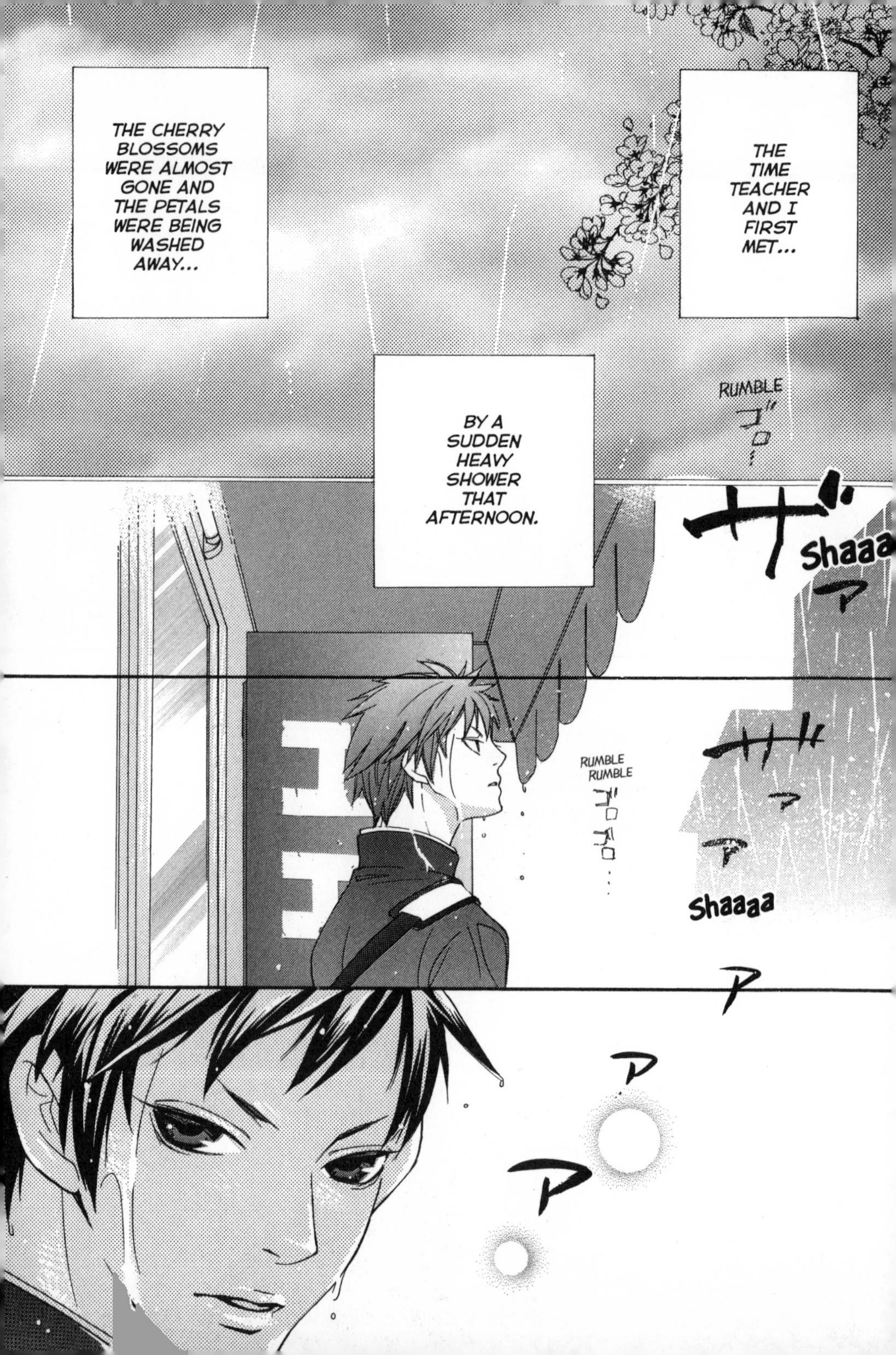
THE TIME TEACHER AND I FIRST MET...
THE CHERRY BLOSSOMS WERE ALMOST GONE AND THE PETALS WERE BEING WASHED AWAY...
RUMBLE
ゴロ…
BY A SUDDEN HEAVY SHOWER THAT AFTERNOON.
ザァ
Shaaa
ザァァァ
Shaaaa
RUMBLE RUMBLE
ゴロゴロ…

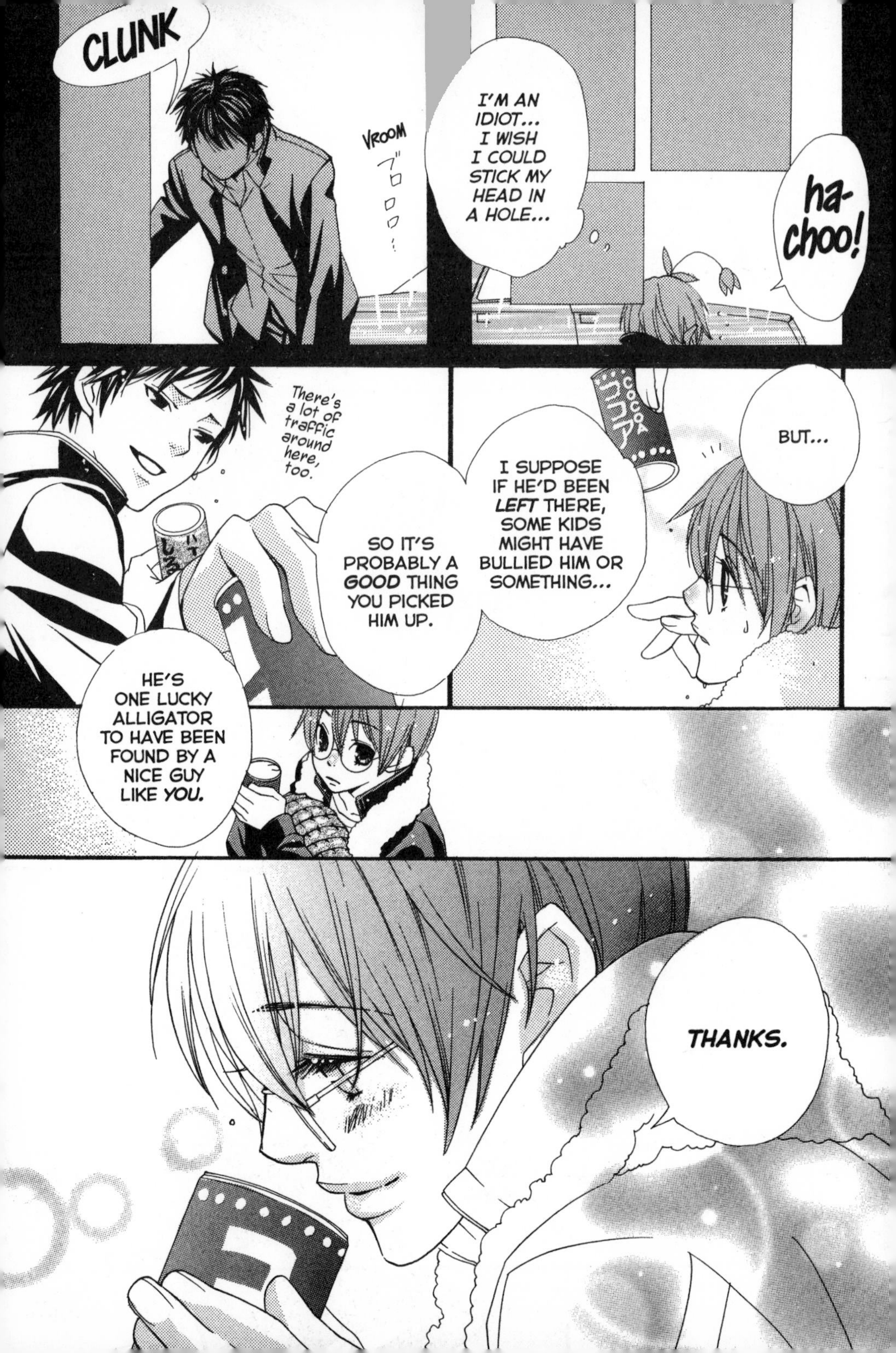
I'M AN IDIOT... I WISH I COULD STICK MY HEAD IN A HOLE...
ha-choo!
CLUNK
VROOM
ブロロロ…
BUT...
COCOA
ココア
I SUPPOSE IF HE'D BEEN *LEFT* THERE, SOME KIDS MIGHT HAVE BULLIED HIM OR SOMETHING...
SO IT'S PROBABLY A *GOOD* THING YOU PICKED HIM UP.
There's a lot of traffic around here, too.
HE'S ONE LUCKY ALLIGATOR TO HAVE BEEN FOUND BY A NICE GUY LIKE *YOU.*
THANKS.

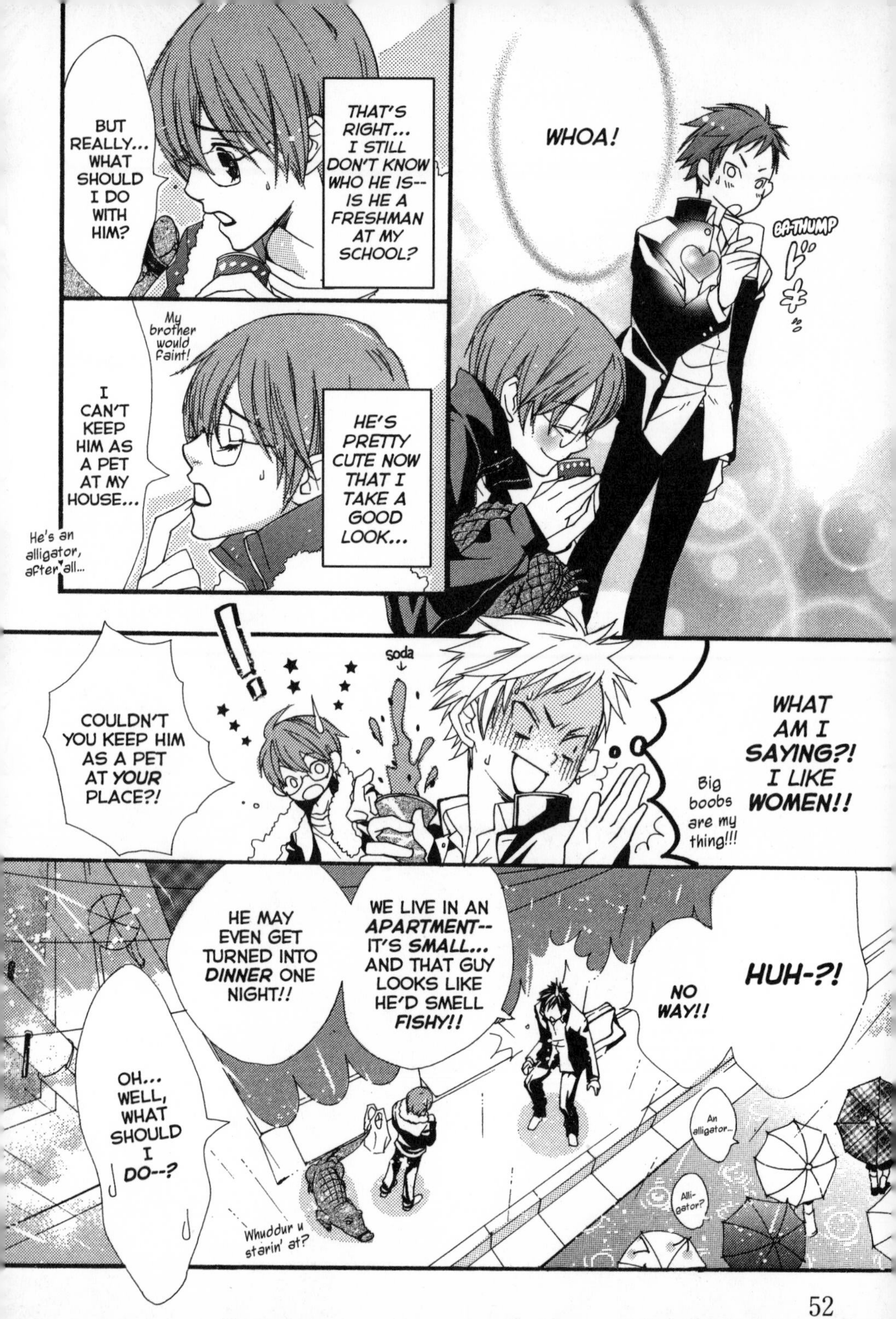
WHOA!
BA-THUMP
THAT'S RIGHT... I STILL DON'T KNOW WHO HE IS-- IS HE A FRESHMAN AT MY SCHOOL?
BUT REALLY... WHAT SHOULD I DO WITH HIM?
HE'S PRETTY CUTE NOW THAT I TAKE A GOOD LOOK...
My brother would faint!
I CAN'T KEEP HIM AS A PET AT MY HOUSE...
He's an alligator, after all...
WHAT AM I SAYING?! I LIKE WOMEN!!
Big boobs are my thing!!!
soda
COULDN'T YOU KEEP HIM AS A PET AT YOUR PLACE?!
HUH-?!
NO WAY!!
WE LIVE IN AN APARTMENT-- IT'S SMALL... AND THAT GUY LOOKS LIKE HE'D SMELL FISHY!!
HE MAY EVEN GET TURNED INTO DINNER ONE NIGHT!!
OH... WELL, WHAT SHOULD I DO--?
An alligator...
Alli-gator?
Whuddur u starin' at?

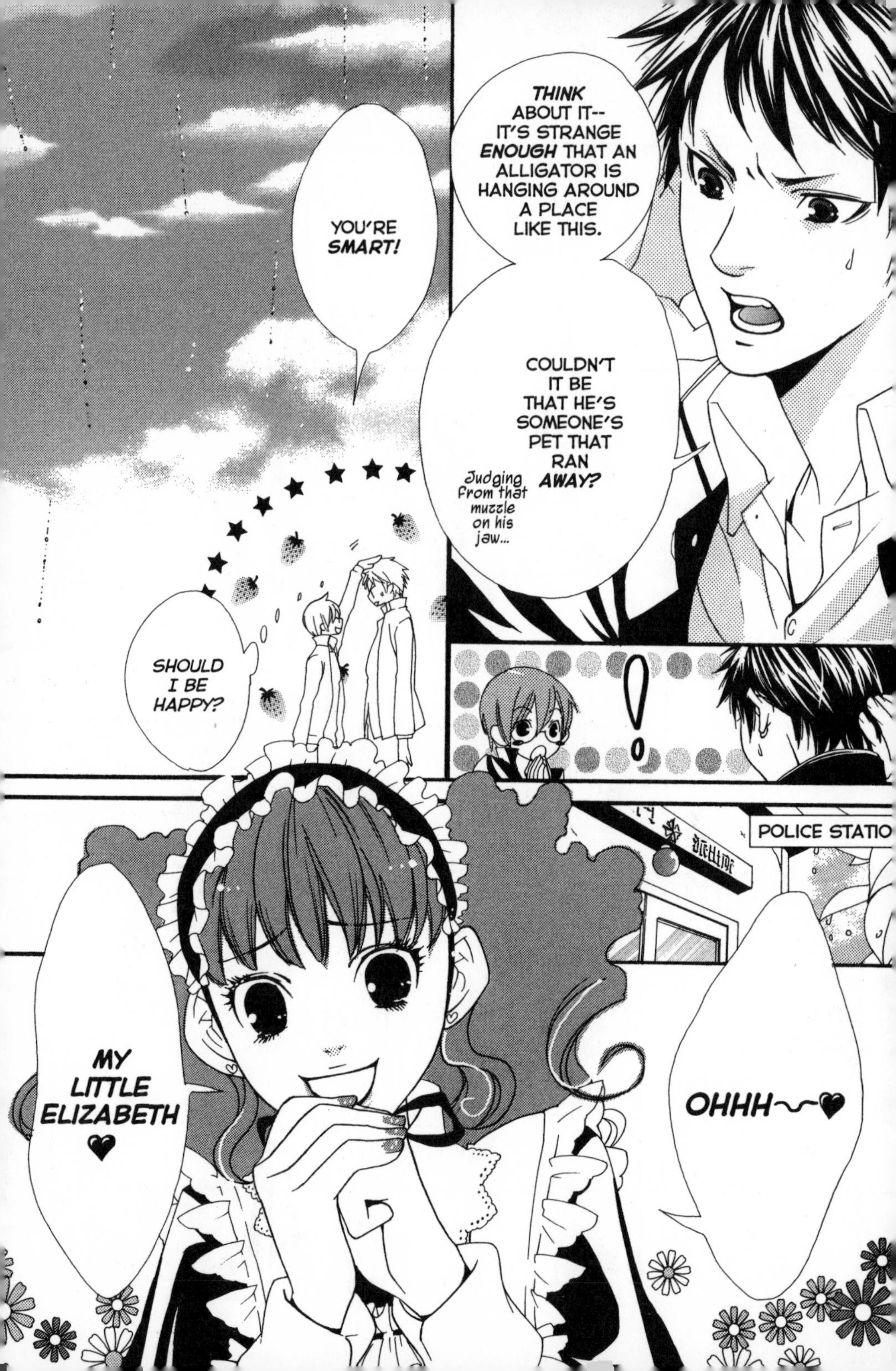
THINK ABOUT IT-- IT'S STRANGE ENOUGH THAT AN ALLIGATOR IS HANGING AROUND A PLACE LIKE THIS.
COULDN'T IT BE THAT HE'S SOMEONE'S PET THAT RAN AWAY?
Judging from that muzzle on his jaw...
!
YOU'RE SMART!
SHOULD I BE HAPPY?
POLICE STATIO
OHHH~~♥
MY LITTLE ELIZABETH ♥

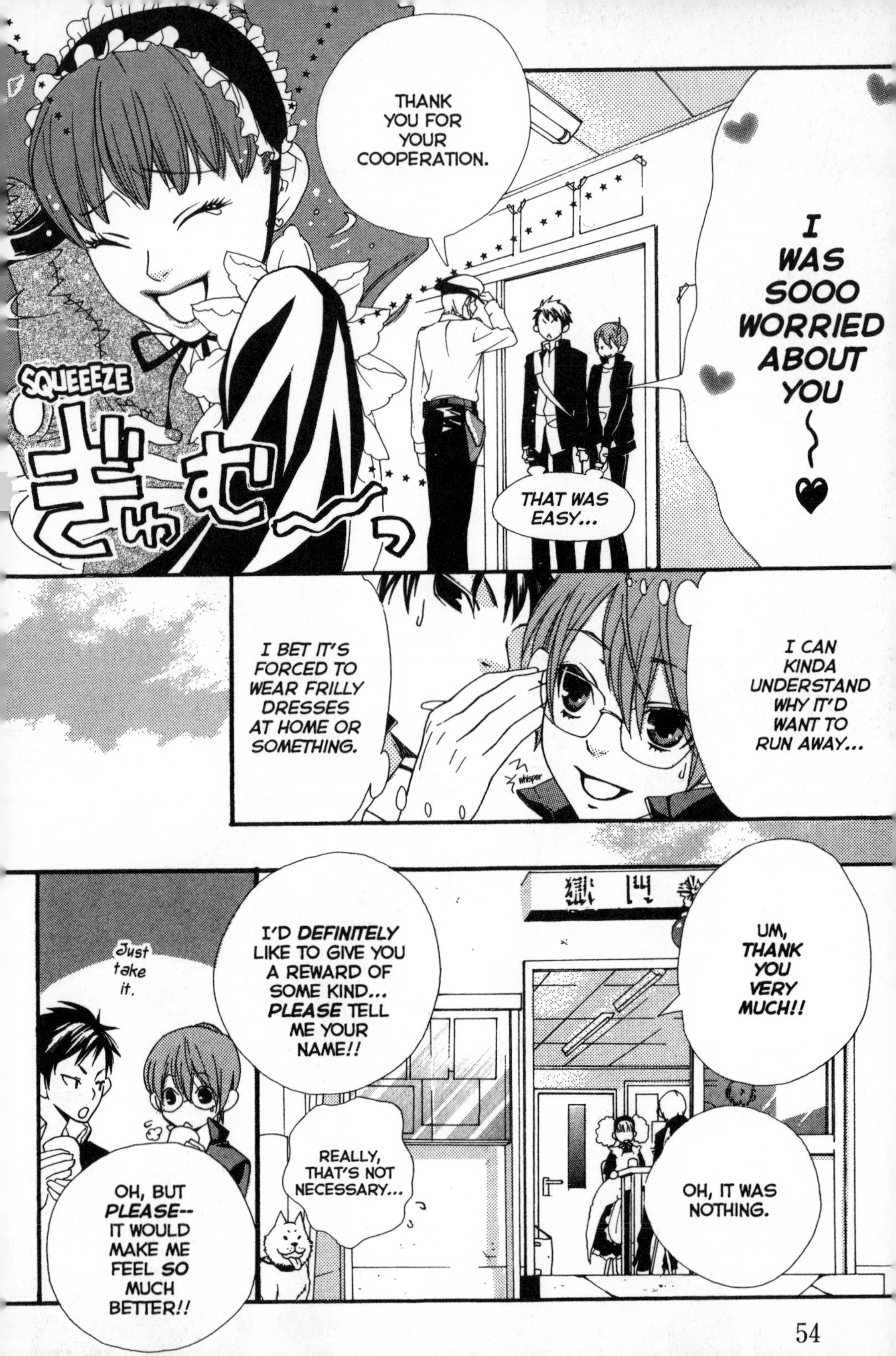
I WAS SOOO WORRIED ABOUT YOU ~ ♥
THANK YOU FOR YOUR COOPERATION.
SQUEEEZE
ぎゅむ～っ
THAT WAS EASY...
I CAN KINDA UNDERSTAND WHY IT'D WANT TO RUN AWAY...
whisper
I BET IT'S FORCED TO WEAR FRILLY DRESSES AT HOME OR SOMETHING.
UM, THANK YOU VERY MUCH!!
OH, IT WAS NOTHING.
I'D DEFINITELY LIKE TO GIVE YOU A REWARD OF SOME KIND... PLEASE TELL ME YOUR NAME!!
REALLY, THAT'S NOT NECESSARY...
Just take it.
OH, BUT PLEASE-- IT WOULD MAKE ME FEEL SO MUCH BETTER!!

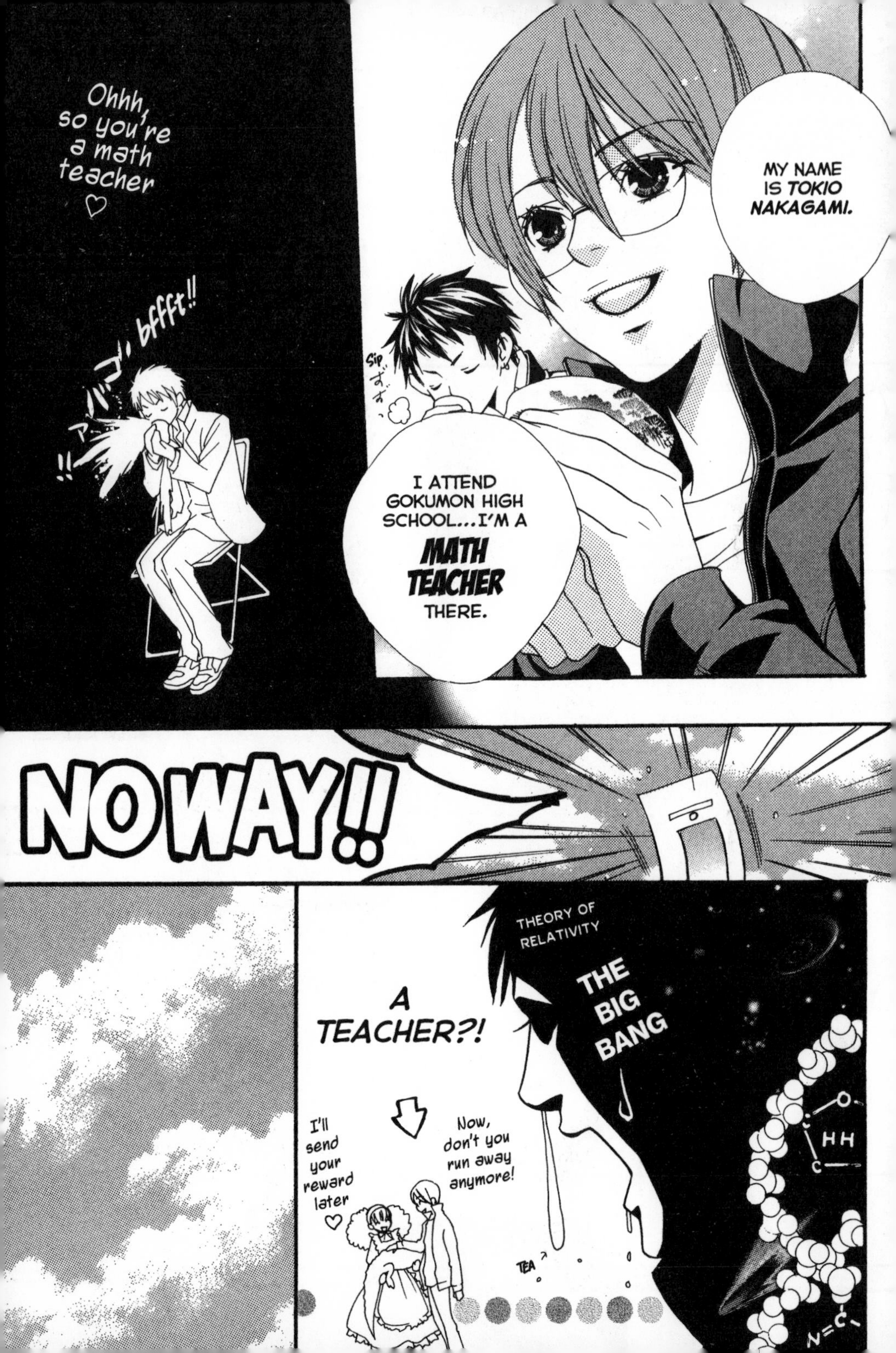
MY NAME IS TOKIO NAKAGAMI.
Sip
I ATTEND GOKUMON HIGH SCHOOL...I'M A MATH TEACHER THERE.
Ohhh, so you're a math teacher ♡
bffft!!
NO WAY!!
THEORY OF RELATIVITY
THE BIG BANG
A TEACHER?!
Now, don't you run away anymore!
I'll send your reward later ♡
TEA

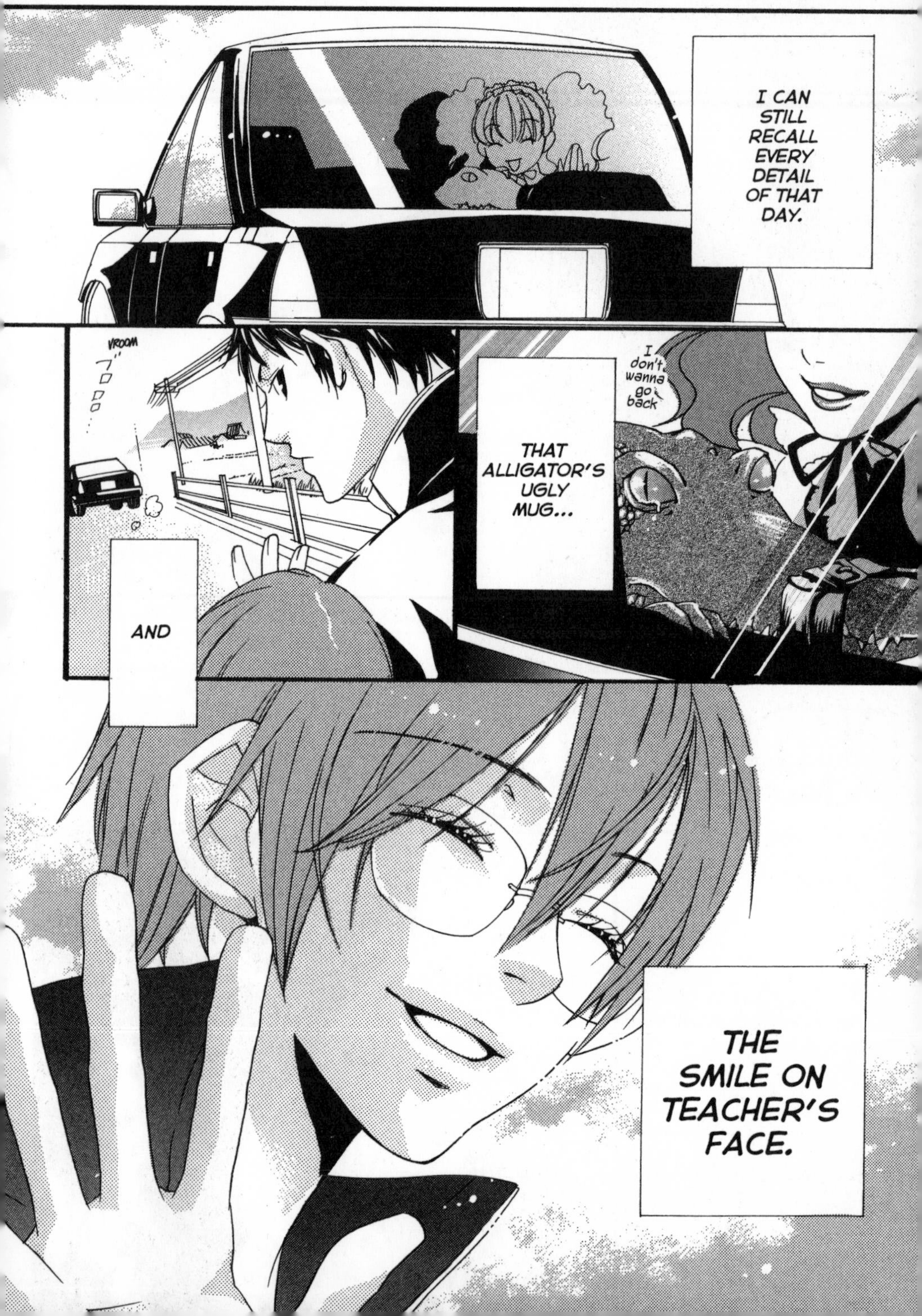
I CAN STILL RECALL EVERY DETAIL OF THAT DAY.
I don't wanna go back
THAT ALLIGATOR'S UGLY MUG...
VROOM
ブロロロ…
AND
THE SMILE ON TEACHER'S FACE.

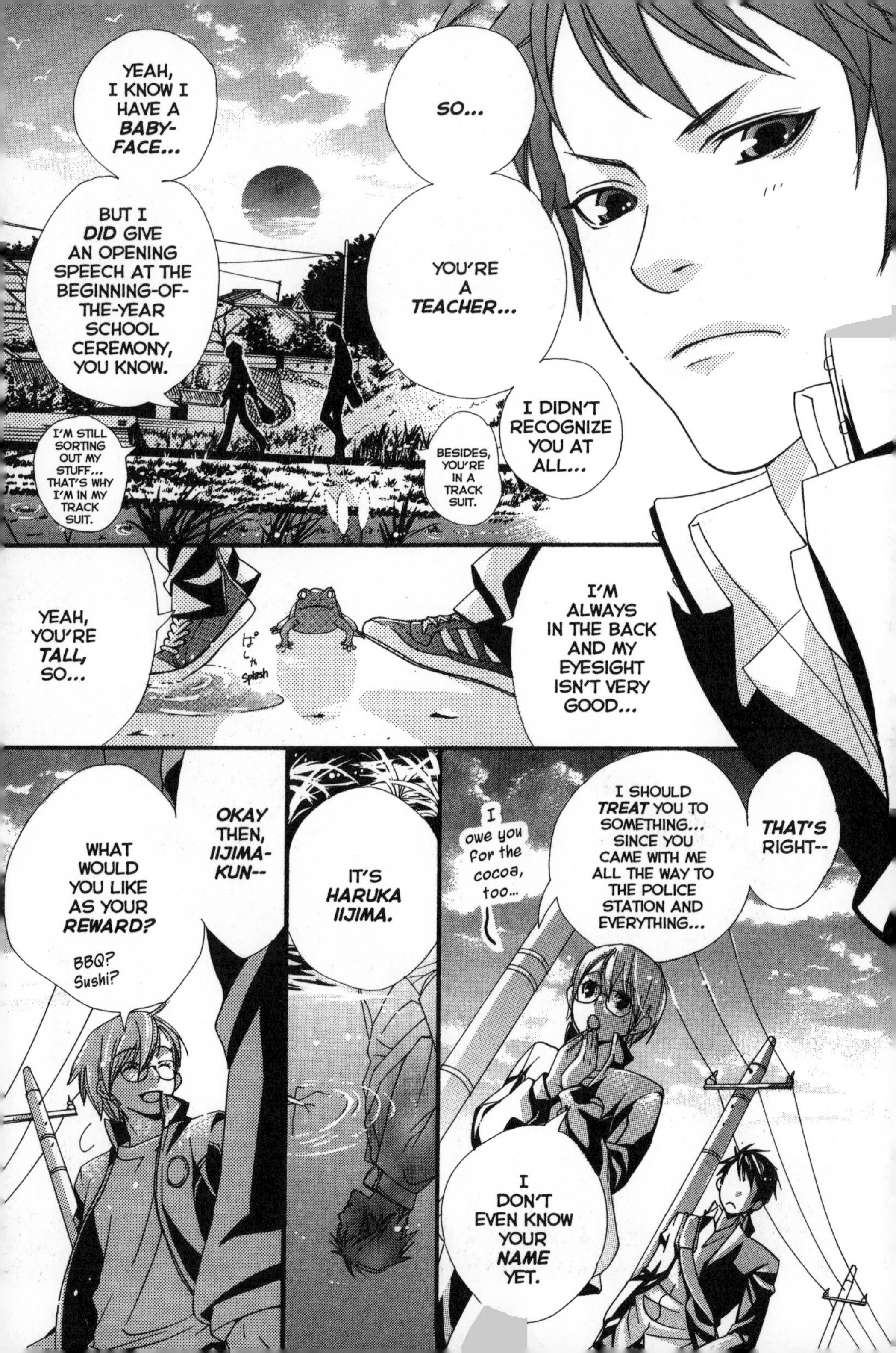
SO...
YOU'RE A *TEACHER*...
I DIDN'T RECOGNIZE YOU AT ALL...
BESIDES, YOU'RE IN A TRACK SUIT.
YEAH, I KNOW I HAVE A *BABY-FACE*...
BUT I *DID* GIVE AN OPENING SPEECH AT THE BEGINNING-OF-THE-YEAR SCHOOL CEREMONY, YOU KNOW.
I'M STILL SORTING OUT MY STUFF... THAT'S WHY I'M IN MY TRACK SUIT.
I'M ALWAYS IN THE BACK AND MY EYESIGHT ISN'T VERY GOOD...
Splash
YEAH, YOU'RE *TALL*, SO...
THAT'S RIGHT--
I SHOULD *TREAT* YOU TO SOMETHING... SINCE YOU CAME WITH ME ALL THE WAY TO THE POLICE STATION AND EVERYTHING...
I owe you for the cocoa, too...
I DON'T EVEN KNOW YOUR *NAME* YET.
IT'S *HARUKA IIJIMA.*
OKAY THEN, *IIJIMA-KUN*--
WHAT WOULD YOU LIKE AS YOUR *REWARD?*
BBQ? Sushi?

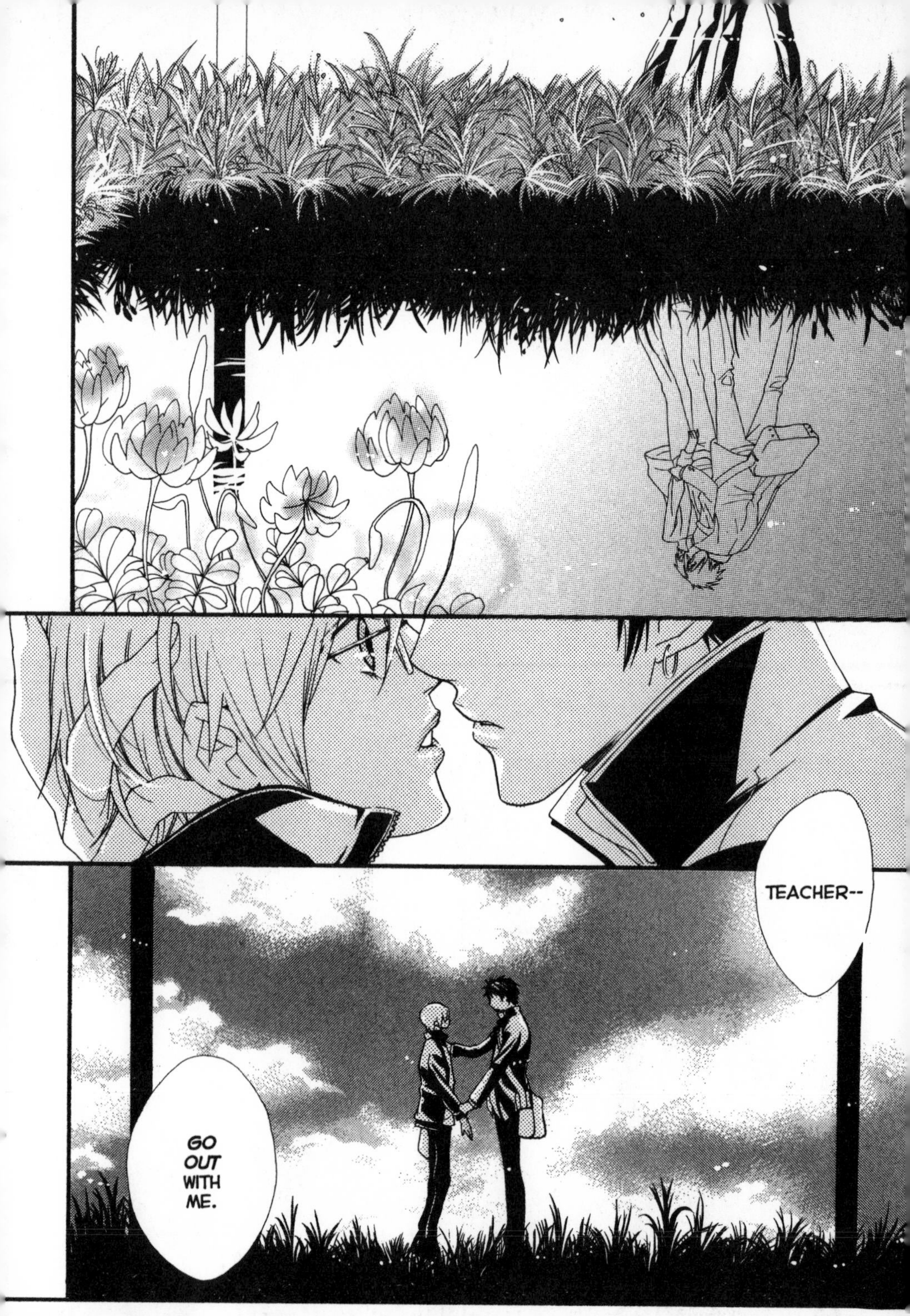
TEACHER--
GO OUT WITH ME.

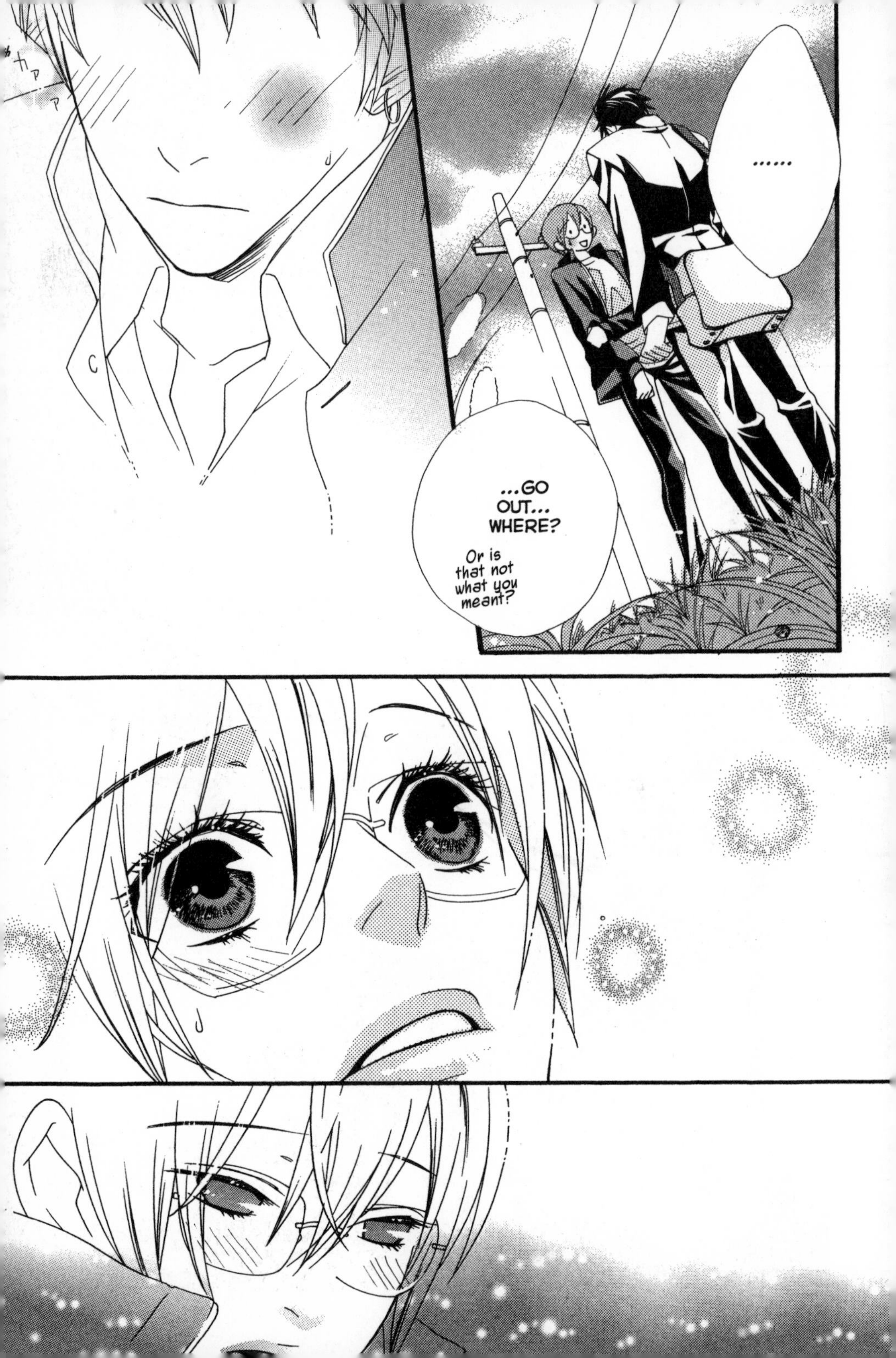
......
...GO OUT... WHERE?
Or is that not what you meant?

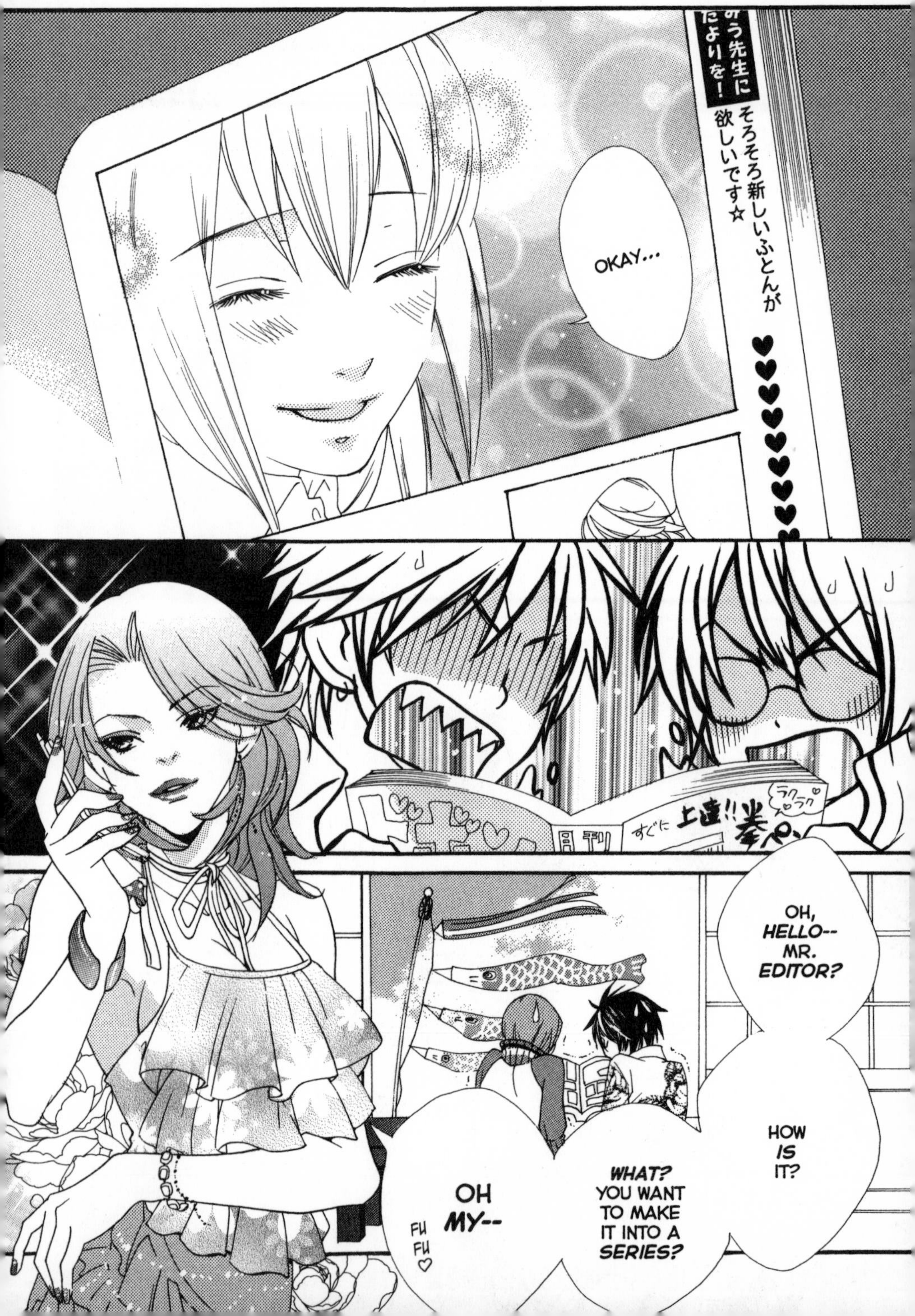

みう先生に
たよりを！
そろそろ新しいふとんが
欲しいです☆
OKAY...
ラクラク
すぐに 上達!!
月刊
OH, HELLO-- MR. EDITOR?
HOW IS IT?
WHAT? YOU WANT TO MAKE IT INTO A SERIES?
OH MY--
FU FU ♡

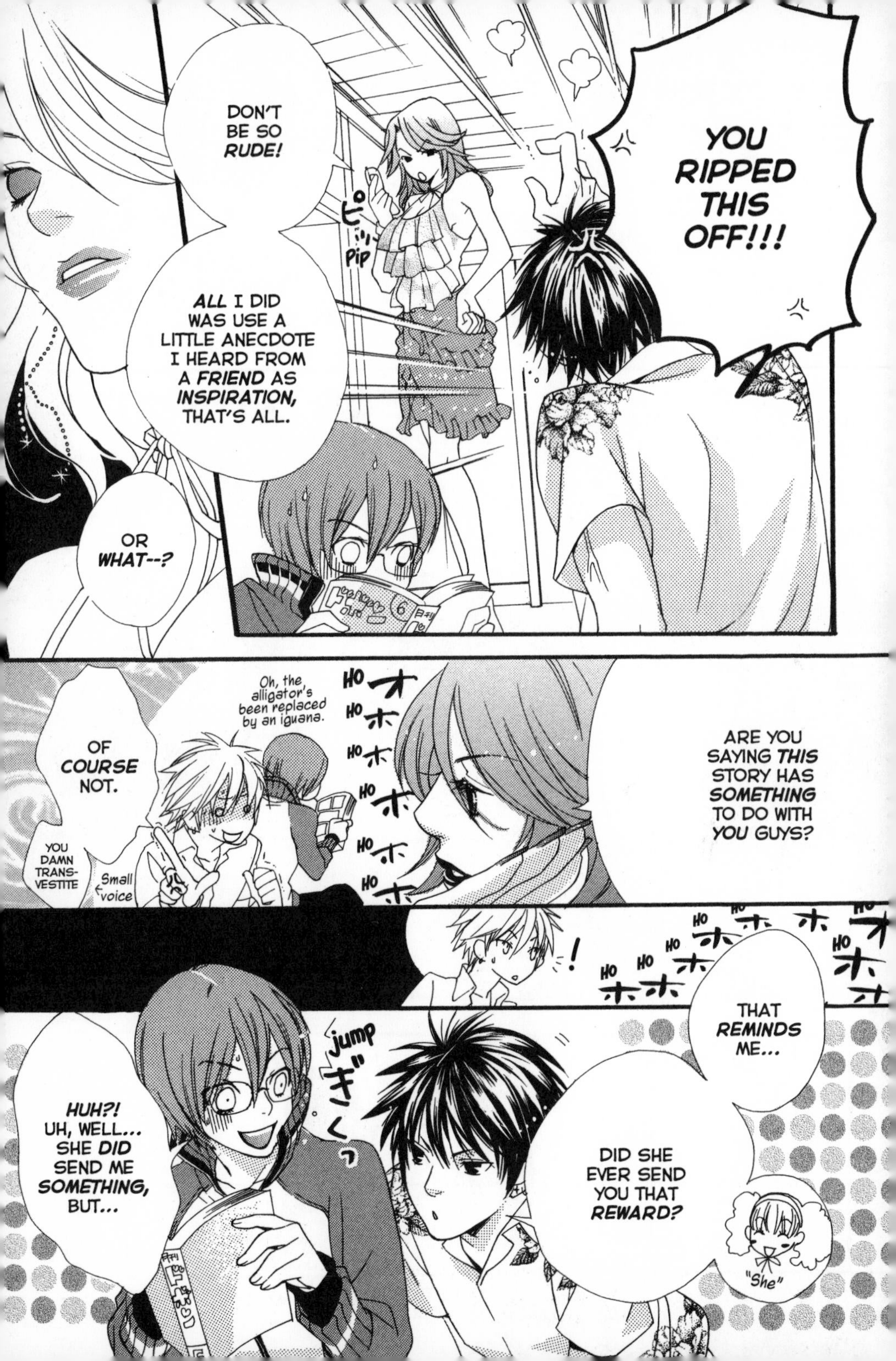
YOU RIPPED THIS OFF!!!
DON'T BE SO RUDE!
Pip
ALL I DID WAS USE A LITTLE ANECDOTE I HEARD FROM A FRIEND AS INSPIRATION, THAT'S ALL.
OR WHAT--?
ARE YOU SAYING THIS STORY HAS SOMETHING TO DO WITH YOU GUYS?
HO HO HO HO HO HO
Oh, the alligator's been replaced by an iguana.
OF COURSE NOT.
YOU DAMN TRANSVESTITE
Small voice
HO HO HO HO HO HO
!
THAT REMINDS ME...
DID SHE EVER SEND YOU THAT REWARD?
"She"
jump
HUH?! UH, WELL... SHE DID SEND ME SOMETHING, BUT...

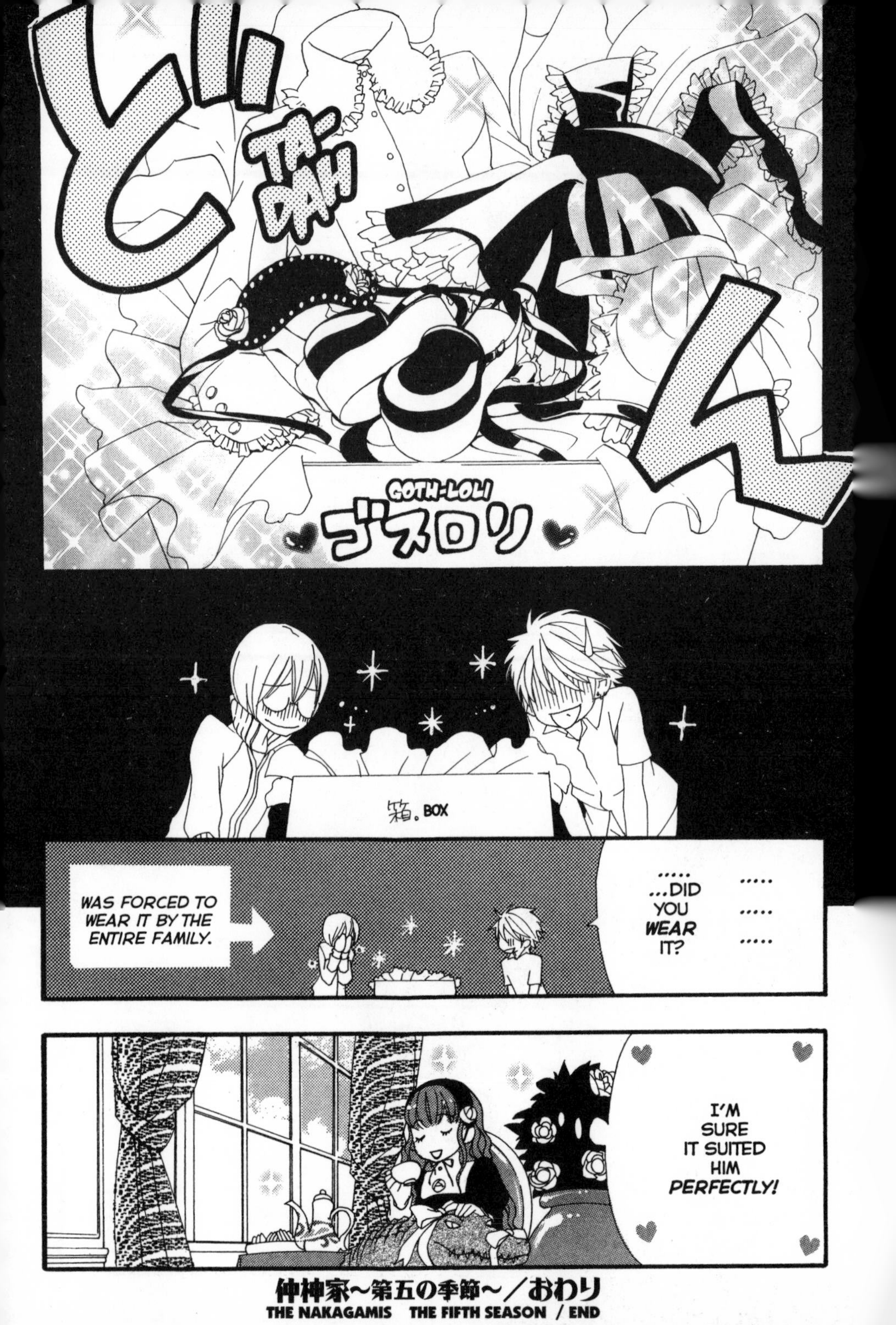
どん
TA-DAH
GOTH-LOLI
ゴスロリ
箱。BOX
....DID YOU WEAR IT?
....
WAS FORCED TO WEAR IT BY THE ENTIRE FAMILY.
I'M SURE IT SUITED HIM PERFECTLY!

仲神家～第五の季節～／おわり
THE NAKAGAMIS THE FIFTH SEASON / END

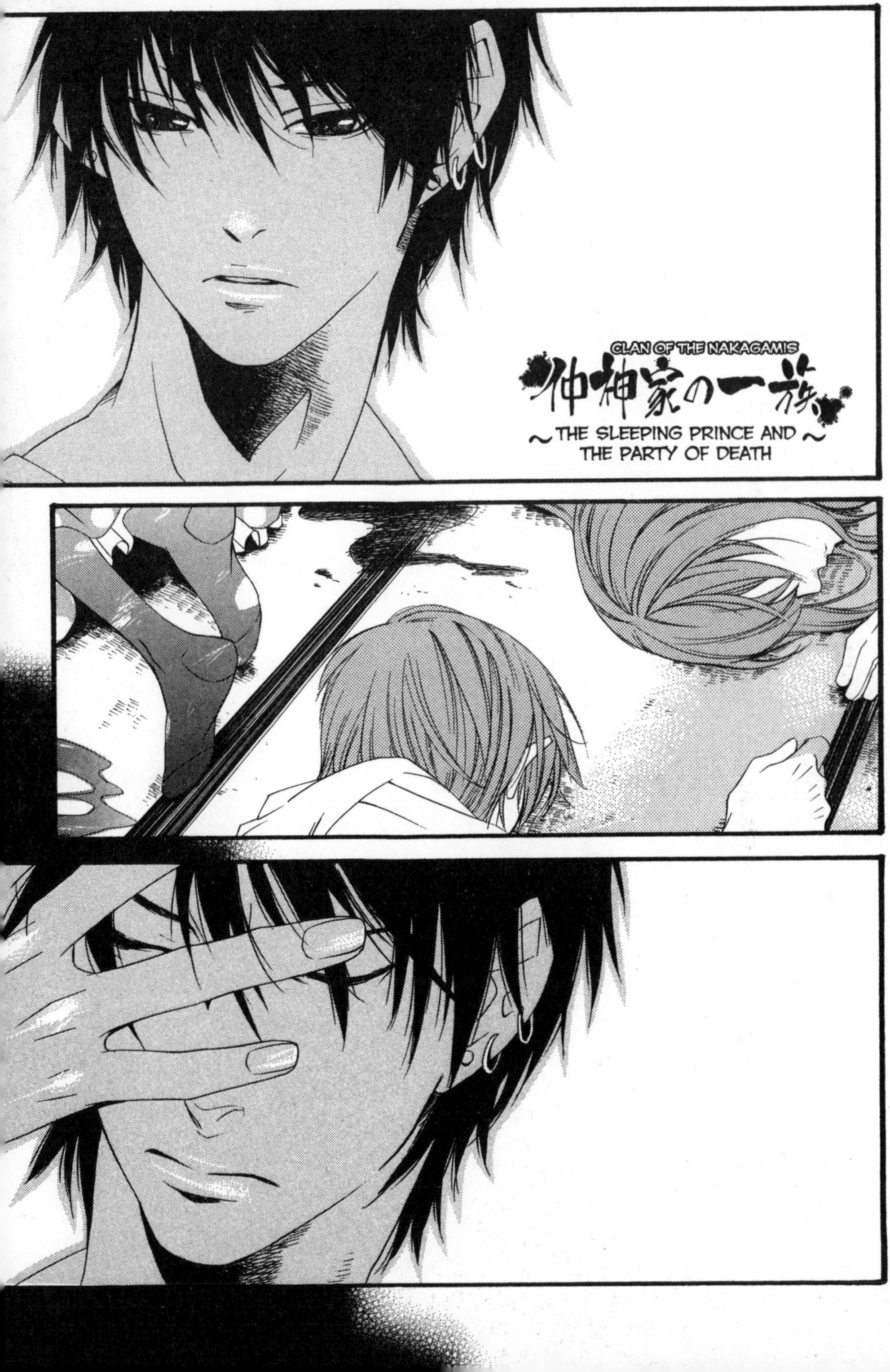
CLAN OF THE NAKAGAMIS
仲神家の一族
~THE SLEEPING PRINCE AND~
THE PARTY OF DEATH

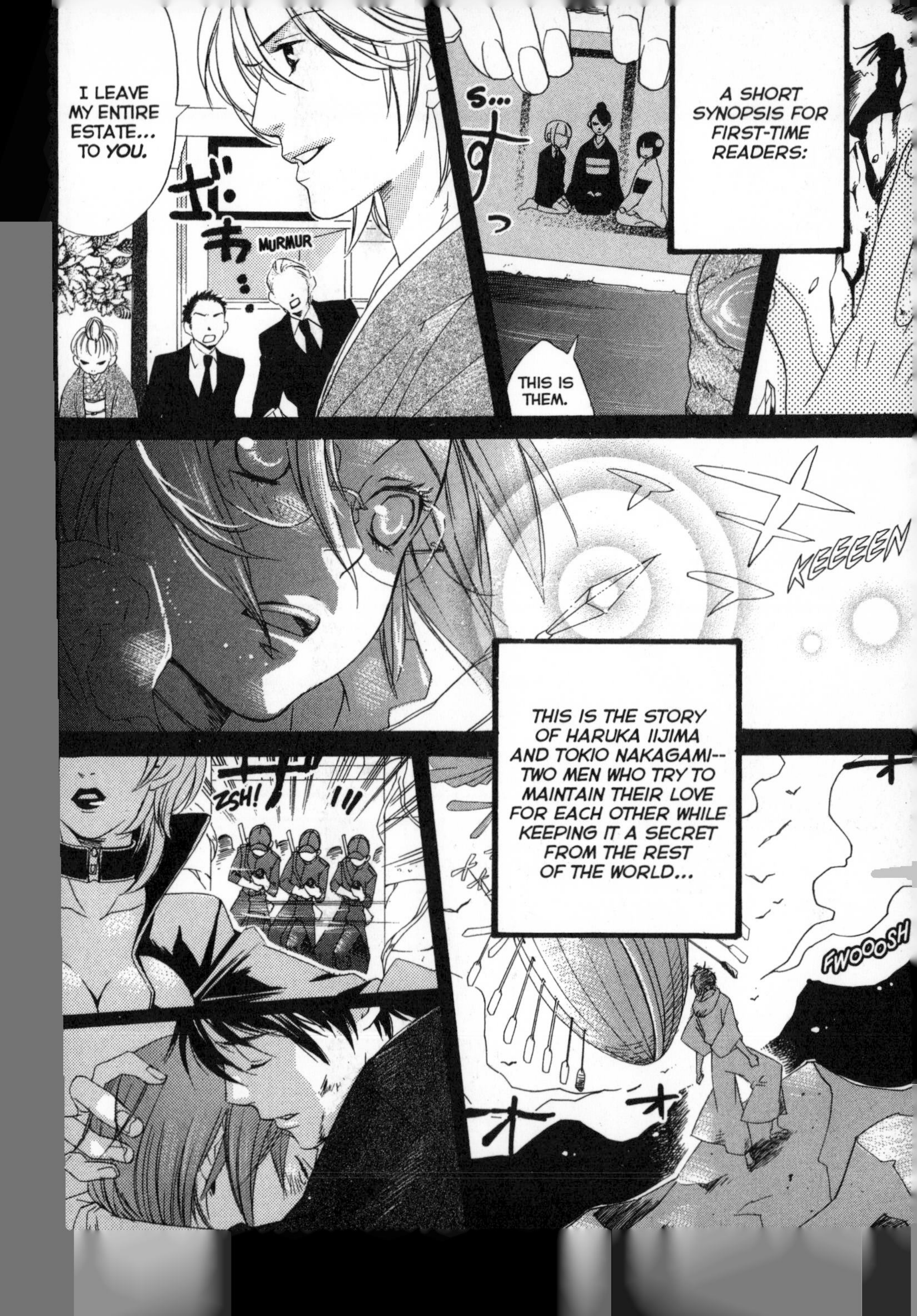
A SHORT SYNOPSIS FOR FIRST-TIME READERS:
S...
THIS IS THEM.
I LEAVE MY ENTIRE ESTATE... TO YOU.
MURMUR
KEEEEN
THIS IS THE STORY OF HARUKA IIJIMA AND TOKIO NAKAGAMI-- TWO MEN WHO TRY TO MAINTAIN THEIR LOVE FOR EACH OTHER WHILE KEEPING IT A SECRET FROM THE REST OF THE WORLD...
FWOOOSH
ZSH!

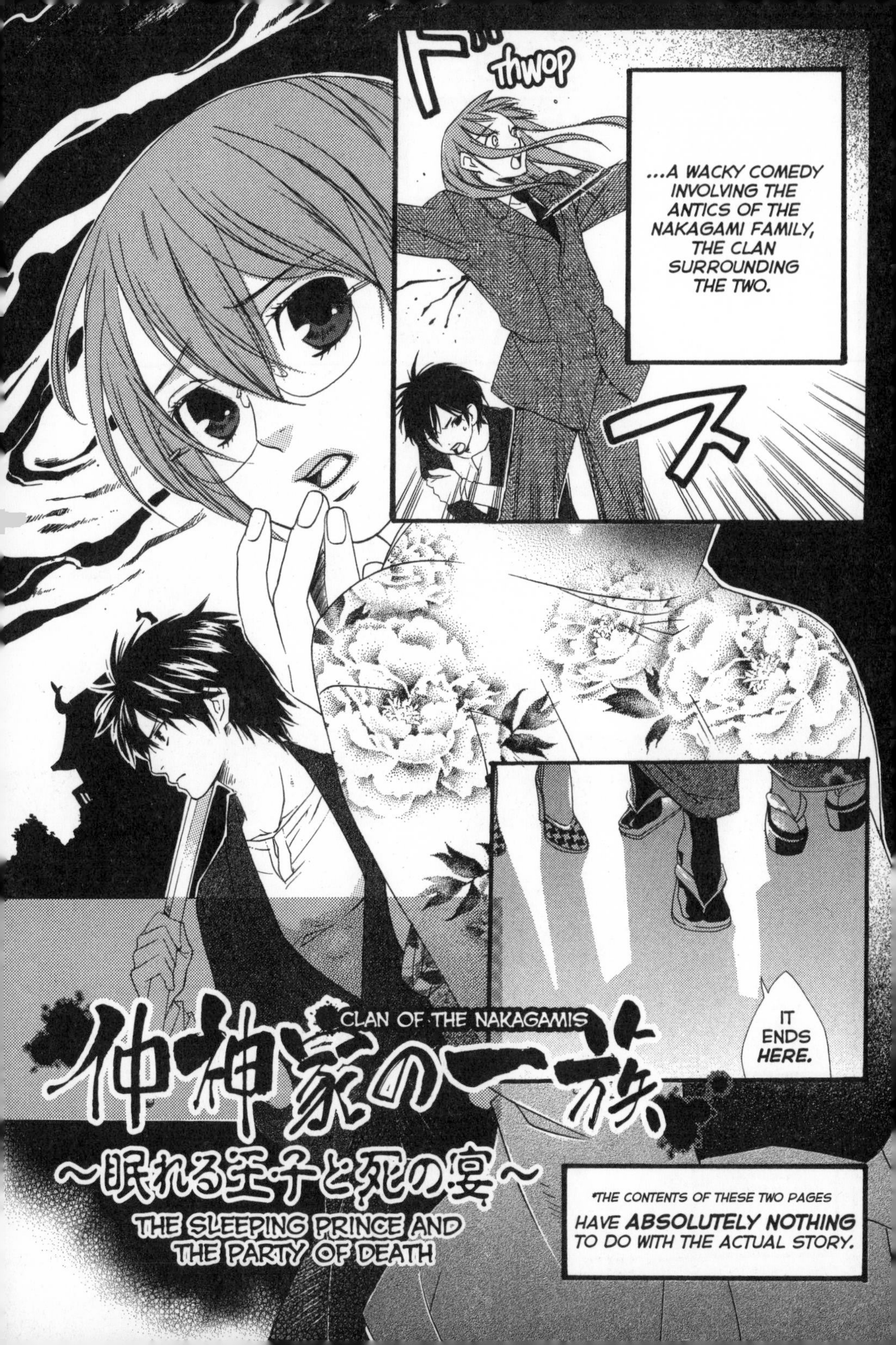
thwop
...A WACKY COMEDY INVOLVING THE ANTICS OF THE NAKAGAMI FAMILY, THE CLAN SURROUNDING THE TWO.
IT ENDS HERE.
仲神家の一族
CLAN OF THE NAKAGAMIS
~眠れる王子と死の宴~
THE SLEEPING PRINCE AND THE PARTY OF DEATH
*THE CONTENTS OF THESE TWO PAGES HAVE ABSOLUTELY NOTHING TO DO WITH THE ACTUAL STORY.

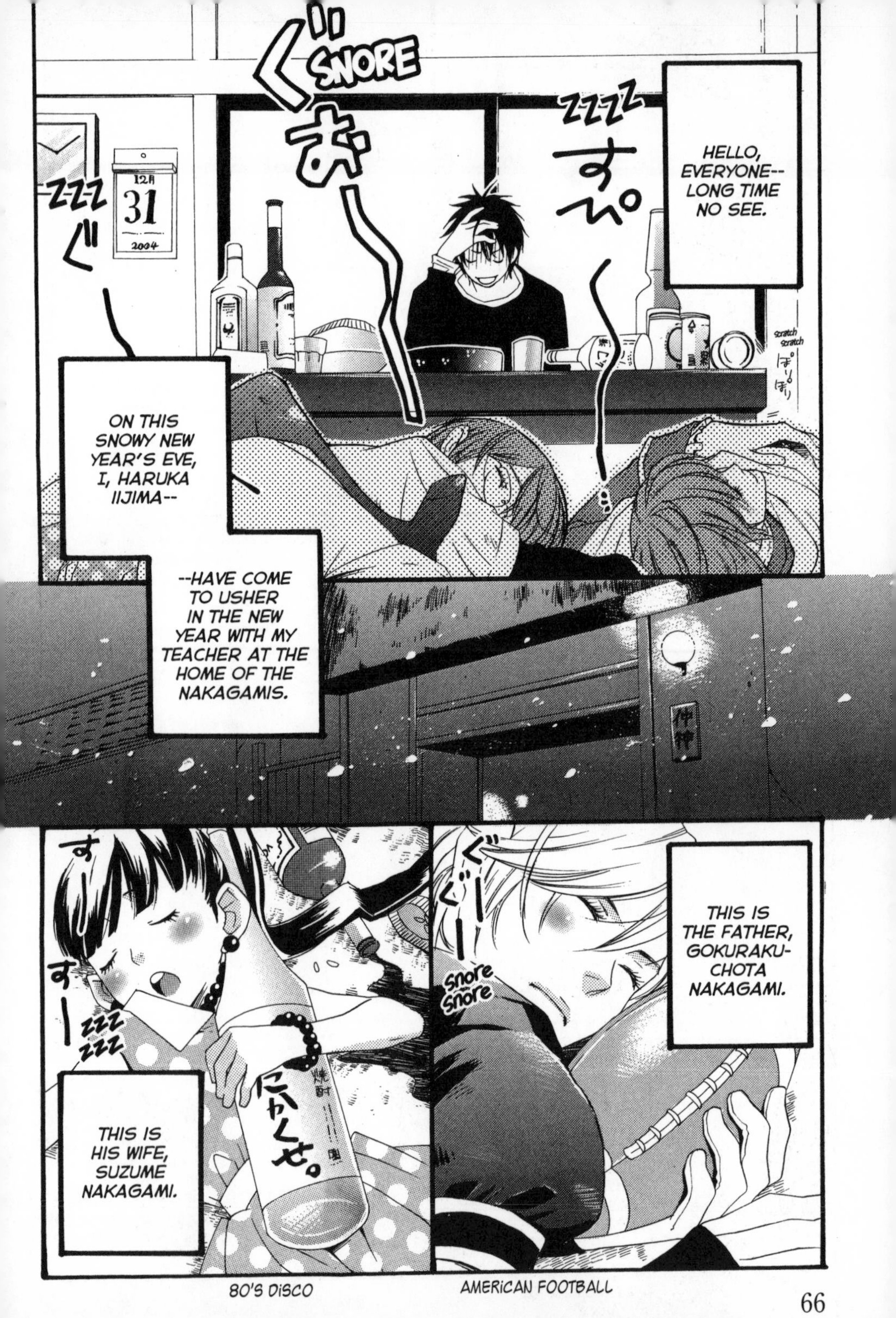
HELLO, EVERYONE-- LONG TIME NO SEE.
ZZZZ
すぴ
SNORE
ぐぉ
scratch scratch
ぽりぽり
12月 31 2004
ZZZZ
ぐ
ON THIS SNOWY NEW YEAR'S EVE, I, HARUKA IIJIMA--
--HAVE COME TO USHER IN THE NEW YEAR WITH MY TEACHER AT THE HOME OF THE NAKAGAMIS.
仲神
THIS IS THE FATHER, GOKURAKUCHOTA NAKAGAMI.
ぐーぐー
snore snore
すーすー
ZZZ ZZZ
焼酎
にかくせ。
THIS IS HIS WIFE, SUZUME NAKAGAMI.

80'S DISCO

AMERICAN FOOTBALL

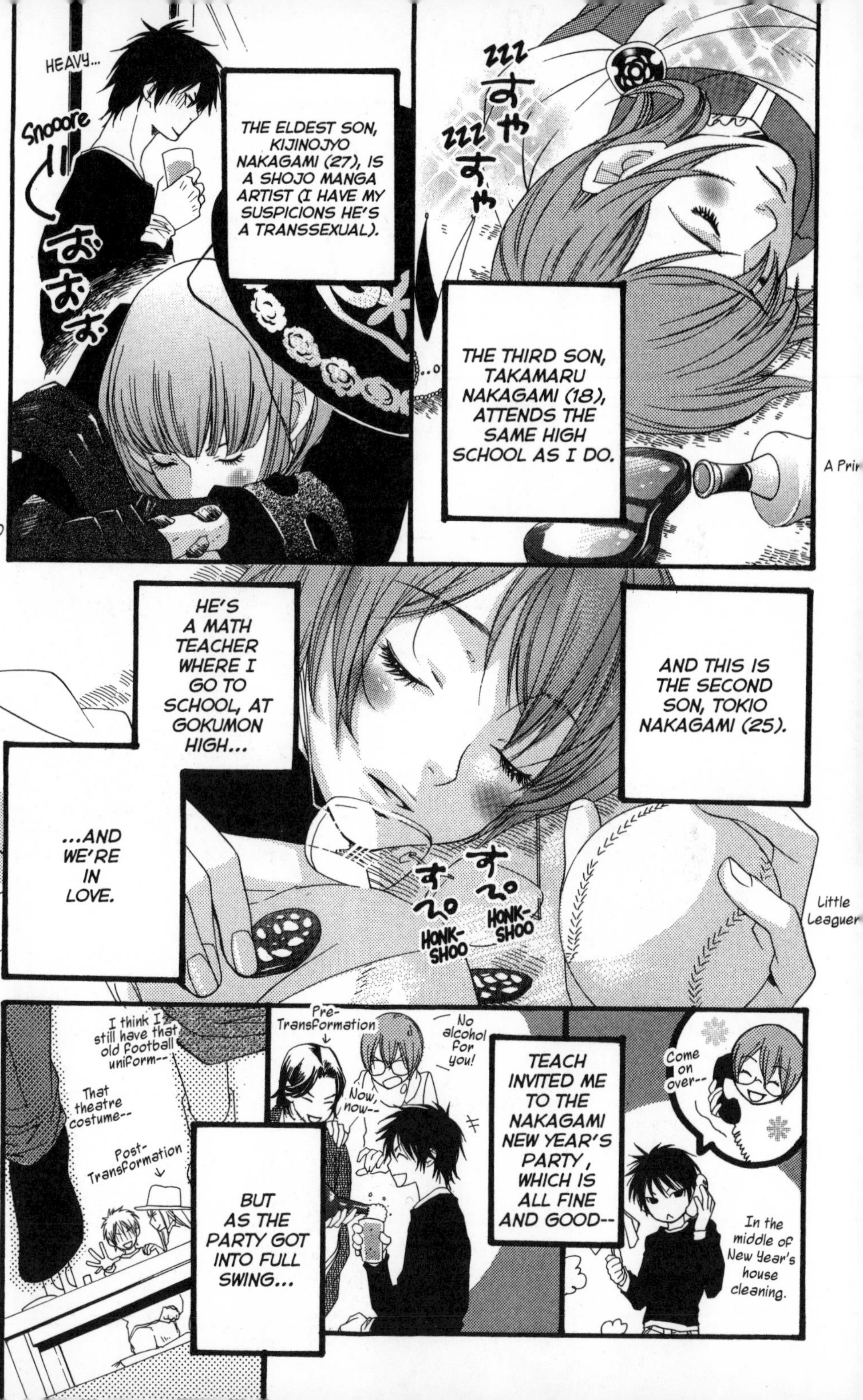

ZZZ すや ZZZ すや
THE THIRD SON, TAKAMARU NAKAGAMI (18), ATTENDS THE SAME HIGH SCHOOL AS I DO.
A Prin
HEAVY...
Snooore
おおす
THE ELDEST SON, KIJINOJYO NAKAGAMI (27), IS A SHOJO MANGA ARTIST (I HAVE MY SUSPICIONS HE'S A TRANSSEXUAL).
MASK OF ZORRO
AND THIS IS THE SECOND SON, TOKIO NAKAGAMI (25).
Little Leaguer
HE'S A MATH TEACHER WHERE I GO TO SCHOOL, AT GOKUMON HIGH...
すぴ HONK-SHOO
すぴ HONK-SHOO
...AND WE'RE IN LOVE.
Come on over--
In the middle of New Year's house cleaning.
TEACH INVITED ME TO THE NAKAGAMI NEW YEAR'S PARTY, WHICH IS ALL FINE AND GOOD--
No alcohol for you!
Pre-Transformation
Now, now--
BUT AS THE PARTY GOT INTO FULL SWING...
I think I still have that old football uniform--
That theatre costume--
Post-Transformation

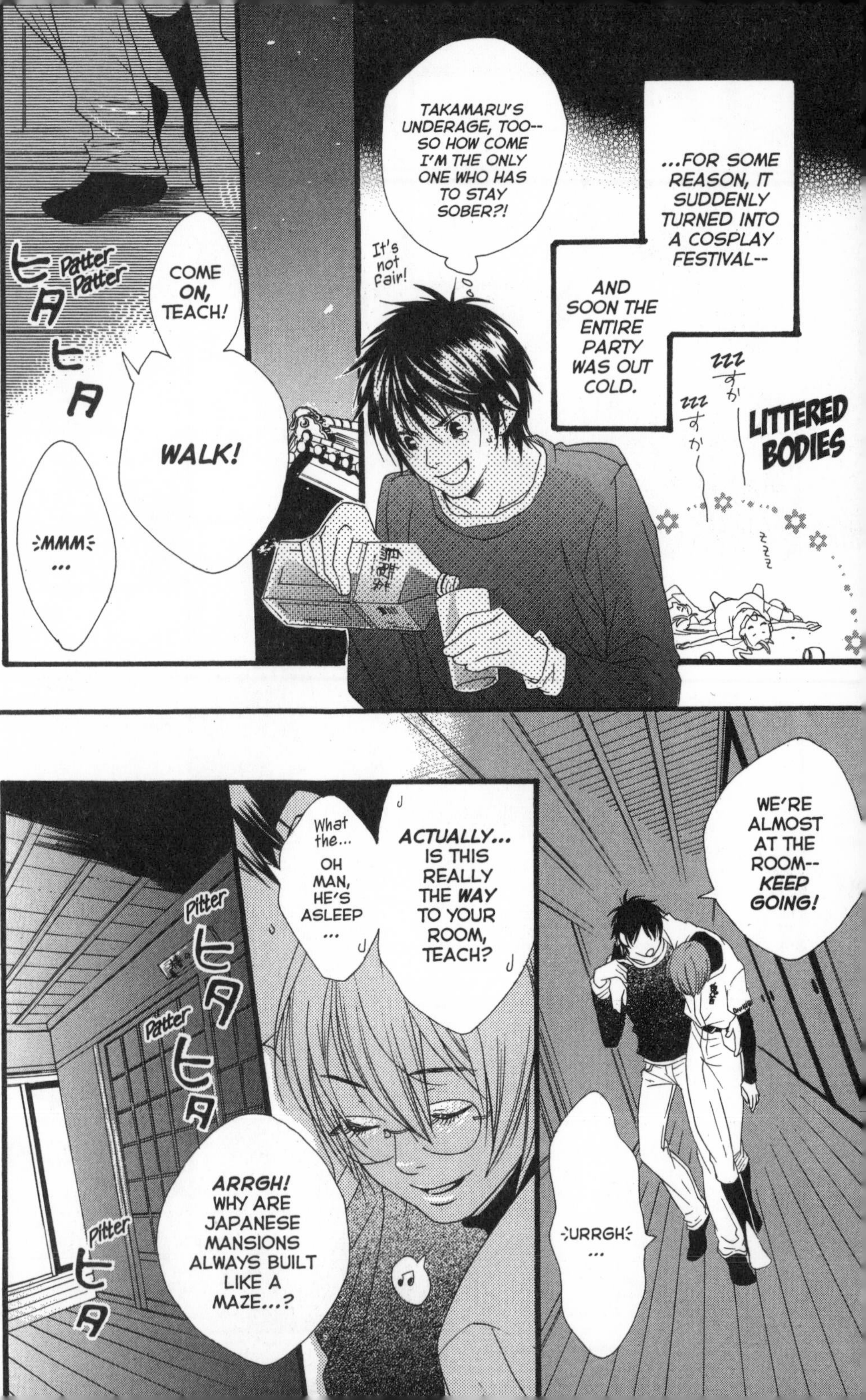
...FOR SOME REASON, IT SUDDENLY TURNED INTO A COSPLAY FESTIVAL--
AND SOON THE ENTIRE PARTY WAS OUT COLD.
LITTERED BODIES
zzz すか
zzz すか
TAKAMARU'S UNDERAGE, TOO-- SO HOW COME I'M THE ONLY ONE WHO HAS TO STAY SOBER?!
It's not fair!
COME ON, TEACH!
WALK!
ヒタ Patter Patter ヒタ
MMM...
WE'RE ALMOST AT THE ROOM-- KEEP GOING!
ACTUALLY... IS THIS REALLY THE WAY TO YOUR ROOM, TEACH?
What the...
OH MAN, HE'S ASLEEP...
URRGH...
ARRGH! WHY ARE JAPANESE MANSIONS ALWAYS BUILT LIKE A MAZE...?
Pitter ヒタ Patter ヒタ
Pitter ヒタ

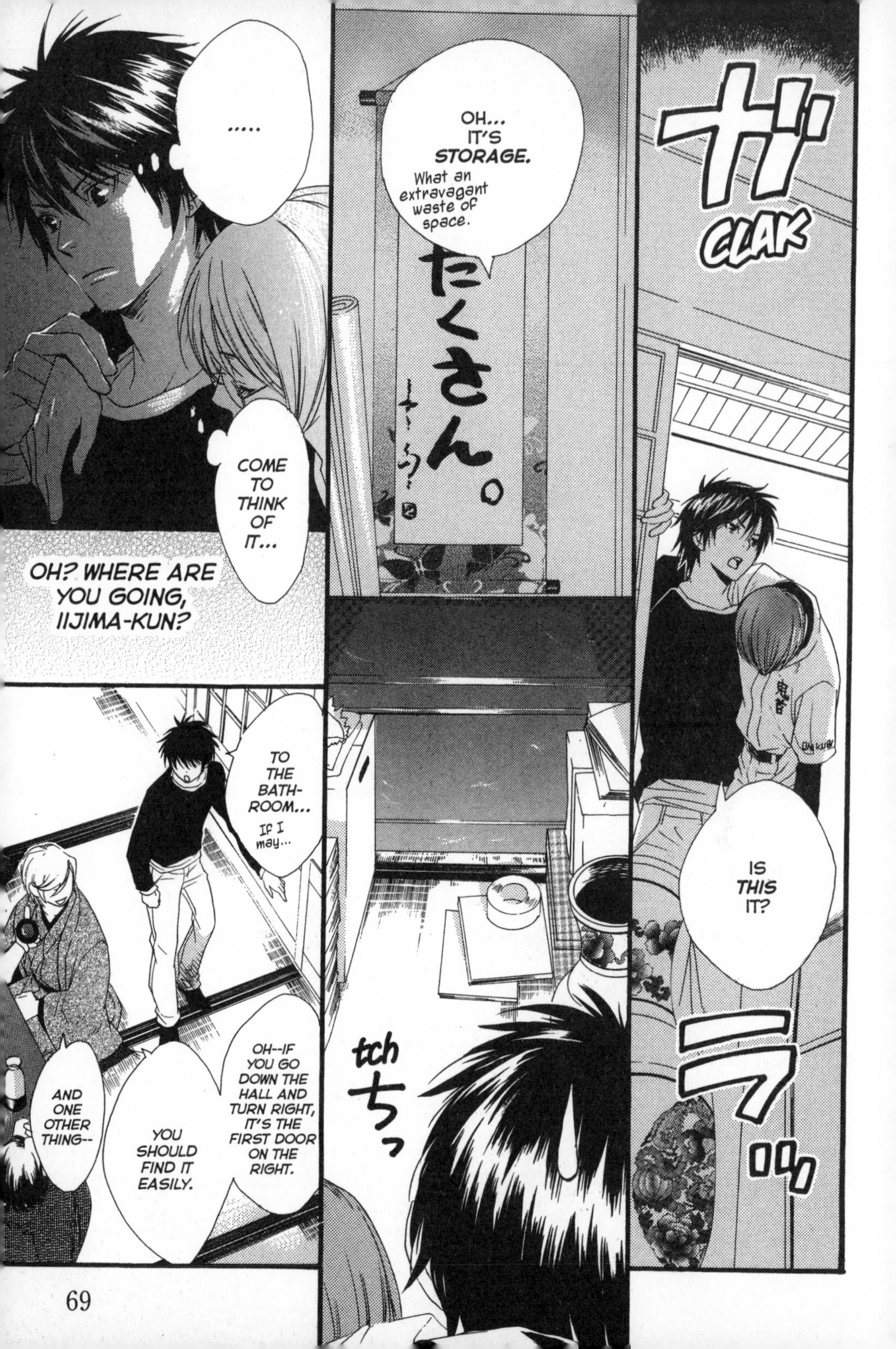

ザ
CLAK
IS THIS IT?
ラ
OH... IT'S **STORAGE.** What an extravagant waste of space.
たくさん。
tch ちっ
.....
COME TO THINK OF IT...
OH? WHERE ARE YOU GOING, IIJIMA-KUN?
TO THE BATH-ROOM... If I may...
OH--IF YOU GO DOWN THE HALL AND TURN RIGHT, IT'S THE FIRST DOOR ON THE RIGHT.
YOU SHOULD FIND IT EASILY.
AND ONE OTHER THING--

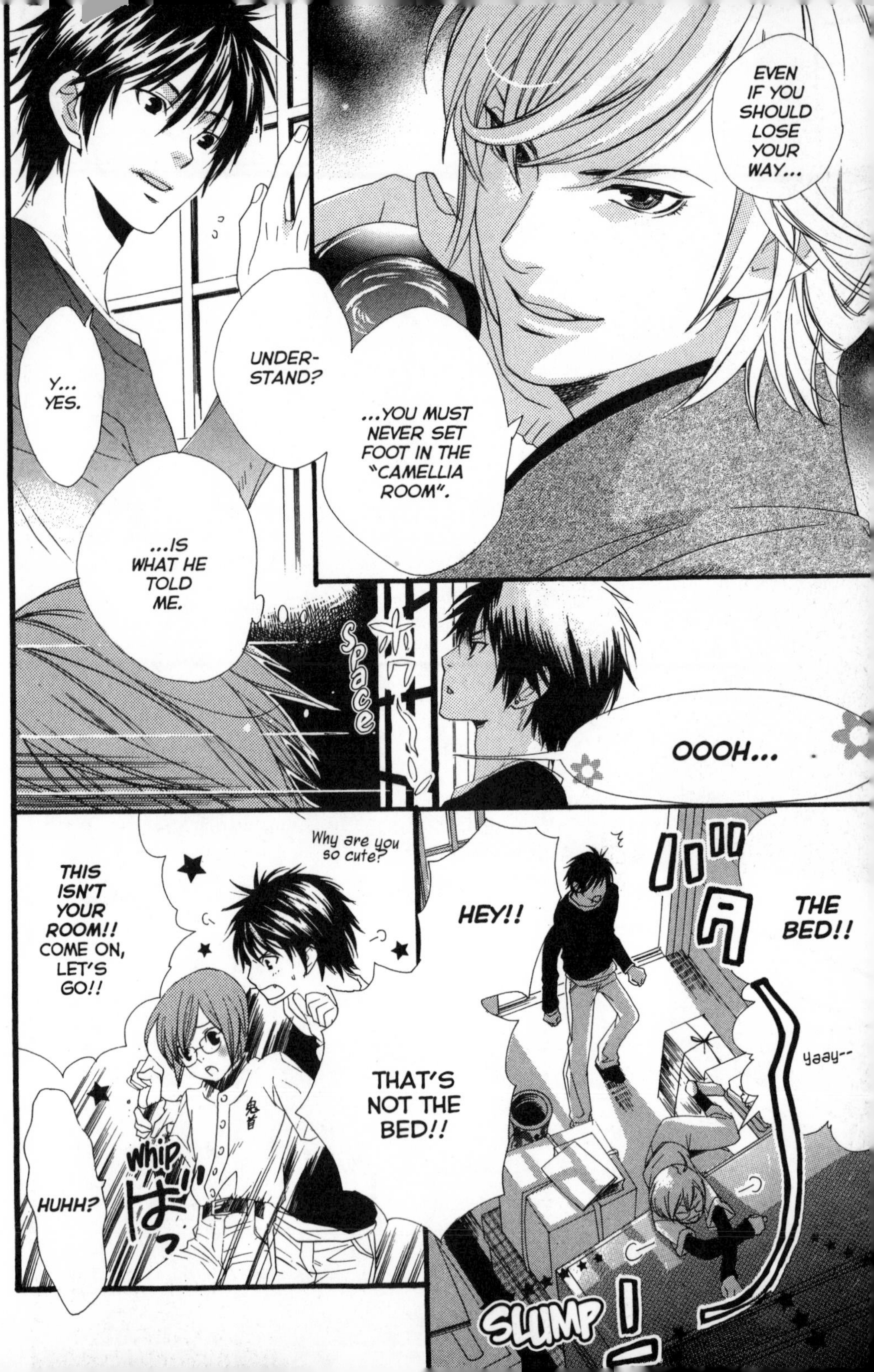
EVEN IF YOU SHOULD LOSE YOUR WAY...
UNDER-STAND?
...YOU MUST NEVER SET FOOT IN THE "CAMELLIA ROOM".
Y... YES.
...IS WHAT HE TOLD ME.
space
OOOH...
THE BED!!
HEY!!
yaay--
SLUMP
Why are you so cute?
THIS ISN'T YOUR ROOM!! COME ON, LET'S GO!!
THAT'S NOT THE BED!!
HUHH?
whip

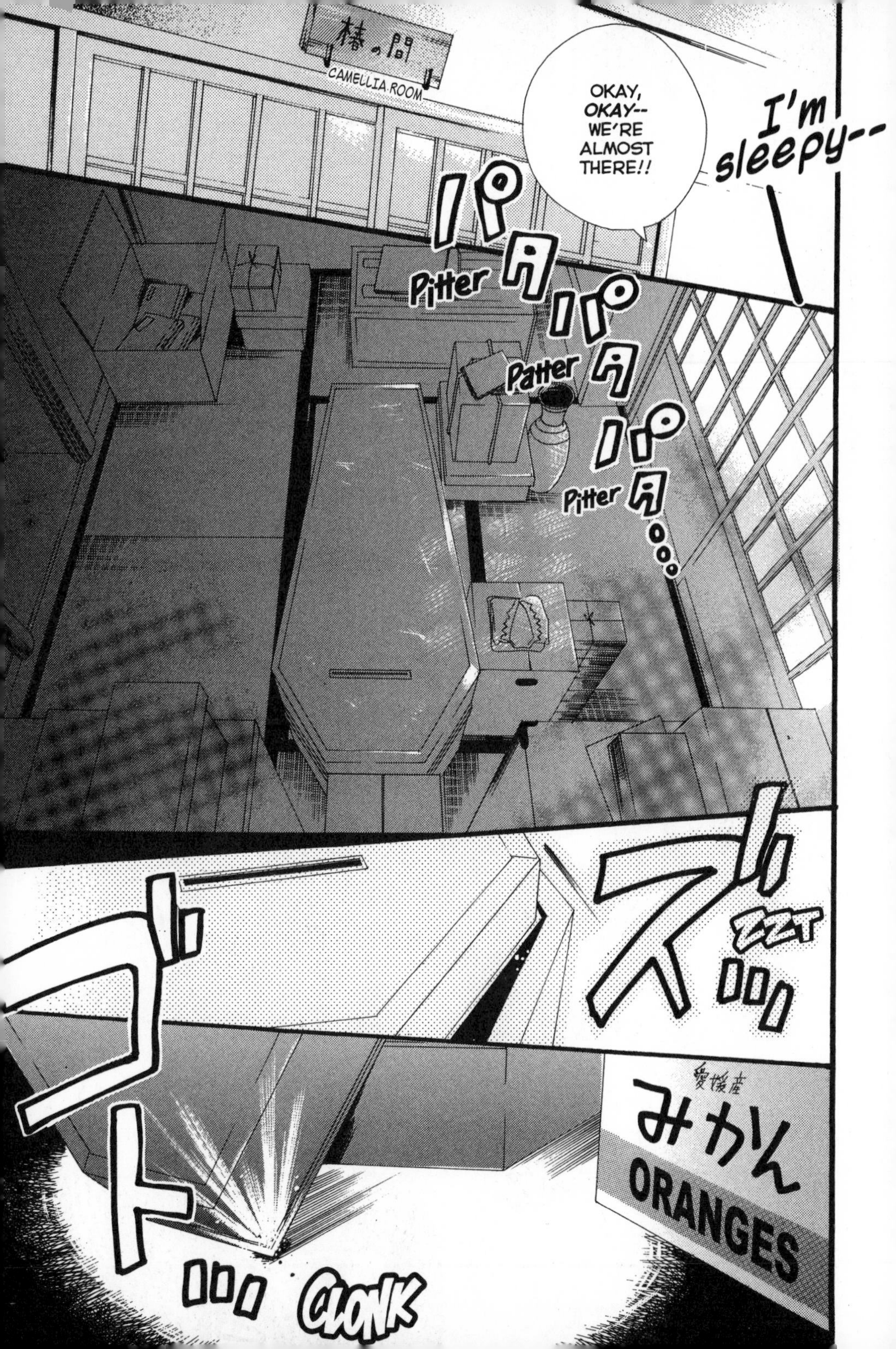
I'm sleepy--
OKAY, OKAY-- WE'RE ALMOST THERE!!
椿の間
CAMELLIA ROOM
パタパタパタ…
Pitter
Patter
Pitter
ズッ
ZZT
愛媛産
みかん
ORANGES
ゴッ
CLONK

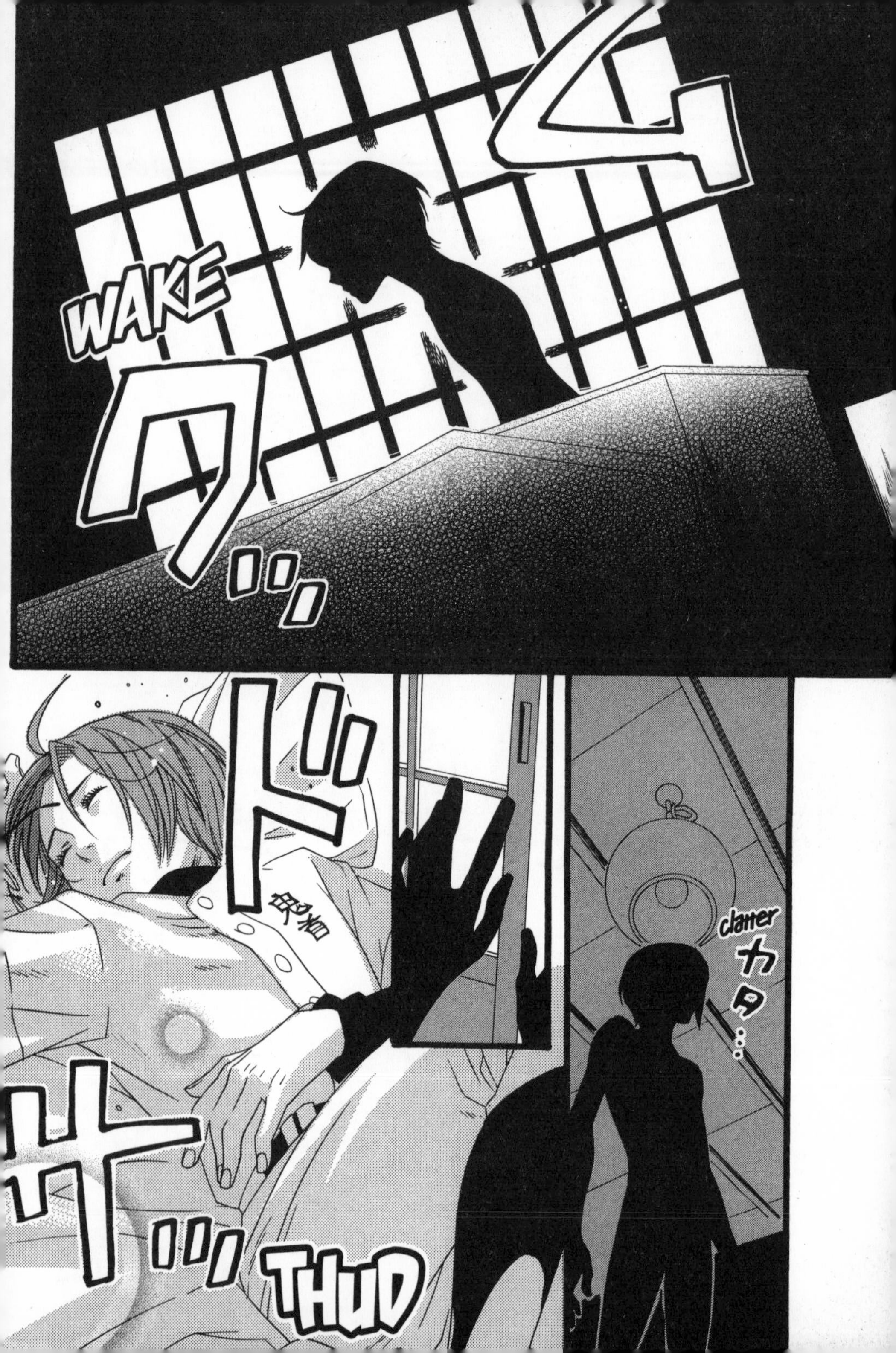
WAKE
clatter
カタ…
ドッ
サッ
THUD

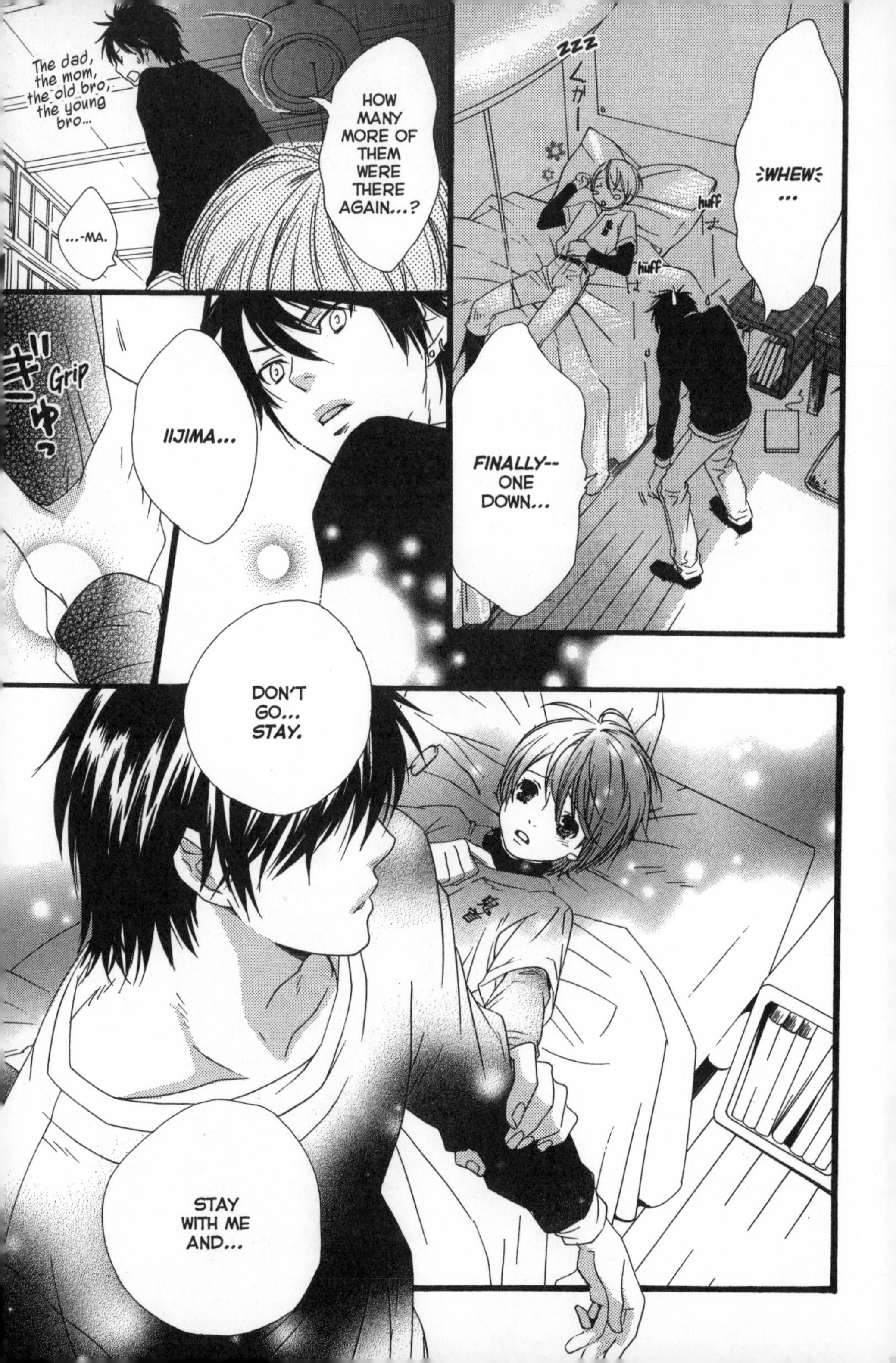
ZZZ
WHEW...
huff
huff
FINALLY--
ONE DOWN...
HOW MANY MORE OF THEM WERE THERE AGAIN...?
The dad, the mom, the old bro, the young bro...
...-MA.
Grip
IIJIMA...
DON'T GO... STAY.
STAY WITH ME AND...

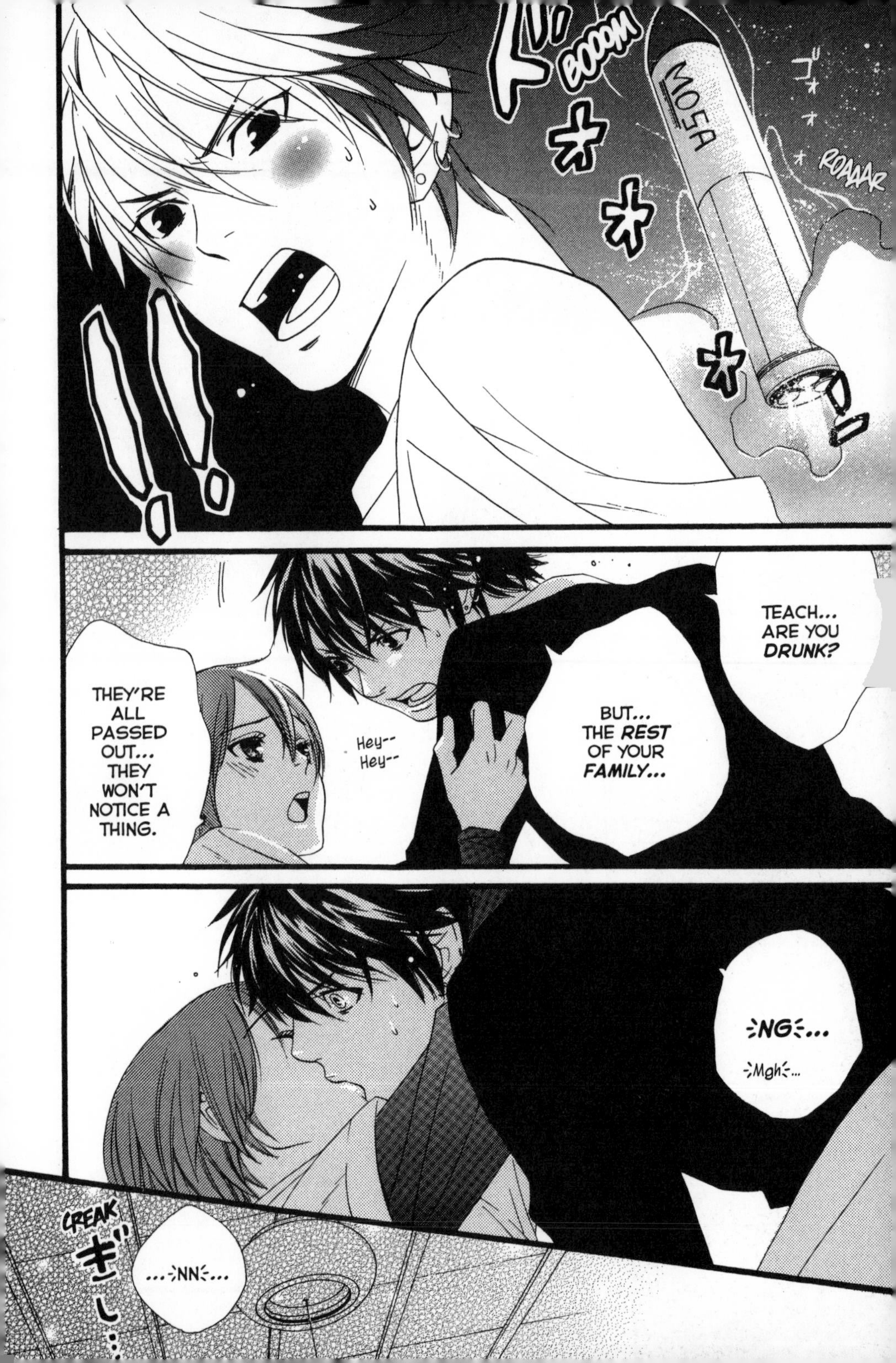
BOOOM
ゴォォォ
ROAAAR
TEACH... ARE YOU DRUNK?
BUT... THE REST OF YOUR FAMILY...
Hey-- Hey--
THEY'RE ALL PASSED OUT... THEY WON'T NOTICE A THING.
NG...
Mgh...
CREAK
ぎし…
...NN...

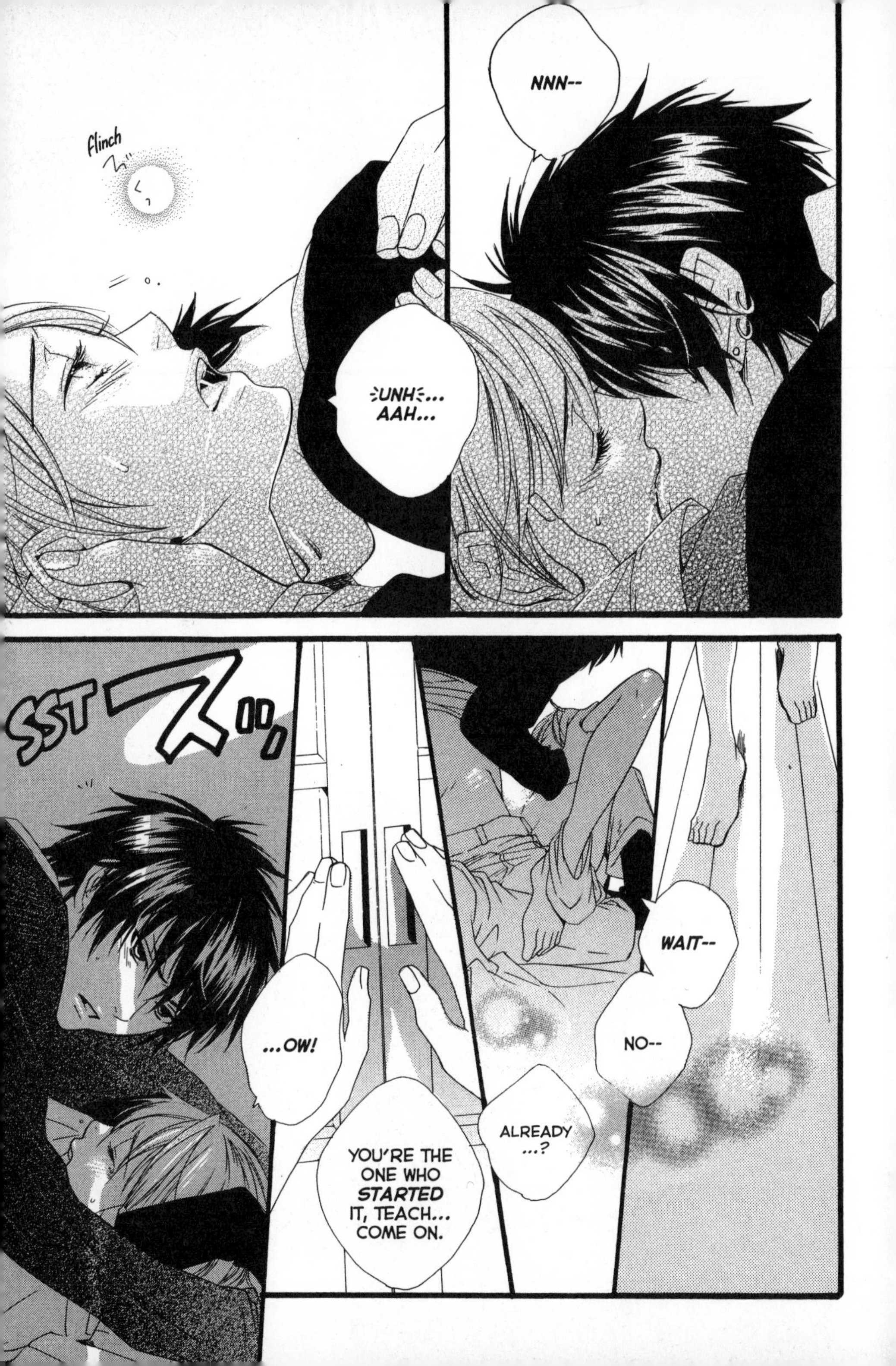
NNN--
Flinch
UNH... AAH...
WAIT--
NO--
ALREADY ...?
...OW!
YOU'RE THE ONE WHO STARTED IT, TEACH... COME ON.
SST

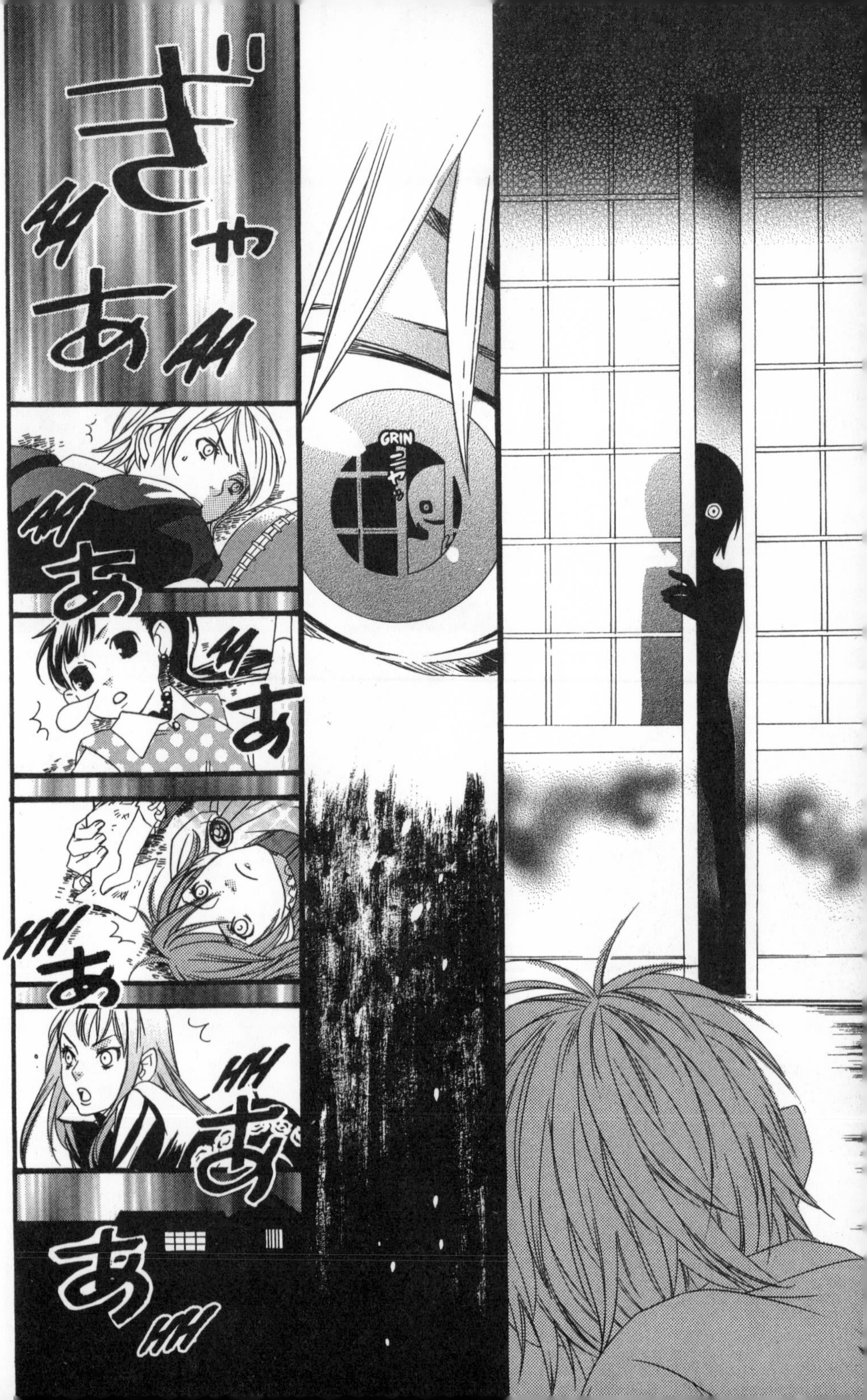
GRIN
ニヤッ
ぎゃあ AAAA
AAA あ
AAA しあ
HH あ
HH あ
あ HH

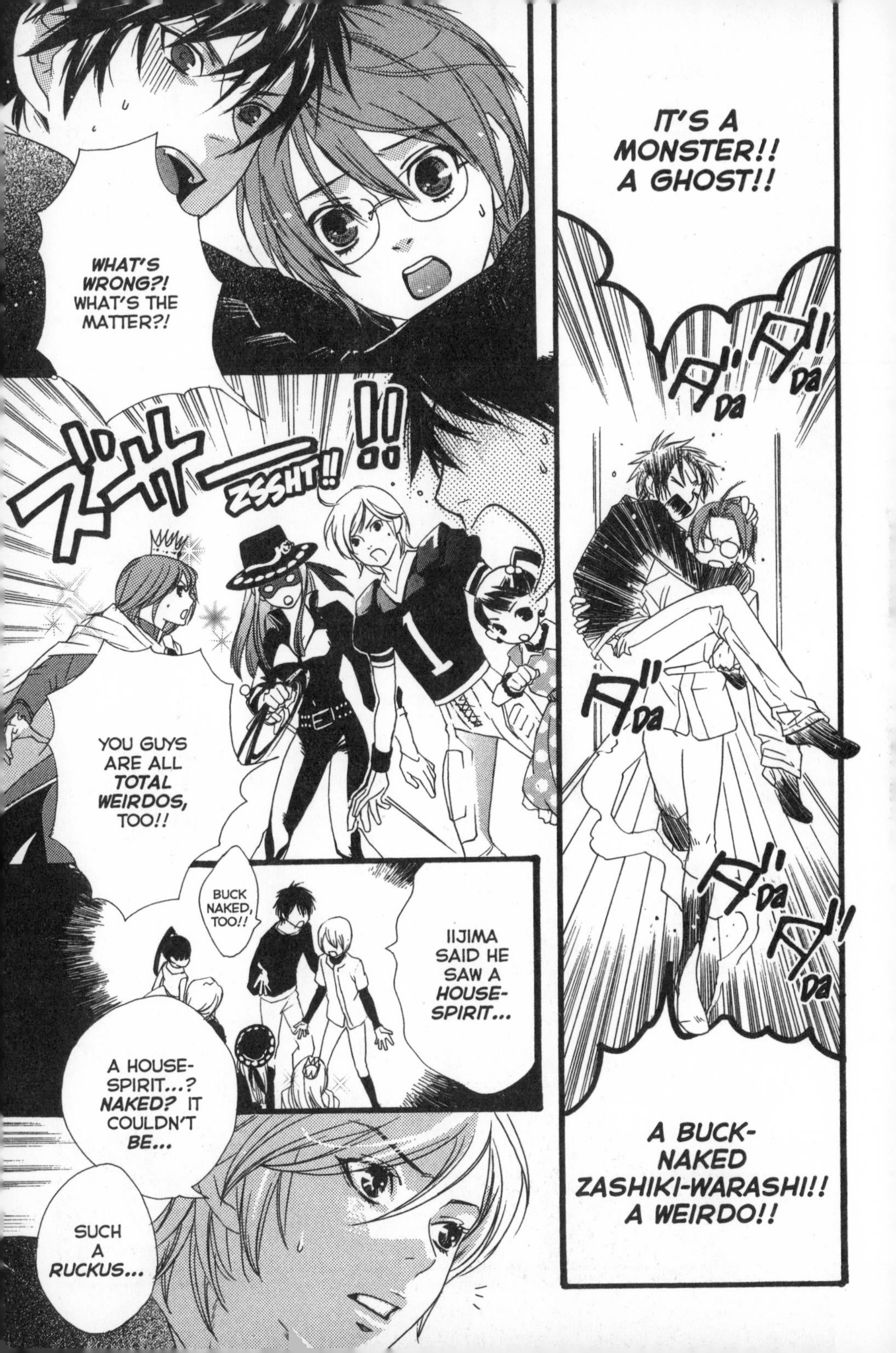
IT'S A MONSTER!! A GHOST!!
ダダ DA DA
ダ DA
ダダ DA DA
A BUCK-NAKED ZASHIKI-WARASHI!! A WEIRDO!!
WHAT'S WRONG?! WHAT'S THE MATTER?!
!!
ズサー ZSSHT!!
YOU GUYS ARE ALL TOTAL WEIRDOS, TOO!!
IIJIMA SAID HE SAW A HOUSE-SPIRIT...
BUCK NAKED, TOO!!
A HOUSE-SPIRIT...? NAKED? IT COULDN'T BE...
SUCH A RUCKUS...

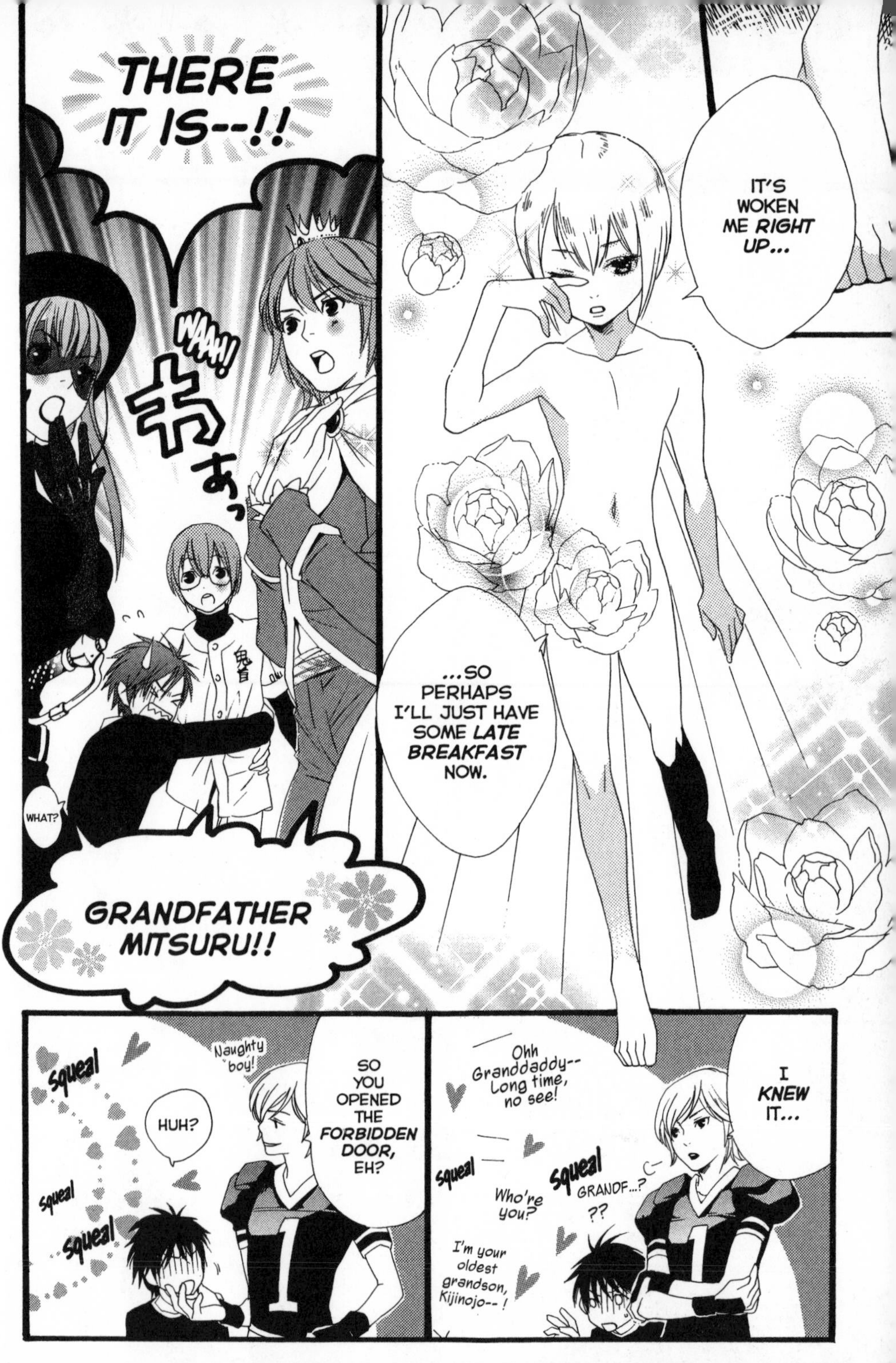
IT'S WOKEN ME RIGHT UP...
...SO PERHAPS I'LL JUST HAVE SOME LATE BREAKFAST NOW.
THERE IT IS--!!
WAAH!
わあっ
WHAT?
GRANDFATHER MITSURU!!
I KNEW IT...
Ohh Granddaddy-- Long time, no see!
squeal
squeal
GRANDF...?
Who're you?
??
I'm your oldest grandson, Kijinojo--!
SO YOU OPENED THE FORBIDDEN DOOR, EH?
Naughty boy!
HUH?
squeal
squeal
squeal

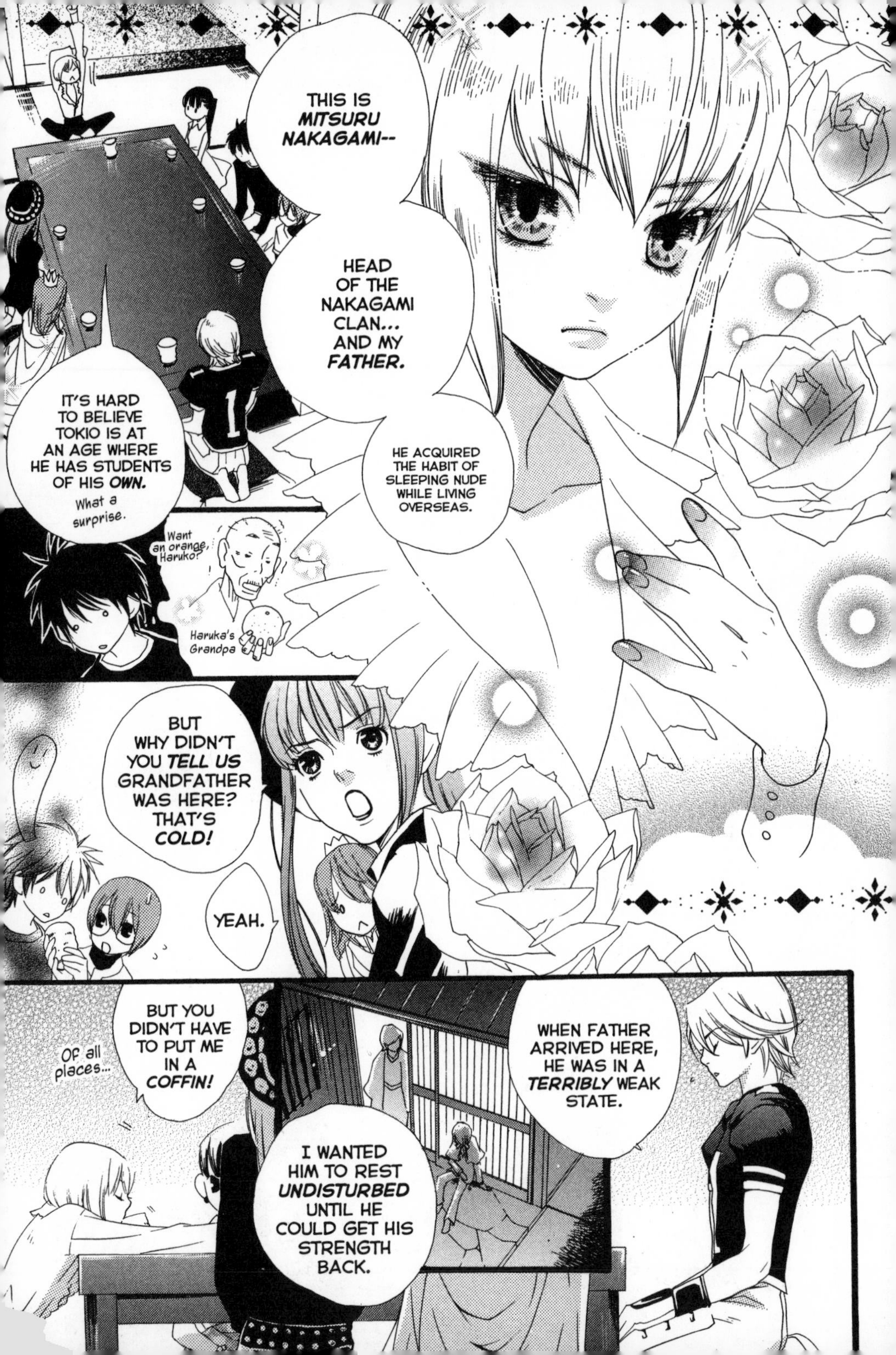

THIS IS MITSURU NAKAGAMI--
HEAD OF THE NAKAGAMI CLAN... AND MY FATHER.
HE ACQUIRED THE HABIT OF SLEEPING NUDE WHILE LIVING OVERSEAS.
IT'S HARD TO BELIEVE TOKIO IS AT AN AGE WHERE HE HAS STUDENTS OF HIS OWN.
What a surprise.
Want an orange, Haruko?
Haruka's Grandpa
BUT WHY DIDN'T YOU TELL US GRANDFATHER WAS HERE? THAT'S COLD!
YEAH.
WHEN FATHER ARRIVED HERE, HE WAS IN A TERRIBLY WEAK STATE.
I WANTED HIM TO REST UNDISTURBED UNTIL HE COULD GET HIS STRENGTH BACK.
BUT YOU DIDN'T HAVE TO PUT ME IN A COFFIN!
Of all places...

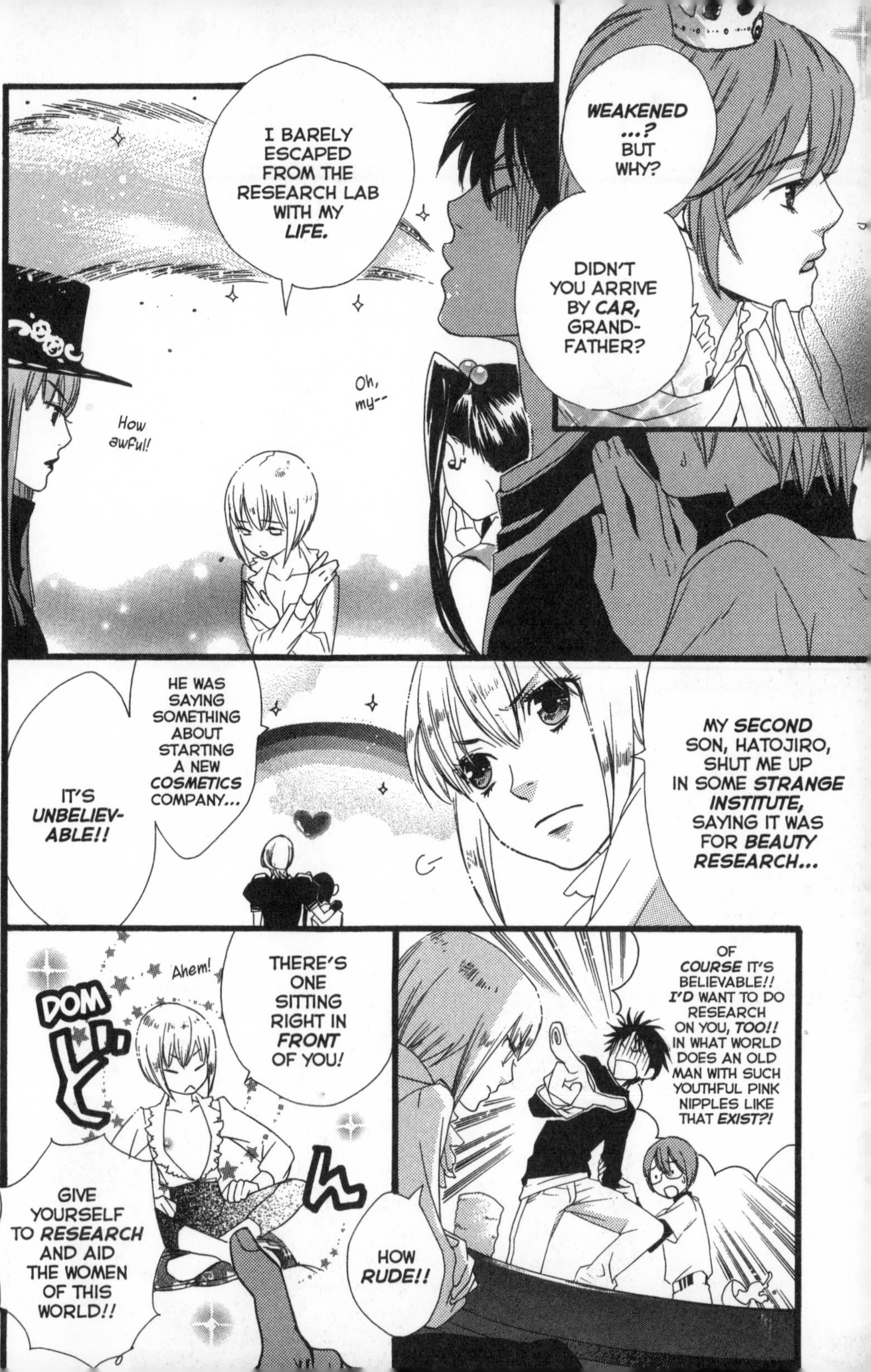
WEAKENED...? BUT WHY?
DIDN'T YOU ARRIVE BY CAR, GRANDFATHER?
I BARELY ESCAPED FROM THE RESEARCH LAB WITH MY LIFE.
Oh, my--
How awful!
MY SECOND SON, HATOJIRO, SHUT ME UP IN SOME STRANGE INSTITUTE, SAYING IT WAS FOR BEAUTY RESEARCH...
HE WAS SAYING SOMETHING ABOUT STARTING A NEW COSMETICS COMPANY...
IT'S UNBELIEVABLE!!
OF COURSE IT'S BELIEVABLE!! I'D WANT TO DO RESEARCH ON YOU, TOO!! IN WHAT WORLD DOES AN OLD MAN WITH SUCH YOUTHFUL PINK NIPPLES LIKE THAT EXIST?!
HOW RUDE!!
THERE'S ONE SITTING RIGHT IN FRONT OF YOU!
Ahem!
DOM
GIVE YOURSELF TO RESEARCH AND AID THE WOMEN OF THIS WORLD!!

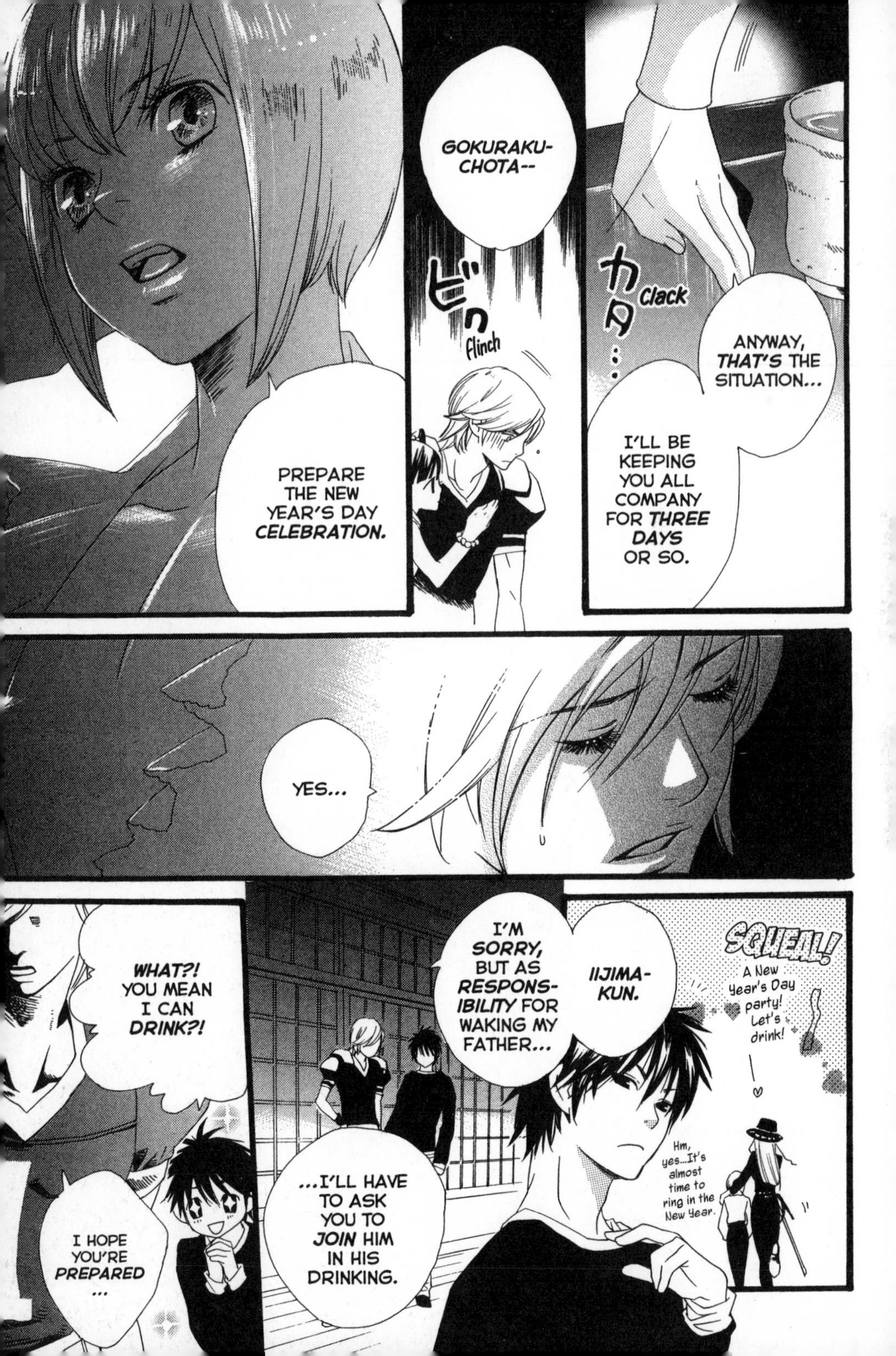
カタ...
Clack
ANYWAY, THAT'S THE SITUATION...
I'LL BE KEEPING YOU ALL COMPANY FOR THREE DAYS OR SO.
GOKURAKU-CHOTA--
ビク
flinch
PREPARE THE NEW YEAR'S DAY CELEBRATION.
YES...
SQUEAL!
A New Year's Day party! Let's drink!
Hm, yes...It's almost time to ring in the New Year.
IIJIMA-KUN.
I'M SORRY, BUT AS RESPONSIBILITY FOR WAKING MY FATHER...
...I'LL HAVE TO ASK YOU TO JOIN HIM IN HIS DRINKING.
WHAT?! YOU MEAN I CAN DRINK?!
I HOPE YOU'RE PREPARED...

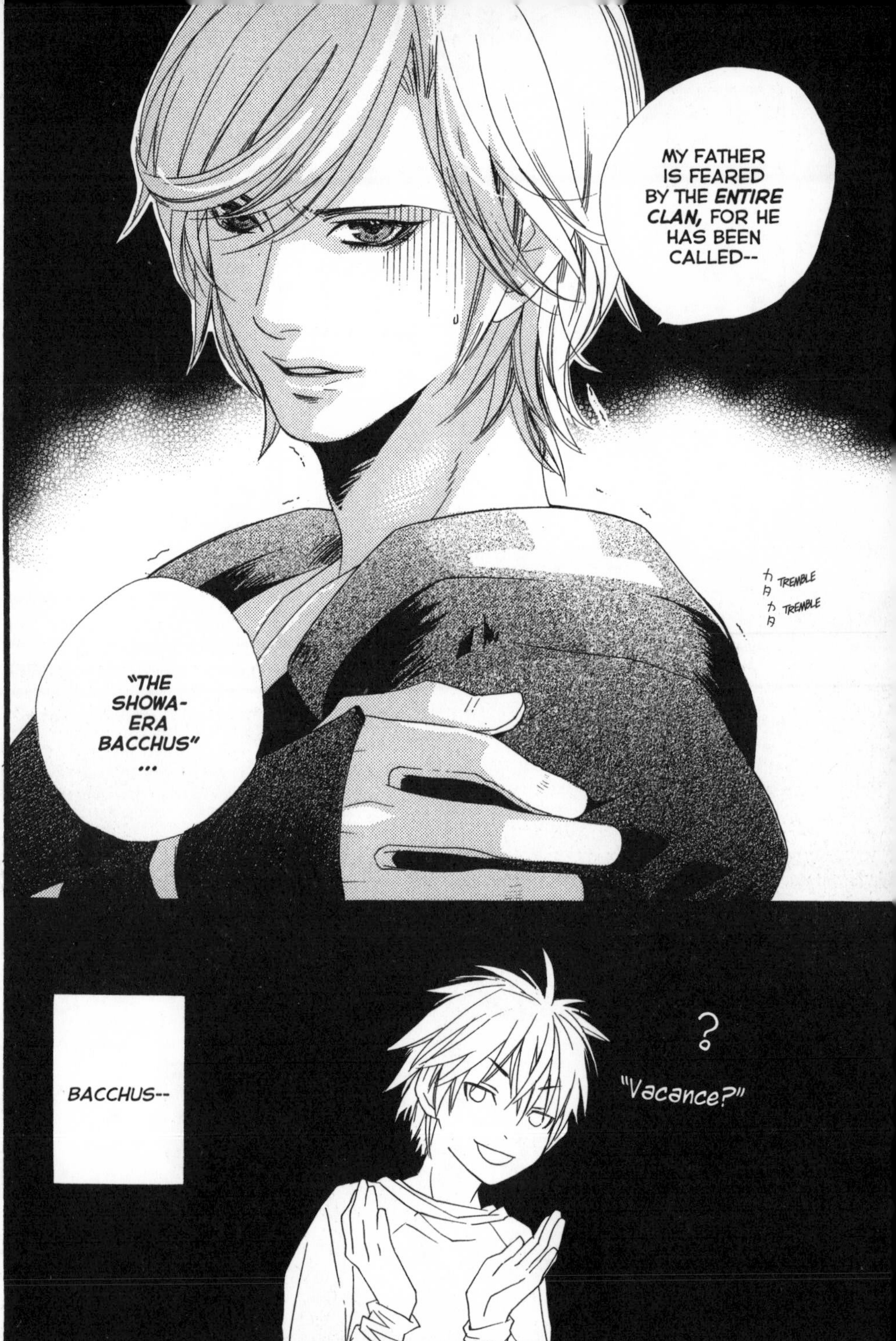
MY FATHER IS FEARED BY THE ENTIRE CLAN, FOR HE HAS BEEN CALLED--
カタ TREMBLE
カタ TREMBLE
"THE SHOWA-ERA BACCHUS" ...
?
"Vacance?"
BACCHUS--

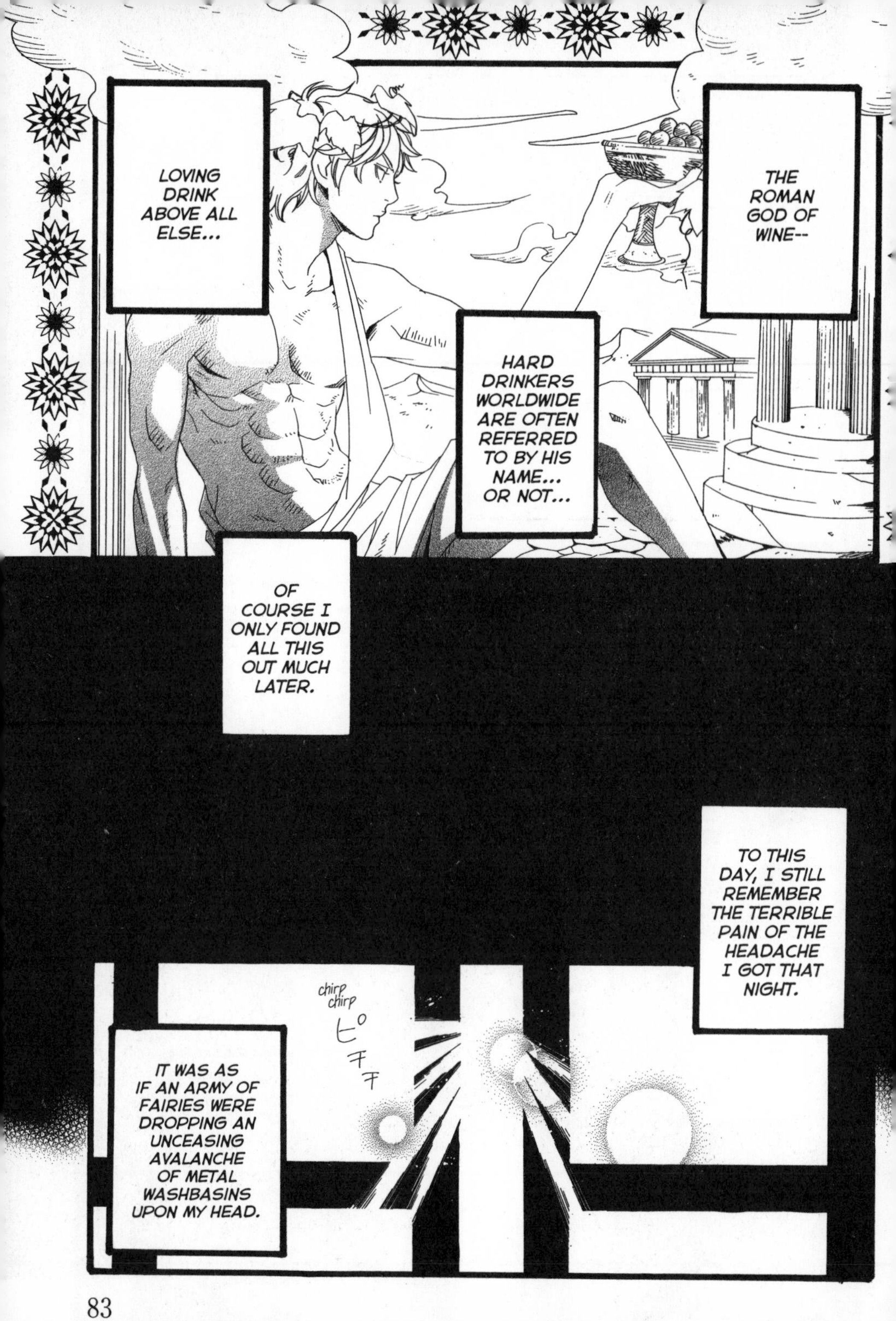
THE ROMAN GOD OF WINE--
LOVING DRINK ABOVE ALL ELSE...
HARD DRINKERS WORLDWIDE ARE OFTEN REFERRED TO BY HIS NAME... OR NOT...
OF COURSE I ONLY FOUND ALL THIS OUT MUCH LATER.
TO THIS DAY, I STILL REMEMBER THE TERRIBLE PAIN OF THE HEADACHE I GOT THAT NIGHT.
chirp chirp
ピチチ
IT WAS AS IF AN ARMY OF FAIRIES WERE DROPPING AN UNCEASING AVALANCHE OF METAL WASHBASINS UPON MY HEAD.

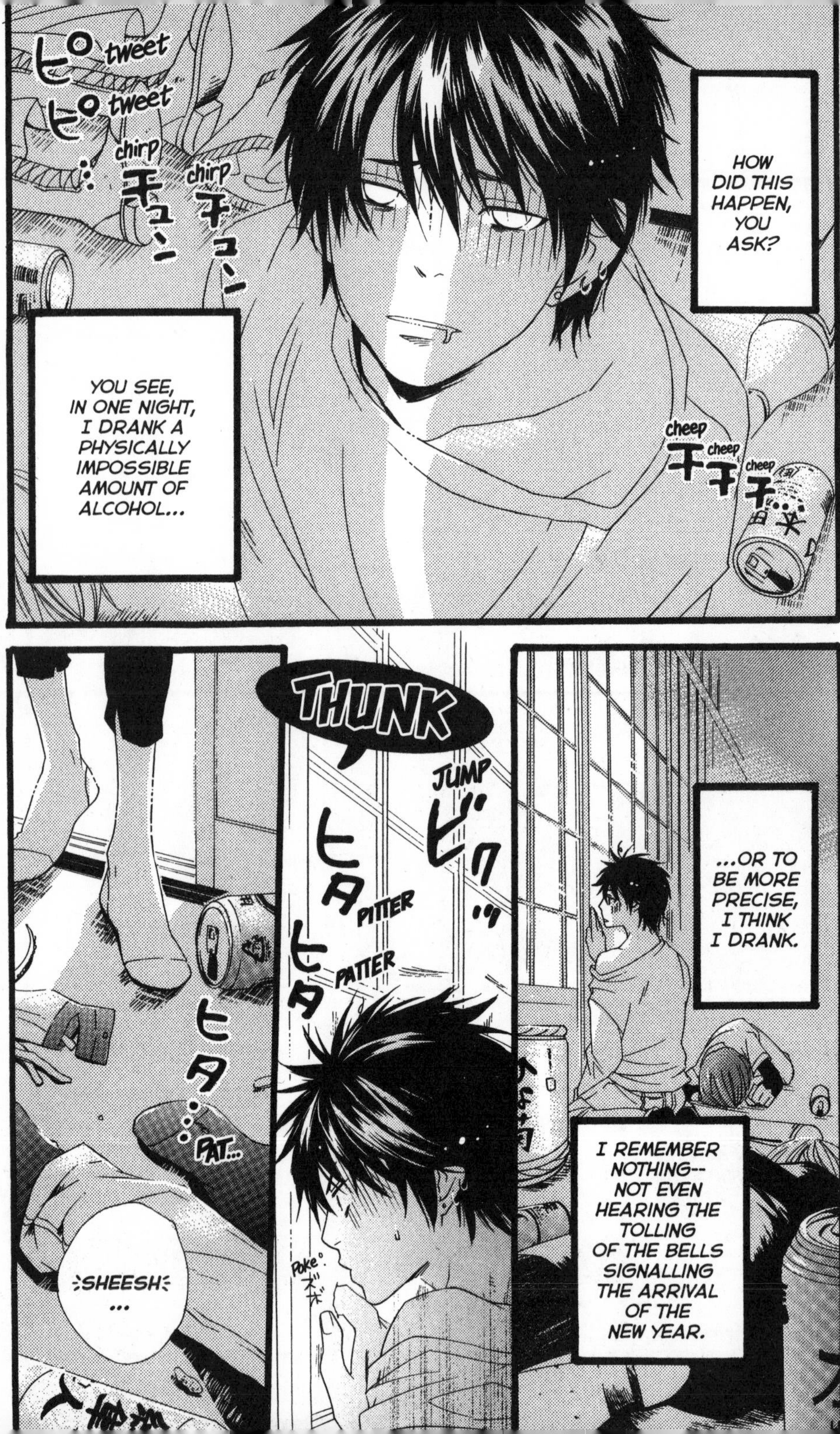
HOW DID THIS HAPPEN, YOU ASK?
tweet
tweet
chirp
chirp
cheep
cheep
cheep
YOU SEE, IN ONE NIGHT, I DRANK A PHYSICALLY IMPOSSIBLE AMOUNT OF ALCOHOL...
...OR TO BE MORE PRECISE, I THINK I DRANK.
I REMEMBER NOTHING-- NOT EVEN HEARING THE TOLLING OF THE BELLS SIGNALLING THE ARRIVAL OF THE NEW YEAR.
THUNK
JUMP
PITTER
PATTER
PAT...
Poke
SHEESH ...

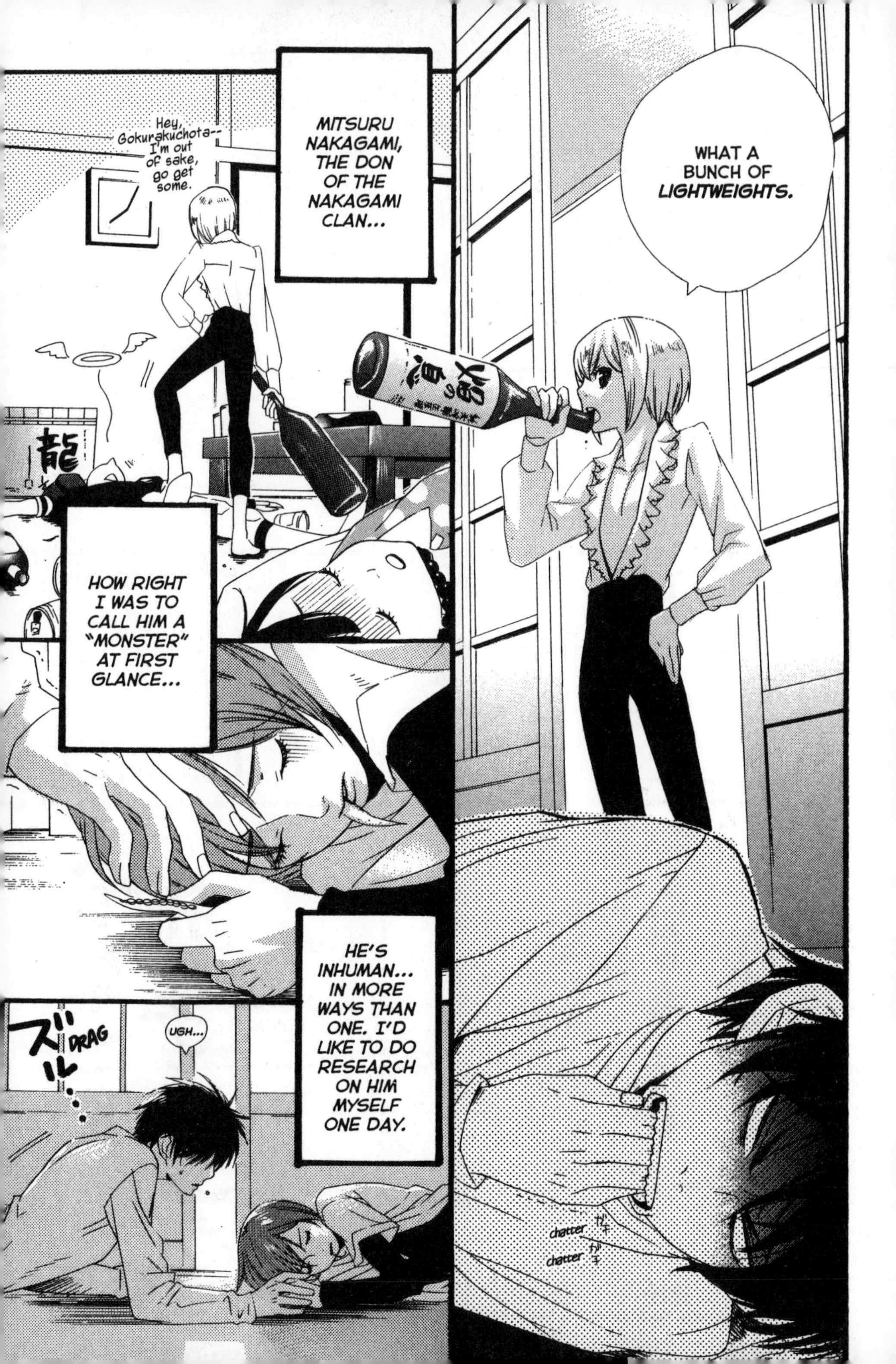
WHAT A BUNCH OF *LIGHTWEIGHTS.*
chatter
chatter
MITSURU NAKAGAMI, THE DON OF THE NAKAGAMI CLAN...
Hey, Gokurakuchota-- I'm out of sake, go get some.
HOW RIGHT I WAS TO CALL HIM A "MONSTER" AT FIRST GLANCE...
HE'S INHUMAN... IN MORE WAYS THAN ONE. I'D LIKE TO DO RESEARCH ON HIM MYSELF ONE DAY.
UGH...
ズル
DRAG

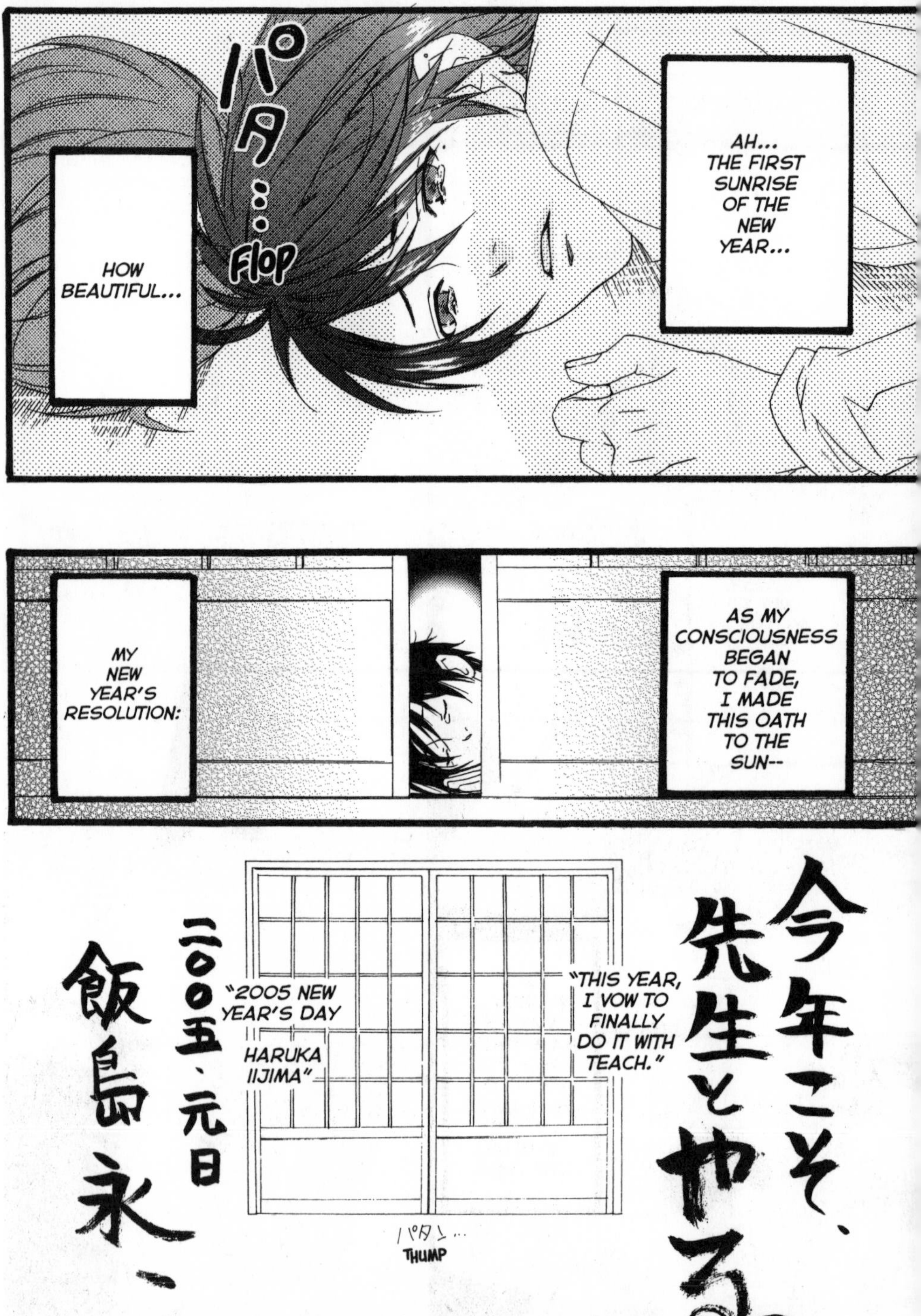
AH... THE FIRST SUNRISE OF THE NEW YEAR...
パタ…
FLOP
HOW BEAUTIFUL...
AS MY CONSCIOUSNESS BEGAN TO FADE, I MADE THIS OATH TO THE SUN--
MY NEW YEAR'S RESOLUTION:
今年こそ、先生とやる。
"THIS YEAR, I VOW TO FINALLY DO IT WITH TEACH."
二〇〇五、元日
飯島永一
"2005 NEW YEAR'S DAY
HARUKA IIJIMA"
パタン…
THUMP

仲神家の一族～眠れる王子と死の宴～／おわり

CLAN OF THE NAKAGAMIS--- THE SLEEPING PRINCE AND THE PARTY OF DEATH/ END

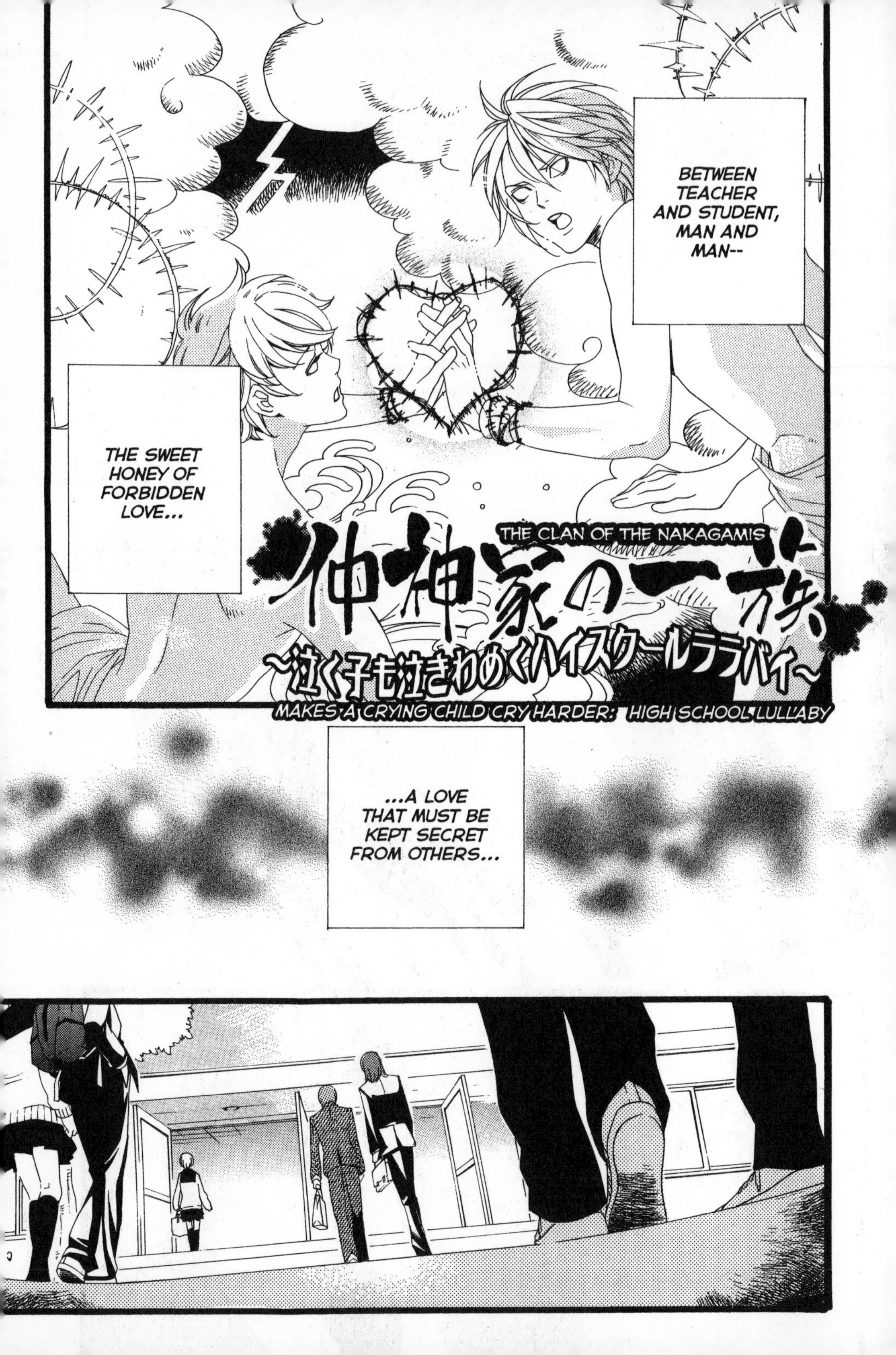

BETWEEN TEACHER AND STUDENT, MAN AND MAN--
THE SWEET HONEY OF FORBIDDEN LOVE...
THE CLAN OF THE NAKAGAMIS
仲神家の一族
~泣く子も泣きわめくハイスクールララバイ~
MAKES A CRYING CHILD CRY HARDER: HIGH SCHOOL LULLABY
...A LOVE THAT MUST BE KEPT SECRET FROM OTHERS...

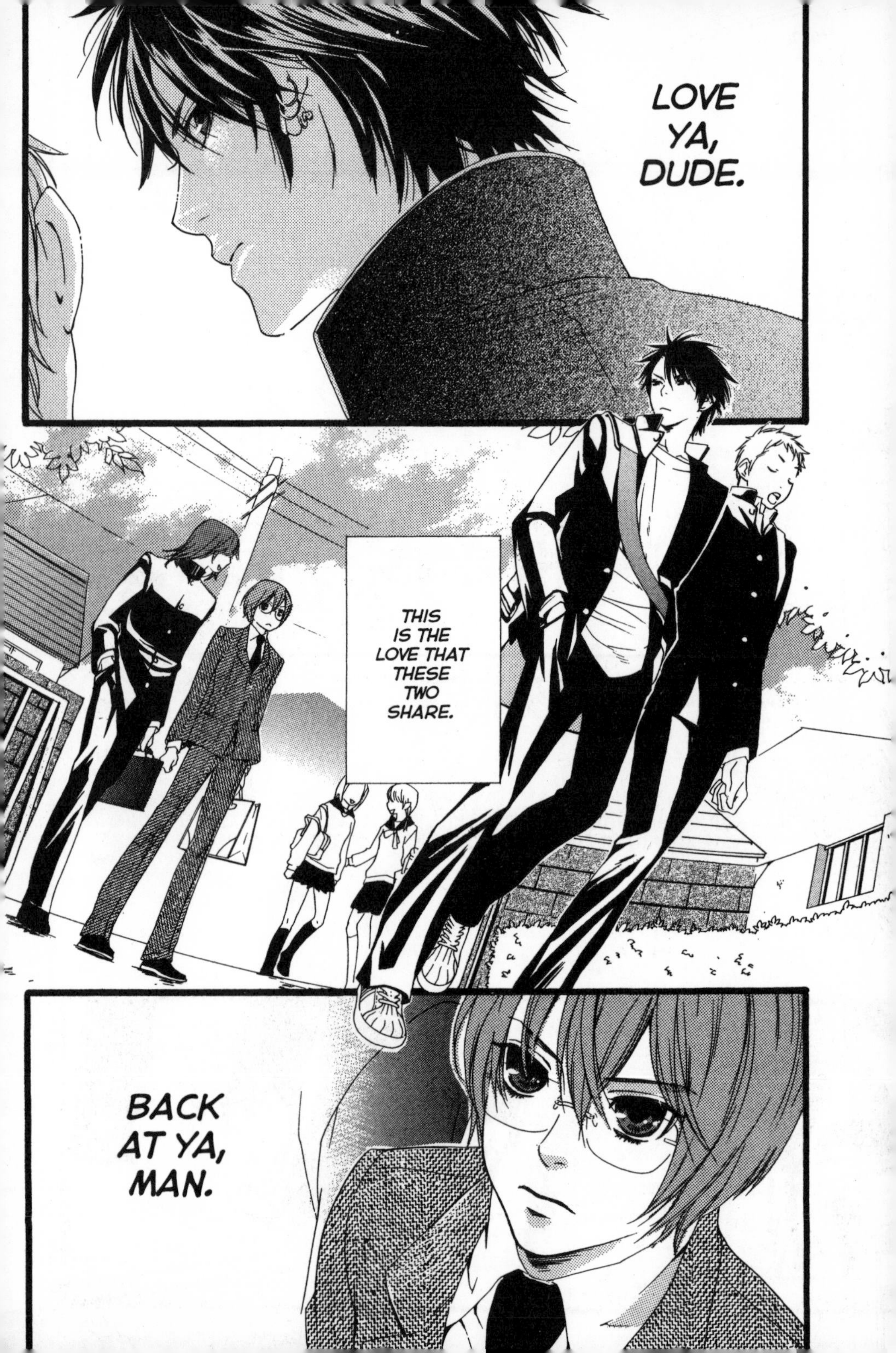
LOVE YA, DUDE.
THIS IS THE LOVE THAT THESE TWO SHARE.
BACK AT YA, MAN.

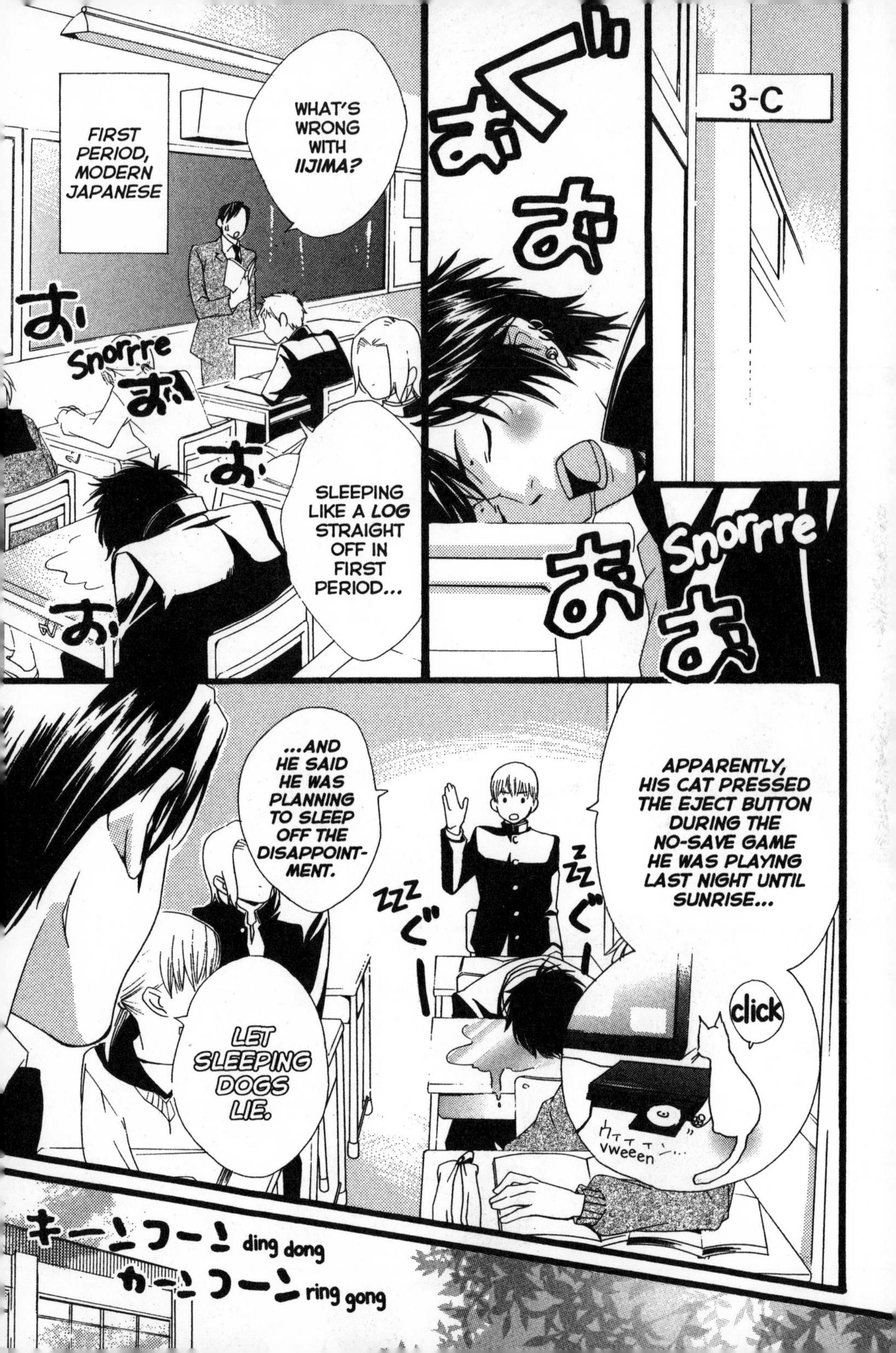
3-C
Snorrre
FIRST PERIOD, MODERN JAPANESE
WHAT'S WRONG WITH IIJIMA?
Snorrre
SLEEPING LIKE A LOG STRAIGHT OFF IN FIRST PERIOD...
APPARENTLY, HIS CAT PRESSED THE EJECT BUTTON DURING THE NO-SAVE GAME HE WAS PLAYING LAST NIGHT UNTIL SUNRISE...
click
vweeen
zzz
zzz
...AND HE SAID HE WAS PLANNING TO SLEEP OFF THE DISAPPOINT-MENT.
LET SLEEPING DOGS LIE.
ding dong
ring gong

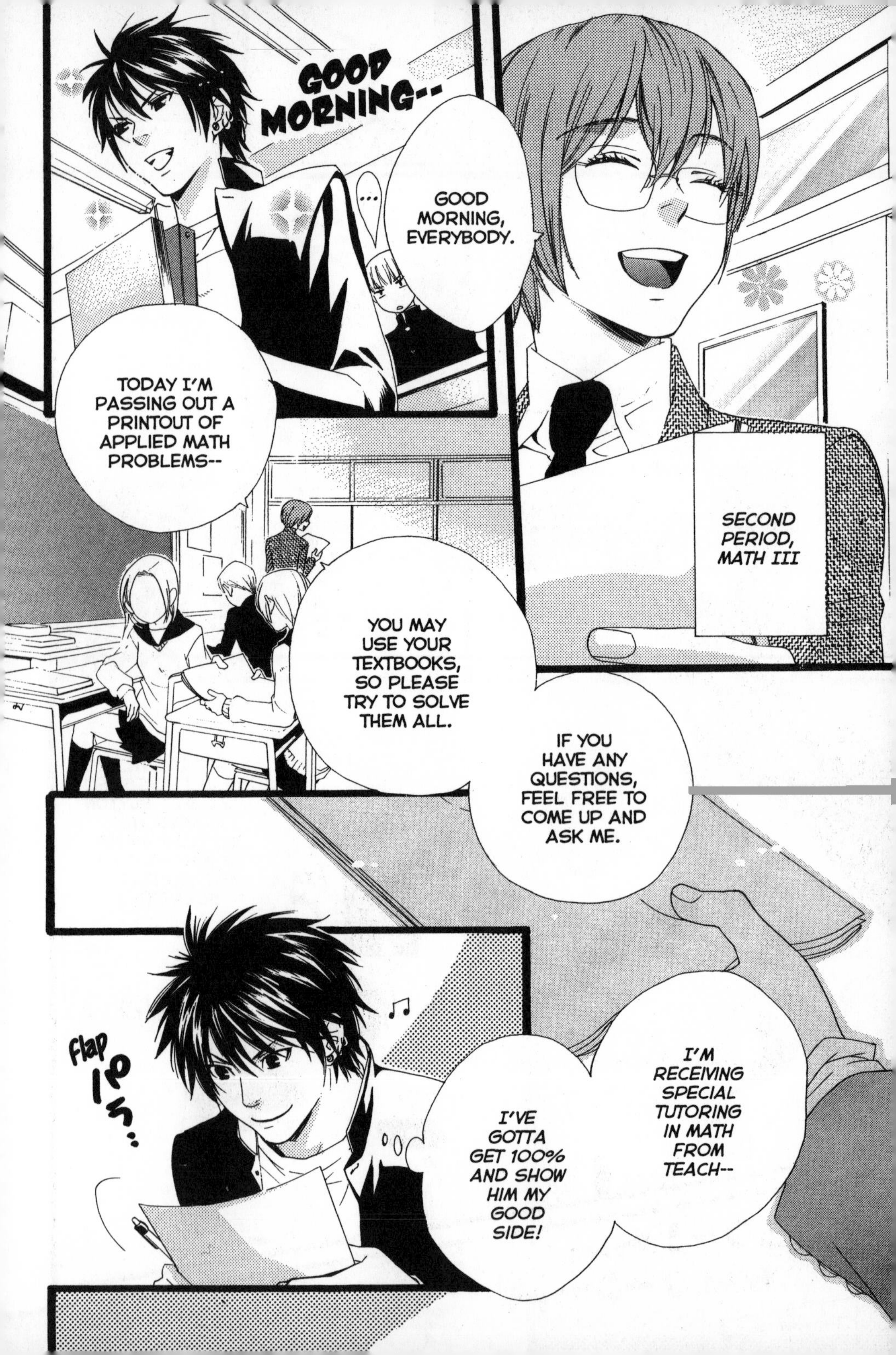

SECOND PERIOD, MATH III
GOOD MORNING, EVERYBODY.
GOOD MORNING--
...
TODAY I'M PASSING OUT A PRINTOUT OF APPLIED MATH PROBLEMS--
YOU MAY USE YOUR TEXTBOOKS, SO PLEASE TRY TO SOLVE THEM ALL.
IF YOU HAVE ANY QUESTIONS, FEEL FREE TO COME UP AND ASK ME.
I'M RECEIVING SPECIAL TUTORING IN MATH FROM TEACH--
I'VE GOTTA GET 100% AND SHOW HIM MY GOOD SIDE!
Flap

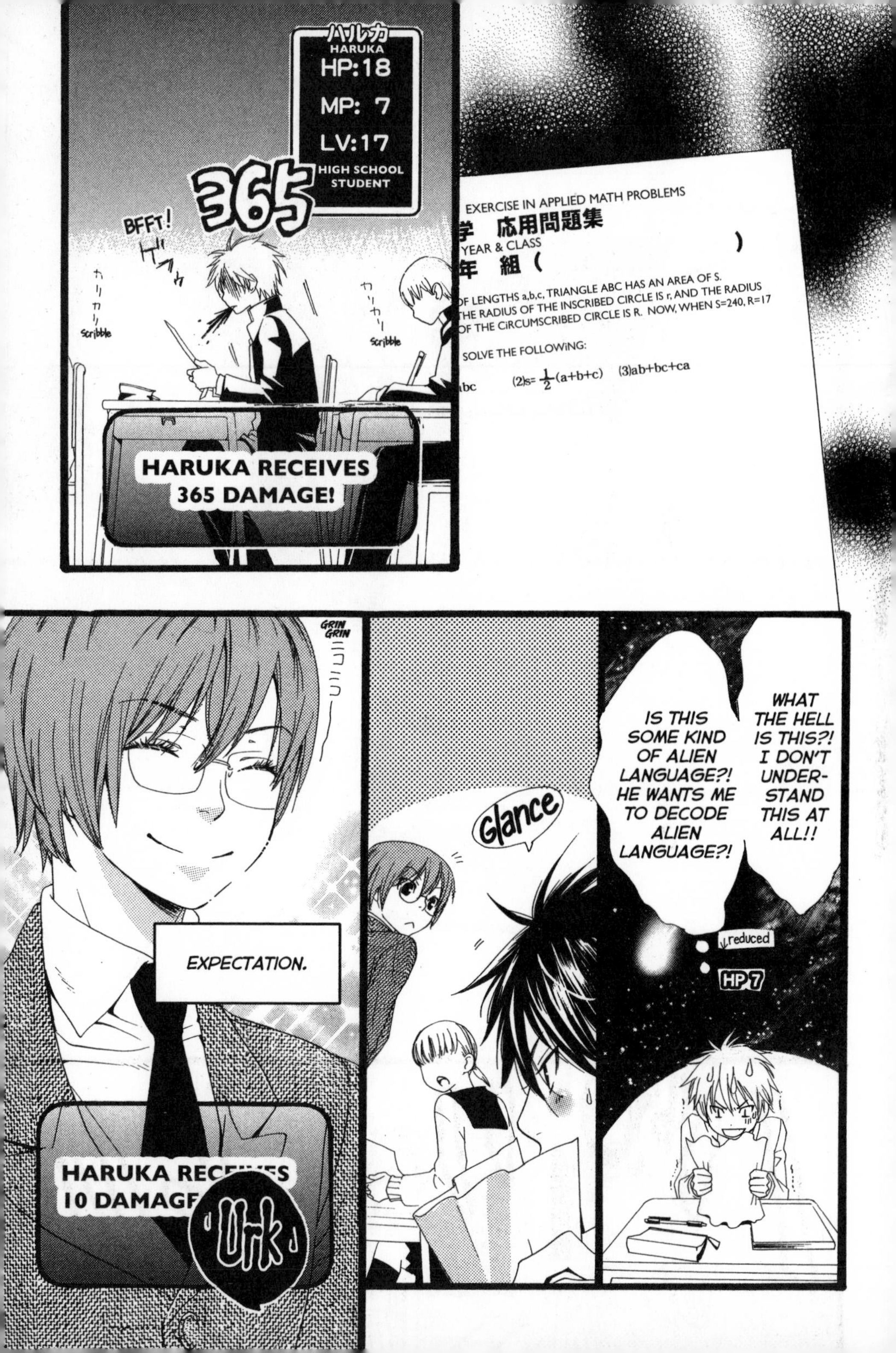

EXERCISE IN APPLIED MATH PROBLEMS
学 応用問題集
YEAR & CLASS
年 組（ ）
OF LENGTHS a,b,c, TRIANGLE ABC HAS AN AREA OF S.
THE RADIUS OF THE INSCRIBED CIRCLE IS r, AND THE RADIUS
OF THE CIRCUMSCRIBED CIRCLE IS R. NOW, WHEN S=240, R=17
SOLVE THE FOLLOWING:
abc (2)s= $\frac{1}{2}$(a+b+c) (3)ab+bc+ca
ハルカ
HARUKA
HP:18
MP: 7
LV:17
HIGH SCHOOL STUDENT
365
BFFT!
カリカリ
scribble
カリカリ
scribble
HARUKA RECEIVES 365 DAMAGE!
WHAT THE HELL IS THIS?! I DON'T UNDER-STAND THIS AT ALL!!
IS THIS SOME KIND OF ALIEN LANGUAGE?! HE WANTS ME TO DECODE ALIEN LANGUAGE?!
reduced
HP 7
Glance
GRIN GRIN
ニコニコ
EXPECTATION.
HARUKA RECEIVES 10 DAMAGE
Urk

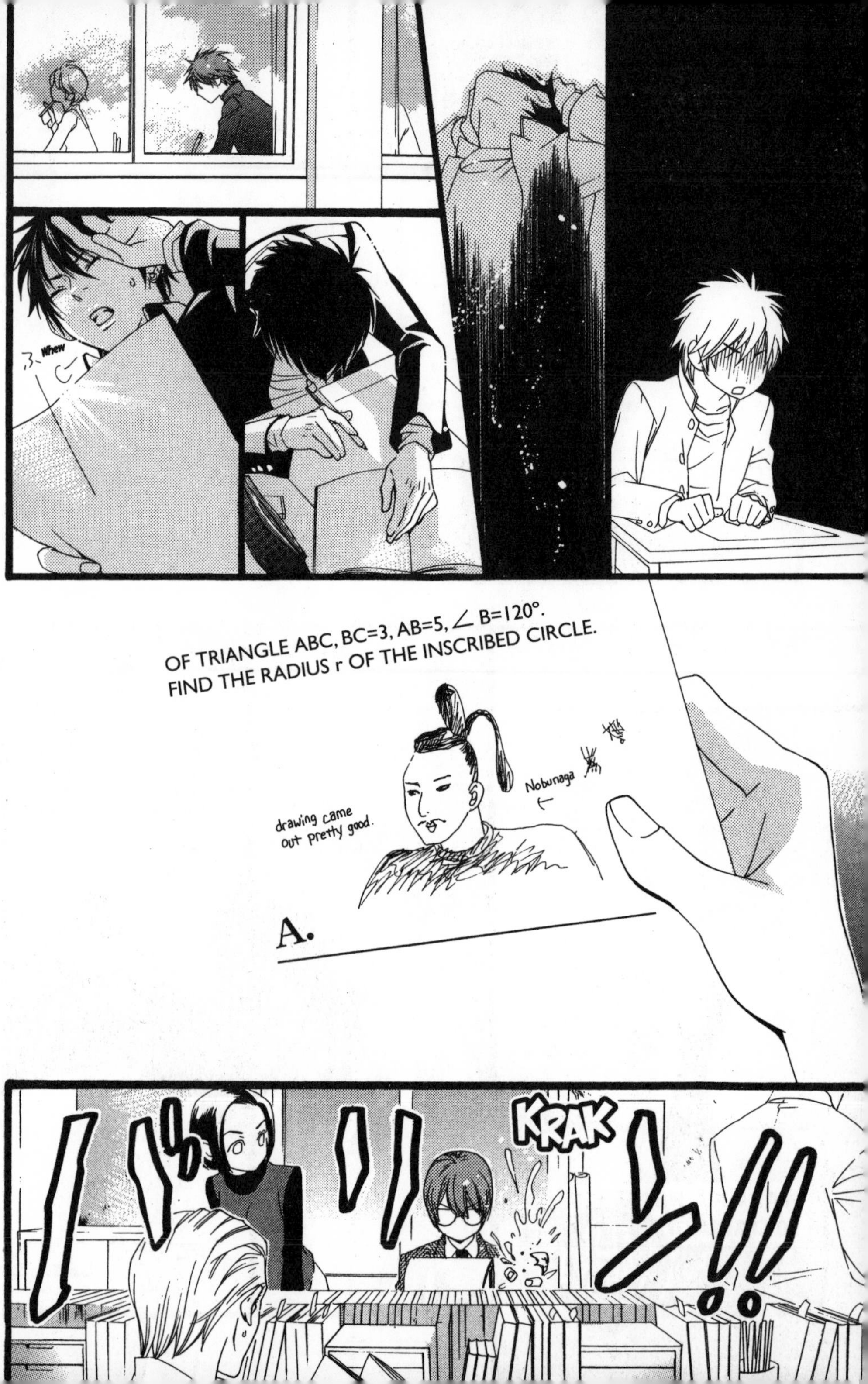
ふ Whew
OF TRIANGLE ABC, BC=3, AB=5, ∠ B=120°.
FIND THE RADIUS r OF THE INSCRIBED CIRCLE.
Nobunaga
drawing came out pretty good.
A.
KRAK

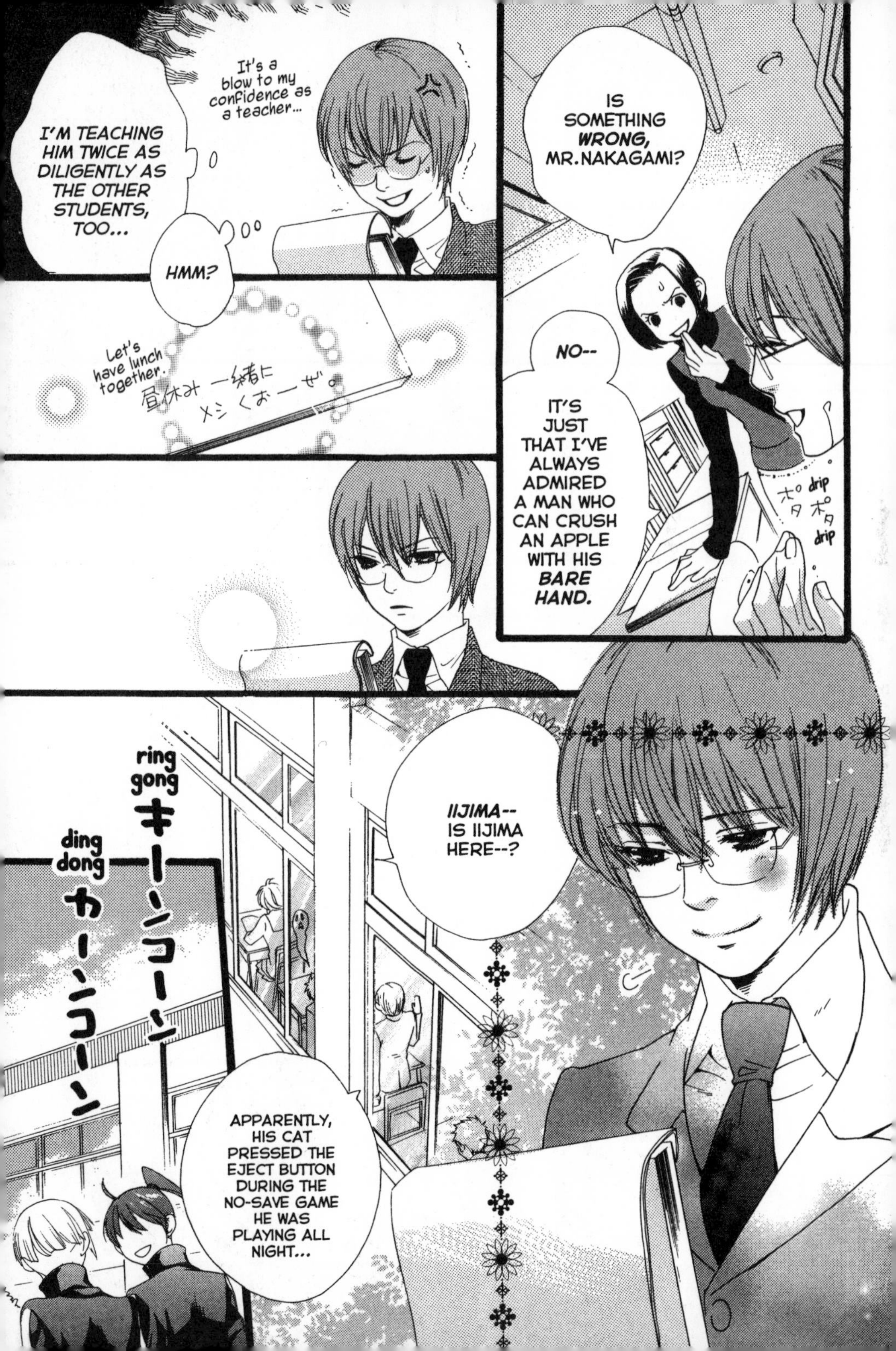
IS SOMETHING WRONG, MR. NAKAGAMI?
NO--
IT'S JUST THAT I'VE ALWAYS ADMIRED A MAN WHO CAN CRUSH AN APPLE WITH HIS BARE HAND.
ポタ drip
ポタ drip
It's a blow to my confidence as a teacher...
I'M TEACHING HIM TWICE AS DILIGENTLY AS THE OTHER STUDENTS, TOO...
HMM?
Let's have lunch together.
昼休み 一緒に メシ くおーぜ。
IIJIMA-- IS IIJIMA HERE--?
APPARENTLY, HIS CAT PRESSED THE EJECT BUTTON DURING THE NO-SAVE GAME HE WAS PLAYING ALL NIGHT...
ring gong キーンコーン
ding dong カーンコーン

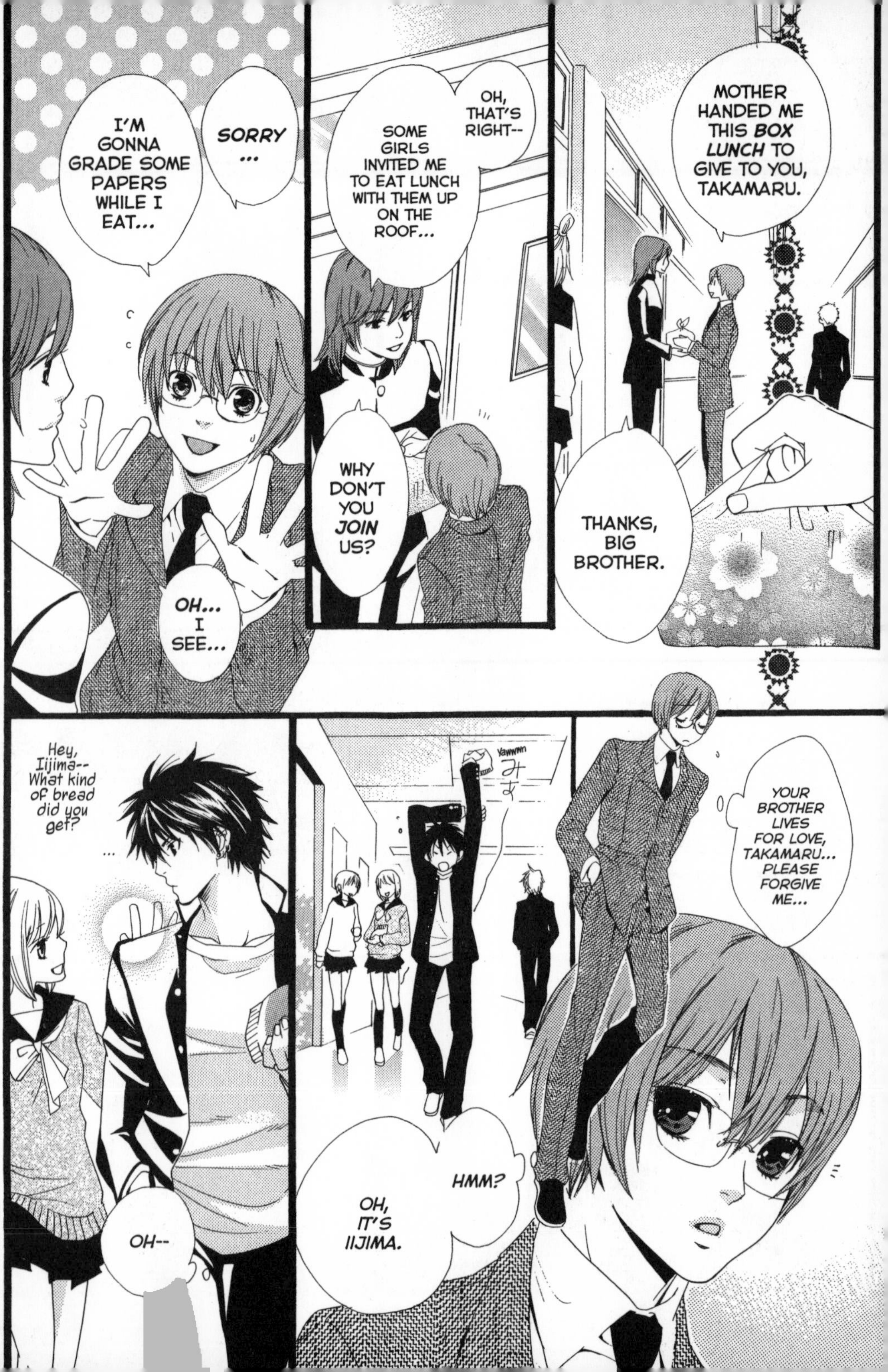
MOTHER HANDED ME THIS **BOX LUNCH** TO GIVE TO YOU, TAKAMARU.
THANKS, BIG BROTHER.
OH, THAT'S RIGHT--
SOME GIRLS INVITED ME TO EAT LUNCH WITH THEM UP ON THE ROOF...
WHY DON'T YOU **JOIN** US?
SORRY...
I'M GONNA GRADE SOME PAPERS WHILE I EAT...
OH... I SEE...
YOUR BROTHER LIVES FOR LOVE, TAKAMARU... PLEASE FORGIVE ME...
Yawwwn
HMM?
OH, IT'S IIJIMA.
Hey, Iijima-- What kind of bread did you get?
...
OH--

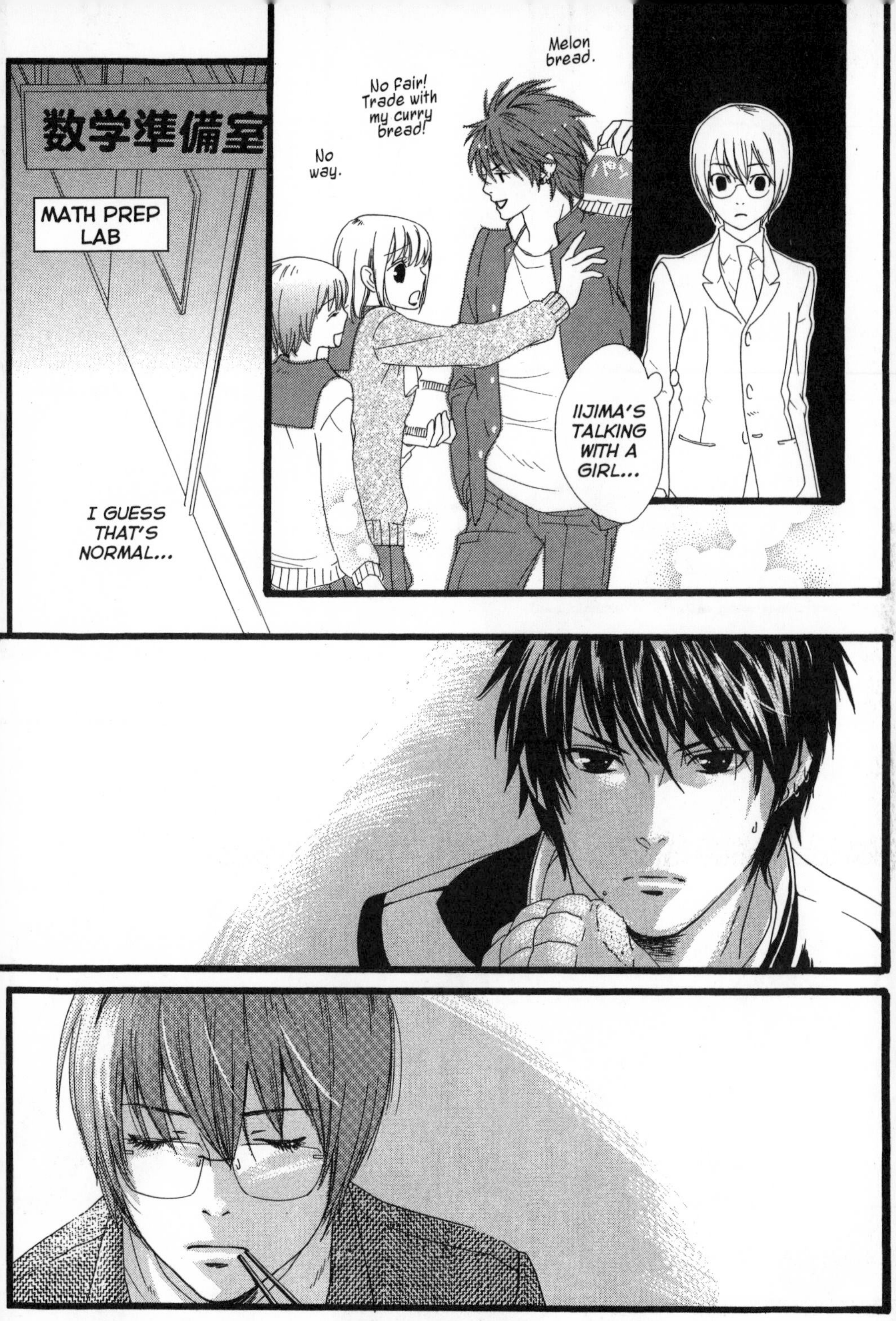
Melon bread.
No fair! Trade with my curry bread!
No way.
IIJIMA'S TALKING WITH A GIRL...
数学準備室
MATH PREP LAB
I GUESS THAT'S NORMAL...

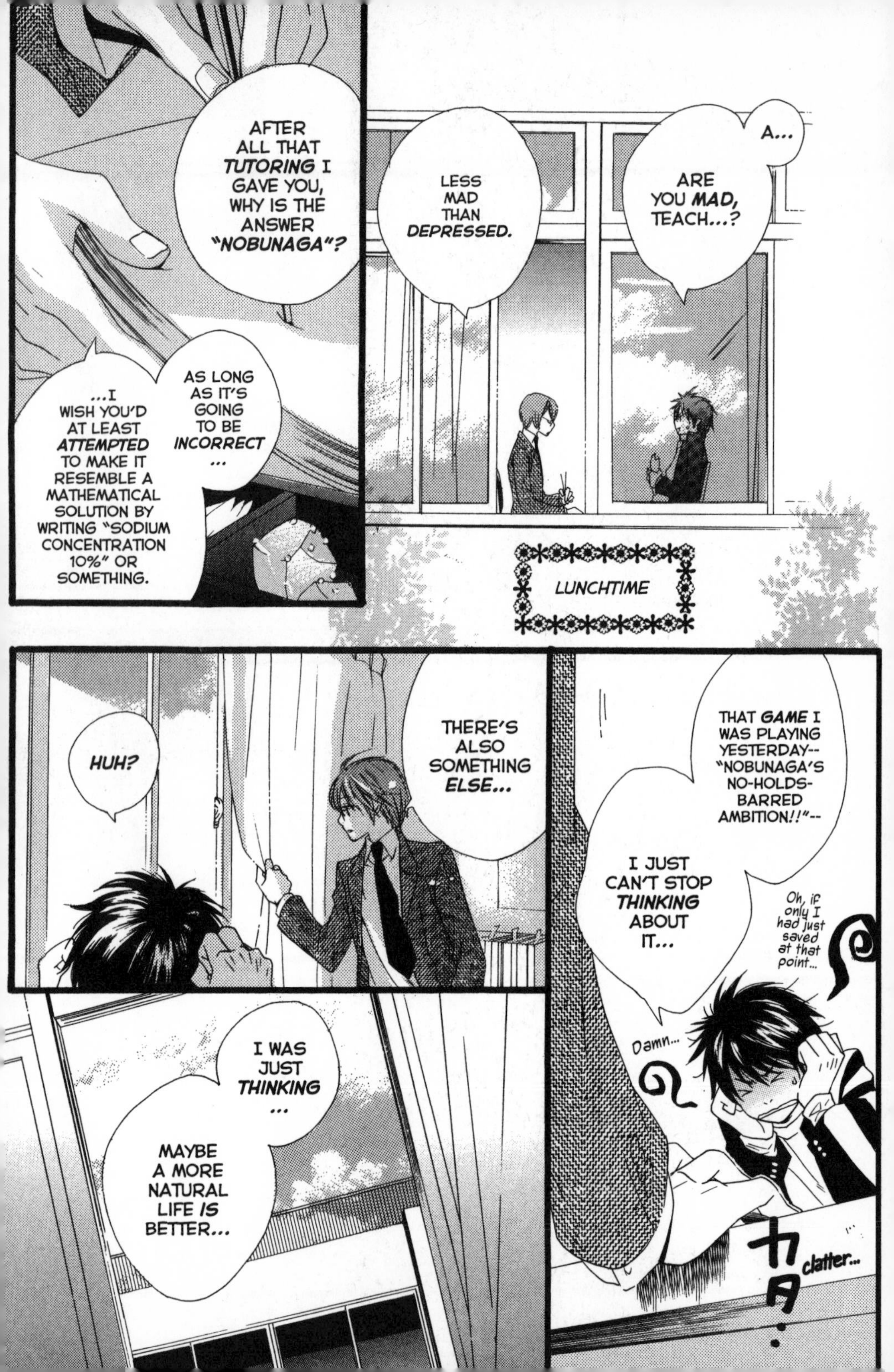
LUNCHTIME
A...
ARE YOU *MAD,* TEACH...?
LESS MAD THAN *DEPRESSED.*
AFTER ALL THAT *TUTORING* I GAVE YOU, WHY IS THE ANSWER *"NOBUNAGA"?*
AS LONG AS IT'S GOING TO BE *INCORRECT* ...
...I WISH YOU'D AT LEAST *ATTEMPTED* TO MAKE IT RESEMBLE A MATHEMATICAL SOLUTION BY WRITING "SODIUM CONCENTRATION 10%" OR SOMETHING.
THAT *GAME* I WAS PLAYING YESTERDAY-- "NOBUNAGA'S NO-HOLDS-BARRED AMBITION!!"--
I JUST CAN'T STOP *THINKING* ABOUT IT...
Oh, if only I had just saved at that point...
Damn...
clatter...
THERE'S ALSO SOMETHING *ELSE...*
HUH?
I WAS JUST *THINKING* ...
MAYBE A MORE NATURAL LIFE *IS* BETTER...

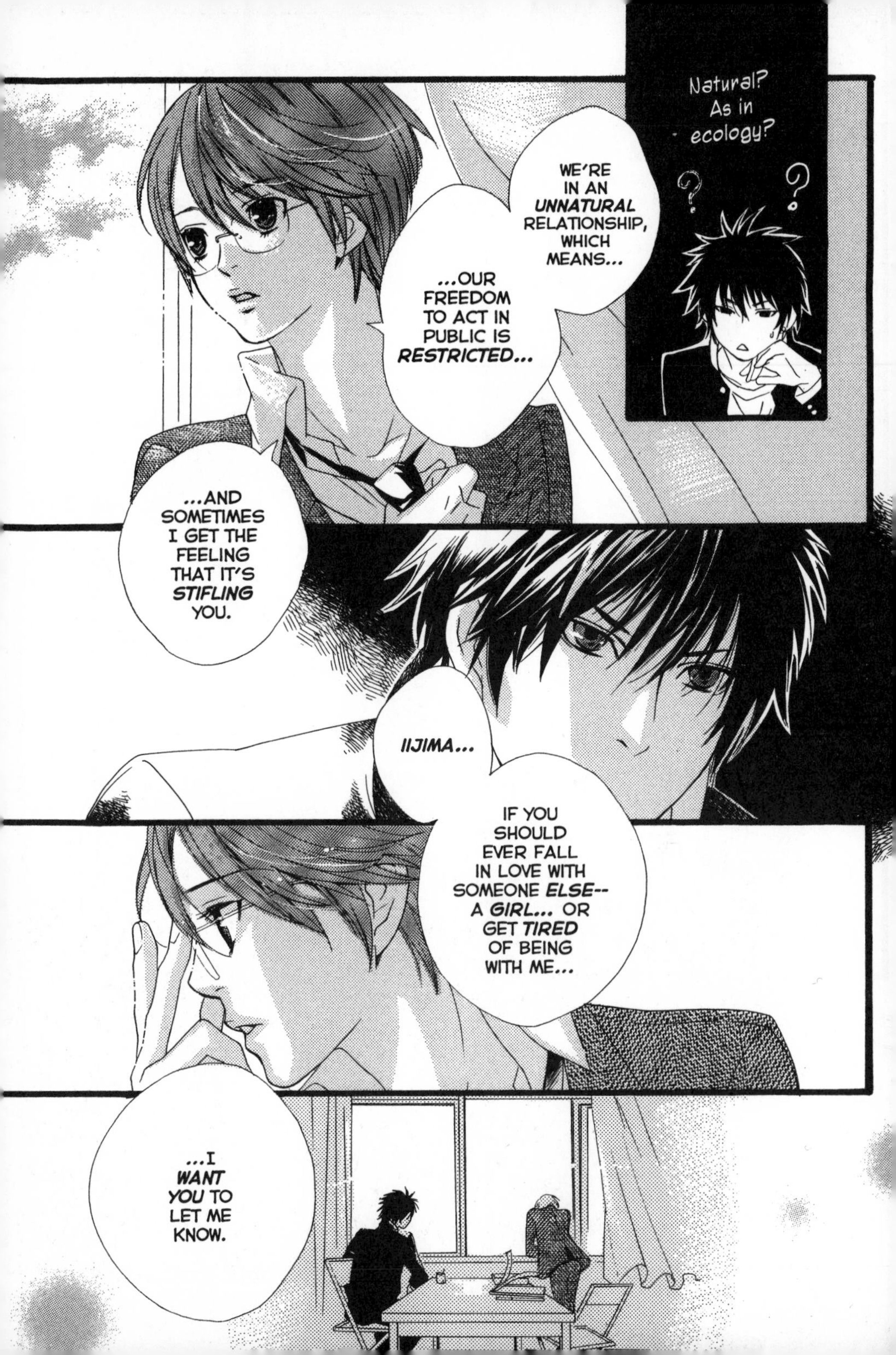
Natural? As in ecology?
?
?
WE'RE IN AN UNNATURAL RELATIONSHIP, WHICH MEANS...
...OUR FREEDOM TO ACT IN PUBLIC IS RESTRICTED...
...AND SOMETIMES I GET THE FEELING THAT IT'S STIFLING YOU.
IIJIMA...
IF YOU SHOULD EVER FALL IN LOVE WITH SOMEONE ELSE-- A GIRL... OR GET TIRED OF BEING WITH ME...
...I WANT YOU TO LET ME KNOW.

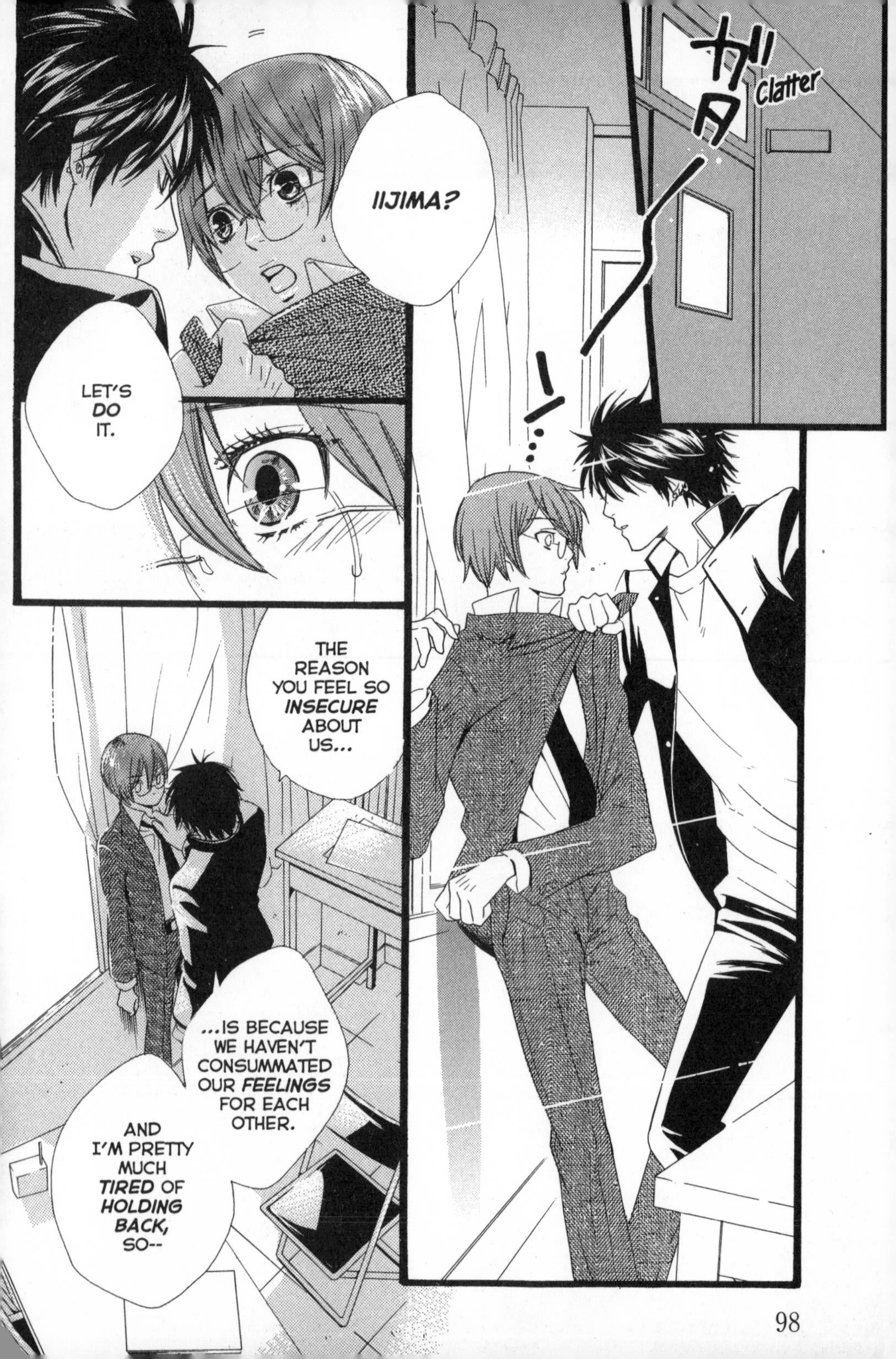
ガタ
Clatter
IIJIMA?
LET'S DO IT.
THE REASON YOU FEEL SO INSECURE ABOUT US...
...IS BECAUSE WE HAVEN'T CONSUMMATED OUR FEELINGS FOR EACH OTHER.
AND I'M PRETTY MUCH TIRED OF HOLDING BACK, SO--

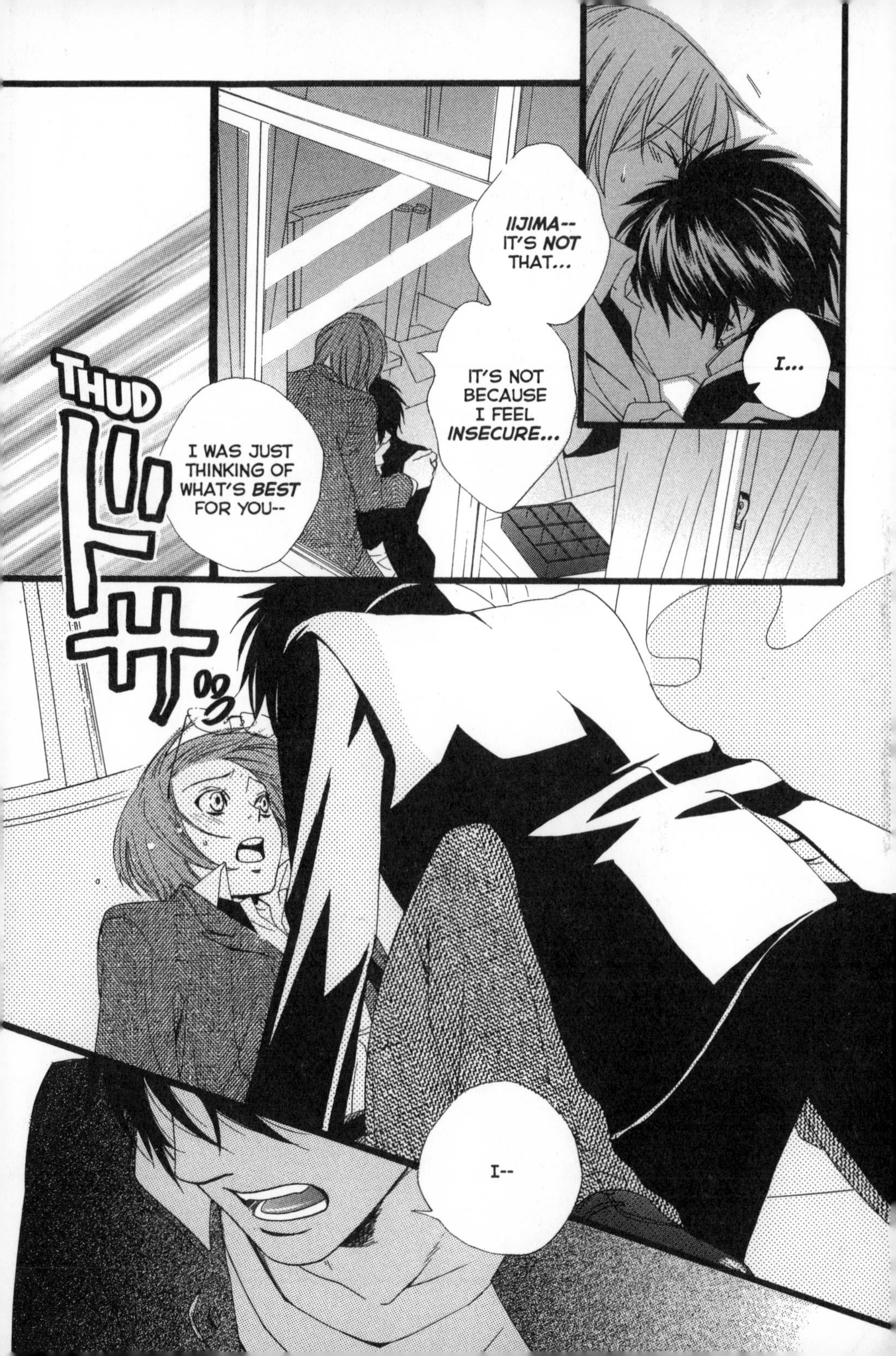
I...
IIJIMA-- IT'S NOT THAT...
IT'S NOT BECAUSE I FEEL INSECURE...
I WAS JUST THINKING OF WHAT'S BEST FOR YOU--
THUD
ドサッ
I--

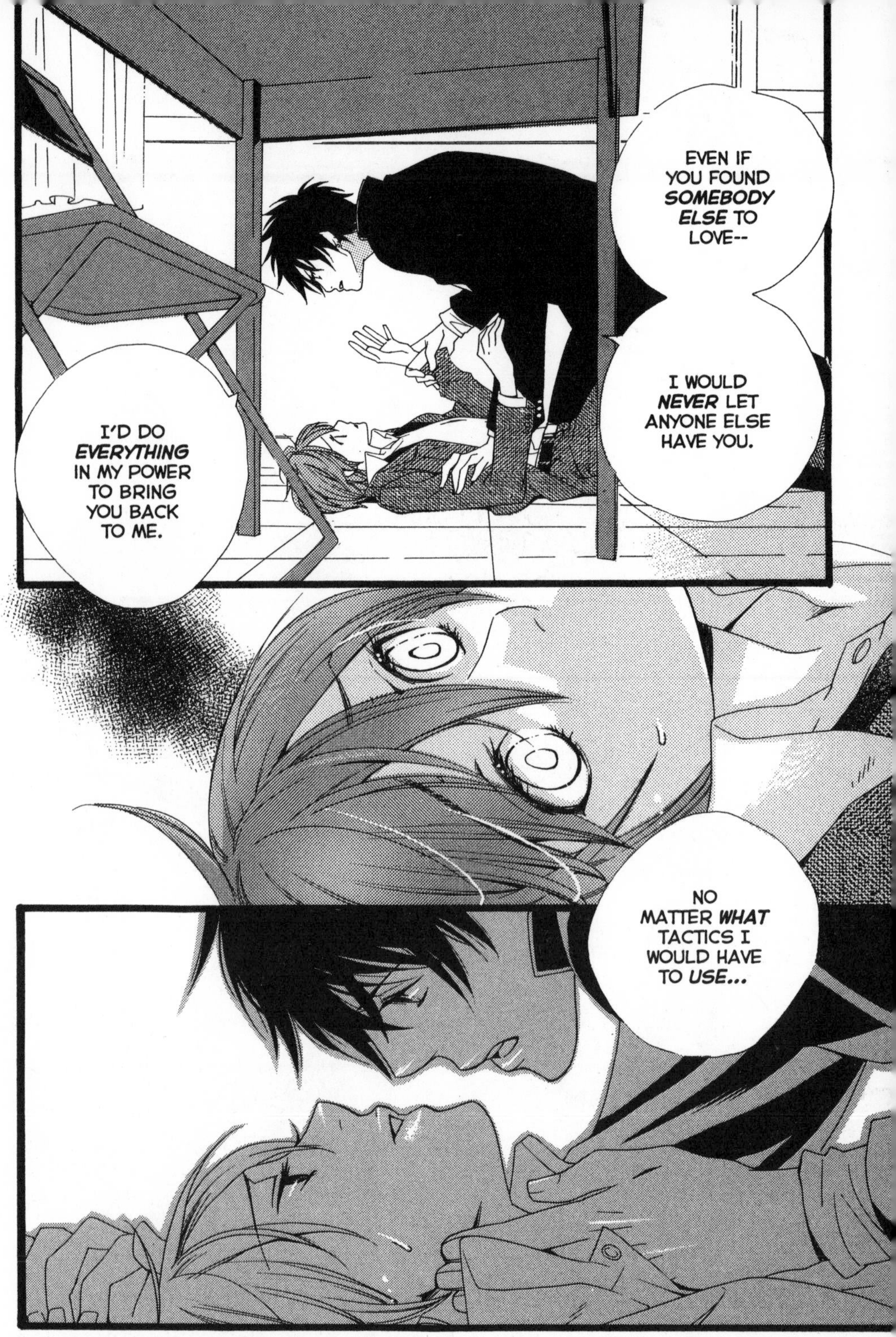
EVEN IF YOU FOUND SOMEBODY ELSE TO LOVE--
I WOULD NEVER LET ANYONE ELSE HAVE YOU.
I'D DO EVERYTHING IN MY POWER TO BRING YOU BACK TO ME.
NO MATTER WHAT TACTICS I WOULD HAVE TO USE...

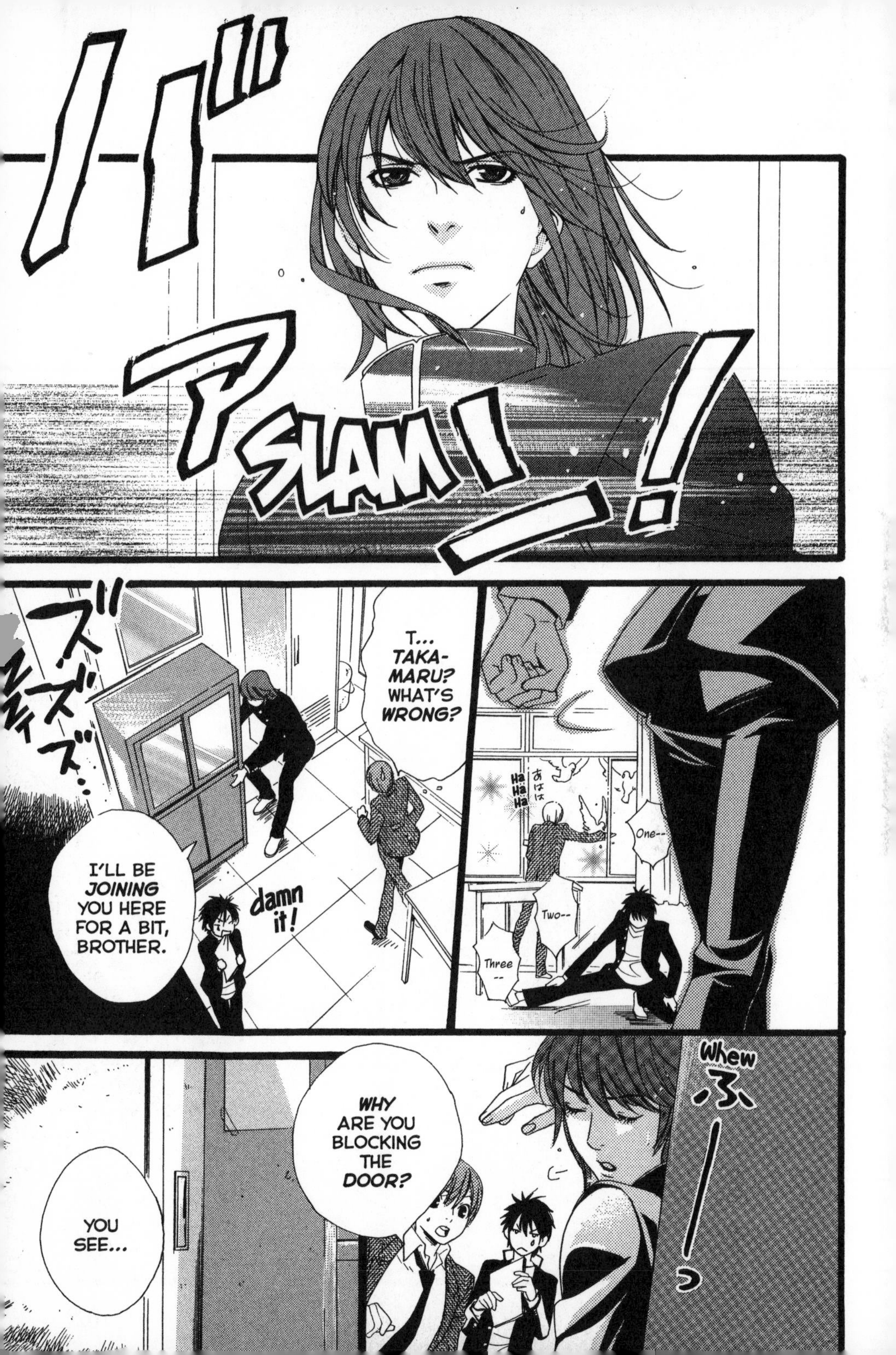
SLAM!
Ha Ha Ha あはは
One--
Two--
Three--
T... TAKA-MARU? WHAT'S WRONG?
I'LL BE JOINING YOU HERE FOR A BIT, BROTHER.
damn it!
Whew ふーっ
WHY ARE YOU BLOCKING THE DOOR?
YOU SEE...

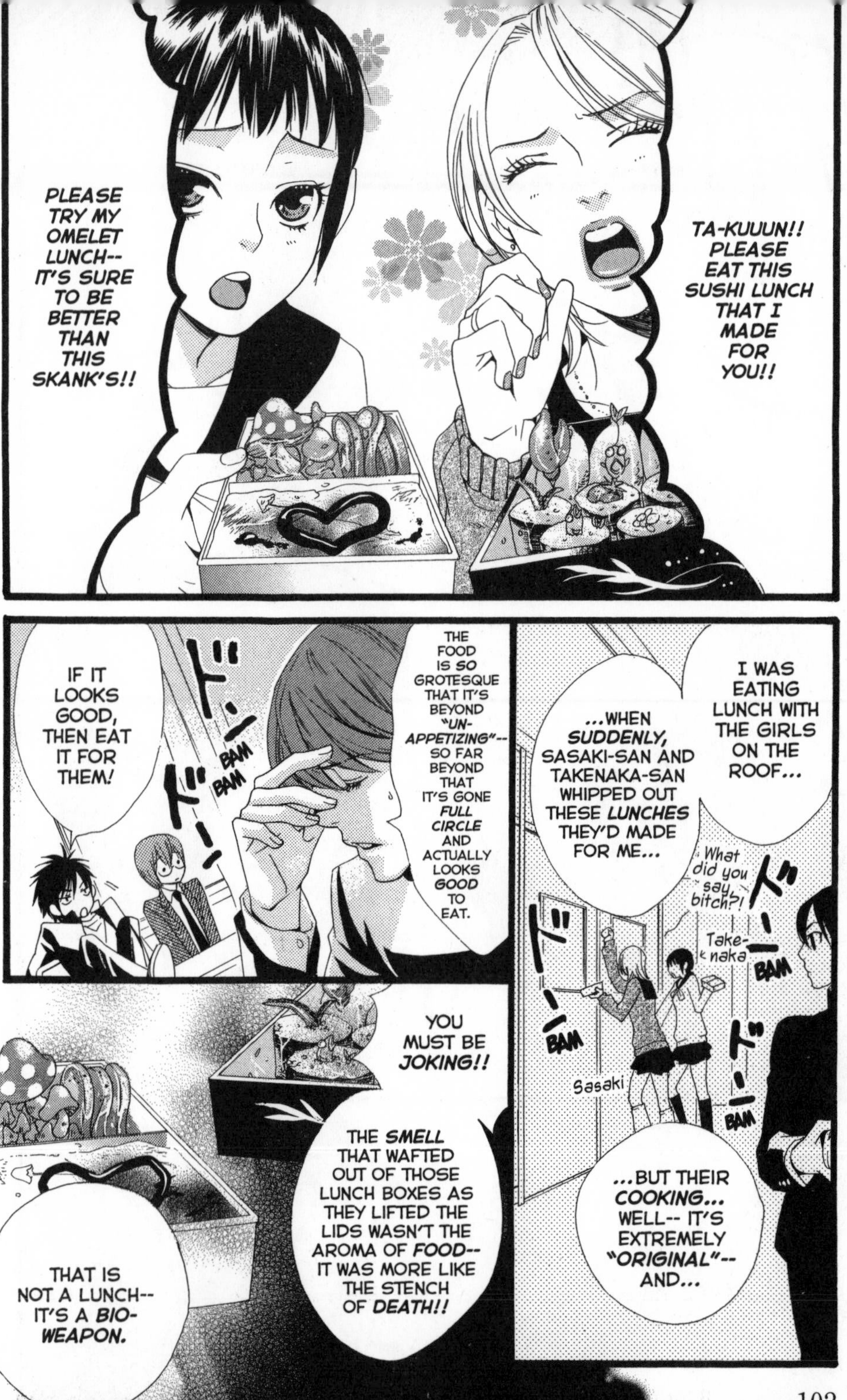
TA-KUUUN!! PLEASE EAT THIS SUSHI LUNCH THAT I MADE FOR YOU!!
PLEASE TRY MY OMELET LUNCH-- IT'S SURE TO BE BETTER THAN THIS SKANK'S!!
I WAS EATING LUNCH WITH THE GIRLS ON THE ROOF...
...WHEN SUDDENLY, SASAKI-SAN AND TAKENAKA-SAN WHIPPED OUT THESE LUNCHES THEY'D MADE FOR ME...
What did you say, bitch?!
Take-naka
BAM
BAM
Sasaki
BAM
...BUT THEIR COOKING... WELL-- IT'S EXTREMELY "ORIGINAL"-- AND...
THE FOOD IS SO GROTESQUE THAT IT'S BEYOND "UN-APPETIZING"-- SO FAR BEYOND THAT IT'S GONE FULL CIRCLE AND ACTUALLY LOOKS GOOD TO EAT.
BAM
BAM
IF IT LOOKS GOOD, THEN EAT IT FOR THEM!
YOU MUST BE JOKING!!
THE SMELL THAT WAFTED OUT OF THOSE LUNCH BOXES AS THEY LIFTED THE LIDS WASN'T THE AROMA OF FOOD-- IT WAS MORE LIKE THE STENCH OF DEATH!!
THAT IS NOT A LUNCH-- IT'S A BIO-WEAPON.

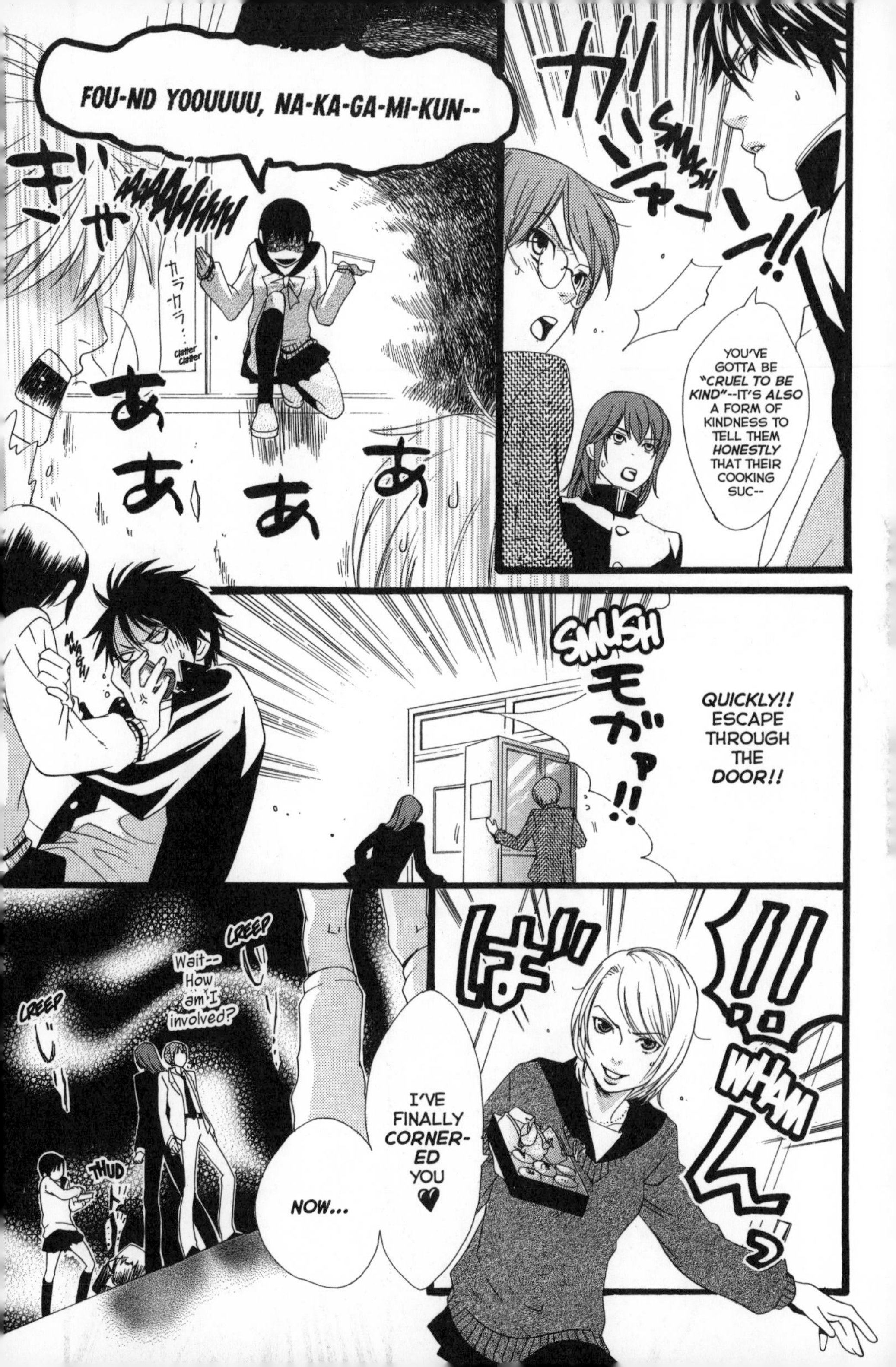

ガシャーン!!
SMASH
YOU'VE GOTTA BE "CRUEL TO BE KIND"--IT'S ALSO A FORM OF KINDNESS TO TELL THEM HONESTLY THAT THEIR COOKING SUC--
FOU-ND YOOUUUU, NA-KA-GA-MI-KUN--
ぎゃ
AAAAAHHHHH
カラカラ…
CLATTER CLATTER
ああああ
QUICKLY!! ESCAPE THROUGH THE DOOR!!
SMUSH
モガァ!!
MWAGH!
WHAM
!!
ばっ
I'VE FINALLY CORNER-ED YOU
NOW...
CREEP
Wait-- How am I involved?
CREEP
THUD

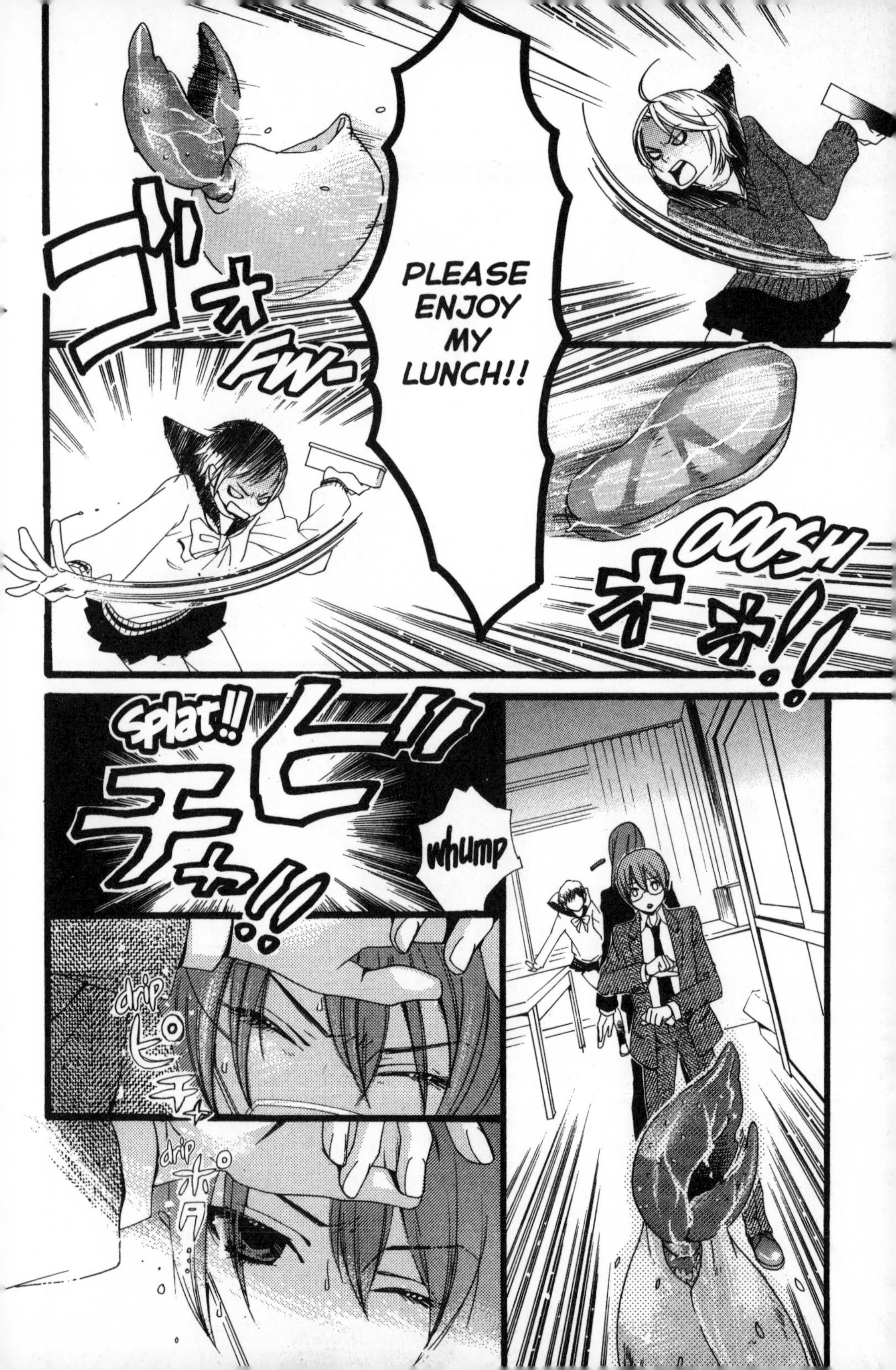
PLEASE ENJOY MY LUNCH!!
FW-
OOOSH
whump
Splat!!
drip
drip

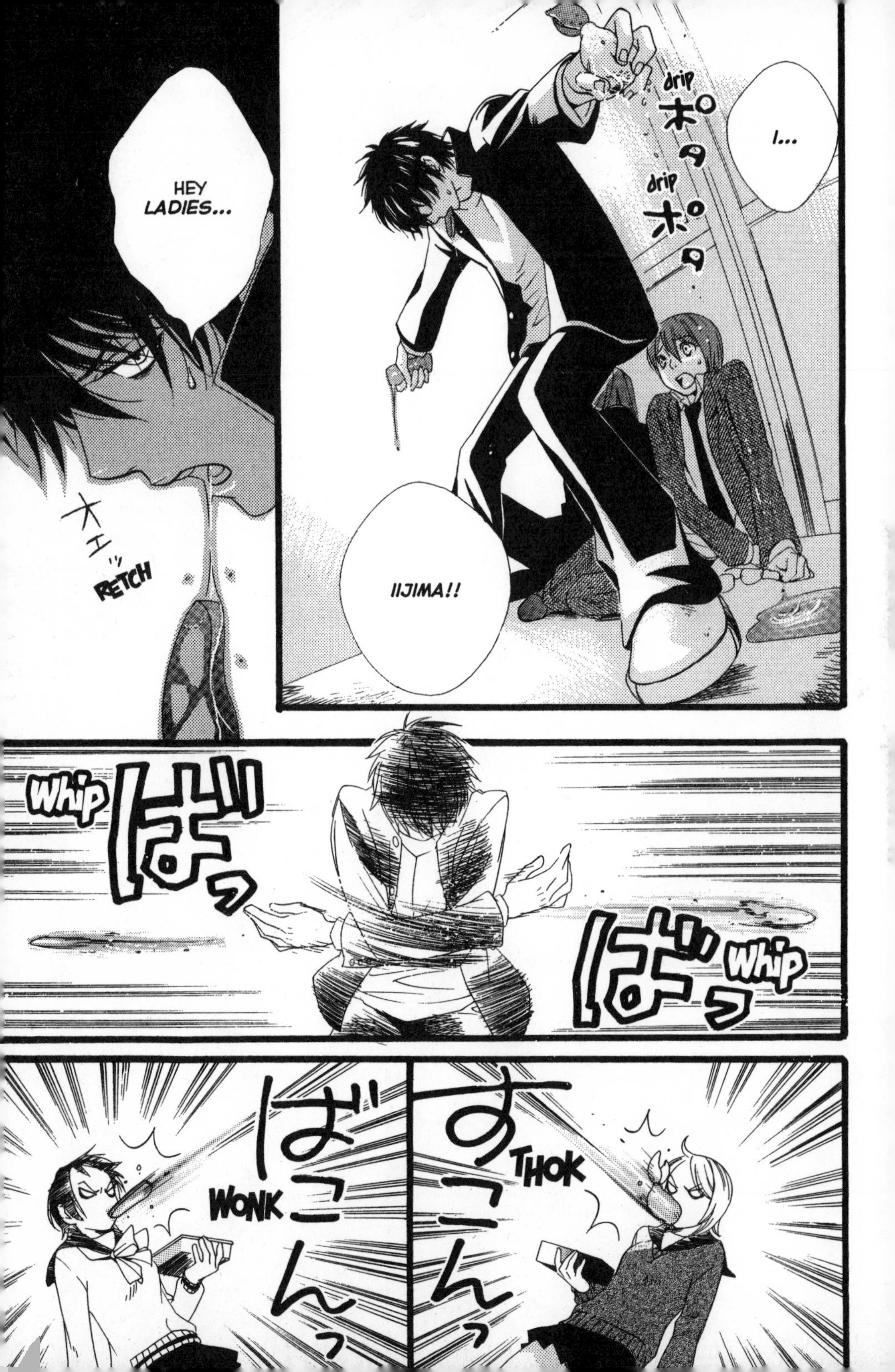

I...
drip ポタ
drip ポタ
IIJIMA!!
HEY LADIES...
オエッ
RETCH
ばっ
whip
ばっ
whip
すこんっ
THOK
ばこんっ
WONK

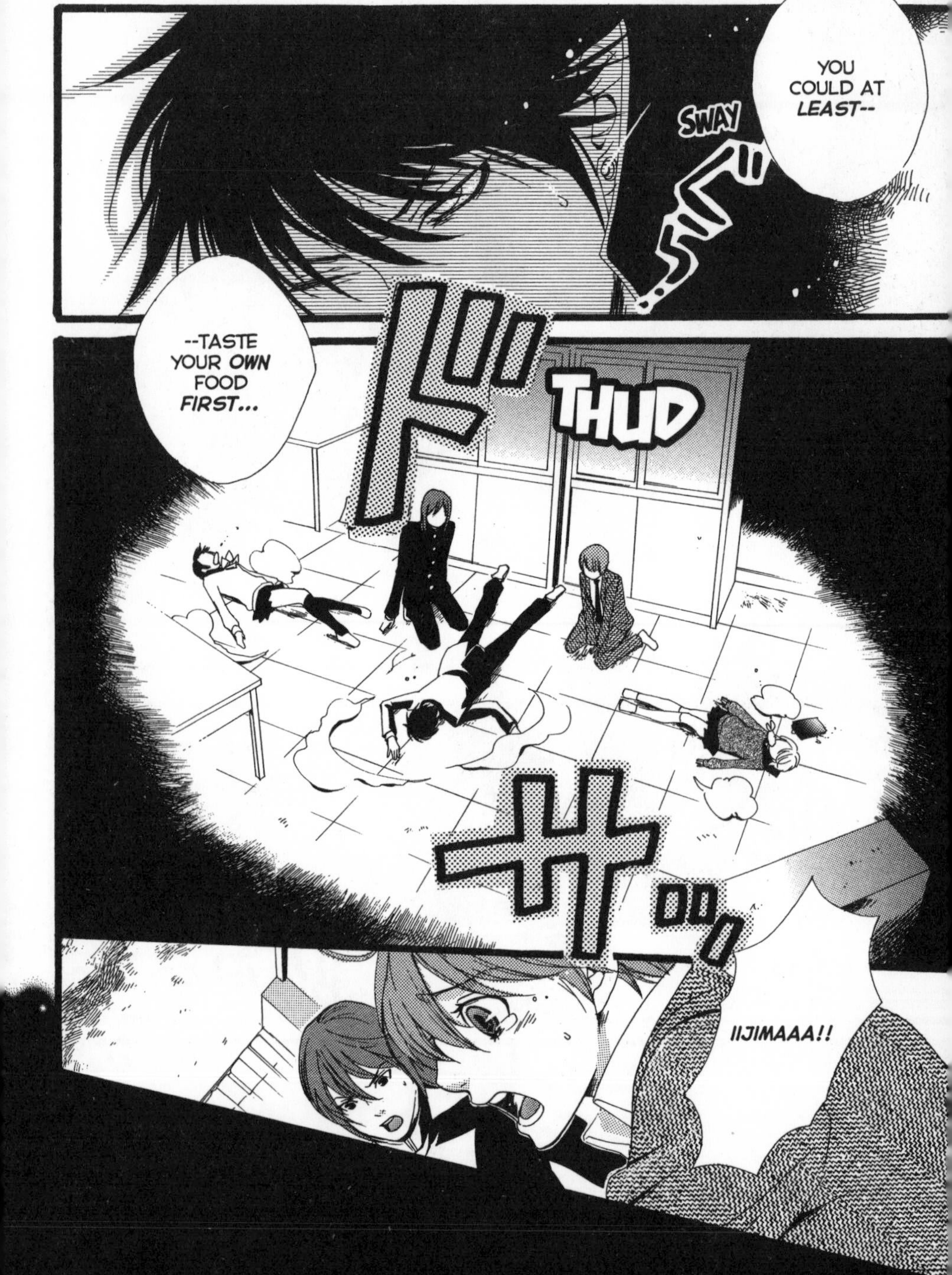
YOU COULD AT LEAST--
SWAY
--TASTE YOUR OWN FOOD FIRST...
THUD
IIJIMAAA!!

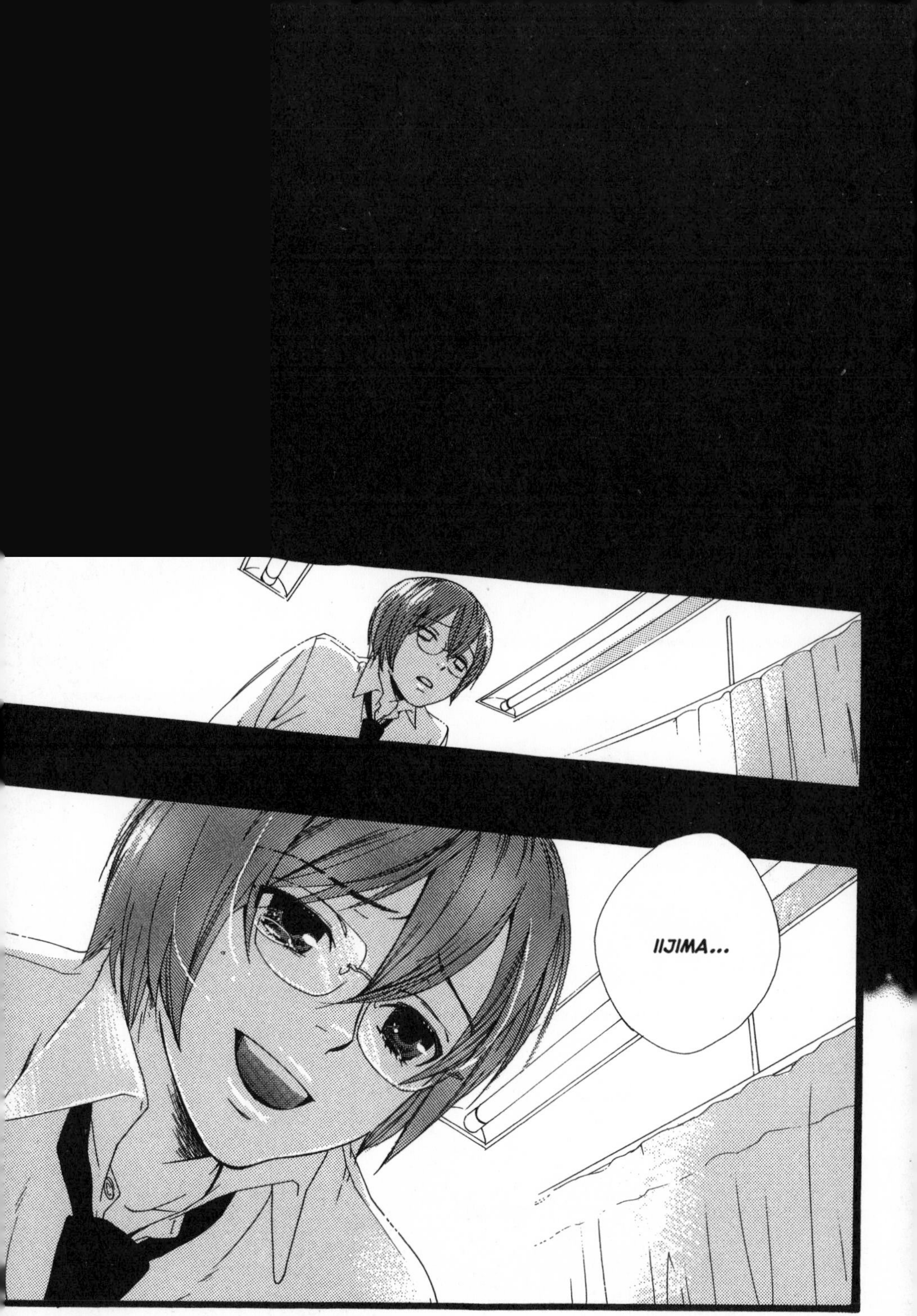
IIJIMA...

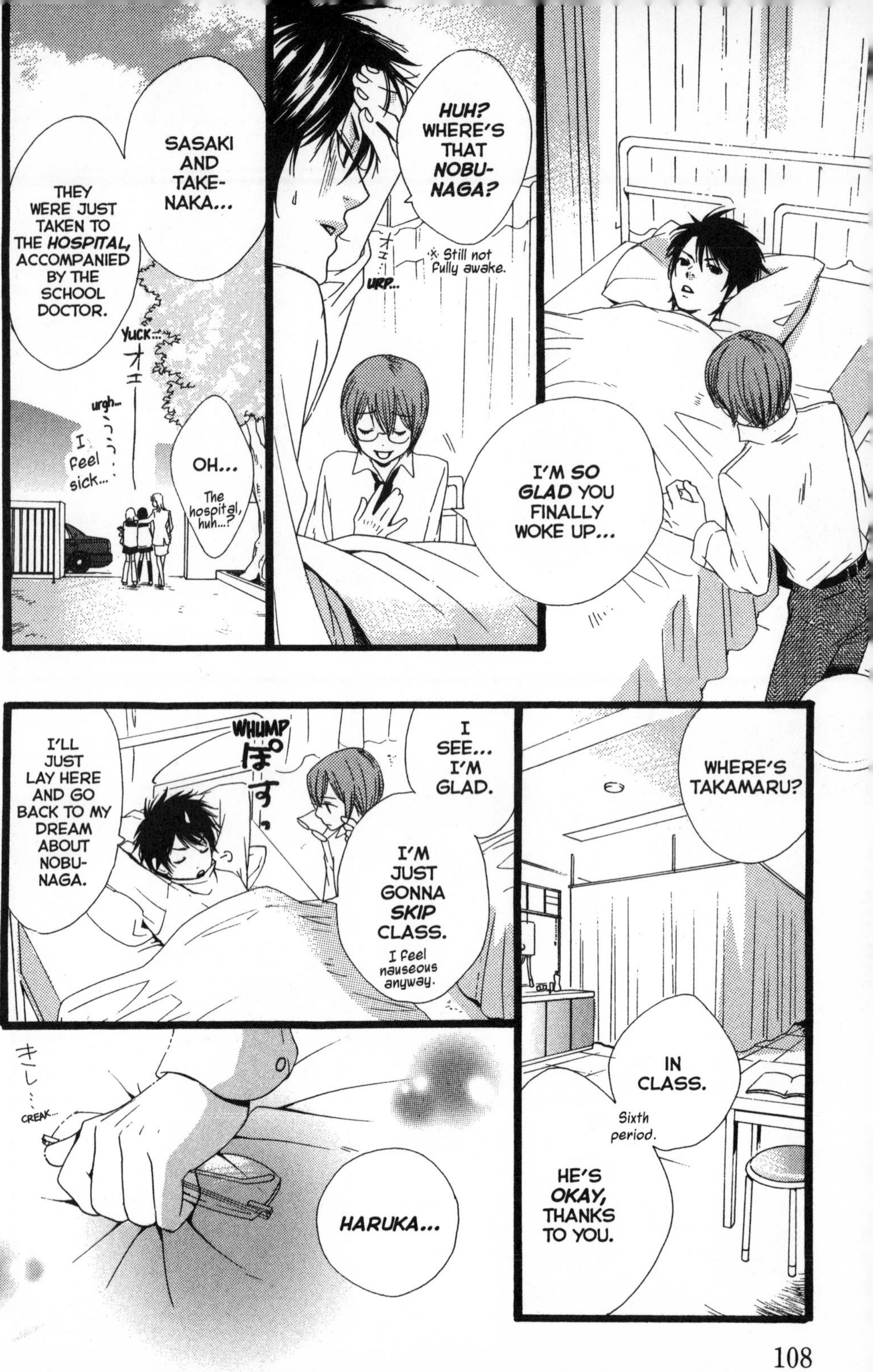
I'M SO GLAD YOU FINALLY WOKE UP...
HUH? WHERE'S THAT NOBU-NAGA?
オェ... URP...
※ Still not fully awake.
SASAKI AND TAKE-NAKA...
THEY WERE JUST TAKEN TO THE HOSPITAL, ACCOMPANIED BY THE SCHOOL DOCTOR.
YUCK... オエー
urgh... ううう
I feel sick...
OH...
The hospital, huh...?
WHERE'S TAKAMARU?
IN CLASS.
Sixth period.
HE'S OKAY, THANKS TO YOU.
I SEE... I'M GLAD.
I'M JUST GONNA SKIP CLASS.
I feel nauseous anyway.
WHUMP ぽすっ
I'LL JUST LAY HERE AND GO BACK TO MY DREAM ABOUT NOBU-NAGA.
きし... CREAK...
HARUKA...

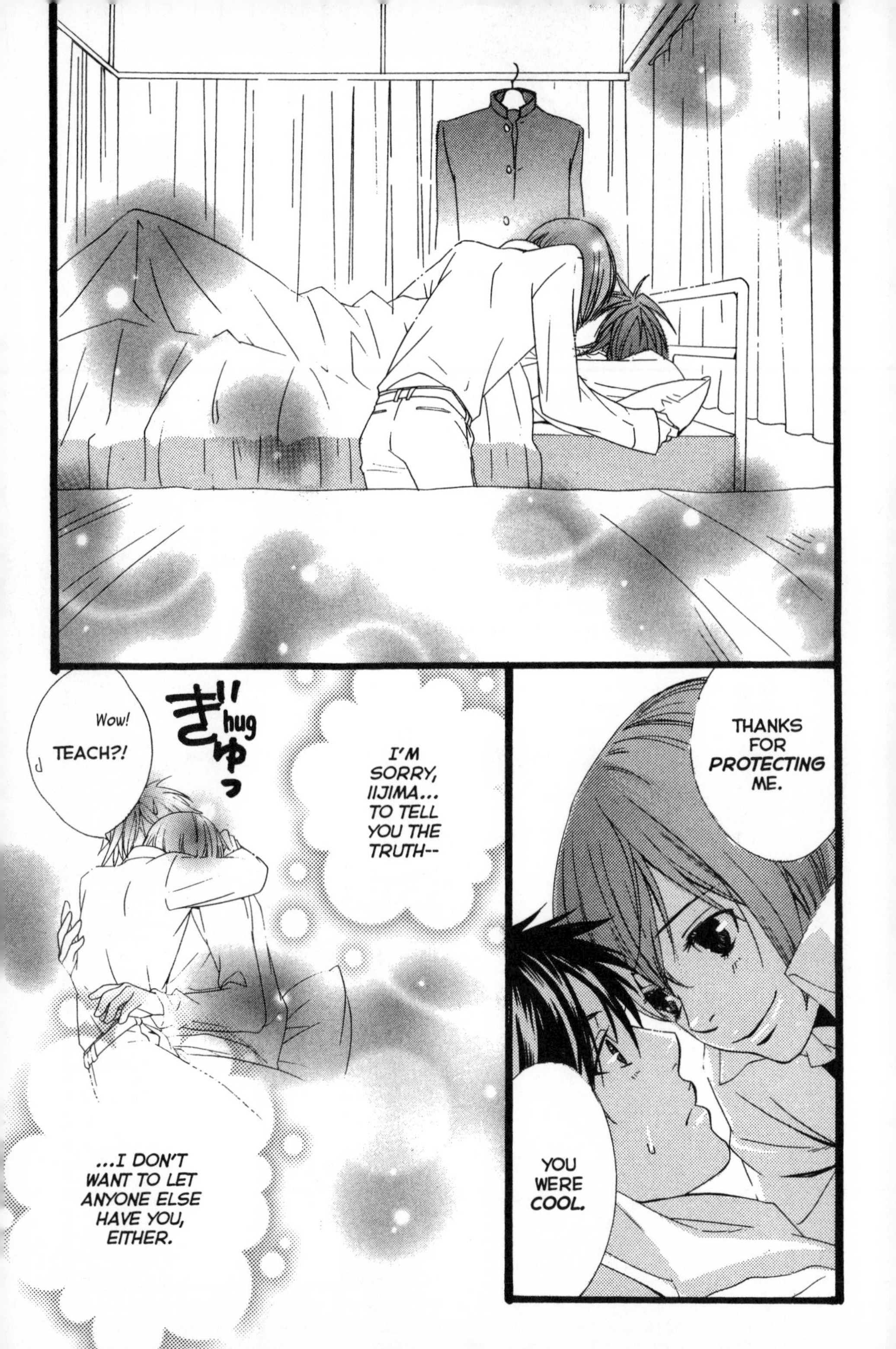
THANKS FOR PROTECTING ME.
YOU WERE COOL.
I'M SORRY, IIJIMA... TO TELL YOU THE TRUTH--
ぎゅっ
hug
Wow!
TEACH?!
...I DON'T WANT TO LET ANYONE ELSE HAVE YOU, EITHER.

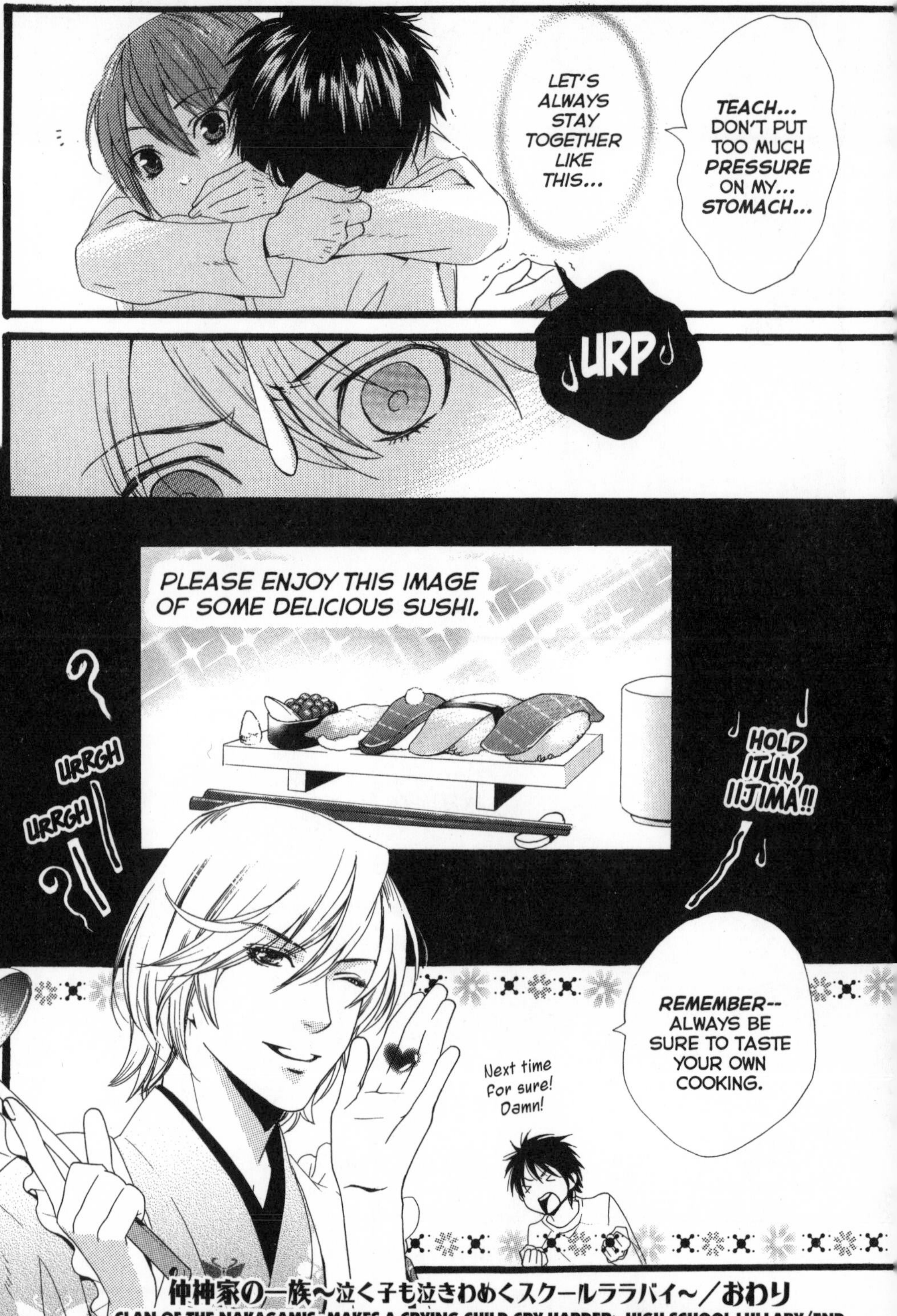
TEACH... DON'T PUT TOO MUCH PRESSURE ON MY... STOMACH...
LET'S ALWAYS STAY TOGETHER LIKE THIS...
URP
PLEASE ENJOY THIS IMAGE OF SOME DELICIOUS SUSHI.
HOLD IT IN, IIJIMA!!
URRGH
URRGH
REMEMBER-- ALWAYS BE SURE TO TASTE YOUR OWN COOKING.
Next time for sure! Damn!

仲神家の一族～泣く子も泣きわめくスクールララバイ～／おわり

CLAN OF THE NAKAGAMIS--MAKES A CRYING CHILD CRY HARDER: HIGH SCHOOL LULLABY/END

登場人物設定資料

CHARACTER DESIGN NOTES

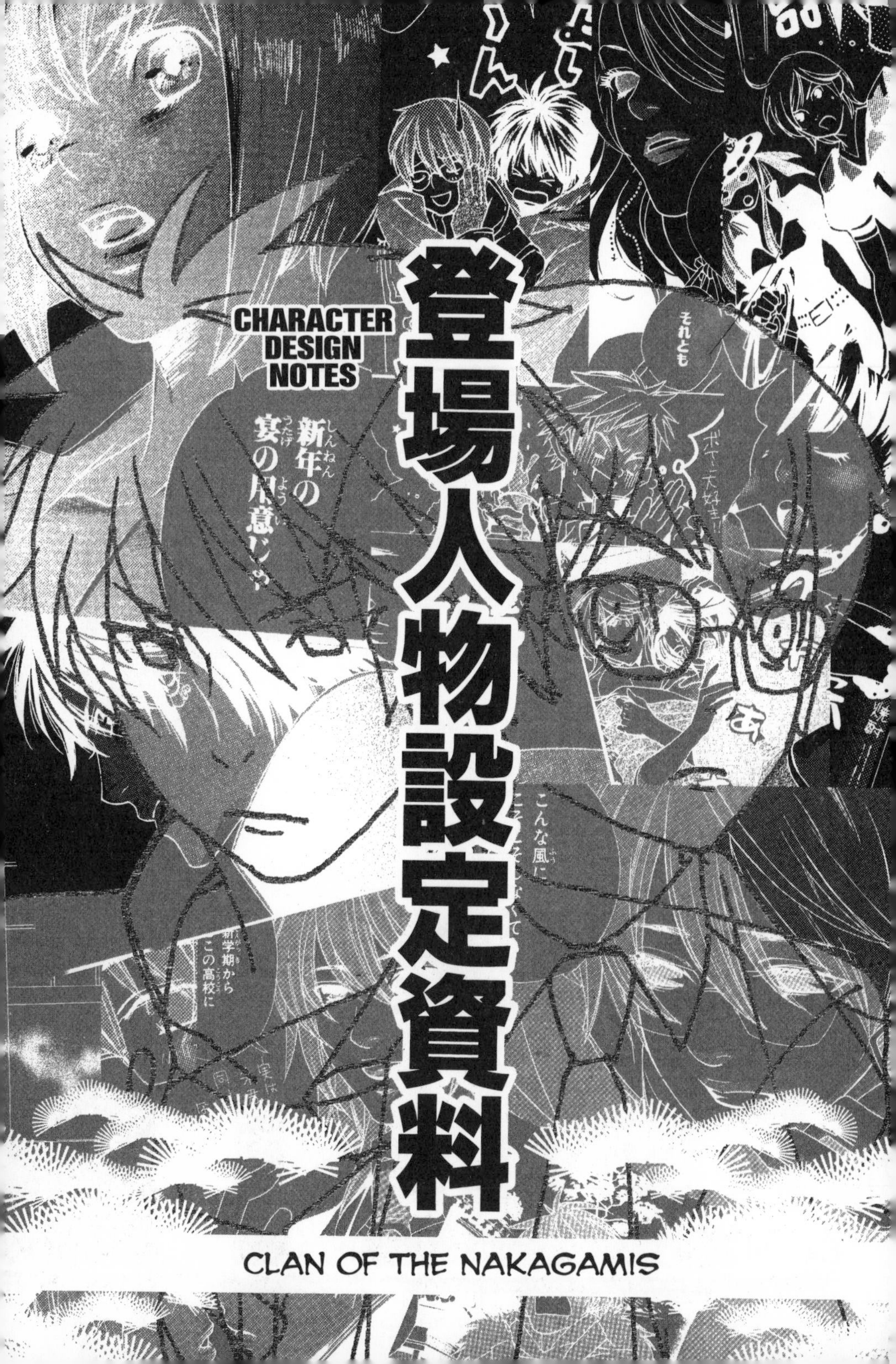
それとも
こんな風に
新学期から
この高校に

CLAN OF THE NAKAGAMIS

飯島永

HARUKA IIJIMA

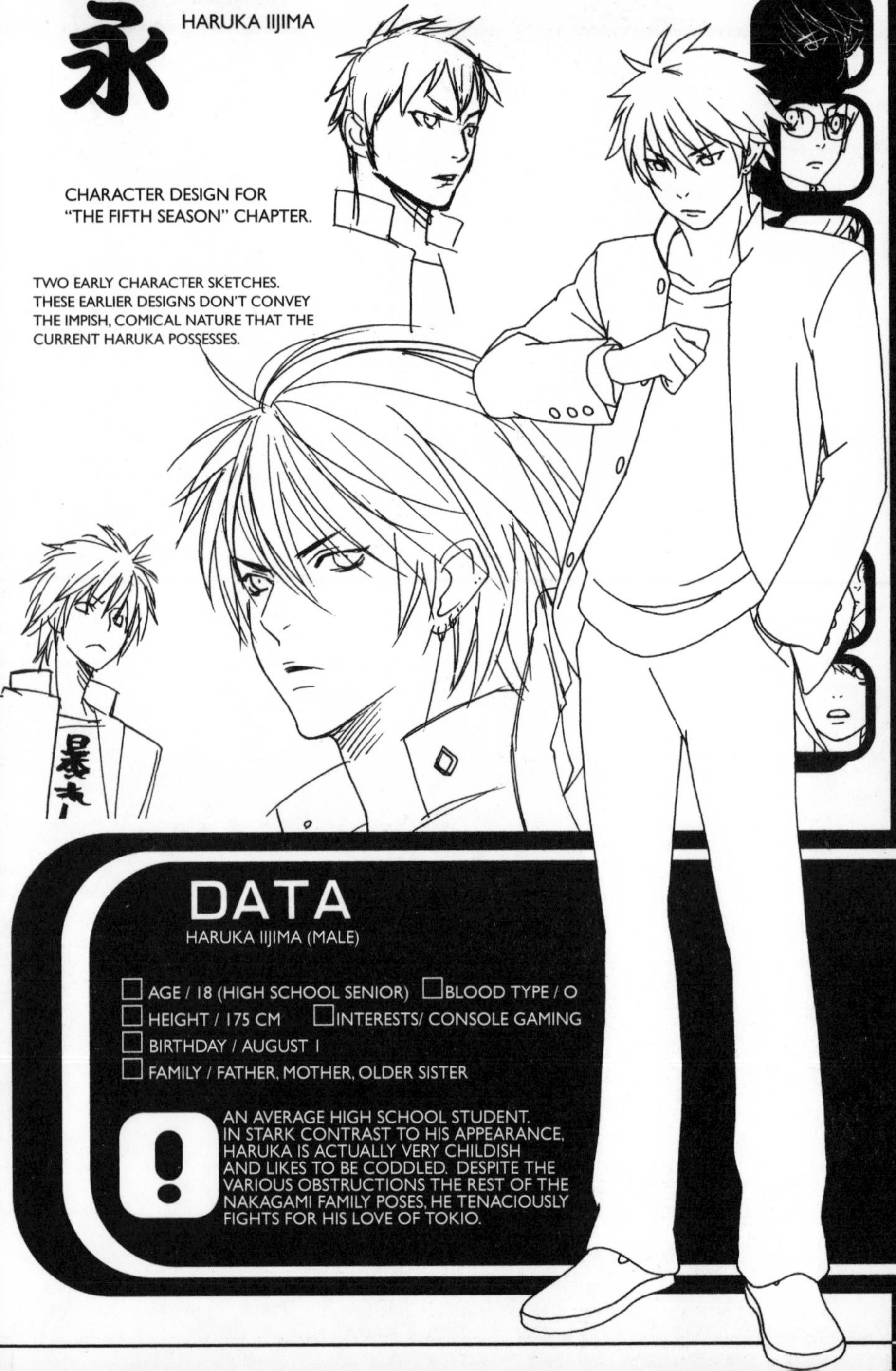

CHARACTER DESIGN FOR "THE FIFTH SEASON" CHAPTER.

TWO EARLY CHARACTER SKETCHES. THESE EARLIER DESIGNS DON'T CONVEY THE IMPISH, COMICAL NATURE THAT THE CURRENT HARUKA POSSESSES.

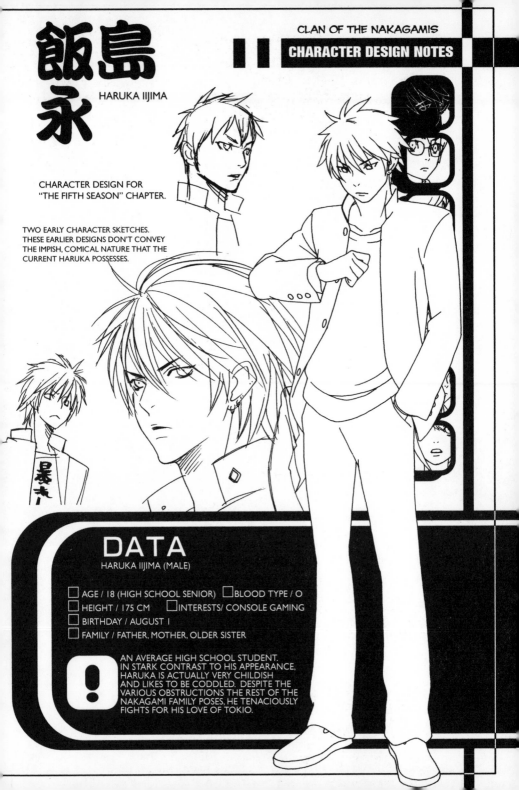

DATA

HARUKA IIJIMA (MALE)

- AGE / 18 (HIGH SCHOOL SENIOR)
- BLOOD TYPE / O
- HEIGHT / 175 CM
- INTERESTS/ CONSOLE GAMING
- BIRTHDAY / AUGUST 1
- FAMILY / FATHER, MOTHER, OLDER SISTER

AN AVERAGE HIGH SCHOOL STUDENT. IN STARK CONTRAST TO HIS APPEARANCE, HARUKA IS ACTUALLY VERY CHILDISH AND LIKES TO BE CODDLED. DESPITE THE VARIOUS OBSTRUCTIONS THE REST OF THE NAKAGAMI FAMILY POSES, HE TENACIOUSLY FIGHTS FOR HIS LOVE OF TOKIO.

CHARACTER DESIGN NOTES 11

仲神 朱鷺緒

TOKIO NAKAGAMI

THESE EARLY DESIGNS SHOW THAT TOKIO'S HAIR WAS MORE UNKEMPT AND HIS FACE MORE MATURE-LOOKING AT FIRST. INITIALLY, HE WAS SUPPOSED TO BE A GEOLOGY TEACHER BUT FOR SOME REASON HIS TEACHING SUBJECT BECAME MATH IN THE END. THE SKETCH AT LEFT ESPECIALL CONTAINS EVIDENCE OF THIS PREVIOUS IDEA.

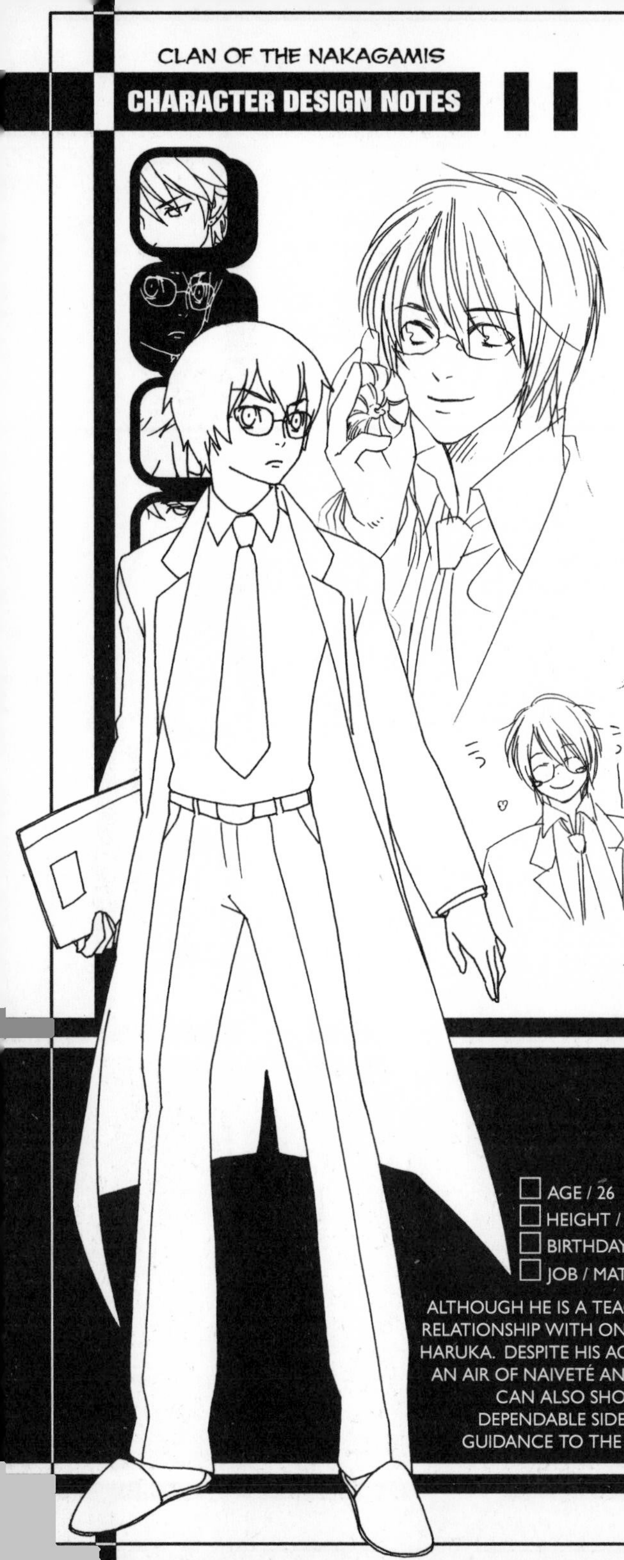

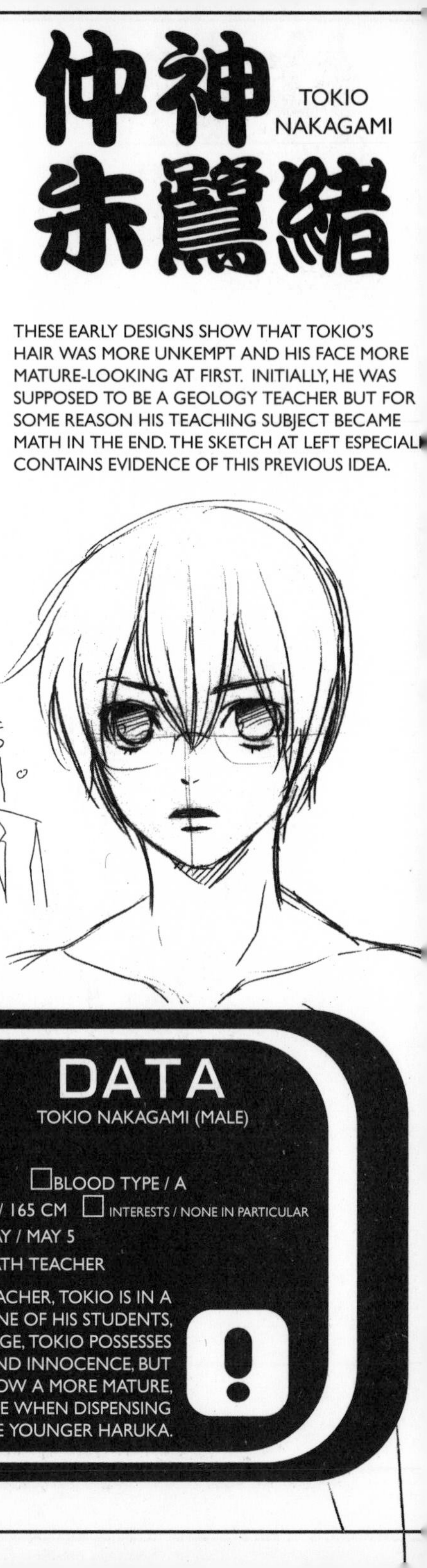

DATA

TOKIO NAKAGAMI (MALE)

- AGE / 26
- BLOOD TYPE / A
- HEIGHT / 165 CM
- INTERESTS / NONE IN PARTICULAR
- BIRTHDAY / MAY 5
- JOB / MATH TEACHER

ALTHOUGH HE IS A TEACHER, TOKIO IS IN A RELATIONSHIP WITH ONE OF HIS STUDENTS, HARUKA. DESPITE HIS AGE, TOKIO POSSESSES AN AIR OF NAIVETÉ AND INNOCENCE, BUT CAN ALSO SHOW A MORE MATURE, DEPENDABLE SIDE WHEN DISPENSING GUIDANCE TO THE YOUNGER HARUKA.

仲神 鷹丸

TAKAMARU NAKAGAMI

CLAN OF THE NAKAGAMIS

CHARACTER DESIGN NOTES

IN CONTRAST TO HIS REFINED APPEARANCE, TAKAMARU HAS THE DECIDEDLY WARPED HOBBY OF TAKING VOYEURISTIC VIDEOS AND PHOTOS. IT IS INTERESTING TO IMAGINE JUST WHAT KIND OF EXPRESSION HE WEARS AS HE GAZES INTO HIS MONITOR…

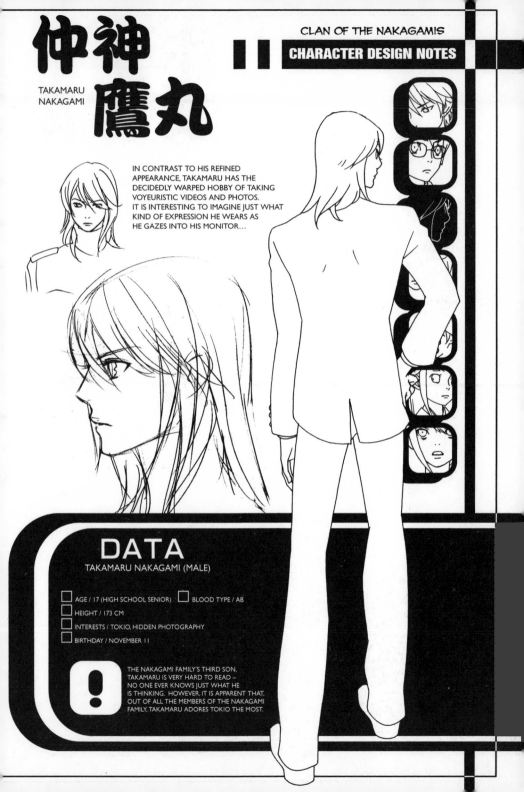

DATA

TAKAMARU NAKAGAMI (MALE)

- AGE / 17 (HIGH SCHOOL SENIOR)
- BLOOD TYPE / AB
- HEIGHT / 173 CM
- INTERESTS / TOKIO, HIDDEN PHOTOGRAPHY
- BIRTHDAY / NOVEMBER 11

!

THE NAKAGAMI FAMILY'S THIRD SON, TAKAMARU IS VERY HARD TO READ – NO ONE EVER KNOWS JUST WHAT HE IS THINKING. HOWEVER, IT IS APPARENT THAT, OUT OF ALL THE MEMBERS OF THE NAKAGAMI FAMILY, TAKAMARU ADORES TOKIO THE MOST.

CLAN OF THE NAKAGAMIS

CHARACTER DESIGN NOTES

仲神雉之丞

KIJINOJYO NAKAGAMI

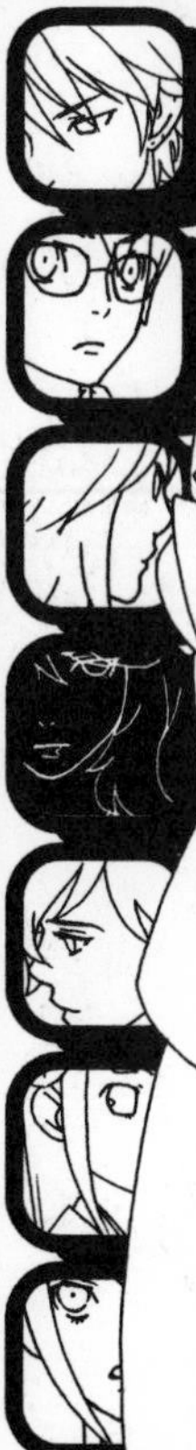

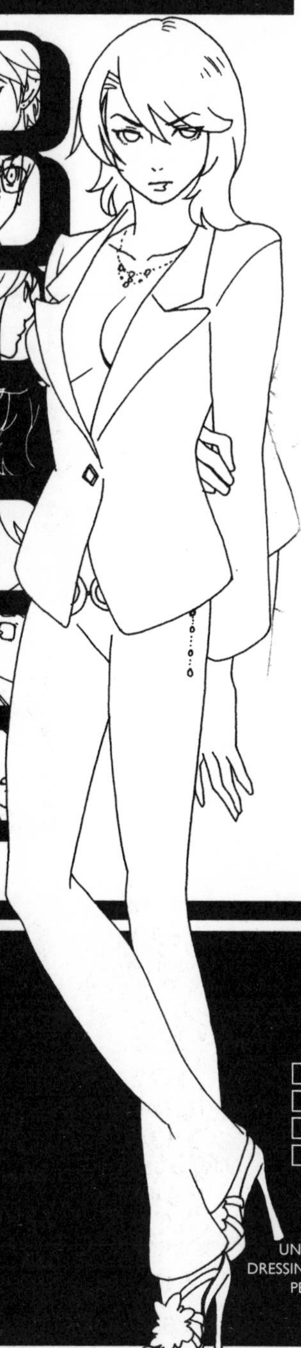

BELOW IS KIJINOJYO IN HIS NORMAL STATE. HE IS A MASTER OF SPECIAL MAKEUP TECHNIQUES- SO MUCH SO THAT THE OTHER FAMILY MEMBERS THINK HE SHOULD HAVE CHOSEN IT AS HIS PROFESSION INSTEAD OF MANGA ARTIST. IN HIS NORMAL STATE, THE RESEMBLANCE TO HIS FATHER GOKURAKUCHOTA IS APPARENT.

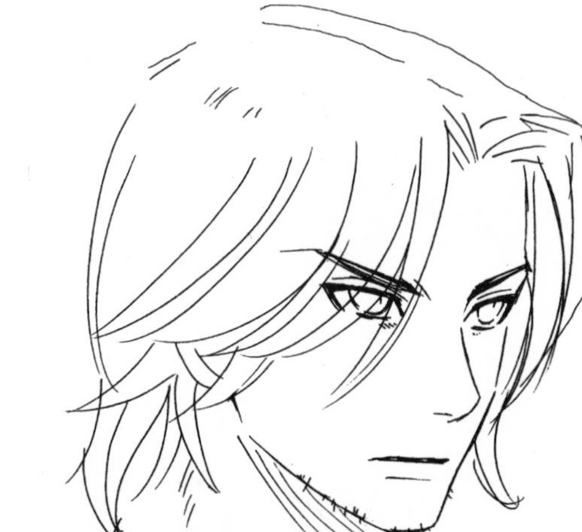

DATA

KIJINOJYO NAKAGAMI (MALE)

- ☐ AGE / 27
- ☐ BLOOD TYPE / O
- ☐ HEIGHT / 181 CM
- ☐ INTERESTS / TOKIO, CROSS-DRESSING
- ☐ BIRTHDAY / NOVEMBER 30
- ☐ JOB / SHOUJO MANGA ARTIST

THE ELDEST SON OF THE NAKAGAMIS, HIS LOVE FOR ALL THINGS ADORABLE ESCALATED UNTIL FINALLY DEVELOPING INTO A PASSION FOR DRESSING AS A WOMAN. HIS TRANSFORMATION IS SO PERFECT THAT THERE IS NO ADEQUATE WAY TO DESCRIBE IT OTHER THAN AS AN "ILLUSION".

!

中神
極楽蝶太

GOKURAKUCHOTA
NAKAGAMI

CLAN OF THE NAKAGAMIS

CHARACTER DESIGN NOTES

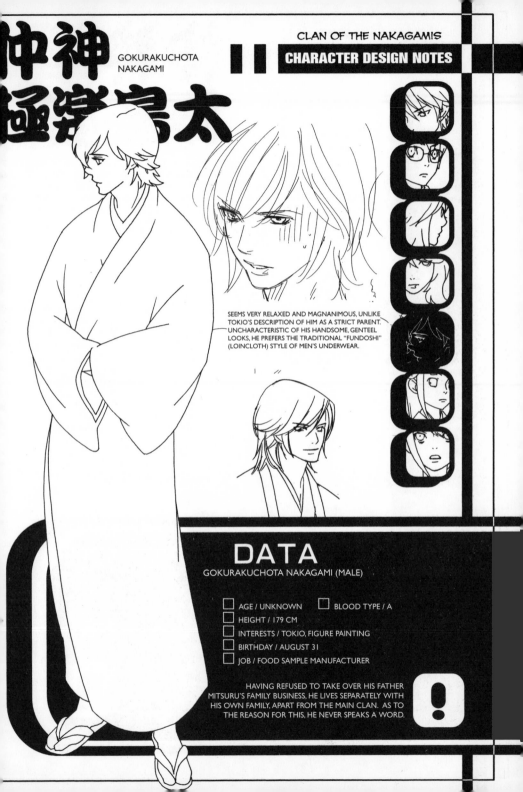

SEEMS VERY RELAXED AND MAGNANIMOUS, UNLIKE TOKIO'S DESCRIPTION OF HIM AS A STRICT PARENT. UNCHARACTERISTIC OF HIS HANDSOME, GENTEEL LOOKS, HE PREFERS THE TRADITIONAL "FUNDOSHI" (LOINCLOTH) STYLE OF MEN'S UNDERWEAR.

DATA

GOKURAKUCHOTA NAKAGAMI (MALE)

- AGE / UNKNOWN
- BLOOD TYPE / A
- HEIGHT / 179 CM
- INTERESTS / TOKIO, FIGURE PAINTING
- BIRTHDAY / AUGUST 31
- JOB / FOOD SAMPLE MANUFACTURER

HAVING REFUSED TO TAKE OVER HIS FATHER MITSURU'S FAMILY BUSINESS, HE LIVES SEPARATELY WITH HIS OWN FAMILY, APART FROM THE MAIN CLAN. AS TO THE REASON FOR THIS, HE NEVER SPEAKS A WORD.

CHARACTER DESIGN NOTES

仲神雀

SUZUME NAKAGAMI

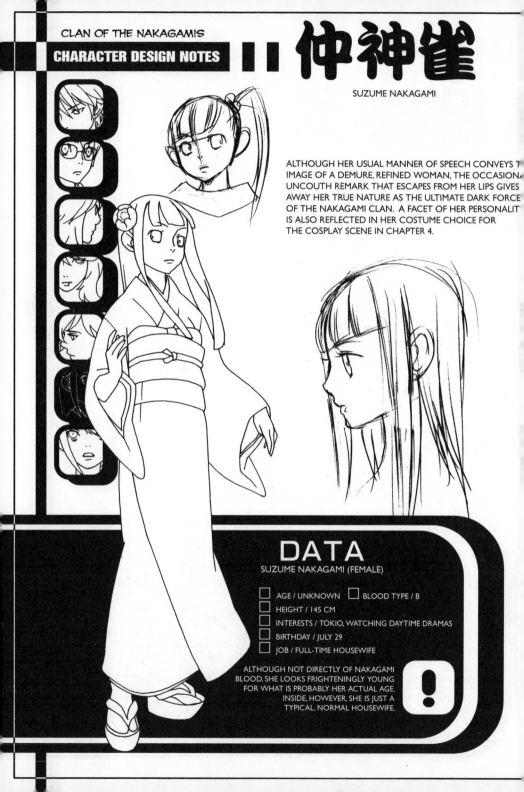

ALTHOUGH HER USUAL MANNER OF SPEECH CONVEYS T
IMAGE OF A DEMURE, REFINED WOMAN, THE OCCASION
UNCOUTH REMARK THAT ESCAPES FROM HER LIPS GIVES
AWAY HER TRUE NATURE AS THE ULTIMATE DARK FORCE
OF THE NAKAGAMI CLAN. A FACET OF HER PERSONALIT
IS ALSO REFLECTED IN HER COSTUME CHOICE FOR
THE COSPLAY SCENE IN CHAPTER 4.

DATA

SUZUME NAKAGAMI (FEMALE)

- [ ] AGE / UNKNOWN [ ] BLOOD TYPE / B
- [ ] HEIGHT / 145 CM
- [ ] INTERESTS / TOKIO, WATCHING DAYTIME DRAMAS
- [ ] BIRTHDAY / JULY 29
- [ ] JOB / FULL-TIME HOUSEWIFE

ALTHOUGH NOT DIRECTLY OF NAKAGAMI
BLOOD, SHE LOOKS FRIGHTENINGLY YOUNG
FOR WHAT IS PROBABLY HER ACTUAL AGE.
INSIDE, HOWEVER, SHE IS JUST A
TYPICAL, NORMAL HOUSEWIFE.

9

仲神美鶴

MITSURU NAKAGAMI

CLAN OF THE NAKAGAMIS

CHARACTER DESIGN NOTES

THE PRELIMINARY DESIGN BELOW SHOWS MITSURU BEFORE HIS CHARACTER WAS FULLY DEVELOPED. IN THE END, THE MORE MATURE VERSION WAS DROPPED BECAUSE HE LOOKED TOO MUCH LIKE TAKAMARU. INITIALLY, THIS CHARACTER WAS NAMED "PHOENIX" BUT HE WAS LATER CHANGED TO A JAPANESE CHARACTER WITH THE NAME "MITSURU" (BEAUTIFUL CRANE). LIKES TO SLEEP IN THE NUDE. HIS ACTUAL AGE IS IN THE LATE SIXTIES.

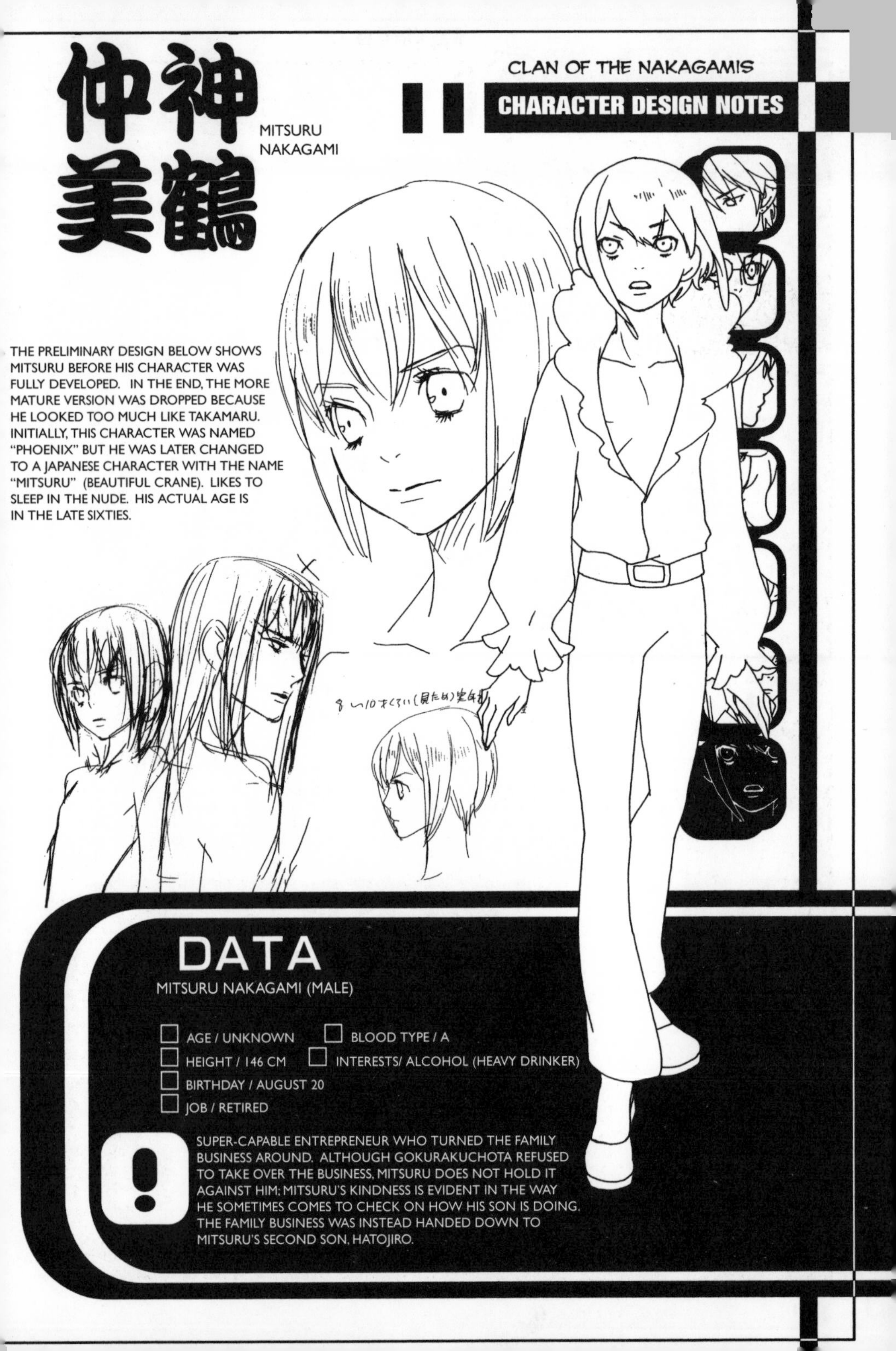

8〜10才くらい(見ため)

DATA

MITSURU NAKAGAMI (MALE)

- ☐ AGE / UNKNOWN
- ☐ BLOOD TYPE / A
- ☐ HEIGHT / 146 CM
- ☐ INTERESTS/ ALCOHOL (HEAVY DRINKER)
- ☐ BIRTHDAY / AUGUST 20
- ☐ JOB / RETIRED

SUPER-CAPABLE ENTREPRENEUR WHO TURNED THE FAMILY BUSINESS AROUND. ALTHOUGH GOKURAKUCHOTA REFUSED TO TAKE OVER THE BUSINESS, MITSURU DOES NOT HOLD IT AGAINST HIM; MITSURU'S KINDNESS IS EVIDENT IN THE WAY HE SOMETIMES COMES TO CHECK ON HOW HIS SON IS DOING. THE FAMILY BUSINESS WAS INSTEAD HANDED DOWN TO MITSURU'S SECOND SON, HATOJIRO.

FATHER

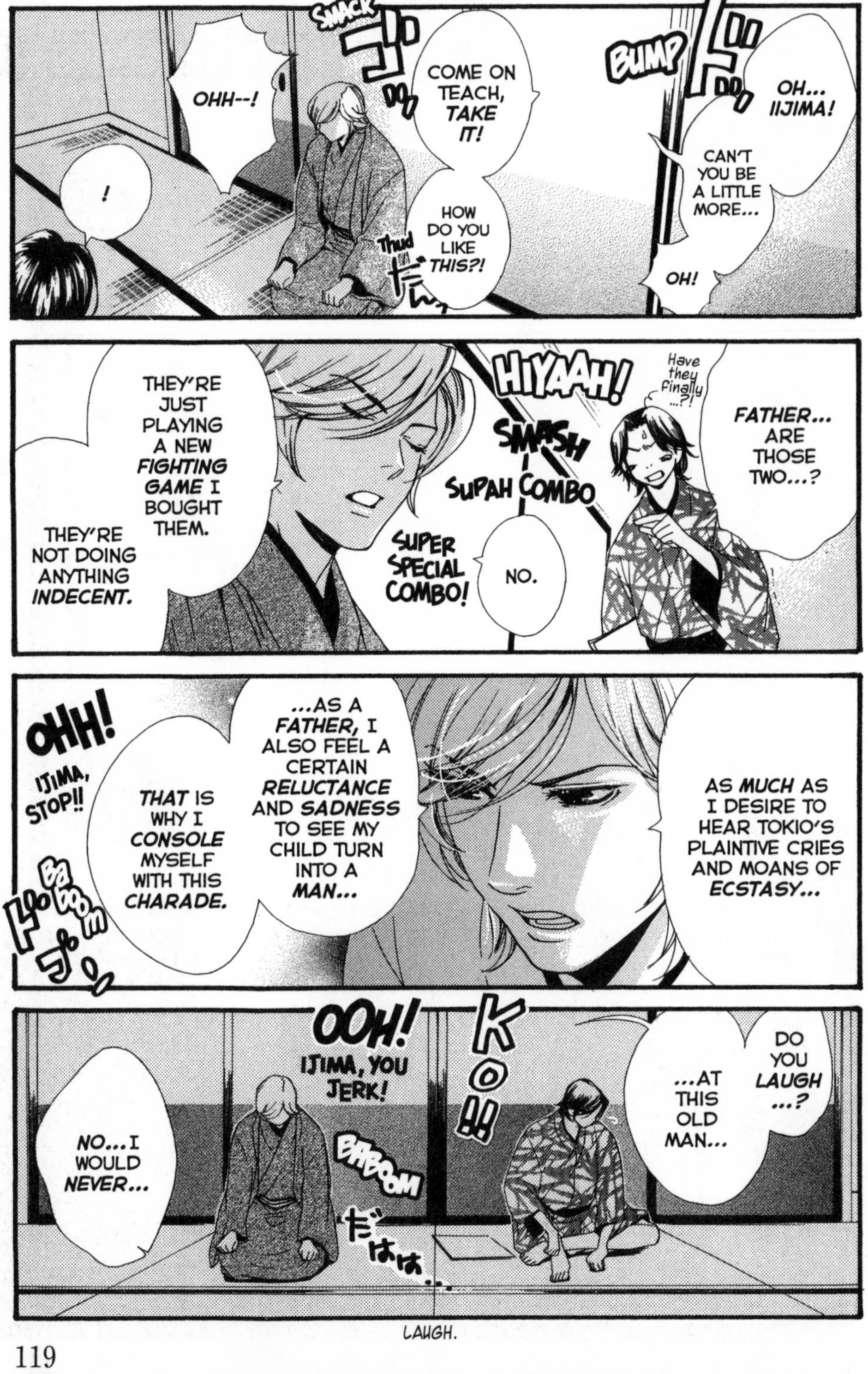
OH... IIJIMA!
CAN'T YOU BE A LITTLE MORE...
OH!
BUMP
COME ON TEACH, TAKE IT!
HOW DO YOU LIKE THIS?!
SMACK
Thud
OHH--!
!
FATHER... ARE THOSE TWO...?
Have they finally...?!
HIYAAH!
SMASH
SUPAH COMBO
NO.
SUPER SPECIAL COMBO!
THEY'RE JUST PLAYING A NEW FIGHTING GAME I BOUGHT THEM.
THEY'RE NOT DOING ANYTHING INDECENT.
AS MUCH AS I DESIRE TO HEAR TOKIO'S PLAINTIVE CRIES AND MOANS OF ECSTASY...
...AS A FATHER, I ALSO FEEL A CERTAIN RELUCTANCE AND SADNESS TO SEE MY CHILD TURN INTO A MAN...
THAT IS WHY I CONSOLE MYSELF WITH THIS CHARADE.
OHH!
IJIMA, STOP!!
Ba boom
DO YOU LAUGH...?
...AT THIS OLD MAN...
K.O.!!
OOH!
IJIMA, YOU JERK!
BABOOM
NO... I WOULD NEVER...

LAUGH.

TELEPATHY

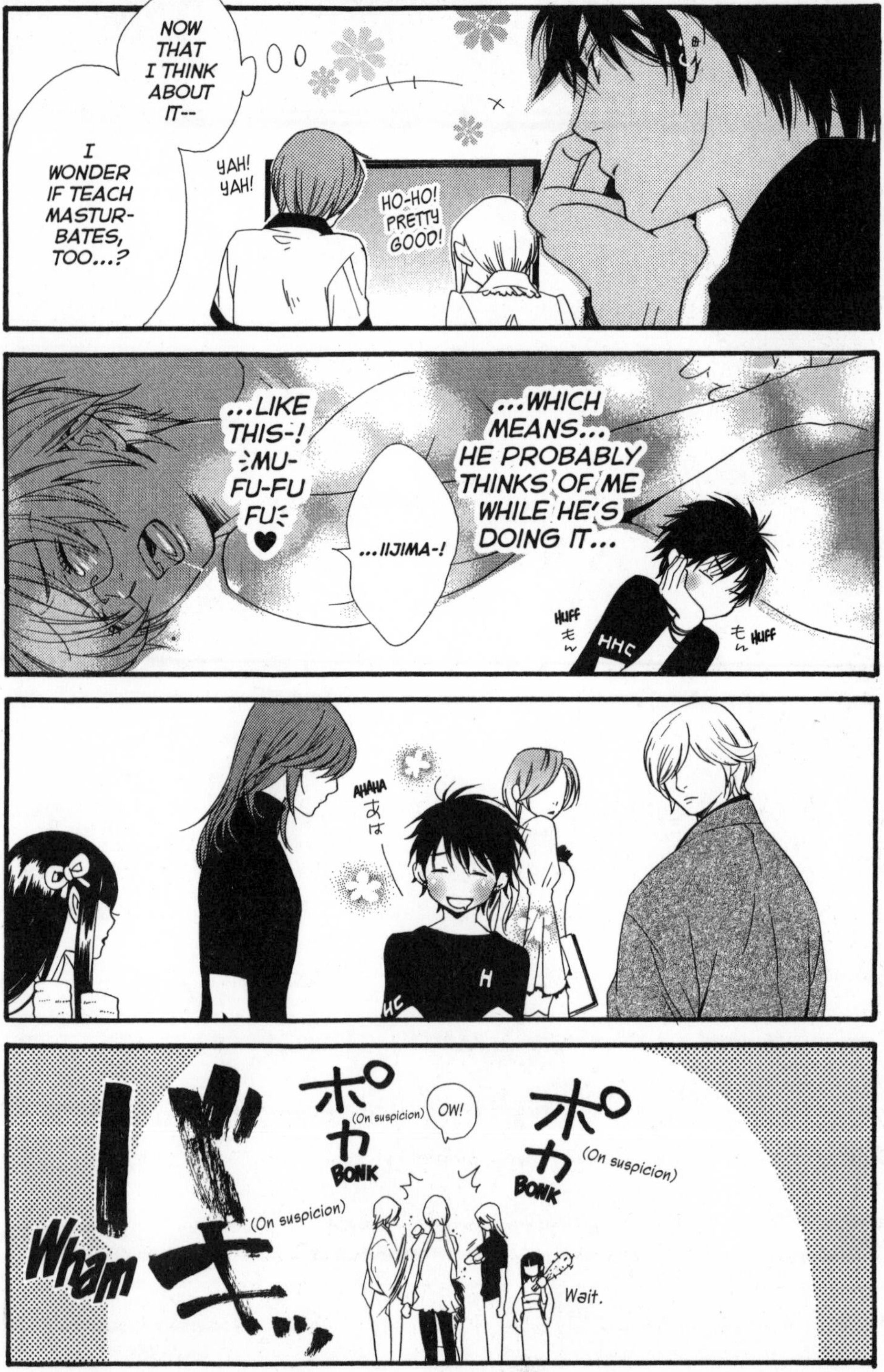
NOW THAT I THINK ABOUT IT--
I WONDER IF TEACH MASTUR-BATES, TOO...?
YAH! YAH!
HO-HO! PRETTY GOOD!
...WHICH MEANS... HE PROBABLY THINKS OF ME WHILE HE'S DOING IT...
HUFF もん
もん HUFF
...IIJIMA-!
...LIKE THIS-! MU-FU-FU FU ♥
AHAHA あは
ポカ BONK
(On suspicion)
OW!
ポカ BONK
(On suspicion)
バキッ Wham
(On suspicion)
Wait.

伸神家の一族

CLAN OF THE NAKAGAMIS

HOMERUN KEN PRESENTS

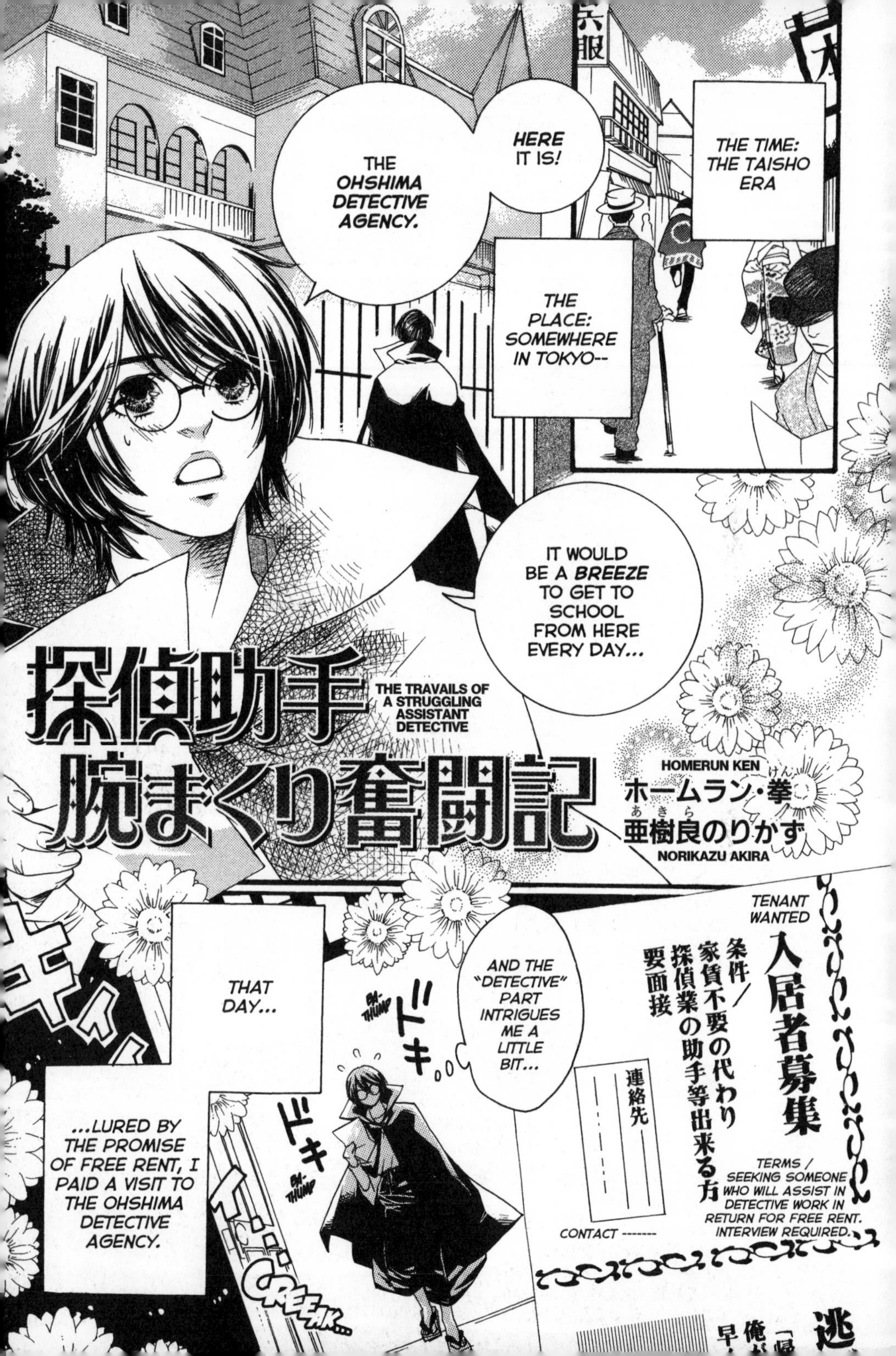
THE TIME: THE TAISHO ERA
THE PLACE: SOMEWHERE IN TOKYO--
HERE IT IS!
THE OHSHIMA DETECTIVE AGENCY.
IT WOULD BE A BREEZE TO GET TO SCHOOL FROM HERE EVERY DAY...
探偵助手腕まくり奮闘記
THE TRAVAILS OF A STRUGGLING ASSISTANT DETECTIVE
ホームラン・拳
HOMERUN KEN
亜樹良のりかず
NORIKAZU AKIRA
入居者募集
TENANT WANTED
条件／家賃不要の代わり探偵業の助手等出来る方要面接
TERMS / SEEKING SOMEONE WHO WILL ASSIST IN DETECTIVE WORK IN RETURN FOR FREE RENT. INTERVIEW REQUIRED.
連絡先
CONTACT -------
AND THE "DETECTIVE" PART INTRIGUES ME A LITTLE BIT...
ドキ
BA-THUMP
ドキ
BA-THUMP
THAT DAY...
...LURED BY THE PROMISE OF FREE RENT, I PAID A VISIT TO THE OHSHIMA DETECTIVE AGENCY.
CREEEAK...

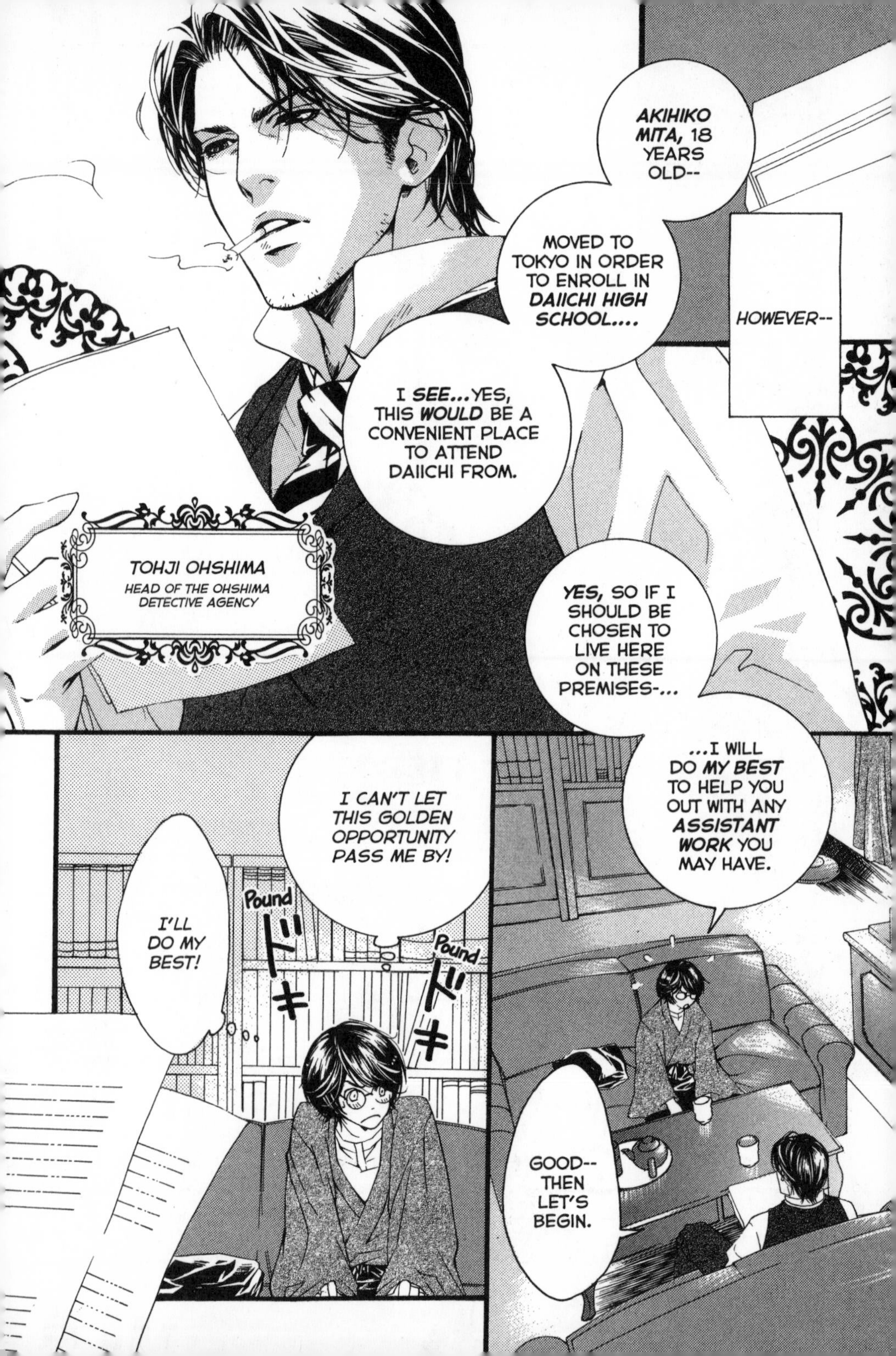

AKIHIKO MITA, 18 YEARS OLD--
MOVED TO TOKYO IN ORDER TO ENROLL IN DAIICHI HIGH SCHOOL....
HOWEVER--
I SEE...YES, THIS WOULD BE A CONVENIENT PLACE TO ATTEND DAIICHI FROM.
TOHJI OHSHIMA
HEAD OF THE OHSHIMA DETECTIVE AGENCY
YES, SO IF I SHOULD BE CHOSEN TO LIVE HERE ON THESE PREMISES-...
...I WILL DO MY BEST TO HELP YOU OUT WITH ANY ASSISTANT WORK YOU MAY HAVE.
GOOD-- THEN LET'S BEGIN.
I CAN'T LET THIS GOLDEN OPPORTUNITY PASS ME BY!
Pound ドキ
Pound ドキ
I'LL DO MY BEST!

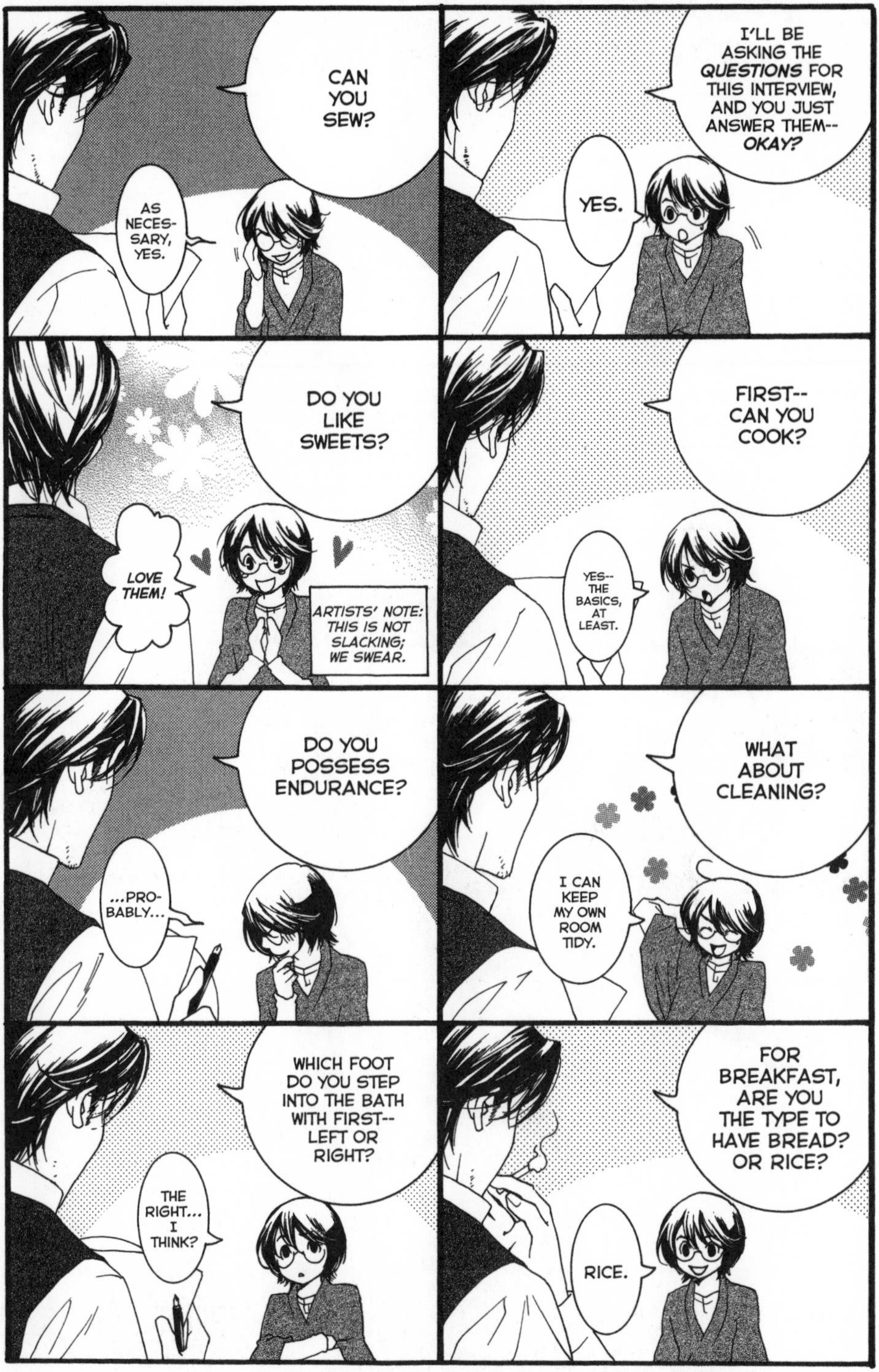
I'LL BE ASKING THE *QUESTIONS* FOR THIS INTERVIEW, AND YOU JUST ANSWER THEM-- *OKAY?*
YES.
CAN YOU SEW?
AS NECES-SARY, YES.
FIRST-- CAN YOU COOK?
YES-- THE BASICS, AT LEAST.
DO YOU LIKE SWEETS?
LOVE THEM!
ARTISTS' NOTE: THIS IS NOT SLACKING; WE SWEAR.
WHAT ABOUT CLEANING?
I CAN KEEP MY OWN ROOM TIDY.
DO YOU POSSESS ENDURANCE?
...PRO-BABLY...
FOR BREAKFAST, ARE YOU THE TYPE TO HAVE BREAD? OR RICE?
RICE.
WHICH FOOT DO YOU STEP INTO THE BATH WITH FIRST-- LEFT OR RIGHT?
THE RIGHT... I THINK?

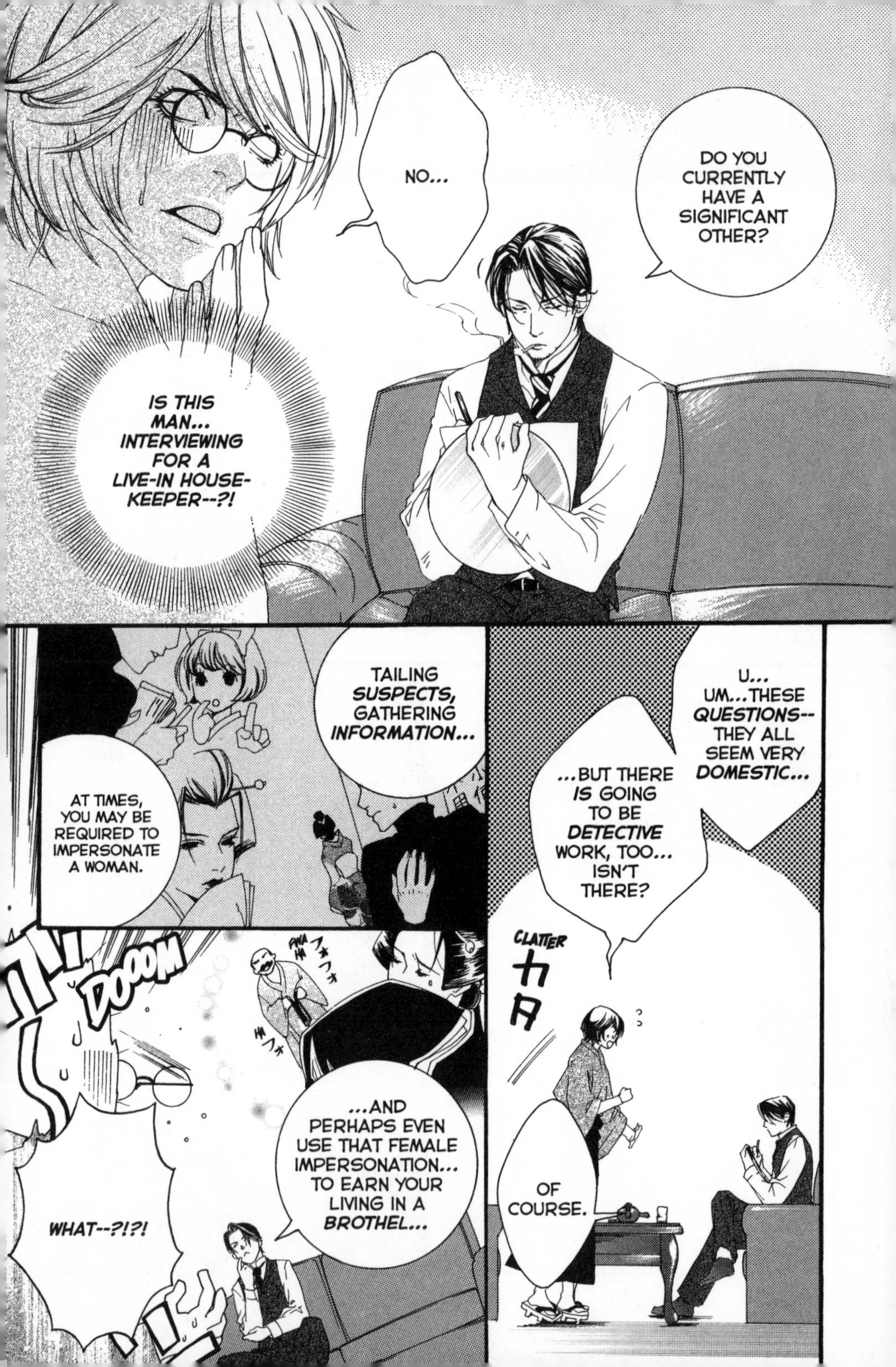

DO YOU CURRENTLY HAVE A SIGNIFICANT OTHER?
NO...
IS THIS MAN... INTERVIEWING FOR A LIVE-IN HOUSE-KEEPER--?!
U... UM...THESE QUESTIONS-- THEY ALL SEEM VERY DOMESTIC...
...BUT THERE IS GOING TO BE DETECTIVE WORK, TOO... ISN'T THERE?
CLATTER
カタ
OF COURSE.
TAILING SUSPECTS, GATHERING INFORMATION...
AT TIMES, YOU MAY BE REQUIRED TO IMPERSONATE A WOMAN.
FWA HA
HA
...AND PERHAPS EVEN USE THAT FEMALE IMPERSONATION... TO EARN YOUR LIVING IN A BROTHEL...
DOOOM
WHAT--?!?!

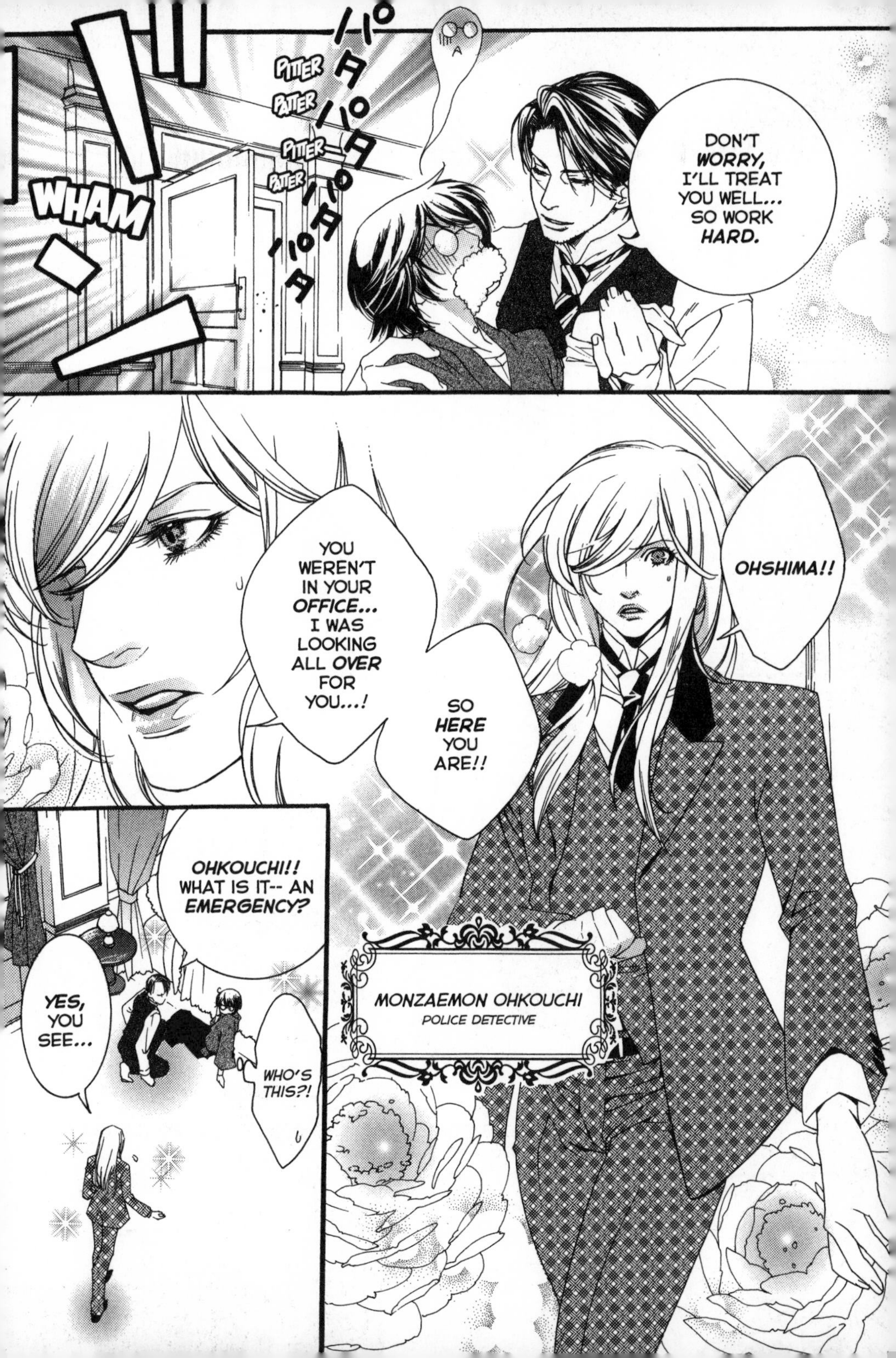

DON'T WORRY, I'LL TREAT YOU WELL... SO WORK HARD.
PITTER PATTER PITTER PATTER
パタパタパタパタ
WHAM
OHSHIMA!!
YOU WEREN'T IN YOUR OFFICE... I WAS LOOKING ALL OVER FOR YOU...!
SO HERE YOU ARE!!
MONZAEMON OHKOUCHI
POLICE DETECTIVE
OHKOUCHI!! WHAT IS IT-- AN EMERGENCY?
WHO'S THIS?!
YES, YOU SEE...

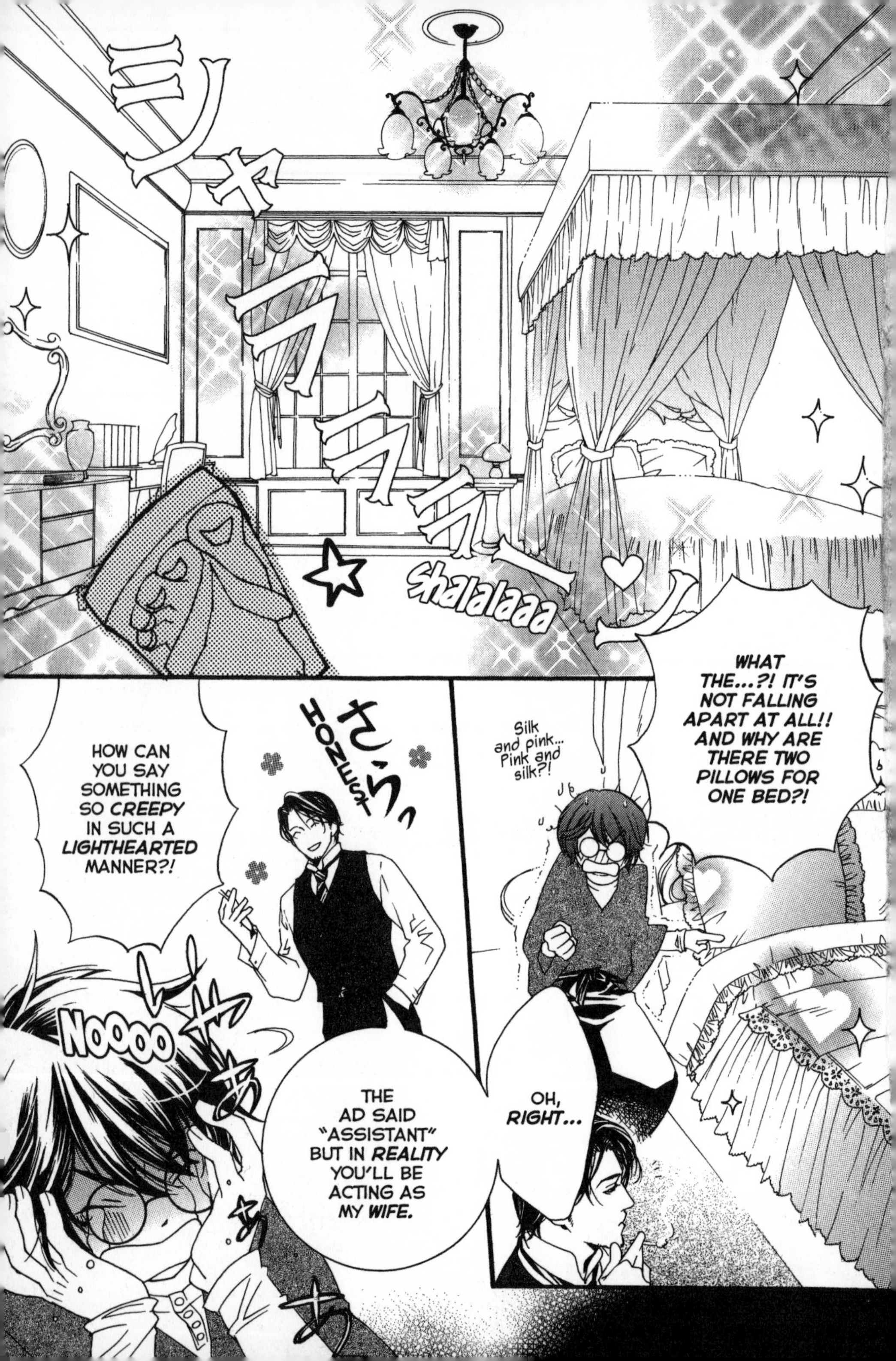
Shalalaaa
WHAT THE...?! IT'S NOT FALLING APART AT ALL!! AND WHY ARE THERE TWO PILLOWS FOR ONE BED?!
Silk and pink... Pink and silk?!
OH, RIGHT...
THE AD SAID "ASSISTANT" BUT IN REALITY YOU'LL BE ACTING AS MY WIFE.
さらっ
HONEST
HOW CAN YOU SAY SOMETHING SO CREEPY IN SUCH A LIGHTHEARTED MANNER?!
NOOOO

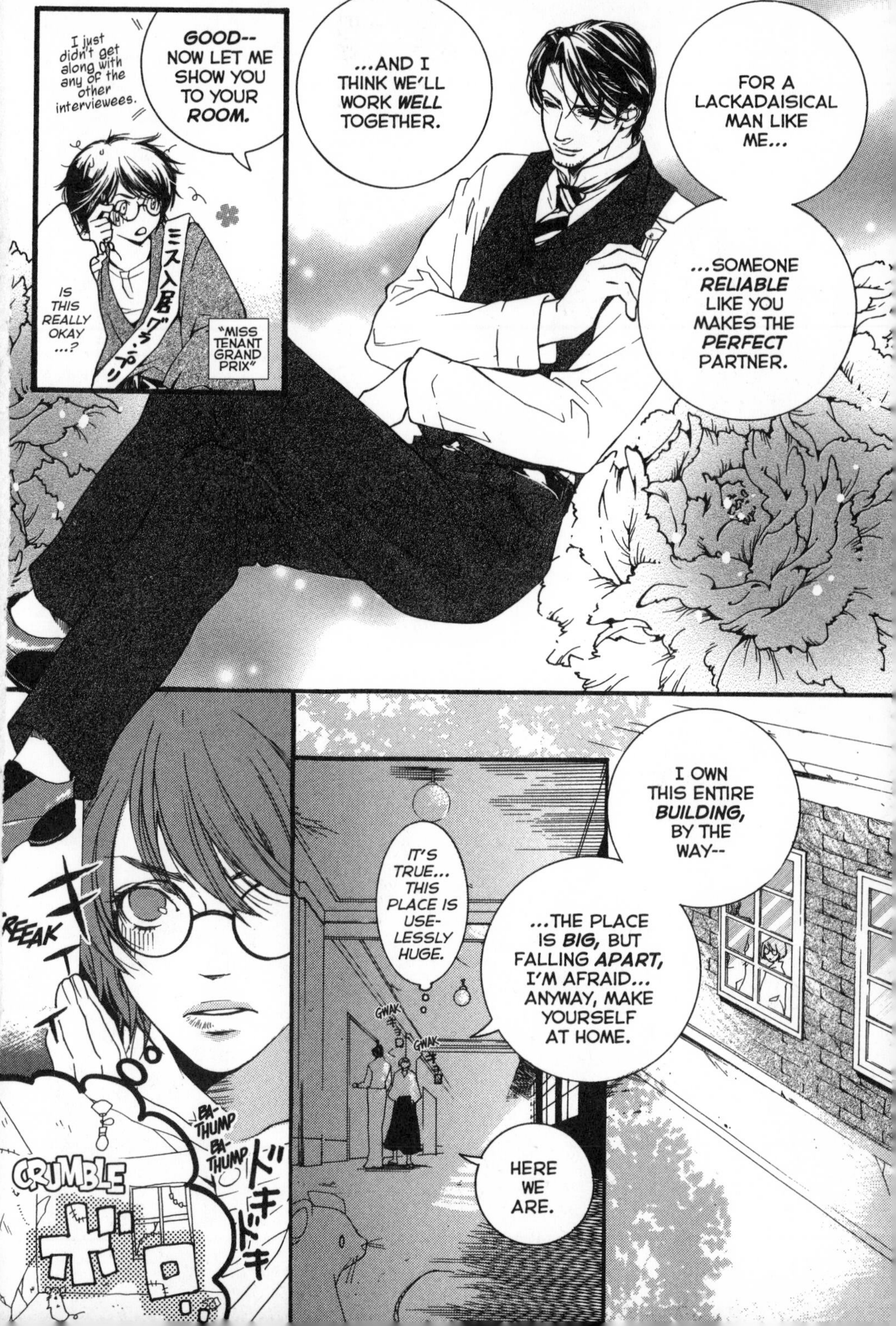
FOR A LACKADAISICAL MAN LIKE ME...
...SOMEONE RELIABLE LIKE YOU MAKES THE PERFECT PARTNER.
...AND I THINK WE'LL WORK WELL TOGETHER.
GOOD-- NOW LET ME SHOW YOU TO YOUR ROOM.
I just didn't get along with any of the other interviewees.
ミス入居グランプリ
"MISS TENANT GRAND PRIX"
IS THIS REALLY OKAY...?
I OWN THIS ENTIRE BUILDING, BY THE WAY--
...THE PLACE IS BIG, BUT FALLING APART, I'M AFRAID... ANYWAY, MAKE YOURSELF AT HOME.
HERE WE ARE.
IT'S TRUE... THIS PLACE IS USE-LESSLY HUGE.
GWAK
GWAK
CREEAK
BA-THUMP BA-THUMP
ドキドキ
CRUMBLE
ボロ

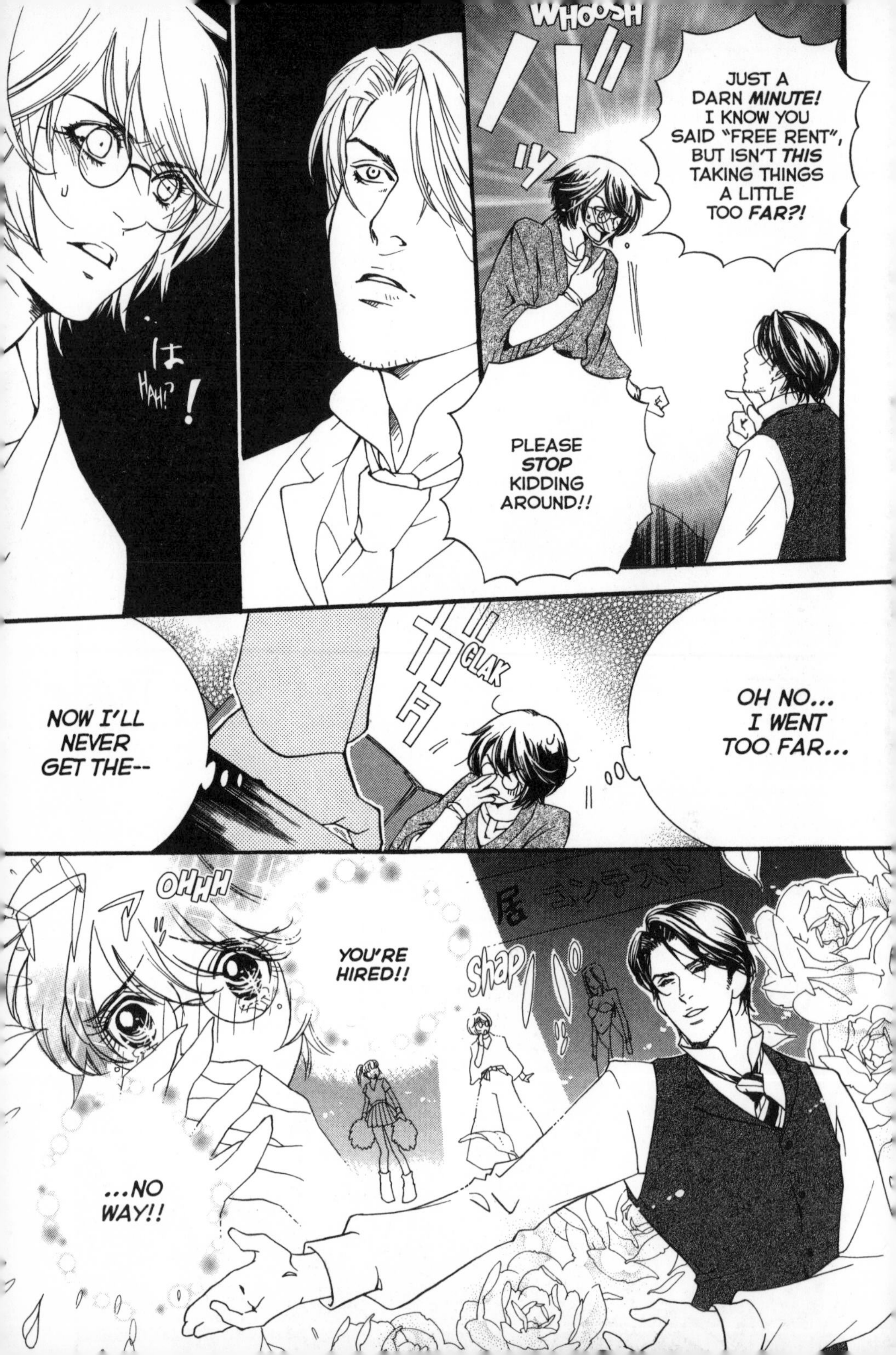
WHOOSH
JUST A DARN *MINUTE!* I KNOW YOU SAID "FREE RENT", BUT ISN'T *THIS* TAKING THINGS A LITTLE TOO *FAR?!*
PLEASE *STOP* KIDDING AROUND!!
は
HAH!?
OH NO... I WENT TOO FAR...
GLAK
NOW I'LL NEVER GET THE--
shap
YOU'RE HIRED!!
OHHH
...NO WAY!!

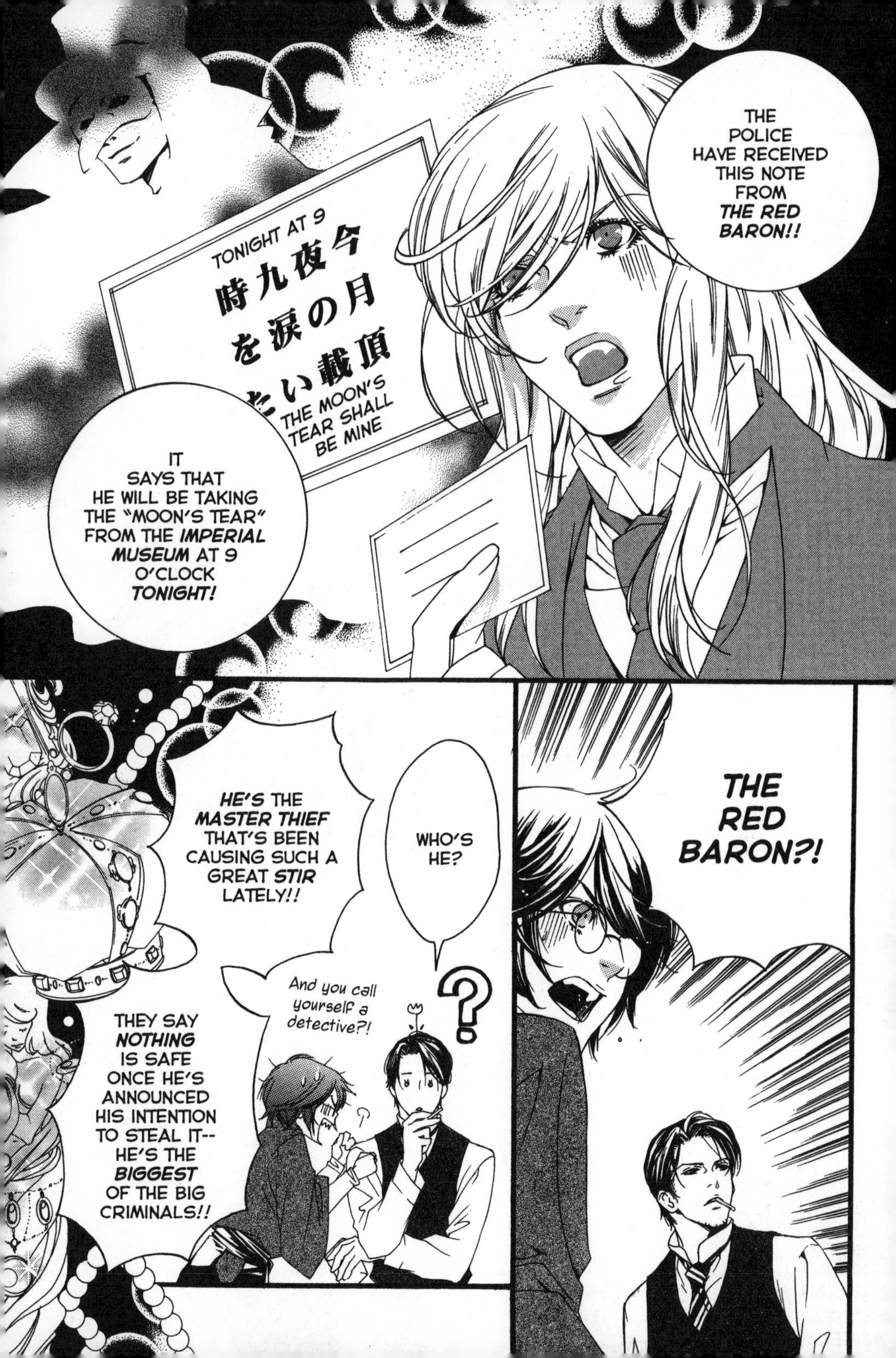
THE POLICE HAVE RECEIVED THIS NOTE FROM THE RED BARON!!
TONIGHT AT 9
今夜九時
月の涙を
頂載い
THE MOON'S TEAR SHALL BE MINE
IT SAYS THAT HE WILL BE TAKING THE "MOON'S TEAR" FROM THE IMPERIAL MUSEUM AT 9 O'CLOCK TONIGHT!
THE RED BARON?!
WHO'S HE?
HE'S THE MASTER THIEF THAT'S BEEN CAUSING SUCH A GREAT STIR LATELY!!
And you call yourself a detective?!
THEY SAY NOTHING IS SAFE ONCE HE'S ANNOUNCED HIS INTENTION TO STEAL IT-- HE'S THE BIGGEST OF THE BIG CRIMINALS!!

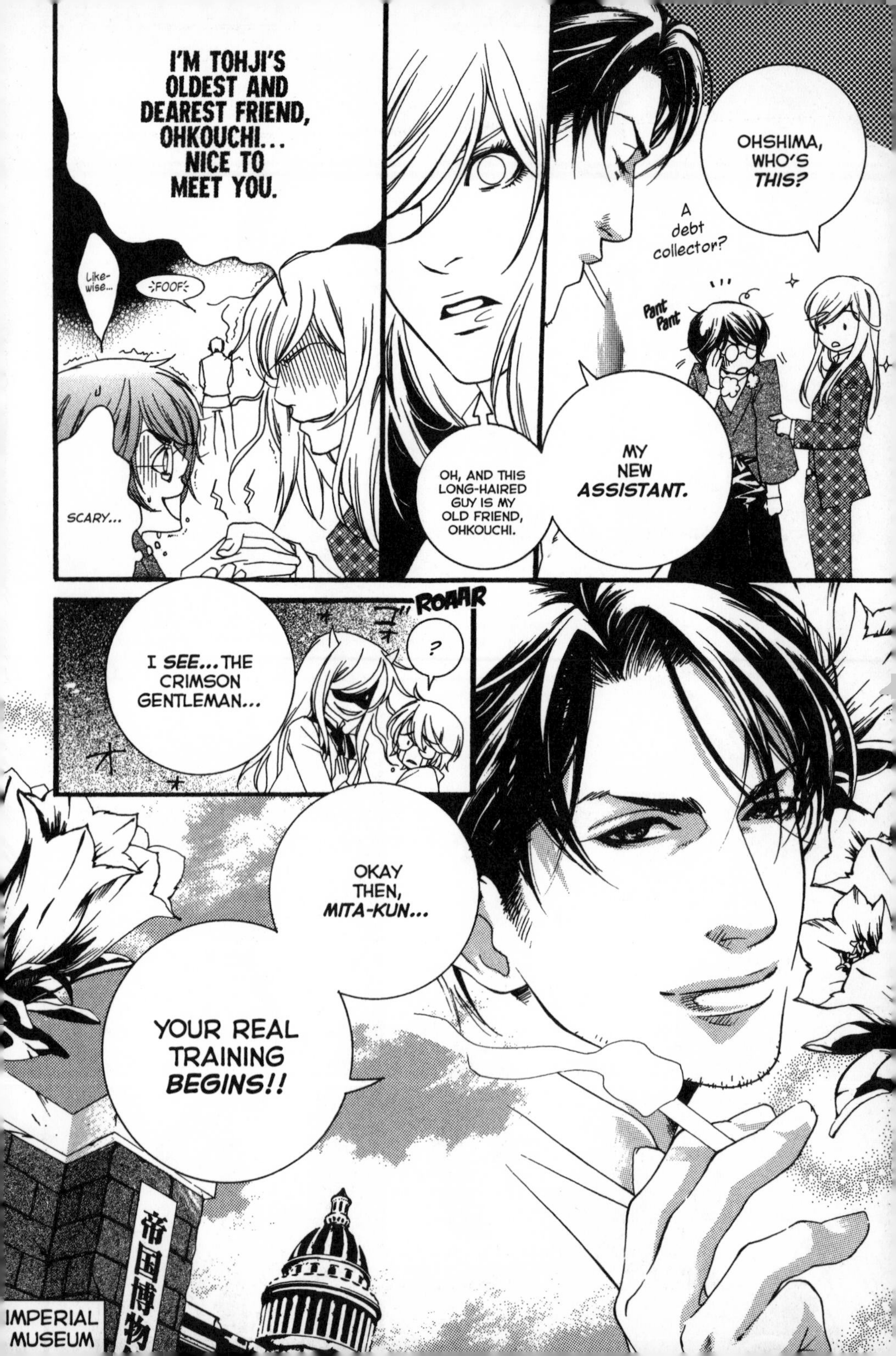
OHSHIMA, WHO'S THIS?
A debt collector?
Pant Pant
MY NEW ASSISTANT.
OH, AND THIS LONG-HAIRED GUY IS MY OLD FRIEND, OHKOUCHI.
I'M TOHJI'S OLDEST AND DEAREST FRIEND, OHKOUCHI... NICE TO MEET YOU.
Like-wise...
FOOF
SCARY...
ROAAR
?
I SEE... THE CRIMSON GENTLEMAN...
OKAY THEN, MITA-KUN...
YOUR REAL TRAINING BEGINS!!
帝国博物
IMPERIAL MUSEUM

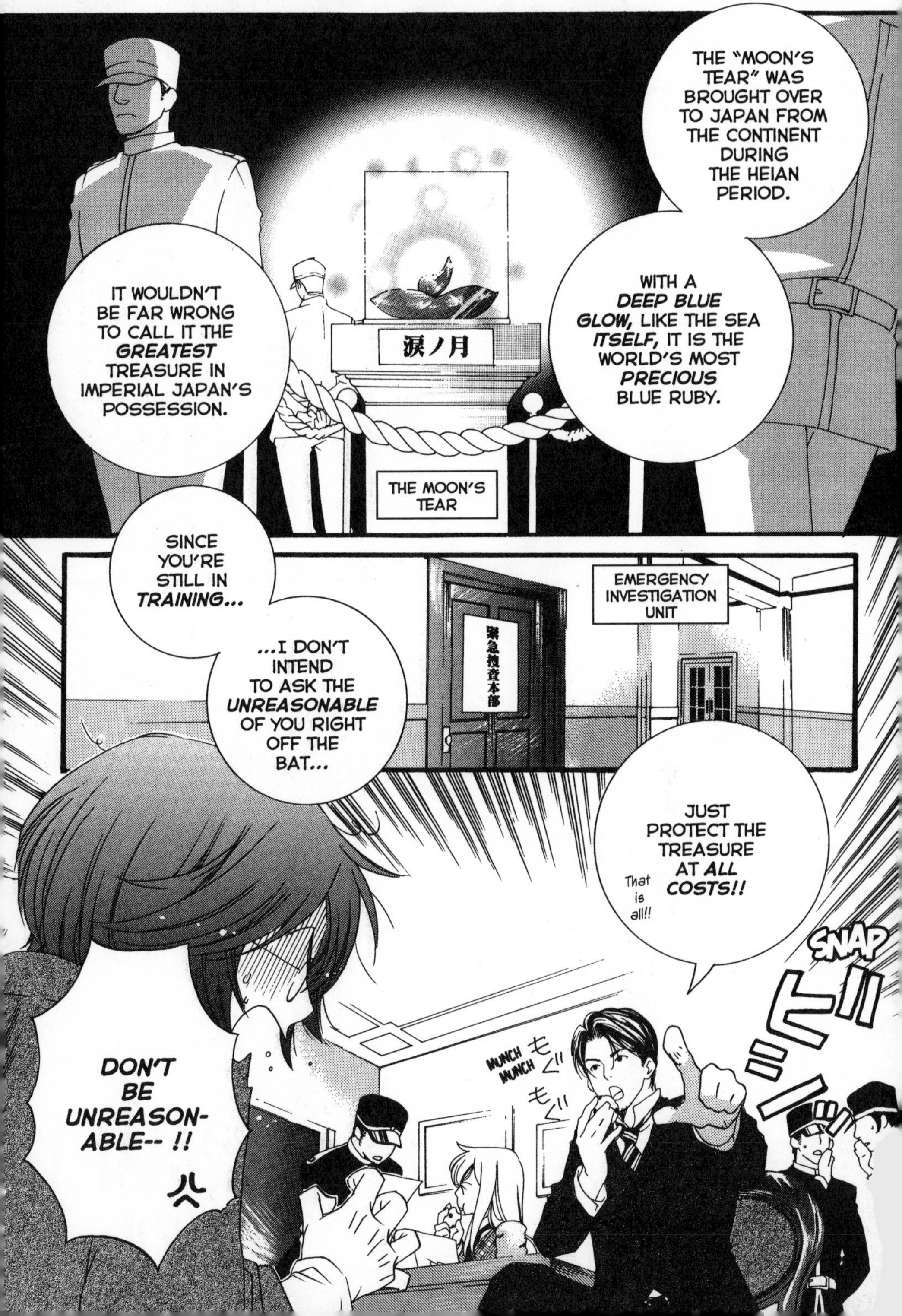
THE "MOON'S TEAR" WAS BROUGHT OVER TO JAPAN FROM THE CONTINENT DURING THE HEIAN PERIOD.
WITH A DEEP BLUE GLOW, LIKE THE SEA ITSELF, IT IS THE WORLD'S MOST PRECIOUS BLUE RUBY.
涙ノ月
IT WOULDN'T BE FAR WRONG TO CALL IT THE GREATEST TREASURE IN IMPERIAL JAPAN'S POSSESSION.
THE MOON'S TEAR
EMERGENCY INVESTIGATION UNIT
緊急捜査本部
SINCE YOU'RE STILL IN TRAINING...
...I DON'T INTEND TO ASK THE UNREASONABLE OF YOU RIGHT OFF THE BAT...
JUST PROTECT THE TREASURE AT ALL COSTS!!
That is all!!
SNAP
MUNCH MUNCH
もぐもぐ
DON'T BE UNREASONABLE-- !!

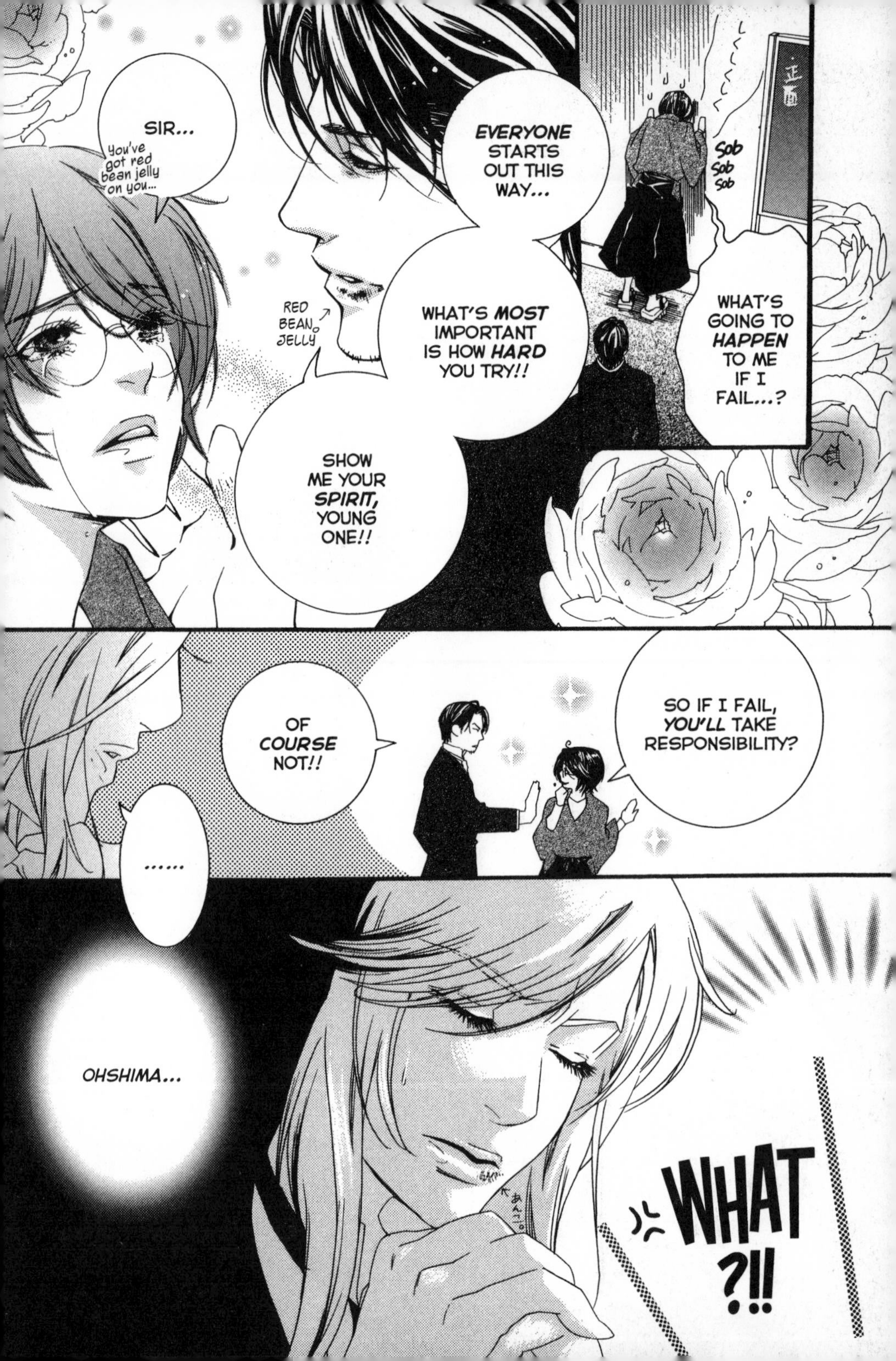
Sob Sob Sob
WHAT'S GOING TO HAPPEN TO ME IF I FAIL...?
EVERYONE STARTS OUT THIS WAY...
WHAT'S MOST IMPORTANT IS HOW HARD YOU TRY!!
SHOW ME YOUR SPIRIT, YOUNG ONE!!
RED BEAN JELLY
SIR...
You've got red bean jelly on you...
SO IF I FAIL, YOU'LL TAKE RESPONSIBILITY?
OF COURSE NOT!!
......
OHSHIMA...
WHAT ?!!

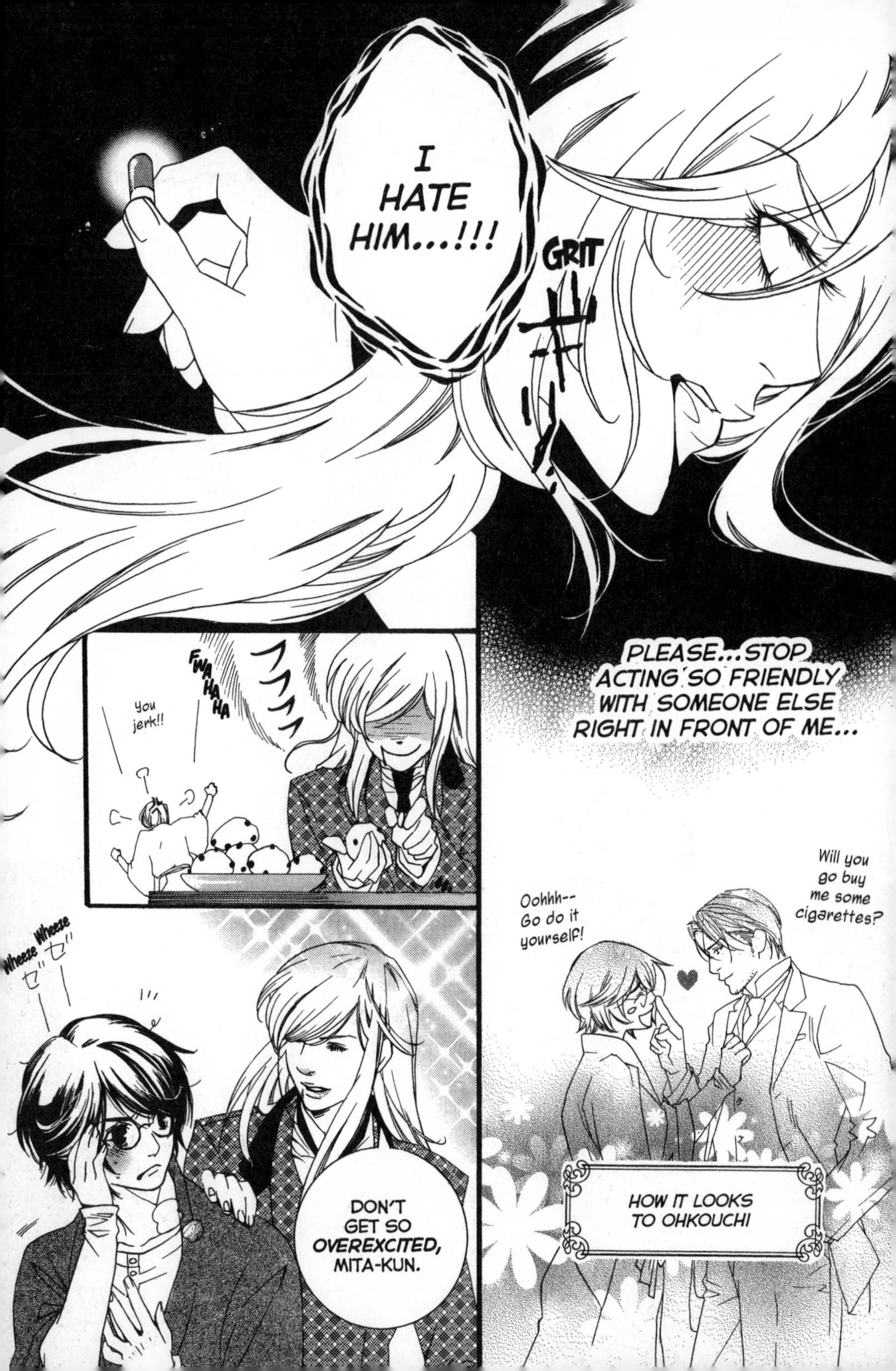
I HATE HIM...!!!
GRIT
PLEASE... STOP ACTING SO FRIENDLY WITH SOMEONE ELSE RIGHT IN FRONT OF ME...
Will you go buy me some cigarettes?
Oohhh-- Go do it yourself!
HOW IT LOOKS TO OHKOUCHI
FWAHAHA
You jerk!!
Wheeze Wheeze
ゼゼ
DON'T GET SO OVEREXCITED, MITA-KUN.

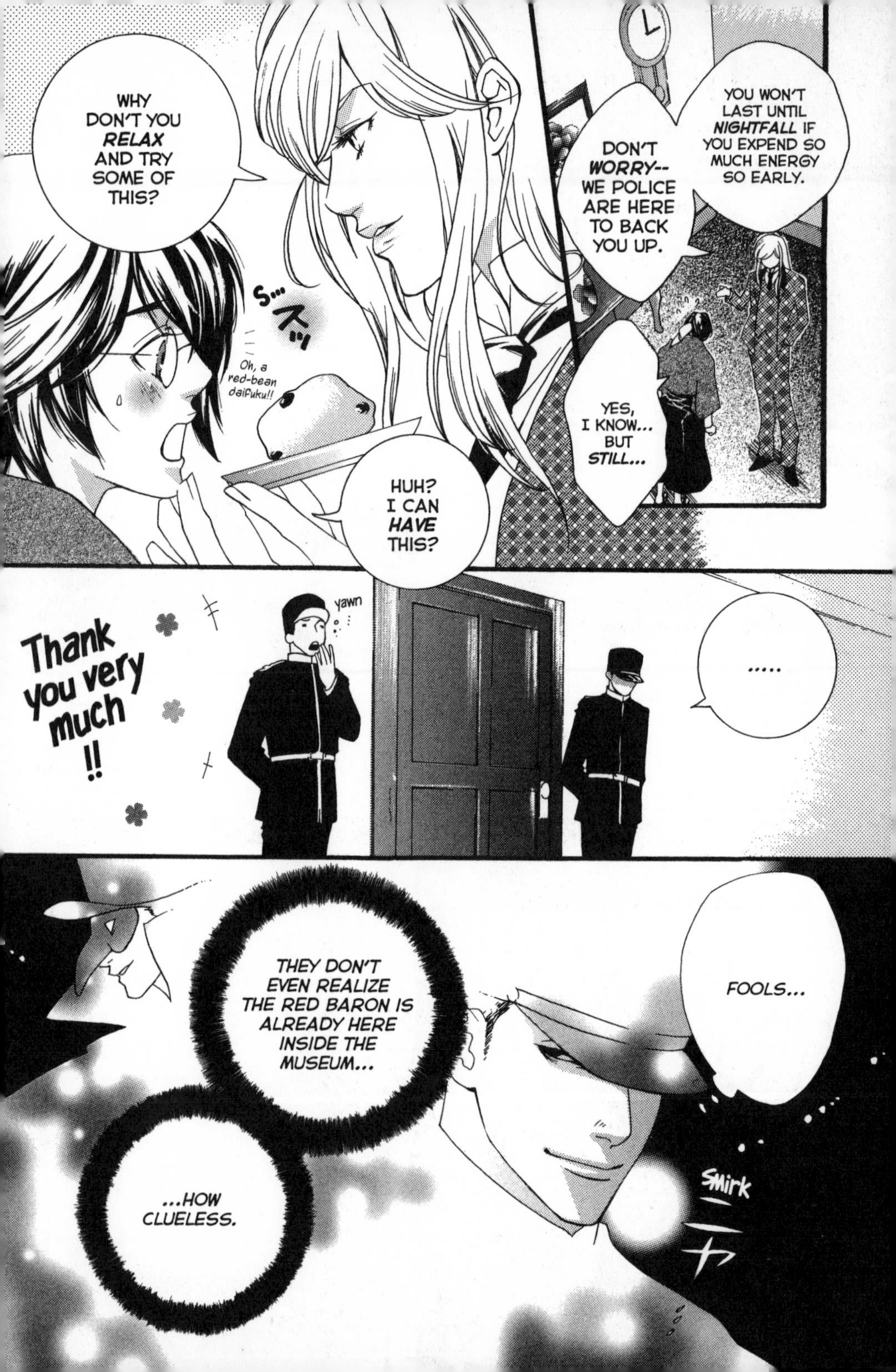
YOU WON'T LAST UNTIL NIGHTFALL IF YOU EXPEND SO MUCH ENERGY SO EARLY.
DON'T WORRY-- WE POLICE ARE HERE TO BACK YOU UP.
YES, I KNOW... BUT STILL...
WHY DON'T YOU RELAX AND TRY SOME OF THIS?
S...
Oh, a red-bean daifuku!!
HUH? I CAN HAVE THIS?
.....
yawn
Thank you very much!!
FOOLS...
THEY DON'T EVEN REALIZE THE RED BARON IS ALREADY HERE INSIDE THE MUSEUM...
...HOW CLUELESS.
Smirk

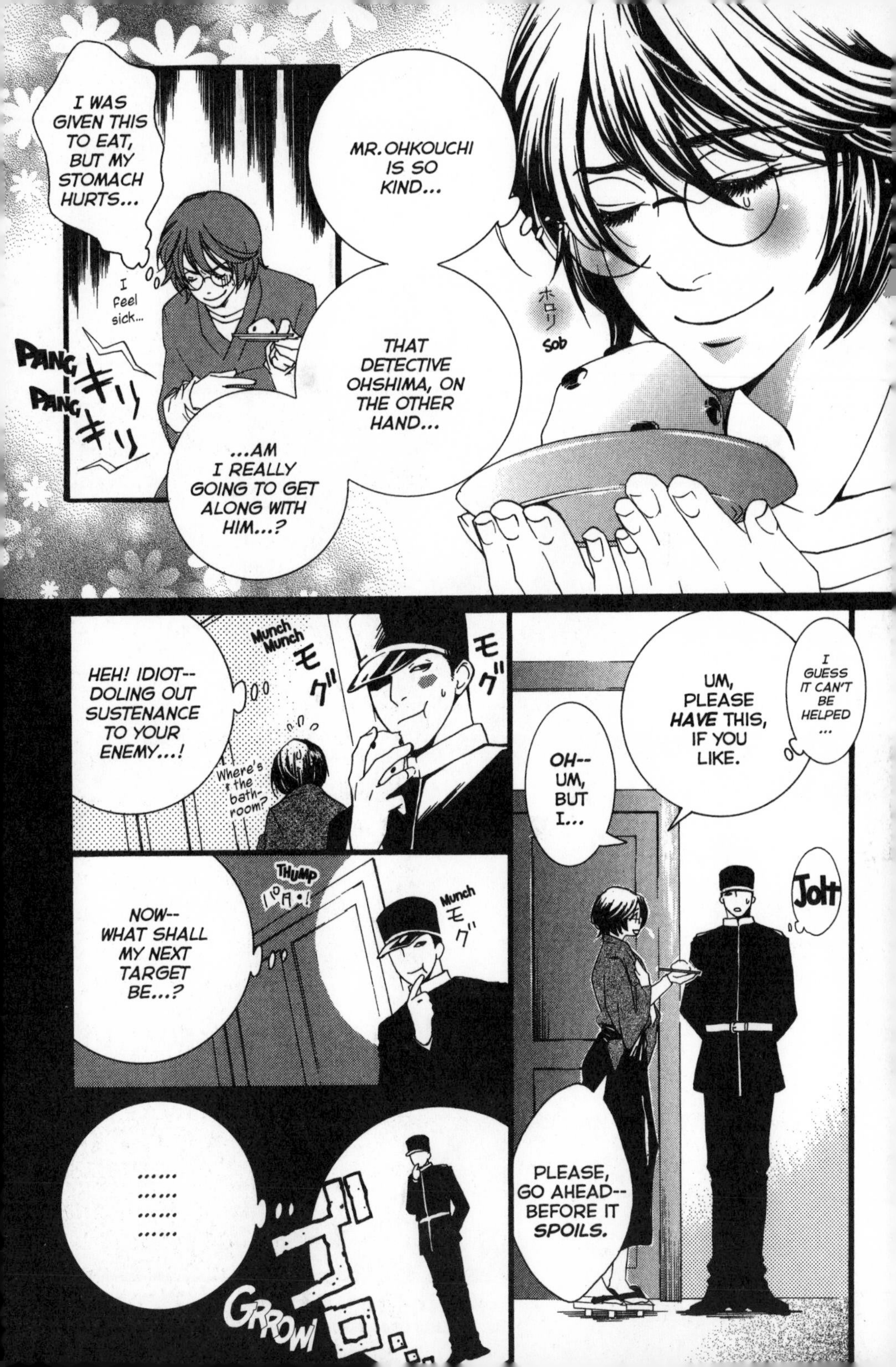
MR.OHKOUCHI IS SO KIND...
ホロリ Sob
THAT DETECTIVE OHSHIMA, ON THE OTHER HAND...
...AM I REALLY GOING TO GET ALONG WITH HIM...?
I WAS GIVEN THIS TO EAT, BUT MY STOMACH HURTS...
I feel sick...
PANG キリ
PANG キリ
I GUESS IT CAN'T BE HELPED...
UM, PLEASE HAVE THIS, IF YOU LIKE.
OH-- UM, BUT I...
Jolt
PLEASE, GO AHEAD-- BEFORE IT SPOILS.
モグ
Munch Munch モグ
HEH! IDIOT-- DOLING OUT SUSTENANCE TO YOUR ENEMY...!
Where's the bathroom?
THUMP パタ・!
Munch モグ
NOW-- WHAT SHALL MY NEXT TARGET BE...?
......
......
......
......
GRROWL ゴロ

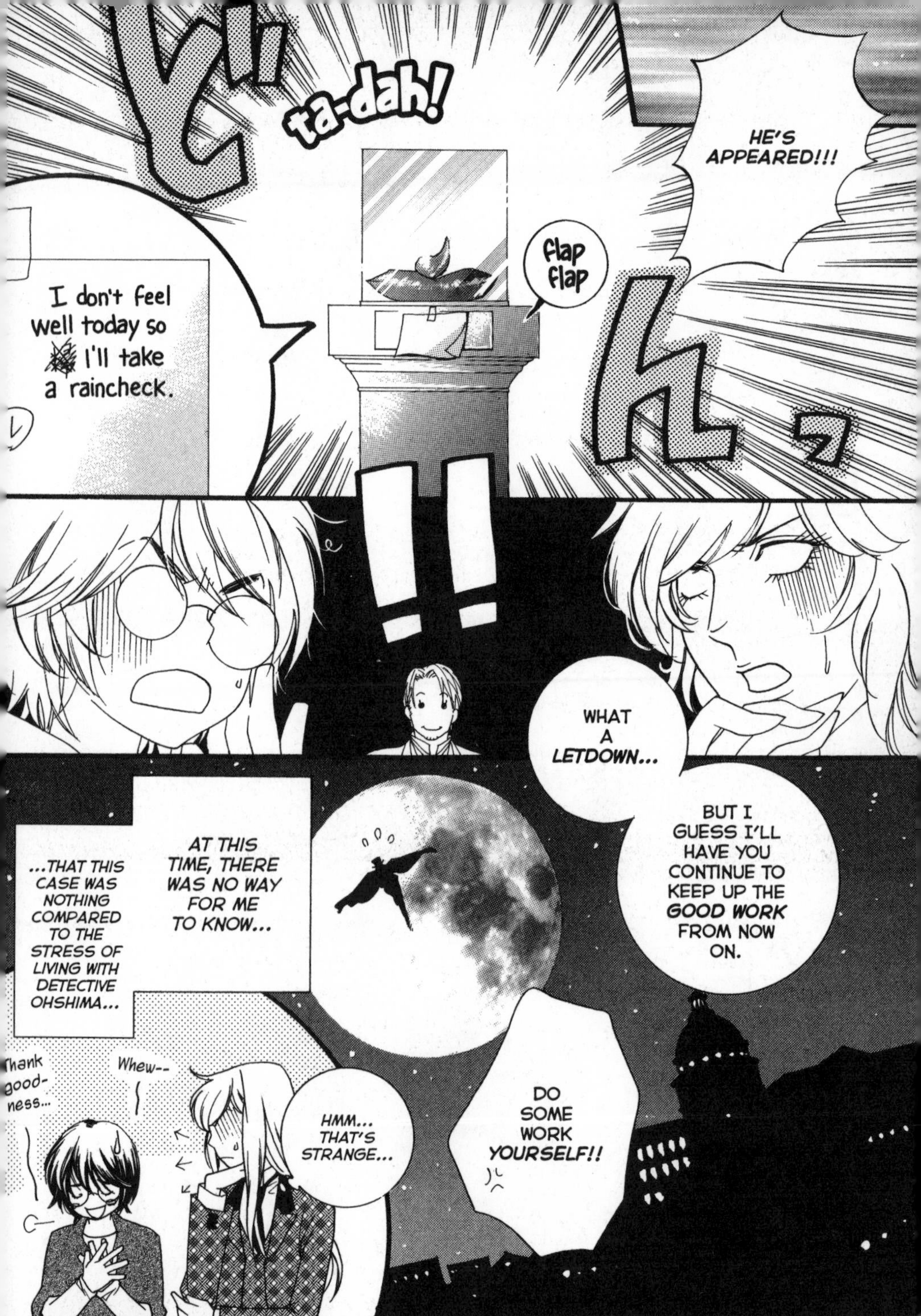
HE'S APPEARED!!!
ta-dah!
flap flap
I don't feel well today so I'll take a raincheck.
!!
WHAT A LETDOWN...
BUT I GUESS I'LL HAVE YOU CONTINUE TO KEEP UP THE GOOD WORK FROM NOW ON.
DO SOME WORK YOURSELF!!
AT THIS TIME, THERE WAS NO WAY FOR ME TO KNOW...
...THAT THIS CASE WAS NOTHING COMPARED TO THE STRESS OF LIVING WITH DETECTIVE OHSHIMA...
HMM... THAT'S STRANGE...
Whew--
Thank goodness...

探偵助手腕まくり奮闘記／おわり
THE TRAVAILS OF A STRUGGLING ASSISTANT DETECTIVE / END

探偵助手腕まくり奮闘記

THE TRAVAILS OF A STRUGGLING ASSISTANT DETECTIVE

HOMERUN KEN PRESENTS

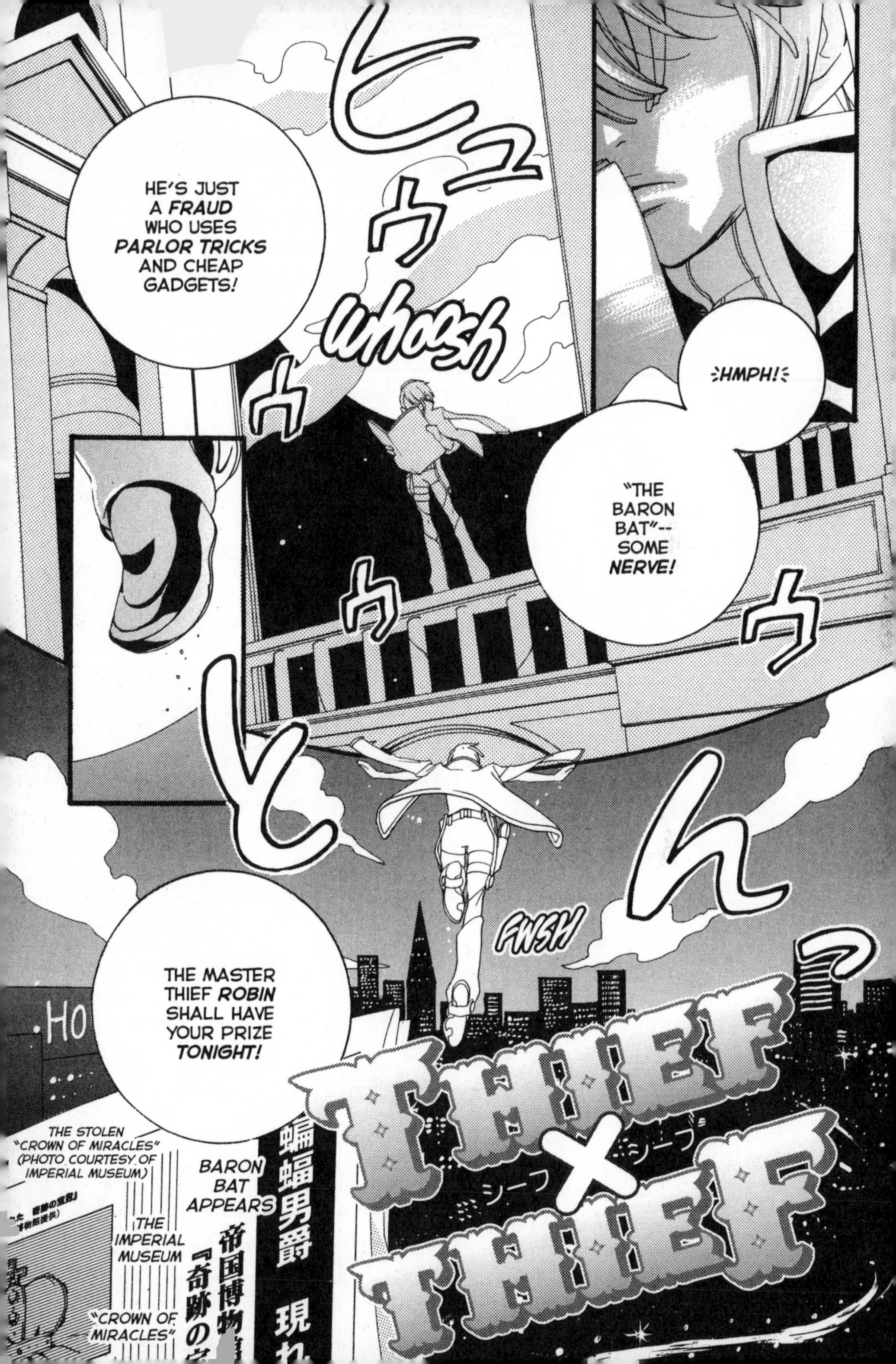
HMPH!
"THE BARON BAT"--SOME NERVE!
HE'S JUST A FRAUD WHO USES PARLOR TRICKS AND CHEAP GADGETS!
ヒュウ
whoosh
ウウウ
とんっ
FWSH
THE MASTER THIEF ROBIN SHALL HAVE YOUR PRIZE TONIGHT!
THIEF × THIEF
シーフ
シーフ
蝙蝠男爵
BARON BAT APPEARS
THE STOLEN "CROWN OF MIRACLES" (PHOTO COURTESY OF IMPERIAL MUSEUM)
THE IMPERIAL MUSEUM
"CROWN OF MIRACLES"

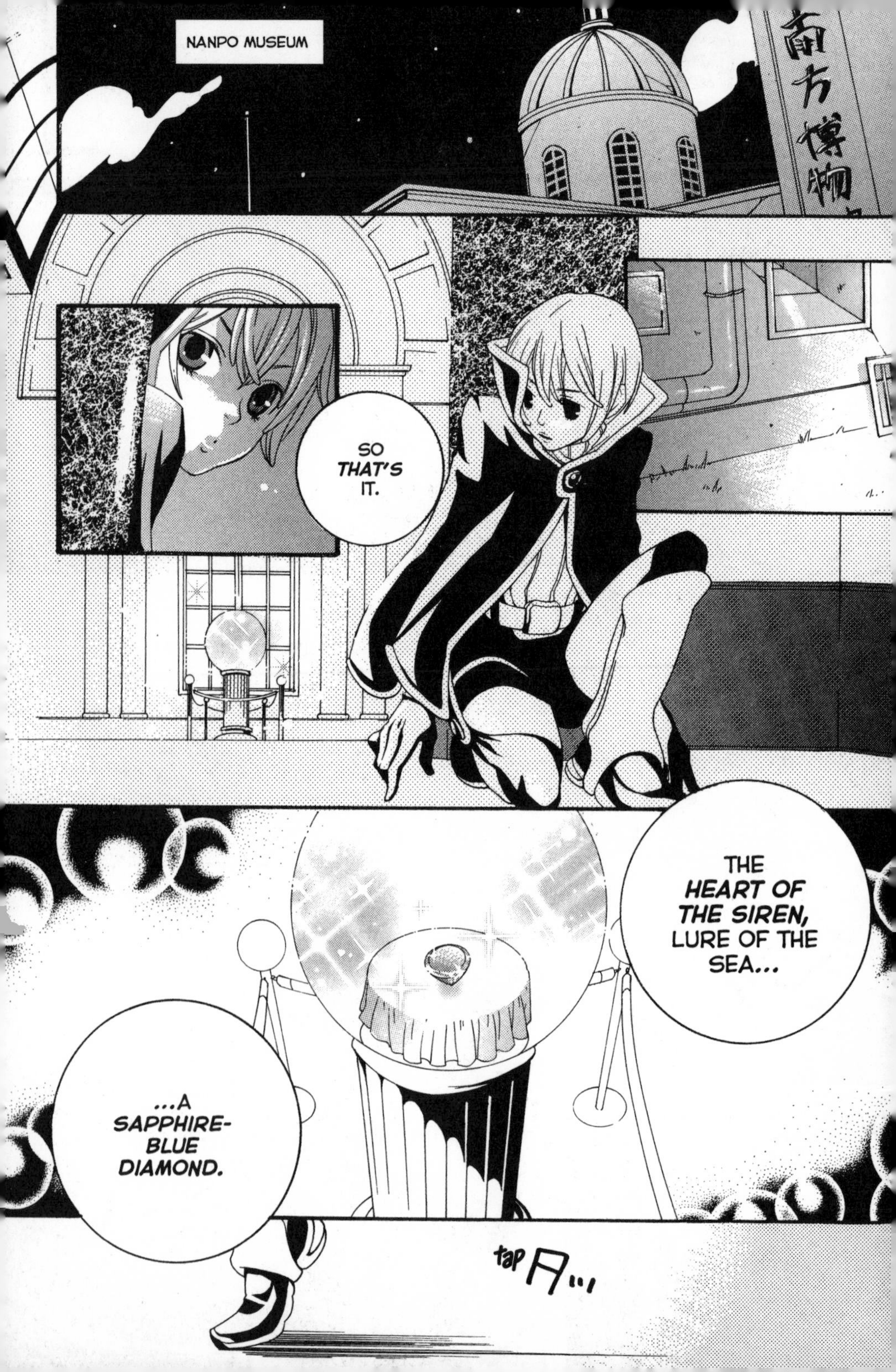
NANPO MUSEUM
SO THAT'S IT.
THE HEART OF THE SIREN, LURE OF THE SEA...
...A SAPPHIRE-BLUE DIAMOND.
tap

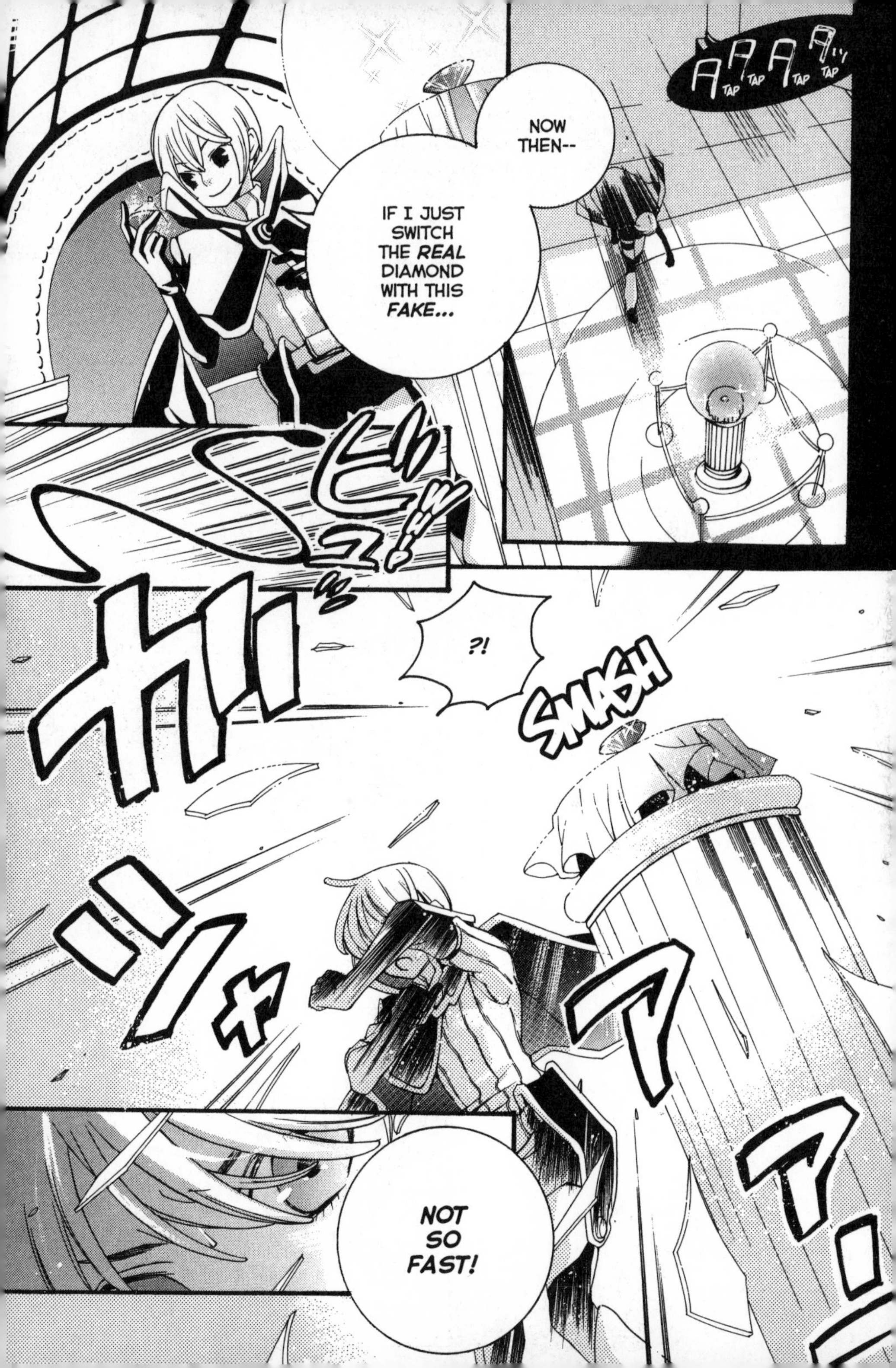
TAP TAP TAP TAP TAP
NOW THEN--
IF I JUST SWITCH THE *REAL* DIAMOND WITH THIS *FAKE*...
WHIP!
?!
SMASH
NOT SO FAST!

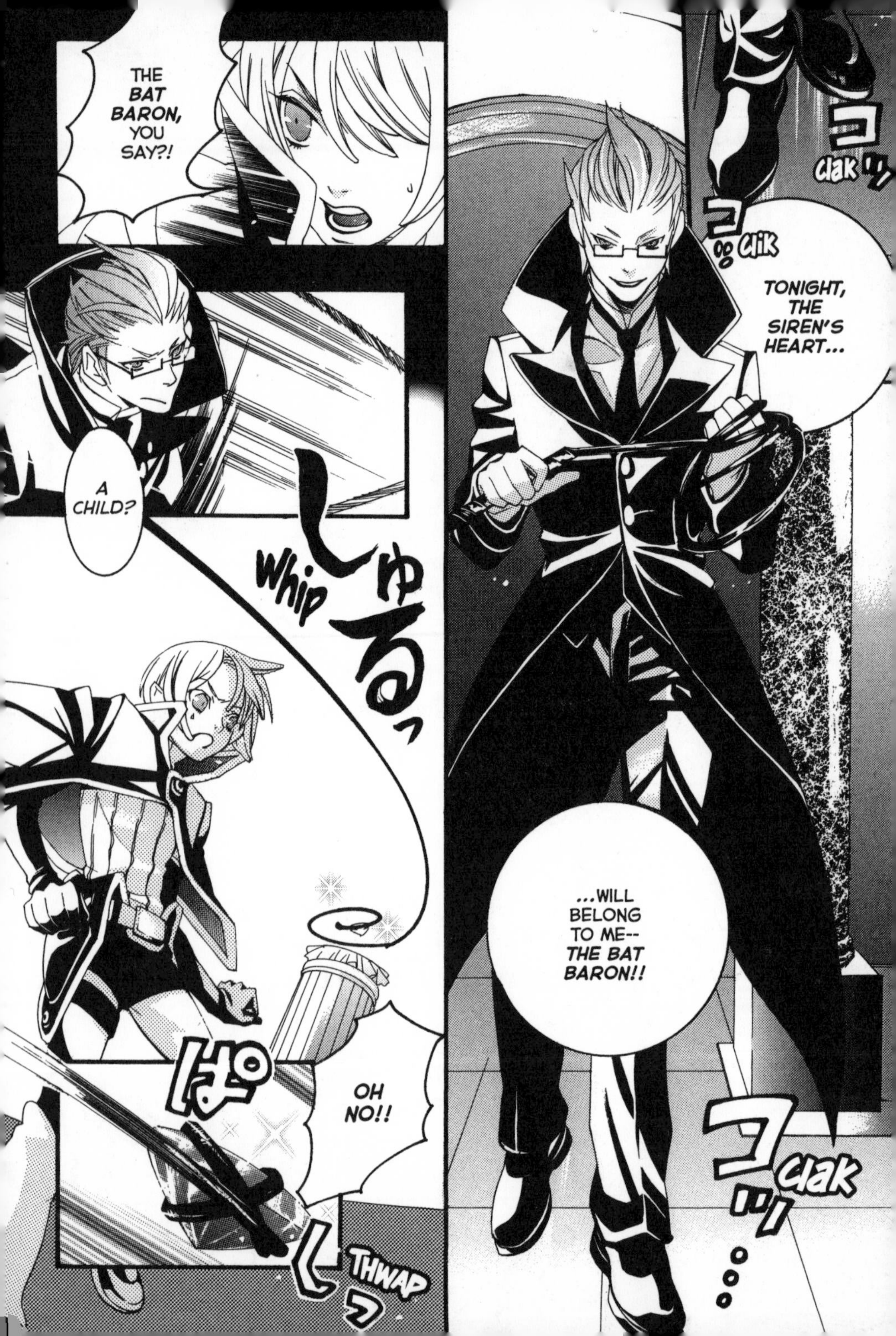
Clak
Clik
TONIGHT, THE SIREN'S HEART...
...WILL BELONG TO ME-- THE BAT BARON!!
Clak
THE BAT BARON, YOU SAY?!
A CHILD?
Whip
OH NO!!
THWAP

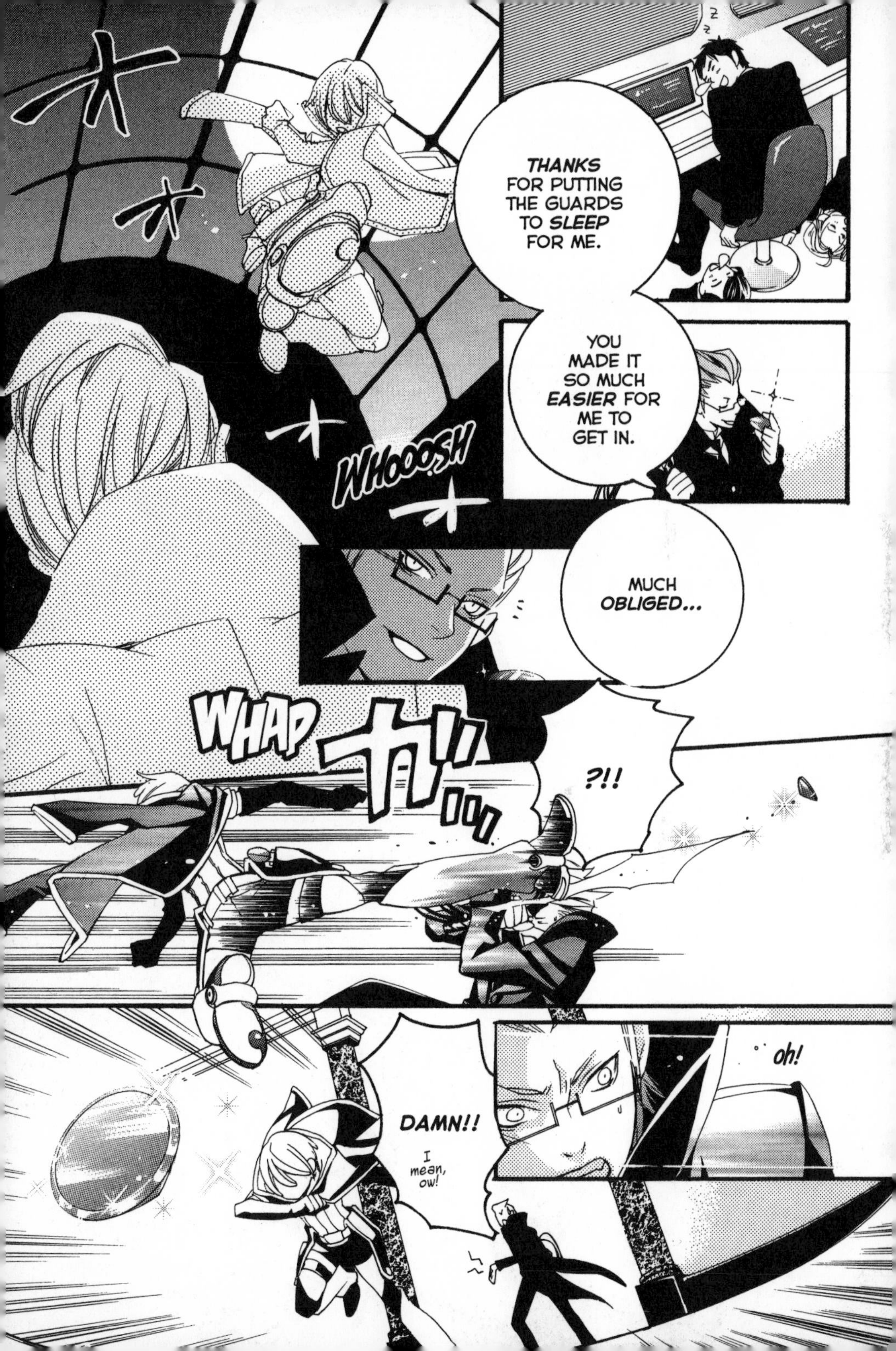

THANKS FOR PUTTING THE GUARDS TO SLEEP FOR ME.
オ
オ
YOU MADE IT SO MUCH EASIER FOR ME TO GET IN.
オ
WHOOOSH
オ
MUCH OBLIGED...
WHAP
カッ
?!!
oh!
DAMN!!
I mean, ow!

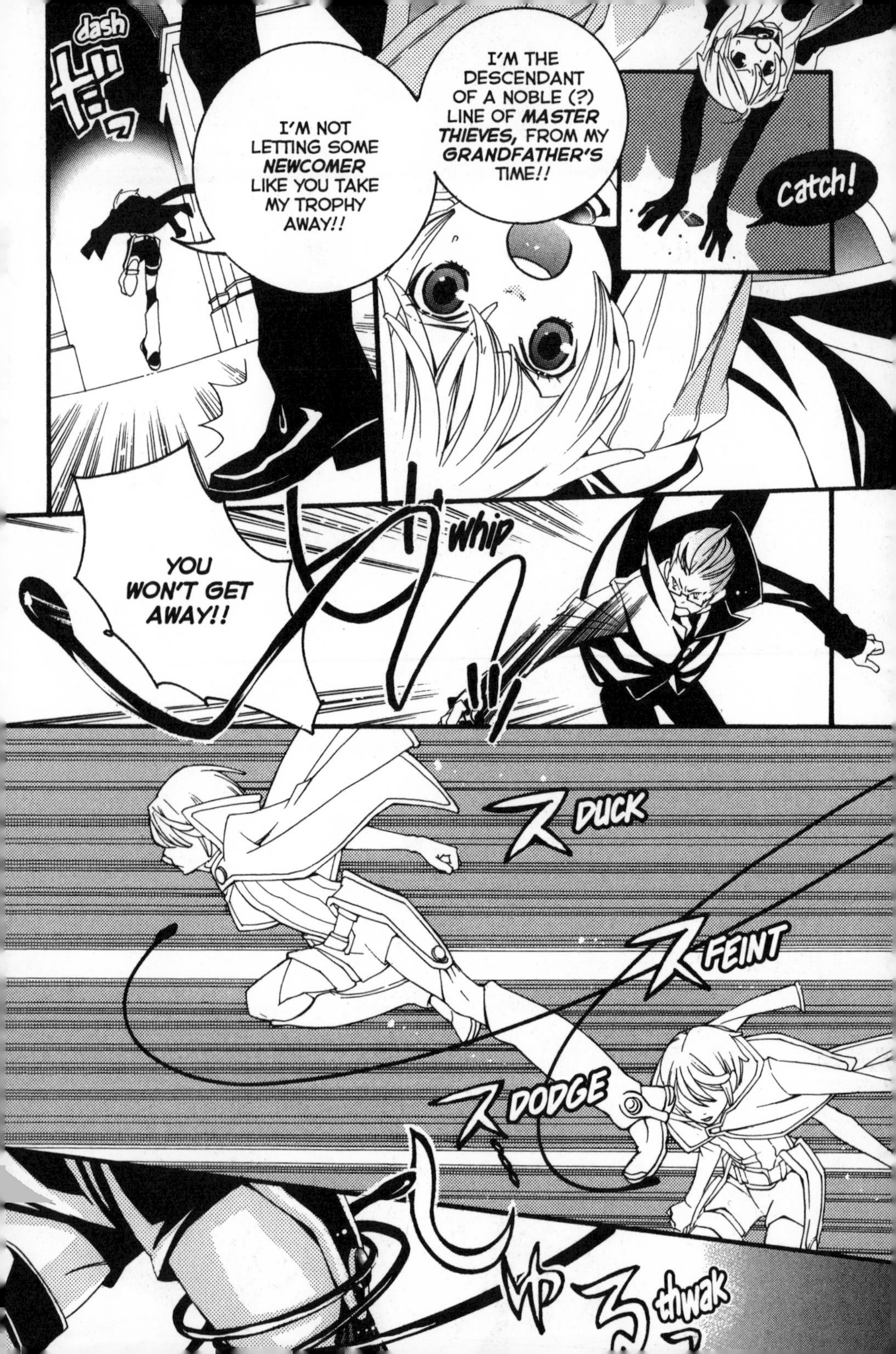
Catch!
I'M THE DESCENDANT OF A NOBLE (?) LINE OF MASTER THIEVES, FROM MY GRANDFATHER'S TIME!!
I'M NOT LETTING SOME NEWCOMER LIKE YOU TAKE MY TROPHY AWAY!!
dash
whip
YOU WON'T GET AWAY!!
DUCK
FEINT
DODGE
thwak

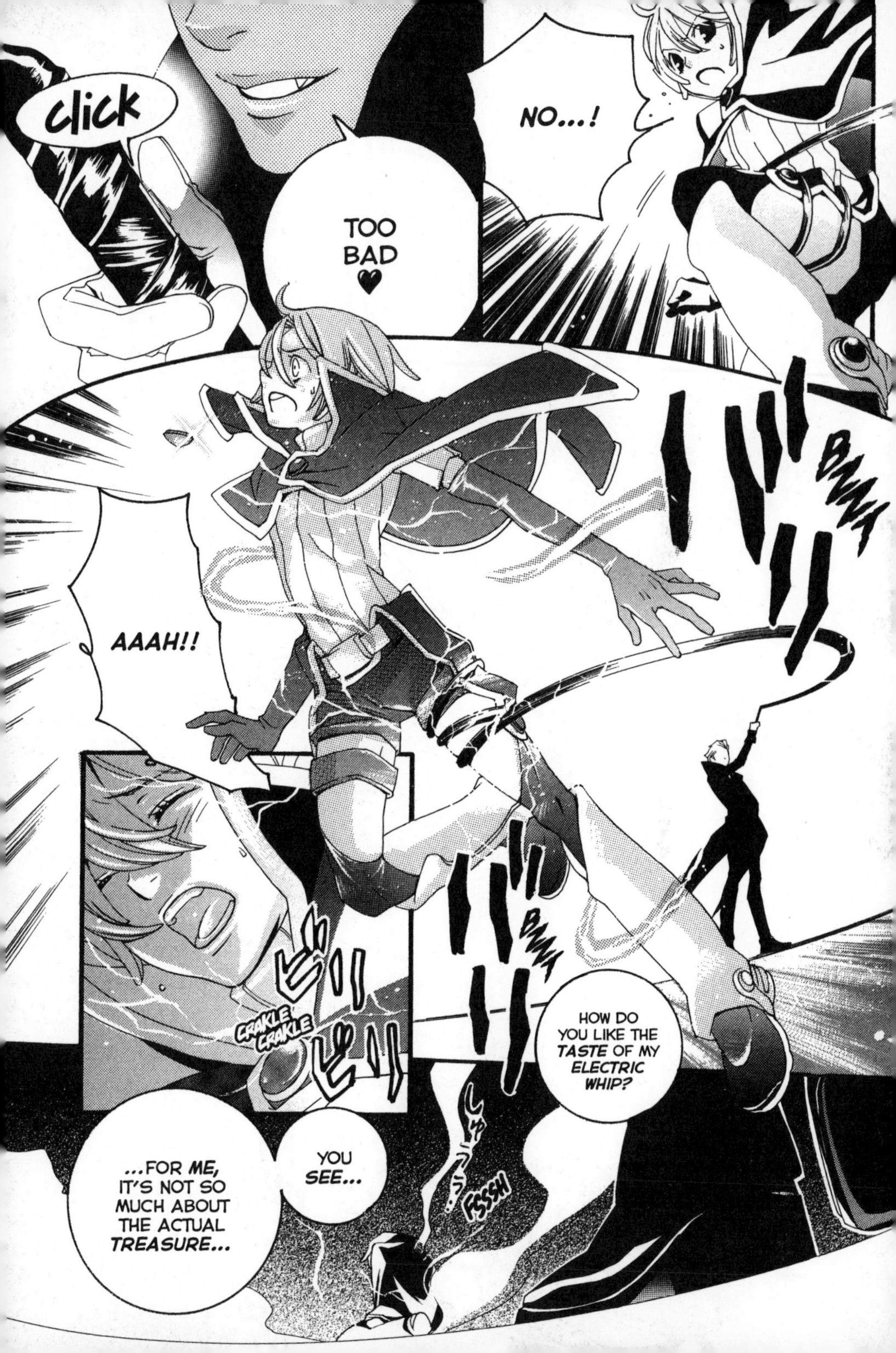
NO...!
Click
TOO BAD ♥
BWAA
AAAH!!
BWAA
HOW DO YOU LIKE THE *TASTE* OF MY *ELECTRIC* WHIP?
CRAKLE CRAKLE
FSSSH
YOU *SEE...*
...FOR *ME,* IT'S NOT SO MUCH ABOUT THE ACTUAL *TREASURE...*

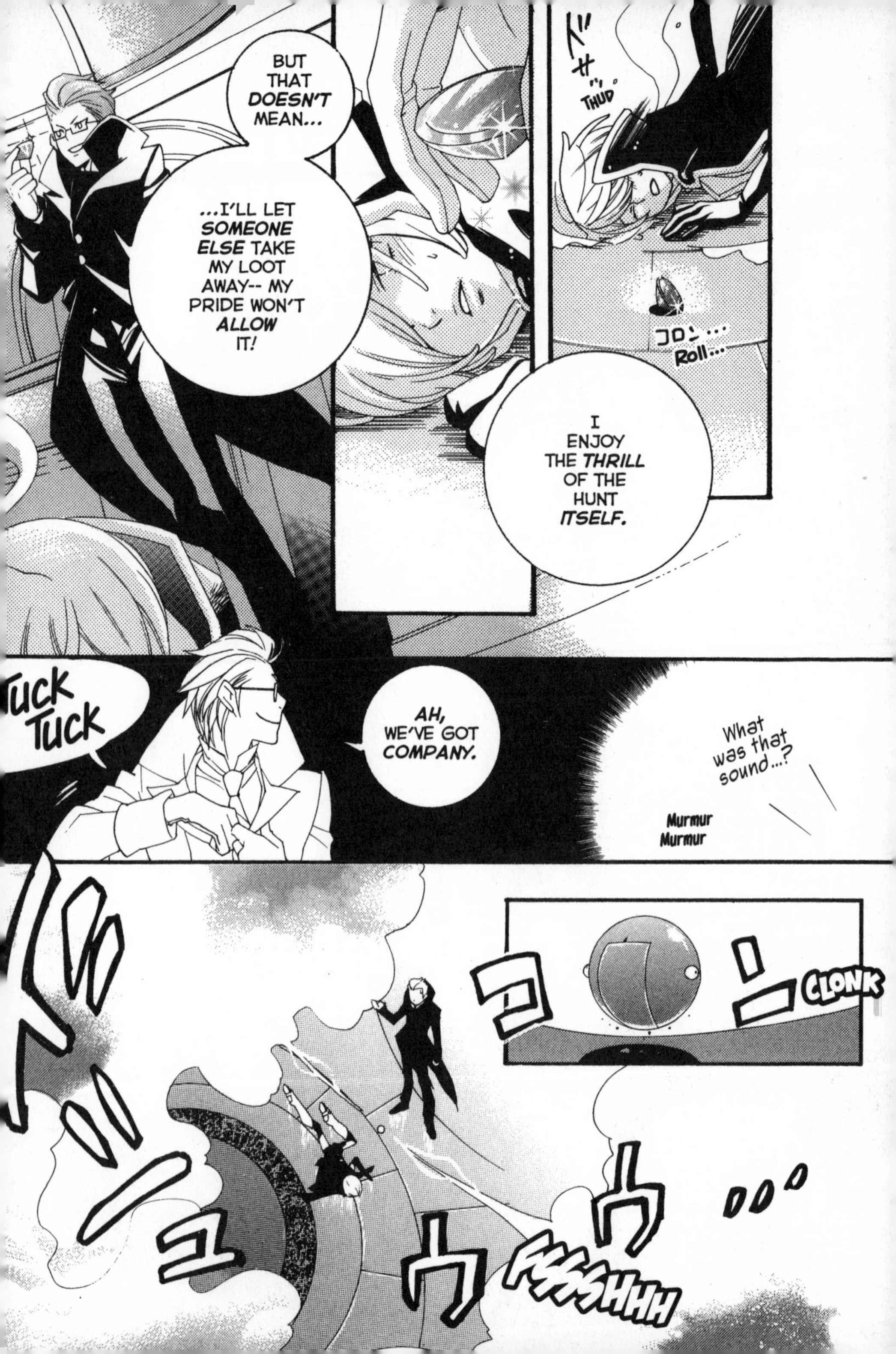
THUD
Roll...
I ENJOY THE THRILL OF THE HUNT ITSELF.
BUT THAT DOESN'T MEAN...
...I'LL LET SOMEONE ELSE TAKE MY LOOT AWAY-- MY PRIDE WON'T ALLOW IT!
What was that sound...?
Murmur Murmur
AH, WE'VE GOT COMPANY.
TUCK TUCK
CLONK
FSSSHHH

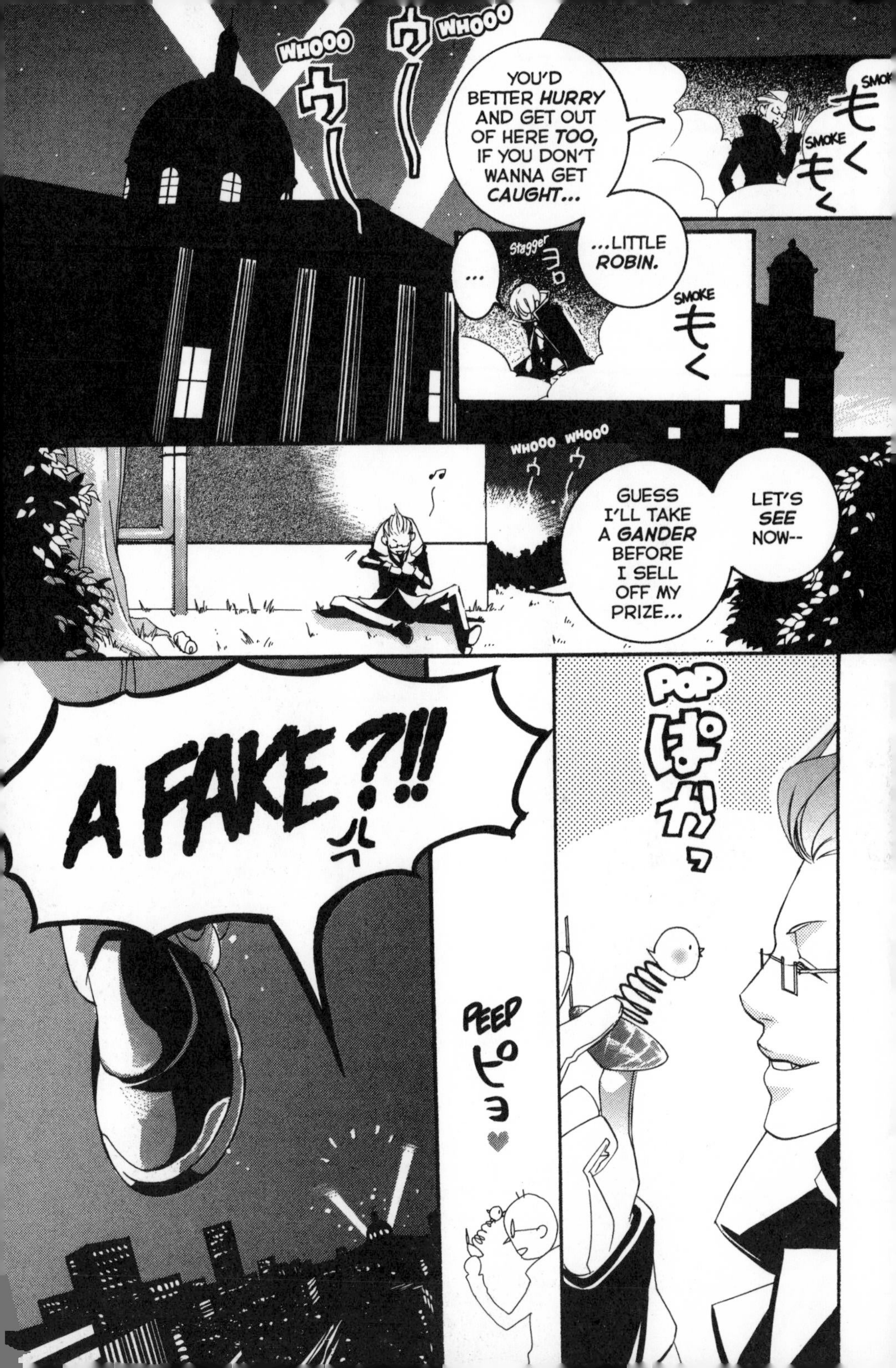
SMOKE
SMOKE
YOU'D BETTER *HURRY* AND GET OUT OF HERE *TOO*, IF YOU DON'T WANNA GET *CAUGHT*...
...LITTLE *ROBIN.*
Stagger
...
SMOKE
WHOOO
WHOOO
WHOOO WHOOO
LET'S *SEE* NOW--
GUESS I'LL TAKE A *GANDER* BEFORE I SELL OFF MY PRIZE...
POP
PEEP
A FAKE?!!

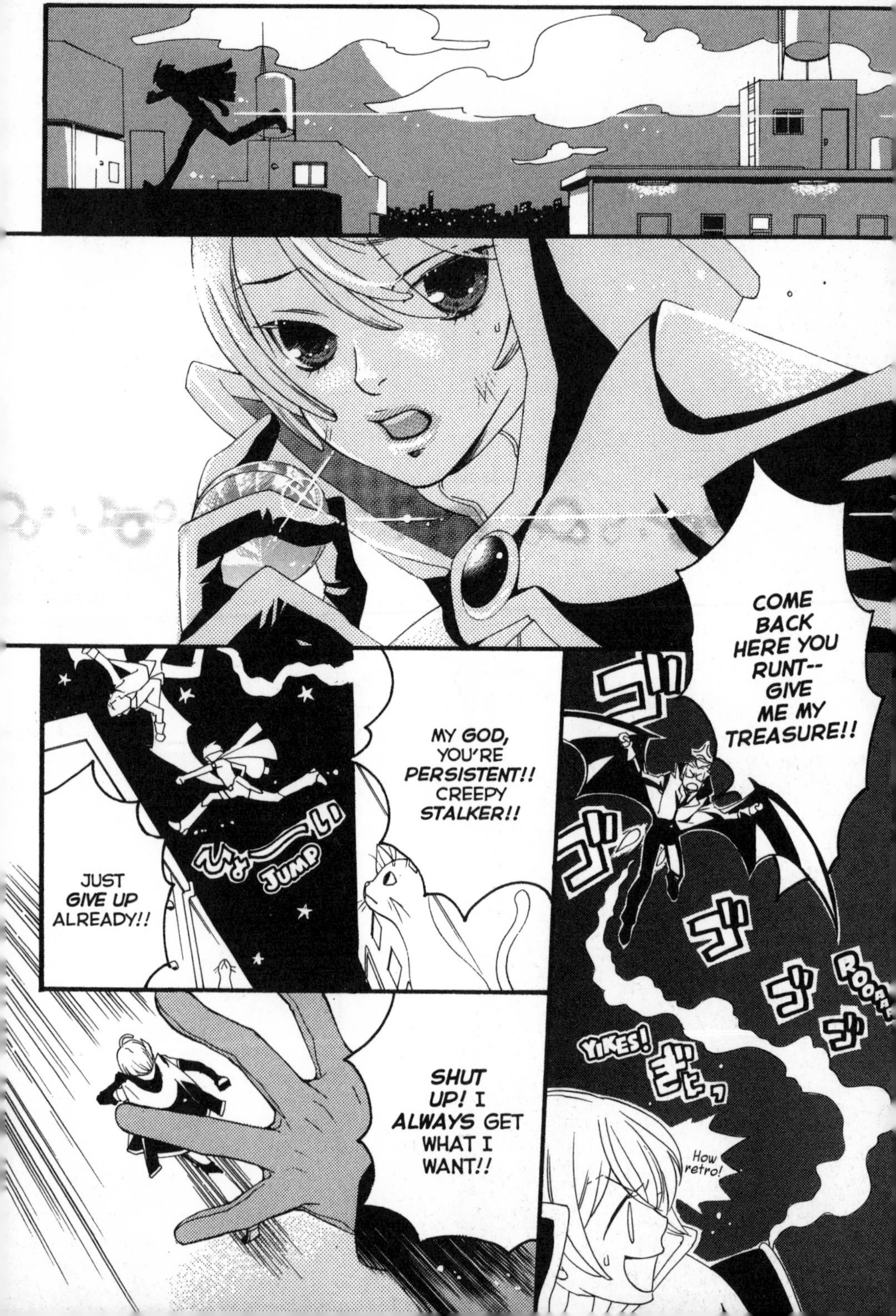
COME BACK HERE YOU RUNT-- GIVE ME MY TREASURE!!
ROOAA
YIKES!
How retro!
MY GOD, YOU'RE PERSISTENT!! CREEPY STALKER!!
JUMP
JUST GIVE UP ALREADY!!
SHUT UP! I ALWAYS GET WHAT I WANT!!

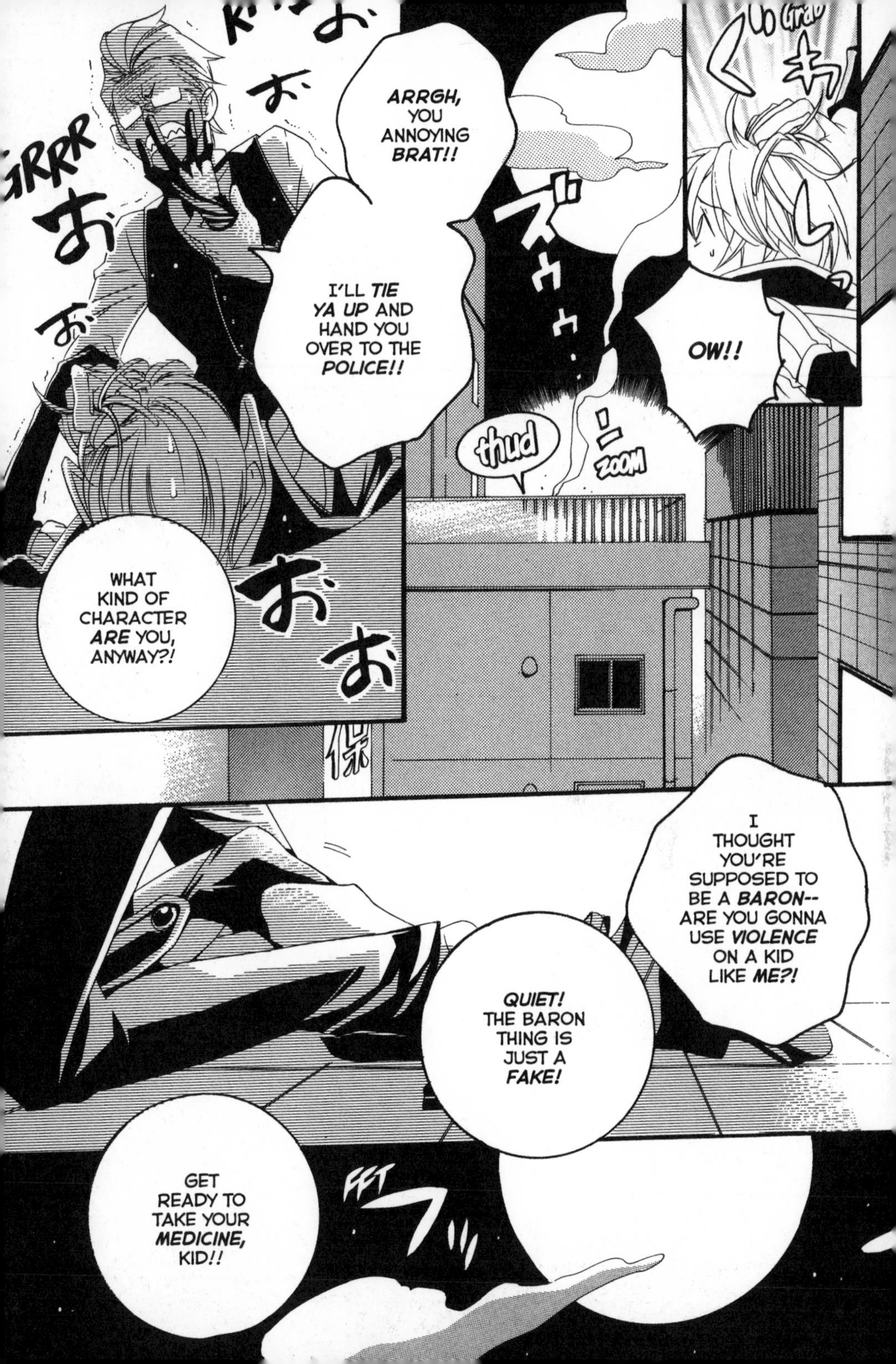
Grab
OW!!
ZOOM
thud
ARRGH, YOU ANNOYING BRAT!!
I'LL TIE YA UP AND HAND YOU OVER TO THE POLICE!!
GRRR
WHAT KIND OF CHARACTER ARE YOU, ANYWAY?!
I THOUGHT YOU'RE SUPPOSED TO BE A BARON-- ARE YOU GONNA USE VIOLENCE ON A KID LIKE ME?!
QUIET! THE BARON THING IS JUST A FAKE!
FFT
GET READY TO TAKE YOUR MEDICINE, KID!!

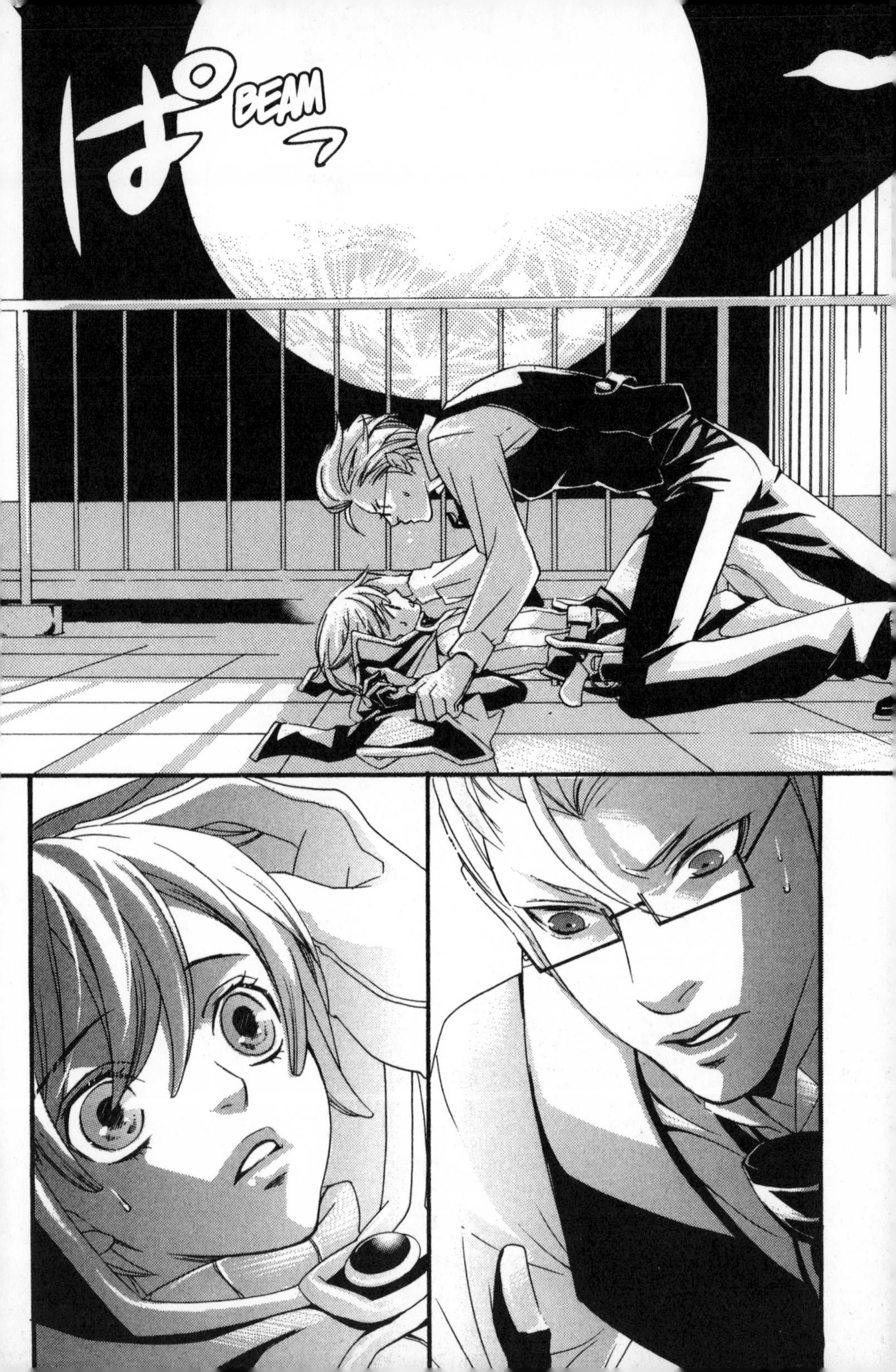
ぱ
BEAM

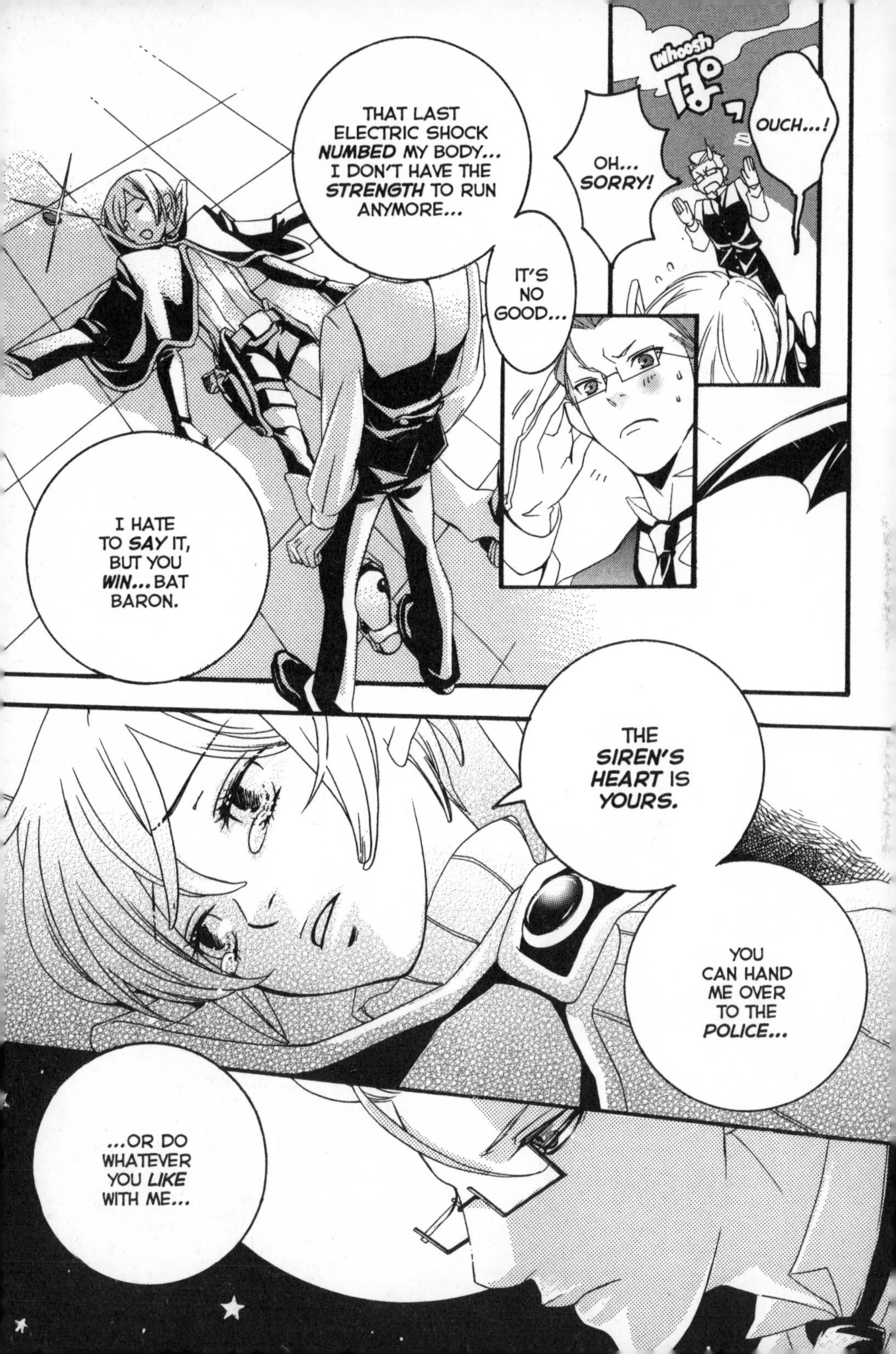
whoosh
ぱっ
OUCH...!
OH... SORRY!
IT'S NO GOOD...
THAT LAST ELECTRIC SHOCK NUMBED MY BODY... I DON'T HAVE THE STRENGTH TO RUN ANYMORE...
I HATE TO SAY IT, BUT YOU WIN... BAT BARON.
THE SIREN'S HEART IS YOURS.
YOU CAN HAND ME OVER TO THE POLICE...
...OR DO WHATEVER YOU LIKE WITH ME...

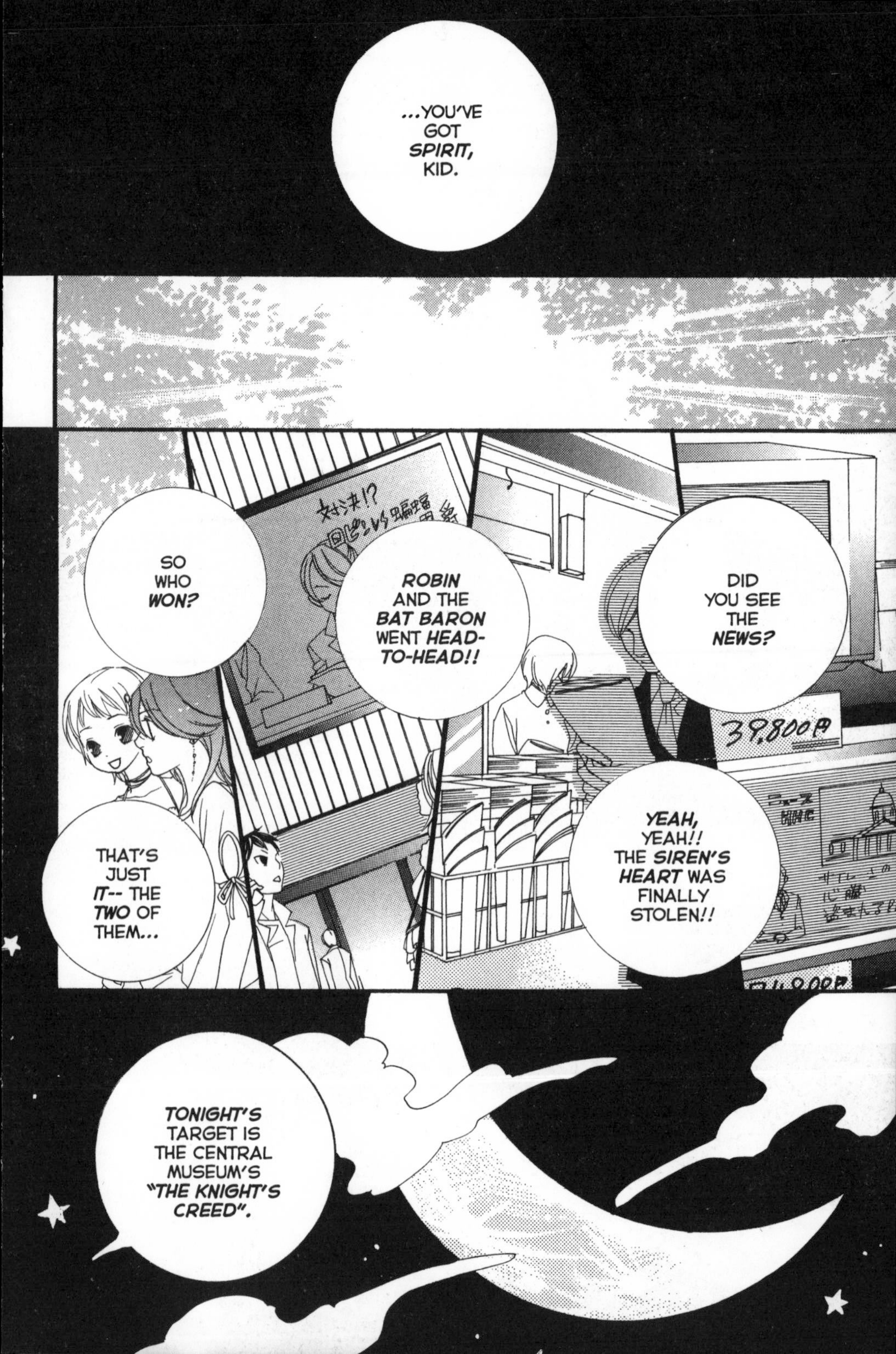
...YOU'VE GOT SPIRIT, KID.
DID YOU SEE THE NEWS?
39,800円
YEAH, YEAH!! THE SIREN'S HEART WAS FINALLY STOLEN!!
ROBIN AND THE BAT BARON WENT HEAD-TO-HEAD!!
SO WHO WON?
THAT'S JUST IT-- THE TWO OF THEM...
TONIGHT'S TARGET IS THE CENTRAL MUSEUM'S "THE KNIGHT'S CREED".

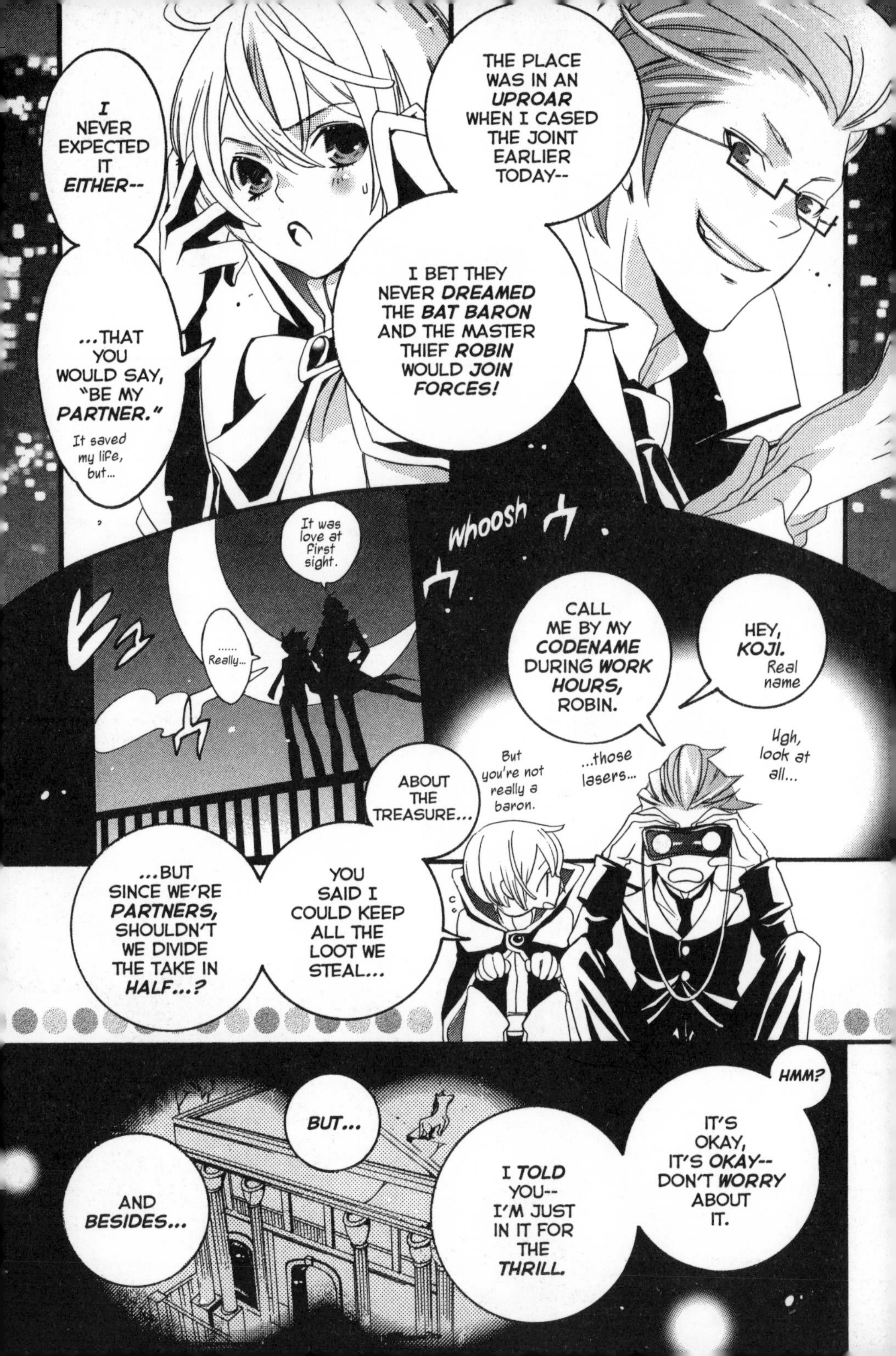
THE PLACE WAS IN AN UPROAR WHEN I CASED THE JOINT EARLIER TODAY--
I BET THEY NEVER DREAMED THE BAT BARON AND THE MASTER THIEF ROBIN WOULD JOIN FORCES!
I NEVER EXPECTED IT EITHER--
...THAT YOU WOULD SAY, "BE MY PARTNER."
It saved my life, but...
Whoosh
HEY, KOJI.
Real name
CALL ME BY MY CODENAME DURING WORK HOURS, ROBIN.
Ugh, look at all...
...those lasers...
But you're not really a baron.
ABOUT THE TREASURE...
YOU SAID I COULD KEEP ALL THE LOOT WE STEAL...
...BUT SINCE WE'RE PARTNERS, SHOULDN'T WE DIVIDE THE TAKE IN HALF...?
It was love at first sight.
......Really...
HMM?
IT'S OKAY, IT'S OKAY-- DON'T WORRY ABOUT IT.
I TOLD YOU-- I'M JUST IN IT FOR THE THRILL.
BUT...
AND BESIDES...

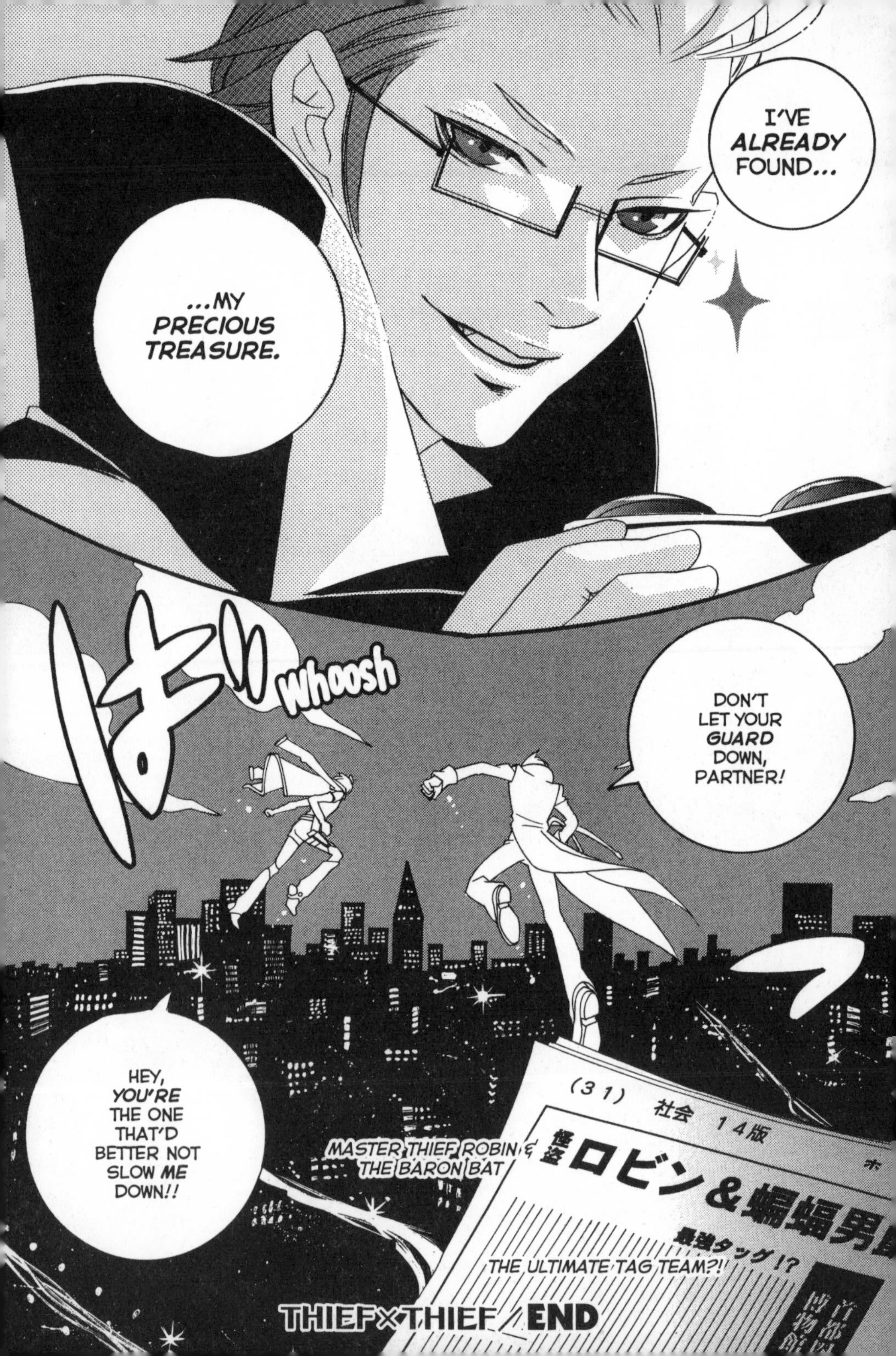
I'VE ALREADY FOUND...
...MY PRECIOUS TREASURE.
DON'T LET YOUR GUARD DOWN, PARTNER!
Whoosh
HEY, YOU'RE THE ONE THAT'D BETTER NOT SLOW ME DOWN!!
(31) 社会 14版
怪盗ロビン＆蝙蝠男
MASTER THIEF ROBIN & THE BARON BAT
最強タッグ!?
THE ULTIMATE TAG TEAM?!
THIEF×THIEF / END

HOMERUN KEN PRESENTS

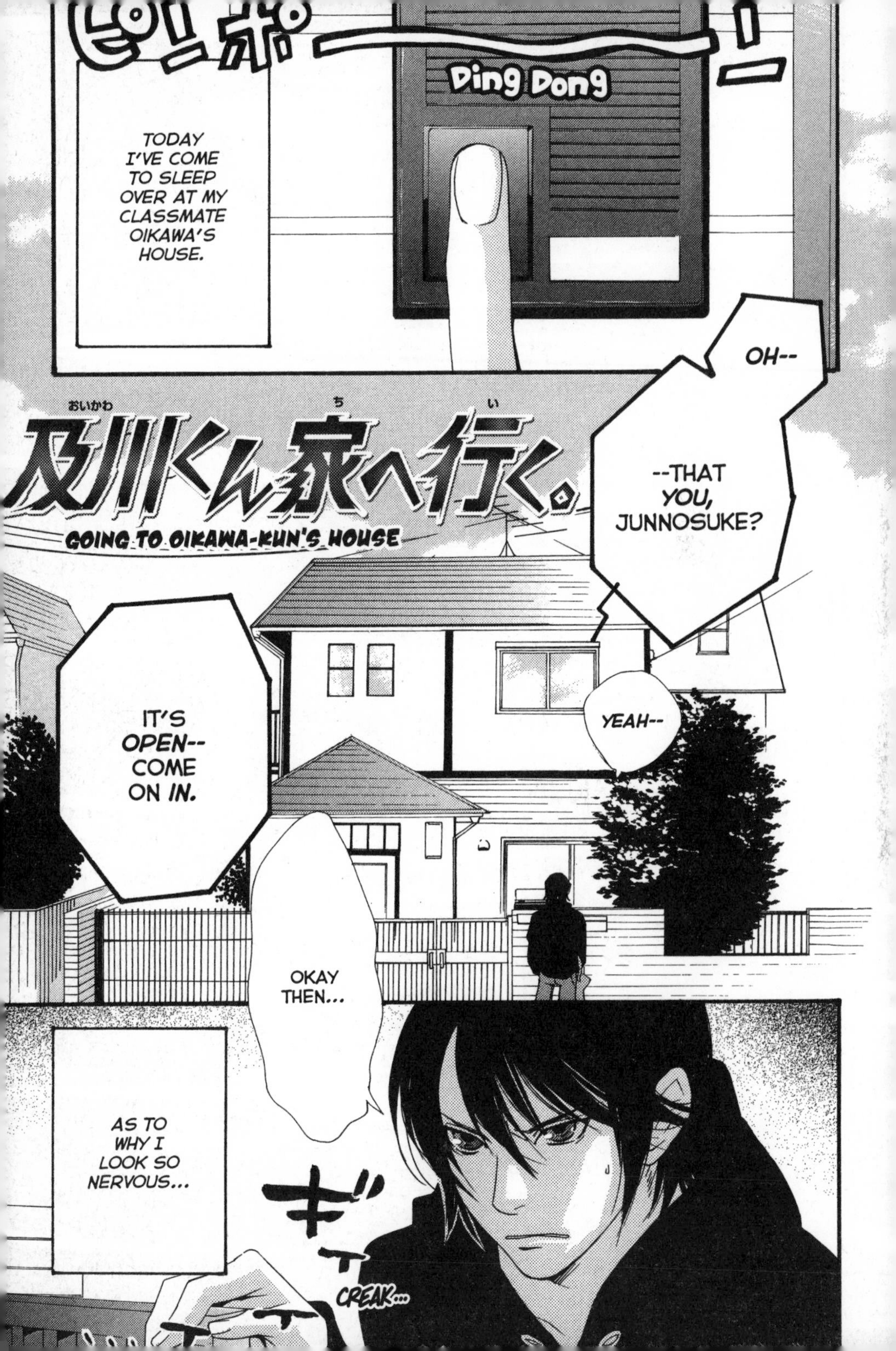
Ding Dong
TODAY I'VE COME TO SLEEP OVER AT MY CLASSMATE OIKAWA'S HOUSE.
及川くん家へ行く。
GOING TO OIKAWA-KUN'S HOUSE
OH--
--THAT YOU, JUNNOSUKE?
YEAH--
IT'S OPEN-- COME ON IN.
OKAY THEN...
AS TO WHY I LOOK SO NERVOUS...
CREAK...

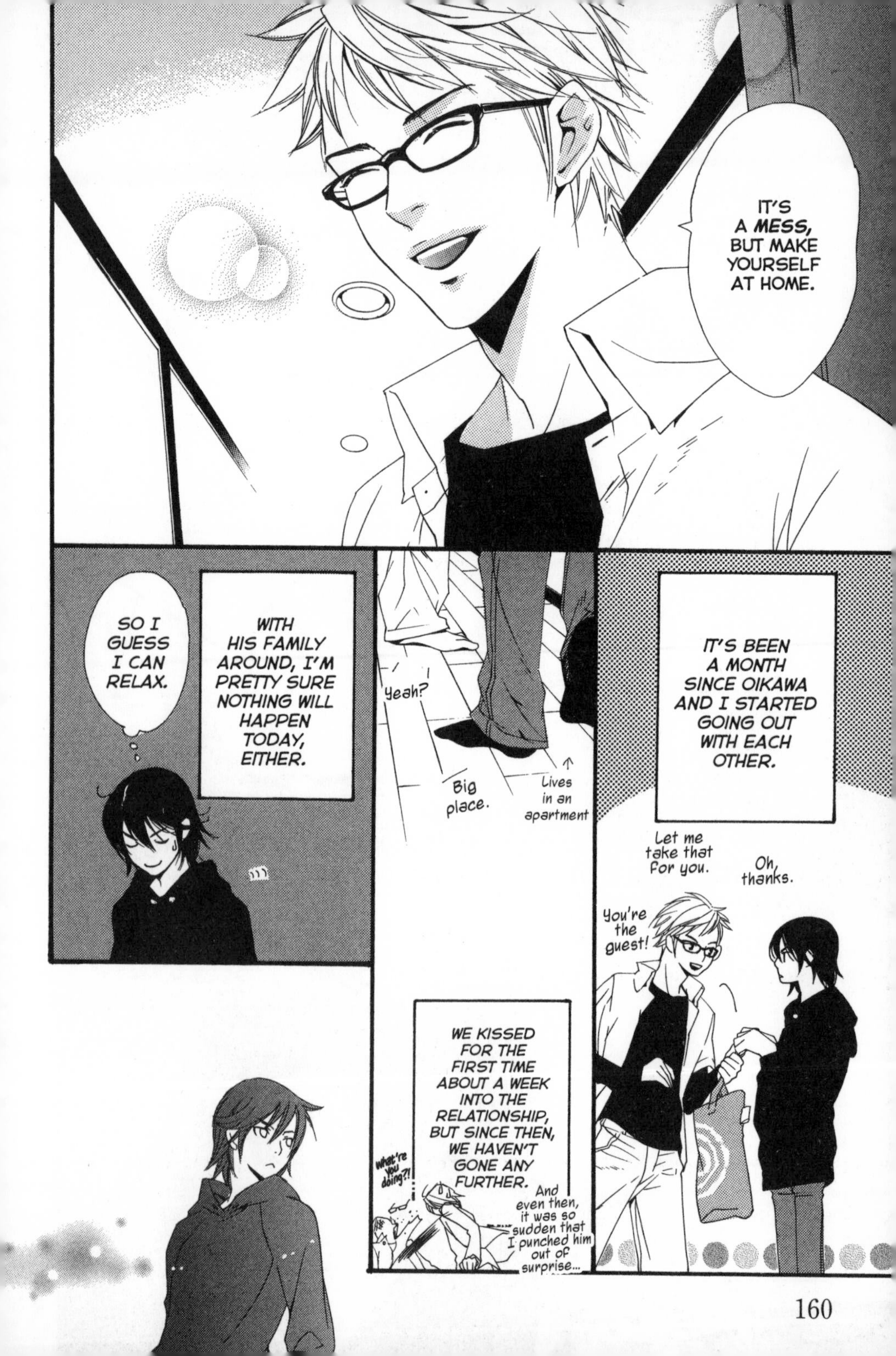
IT'S A MESS, BUT MAKE YOURSELF AT HOME.
IT'S BEEN A MONTH SINCE OIKAWA AND I STARTED GOING OUT WITH EACH OTHER.
Let me take that for you.
Oh, thanks.
You're the guest!
Yeah?
Big place.
Lives in an apartment
WE KISSED FOR THE FIRST TIME ABOUT A WEEK INTO THE RELATIONSHIP, BUT SINCE THEN, WE HAVEN'T GONE ANY FURTHER.
what're you doing?!
And even then, it was so sudden that I punched him out of surprise...
WITH HIS FAMILY AROUND, I'M PRETTY SURE NOTHING WILL HAPPEN TODAY, EITHER.
SO I GUESS I CAN RELAX.

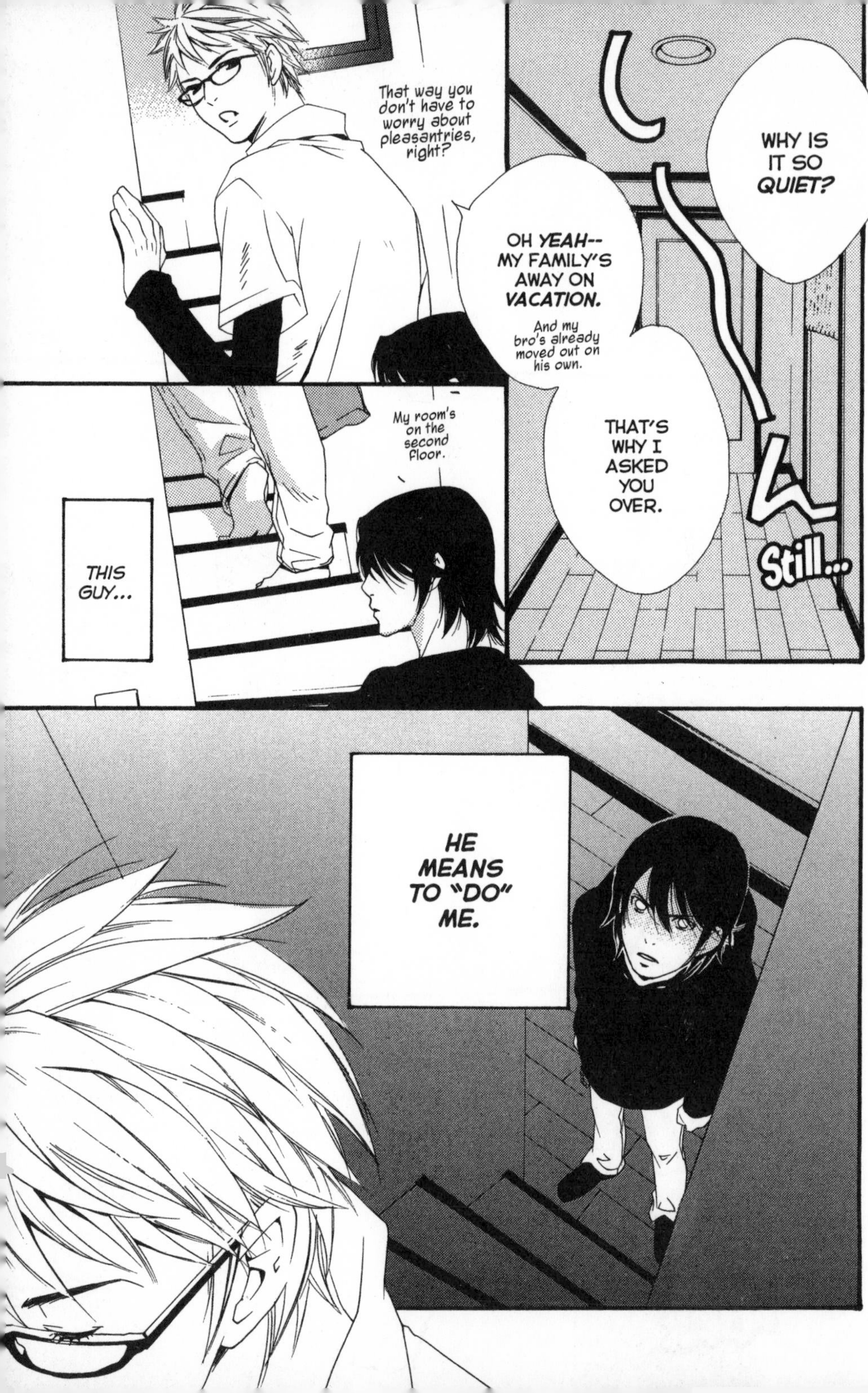

WHY IS IT SO QUIET?
しーん
Still...
OH YEAH-- MY FAMILY'S AWAY ON VACATION.
And my bro's already moved out on his own.
THAT'S WHY I ASKED YOU OVER.
That way you don't have to worry about pleasantries, right?
My room's on the second floor.
THIS GUY...
HE MEANS TO "DO" ME.

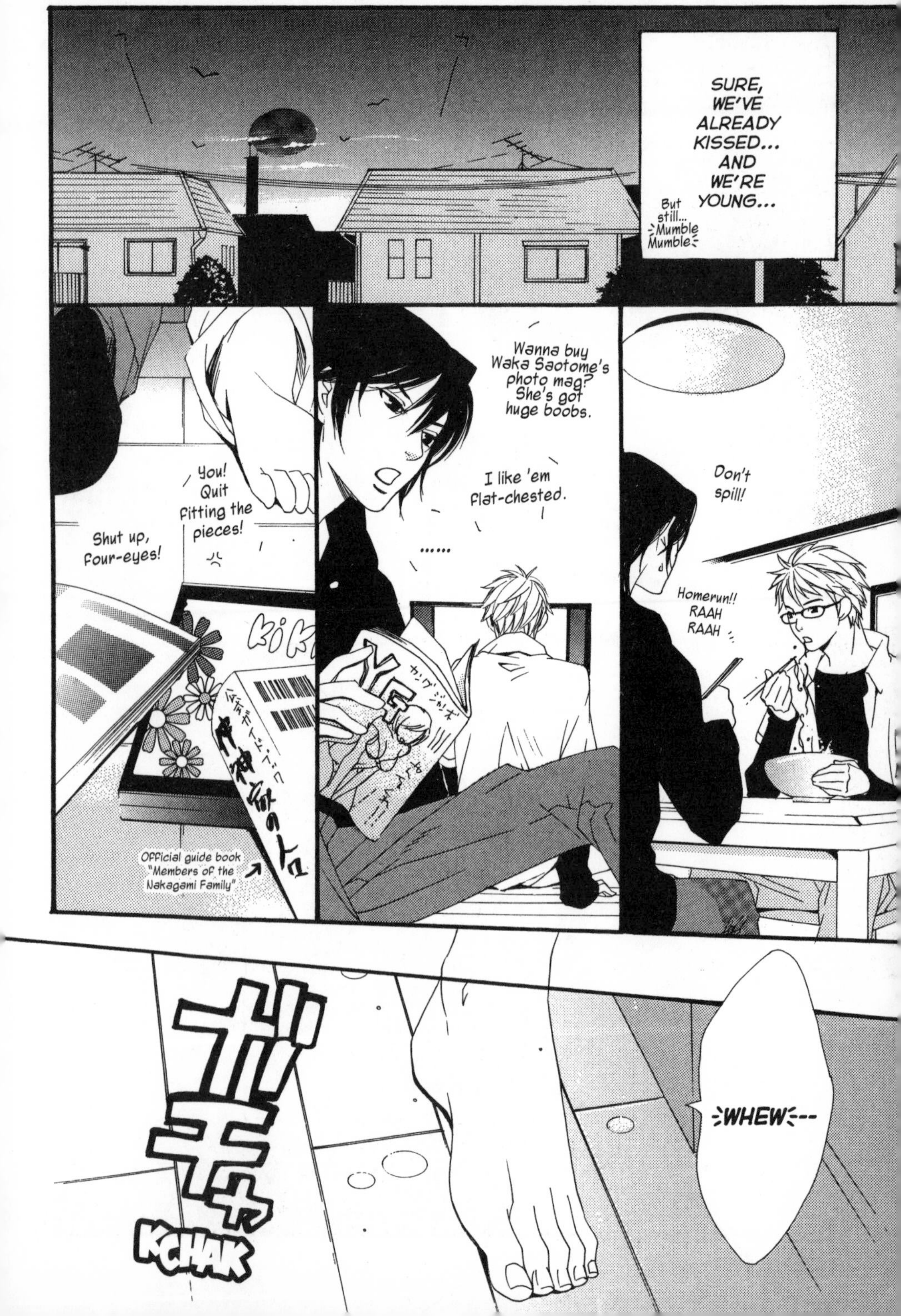
SURE, WE'VE ALREADY KISSED... AND WE'RE YOUNG...
But still... Mumble Mumble
Don't spill!
Homerun!! RAAH RAAH
Wanna buy Waka Saotome's photo mag? She's got huge boobs.
I like 'em flat-chested.
......
You! Quit fitting the pieces!
Shut up, four-eyes!
Official guide book "Members of the Nakagami Family"
WHEW---
KCHAK

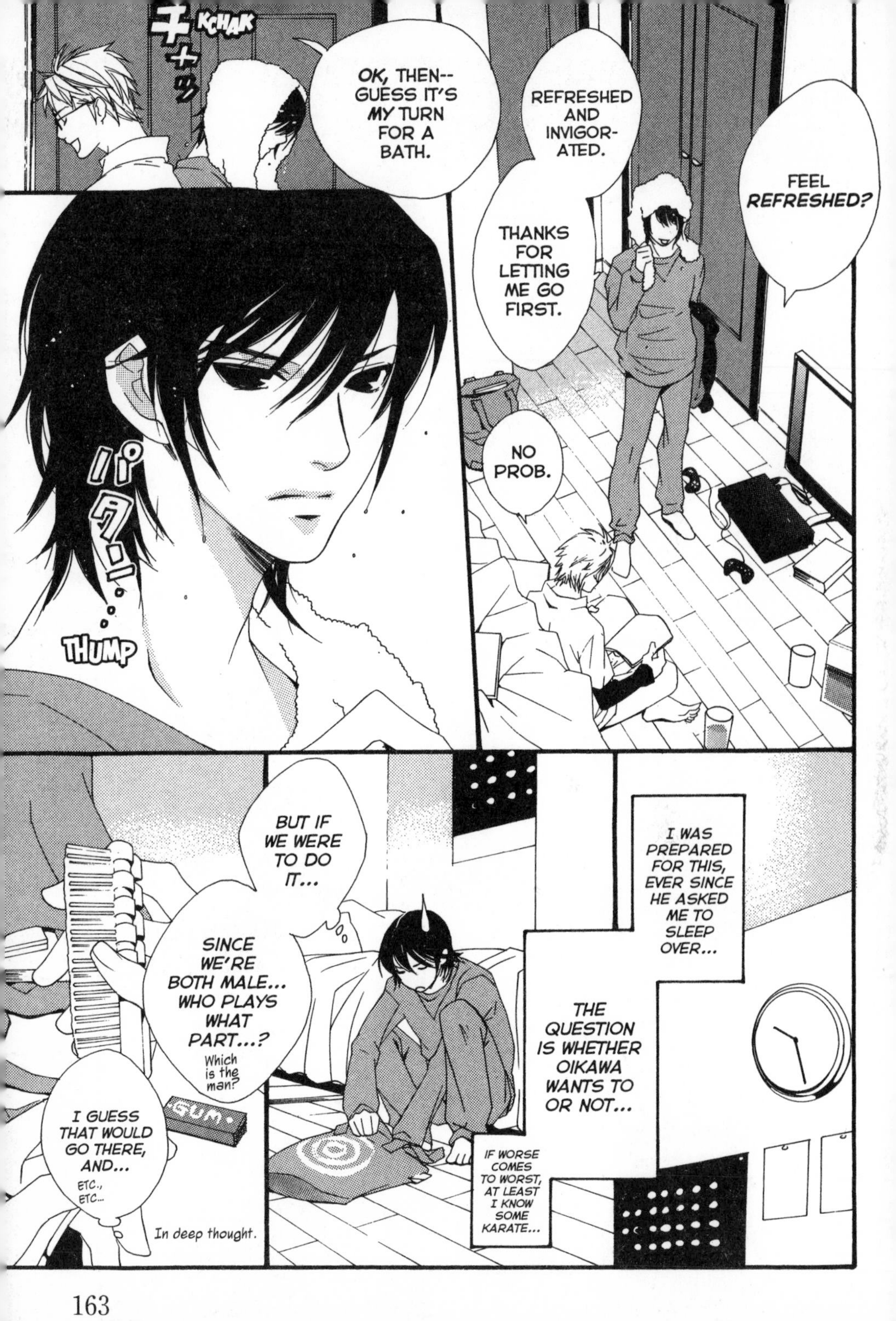
FEEL REFRESHED?
REFRESHED AND INVIGORATED.
THANKS FOR LETTING ME GO FIRST.
NO PROB.
KCHAK
OK, THEN-- GUESS IT'S MY TURN FOR A BATH.
THUMP
I WAS PREPARED FOR THIS, EVER SINCE HE ASKED ME TO SLEEP OVER...
THE QUESTION IS WHETHER OIKAWA WANTS TO OR NOT...
IF WORSE COMES TO WORST, AT LEAST I KNOW SOME KARATE...
BUT IF WE WERE TO DO IT...
SINCE WE'RE BOTH MALE... WHO PLAYS WHAT PART...?
Which is the man?
GUM
I GUESS THAT WOULD GO THERE, AND...
ETC., ETC...
In deep thought.

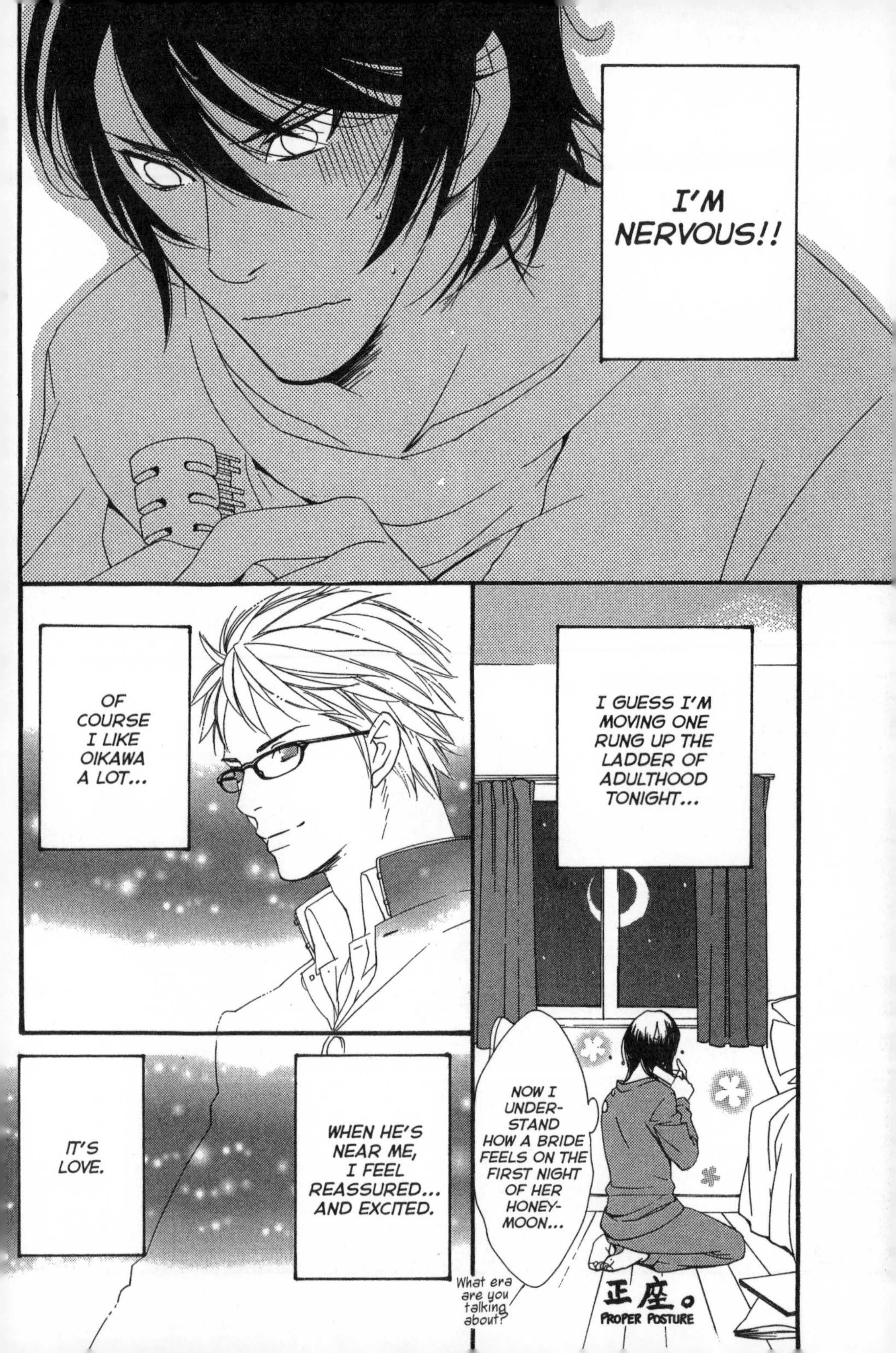
I'M NERVOUS!!
I GUESS I'M MOVING ONE RUNG UP THE LADDER OF ADULTHOOD TONIGHT...
NOW I UNDERSTAND HOW A BRIDE FEELS ON THE FIRST NIGHT OF HER HONEYMOON...
What era are you talking about?
正座。
PROPER POSTURE
OF COURSE I LIKE OIKAWA A LOT...
WHEN HE'S NEAR ME, I FEEL REASSURED... AND EXCITED.
IT'S LOVE.

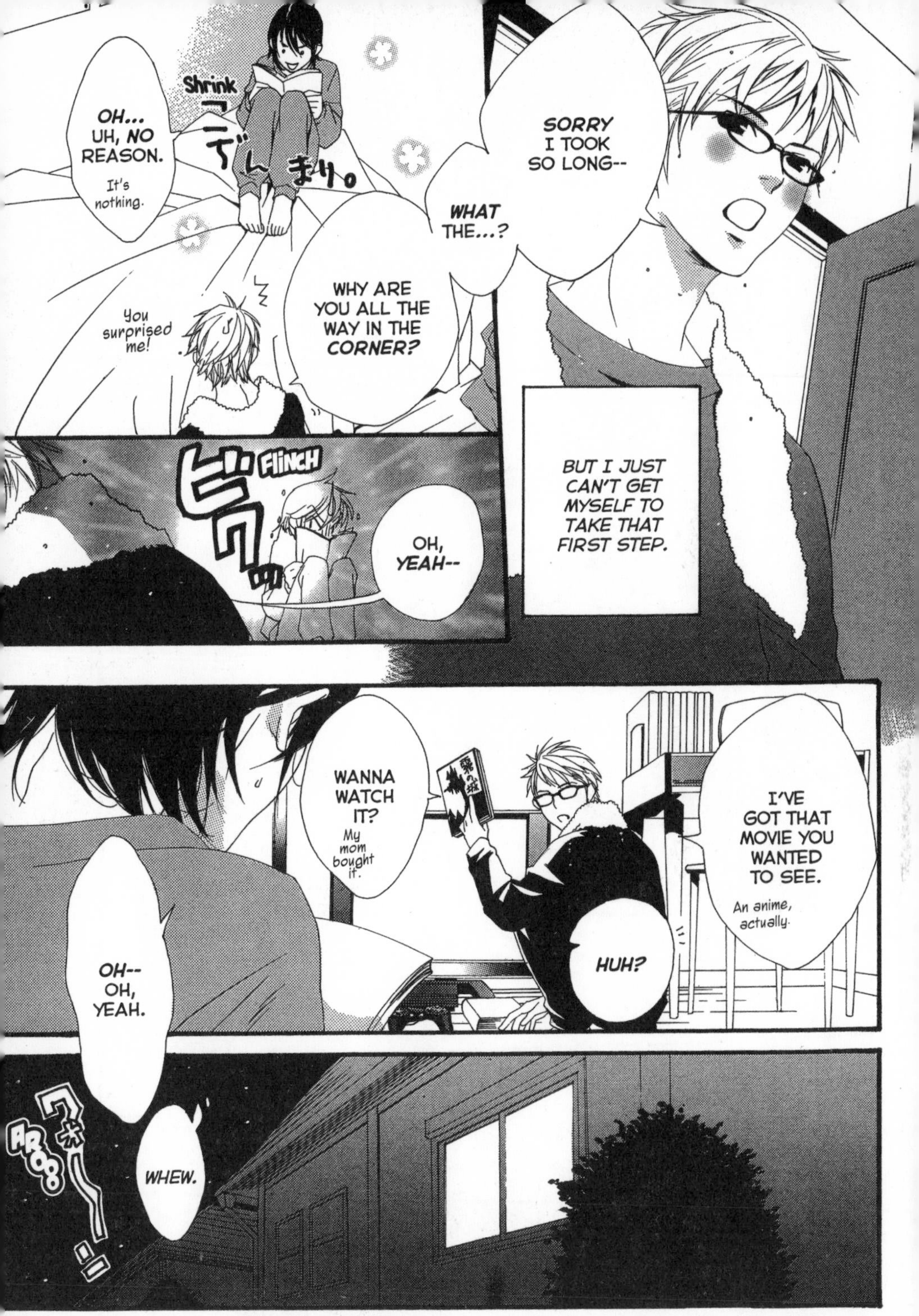
SORRY I TOOK SO LONG--
WHAT THE...?
WHY ARE YOU ALL THE WAY IN THE CORNER?
You surprised me!
Shrink
OH... UH, NO REASON.
It's nothing.
BUT I JUST CAN'T GET MYSELF TO TAKE THAT FIRST STEP.
FLINCH
OH, YEAH--
I'VE GOT THAT MOVIE YOU WANTED TO SEE.
An anime, actually.
HUH?
WANNA WATCH IT?
My mom bought it.
OH-- OH, YEAH.
WHEW.
AROO

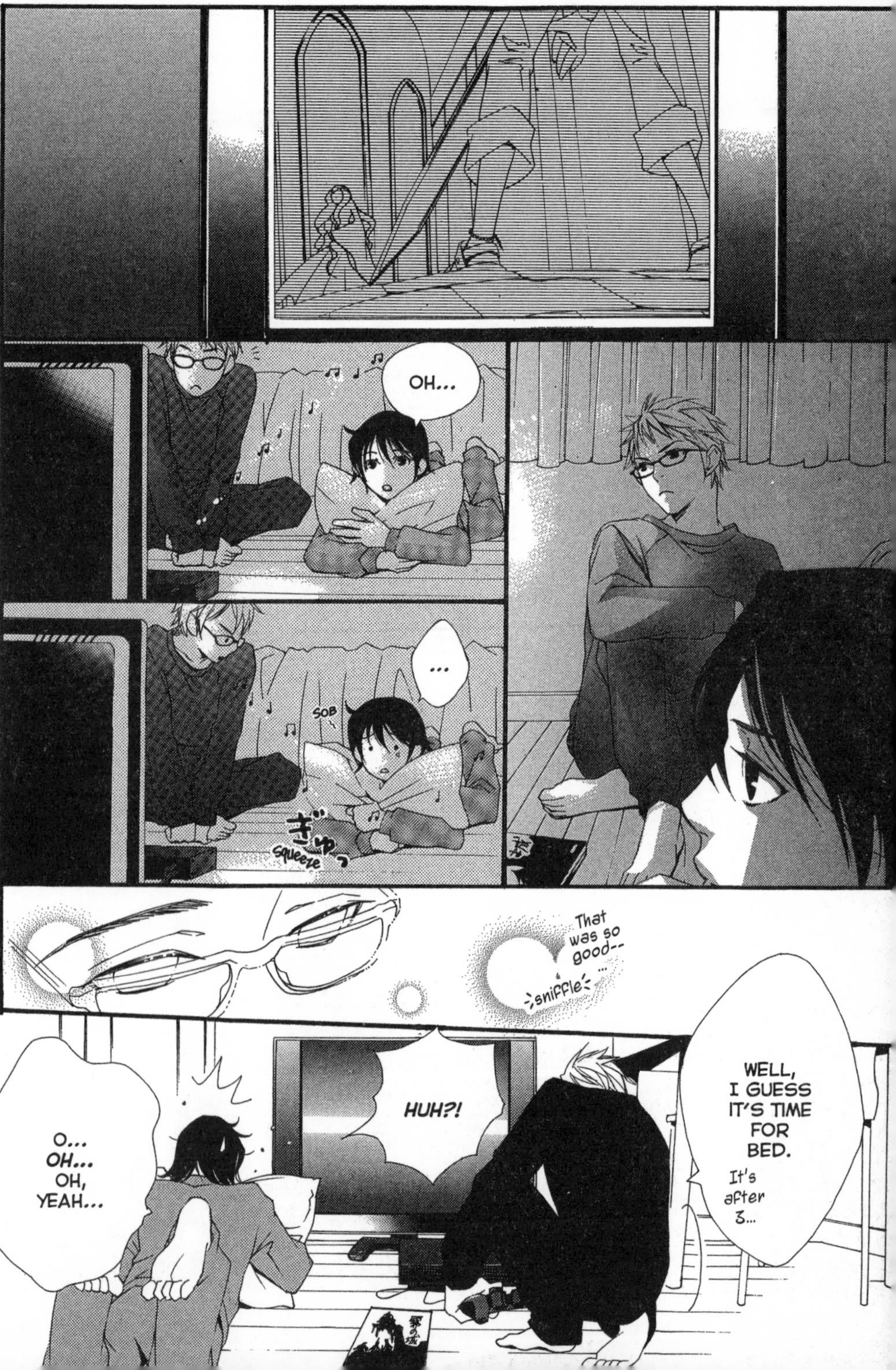
OH...
SOB
...
ぎゅっ
squeeze
That was so good-- ...
sniffle
WELL, I GUESS IT'S TIME FOR BED.
It's after 3...
HUH?!
O... OH... OH, YEAH...

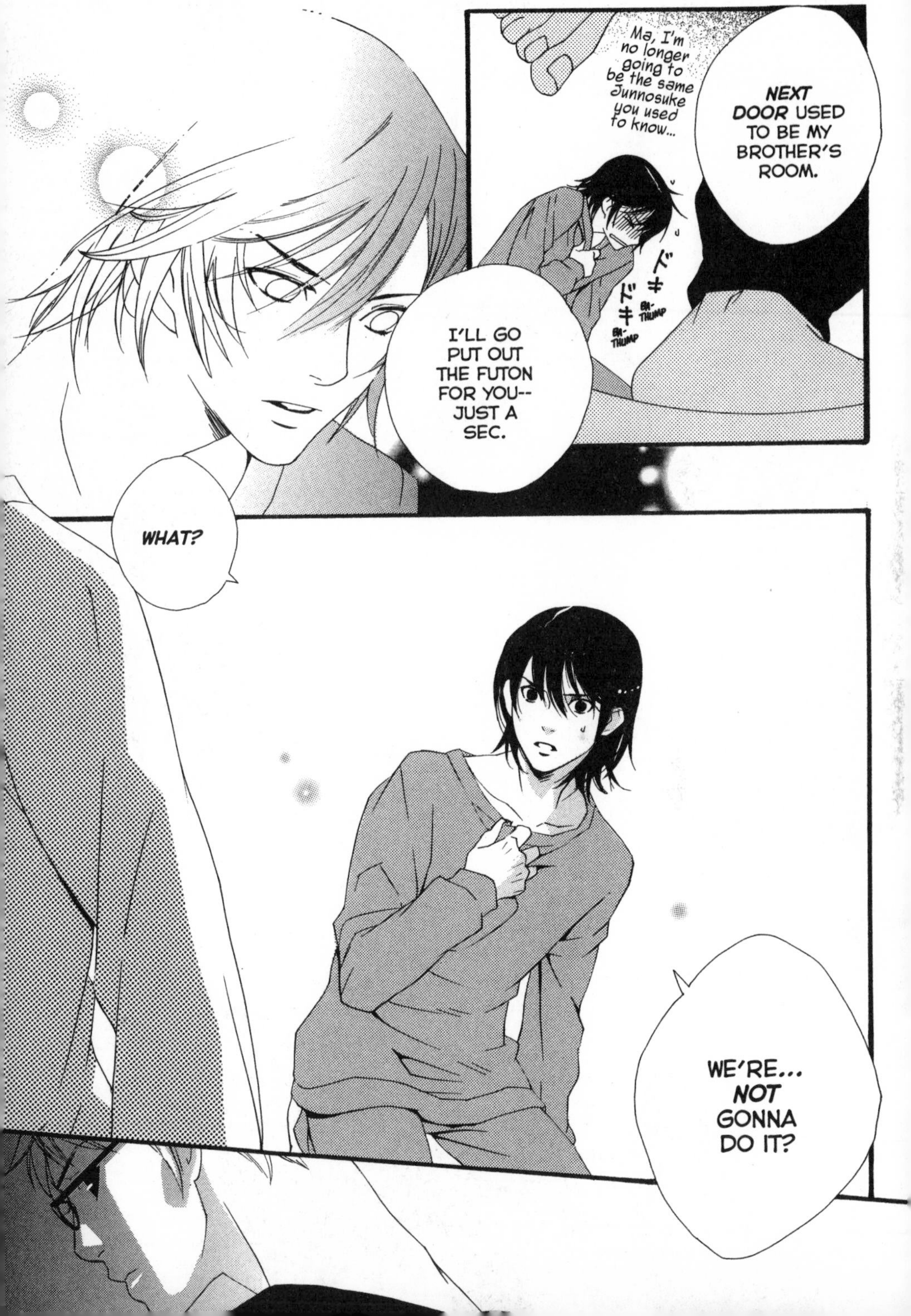
NEXT DOOR USED TO BE MY BROTHER'S ROOM.
Ma, I'm no longer going to be the same Junnosuke you used to know...
ドキドキ
BA-THUMP BA-THUMP
I'LL GO PUT OUT THE FUTON FOR YOU-- JUST A SEC.
WHAT?
WE'RE... NOT GONNA DO IT?

<NOTE: IN JAPANESE, THE "JUN" IN JUNNOSUKE MEANS "PURE, INNOCENT, NAÏVE".>

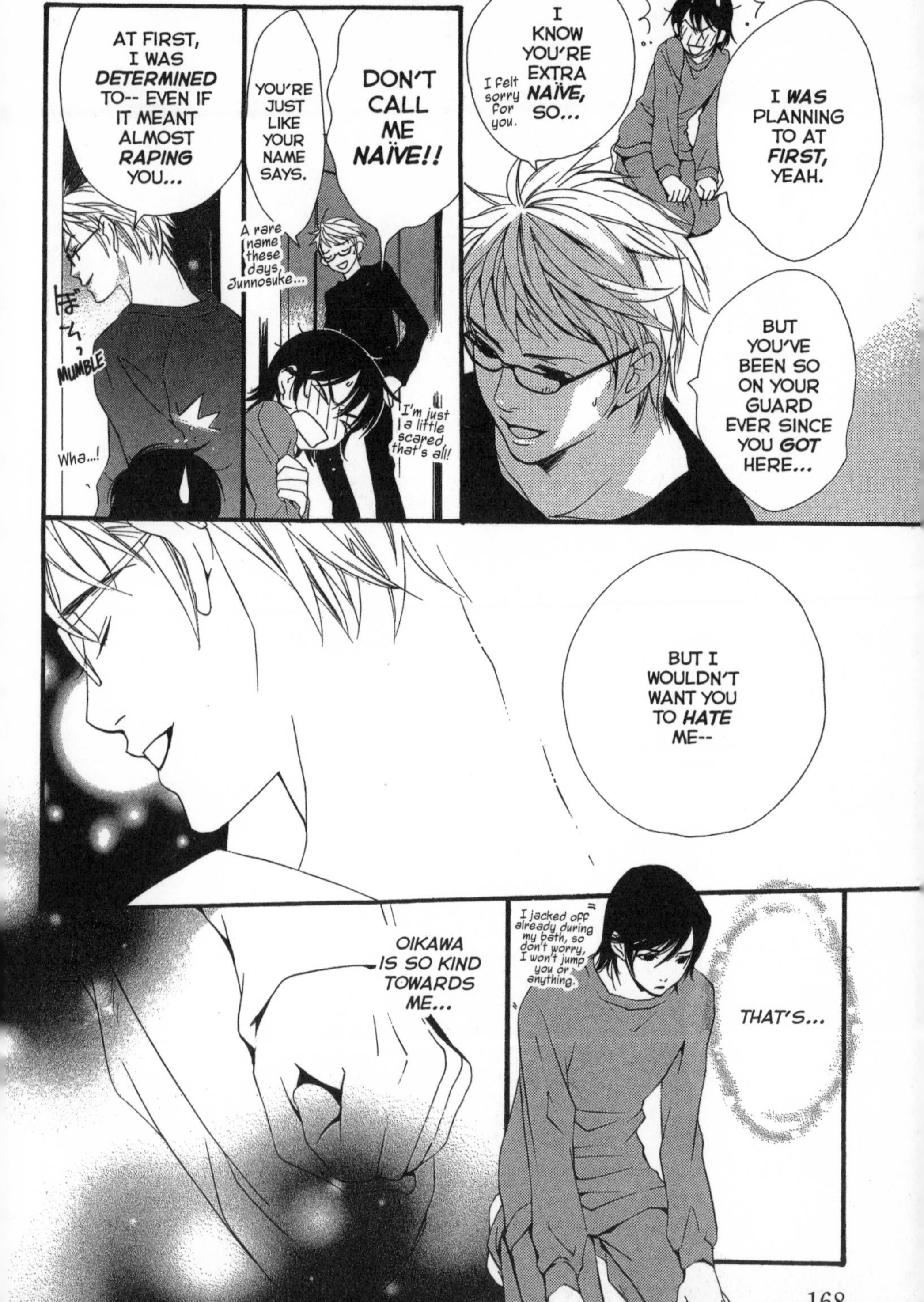

I WAS PLANNING TO AT FIRST, YEAH.
I KNOW YOU'RE EXTRA NAÏVE, SO...
I felt sorry for you.
BUT YOU'VE BEEN SO ON YOUR GUARD EVER SINCE YOU GOT HERE...
DON'T CALL ME NAÏVE!!
YOU'RE JUST LIKE YOUR NAME SAYS.
A rare name these days, Junnosuke...
I'm just a little scared that's all!
AT FIRST, I WAS DETERMINED TO-- EVEN IF IT MEANT ALMOST RAPING YOU...
ぼそ
MUMBLE
Wha...!
BUT I WOULDN'T WANT YOU TO HATE ME--
THAT'S...
I jacked off already during my bath, so don't worry, I won't jump you or anything.
OIKAWA IS SO KIND TOWARDS ME...

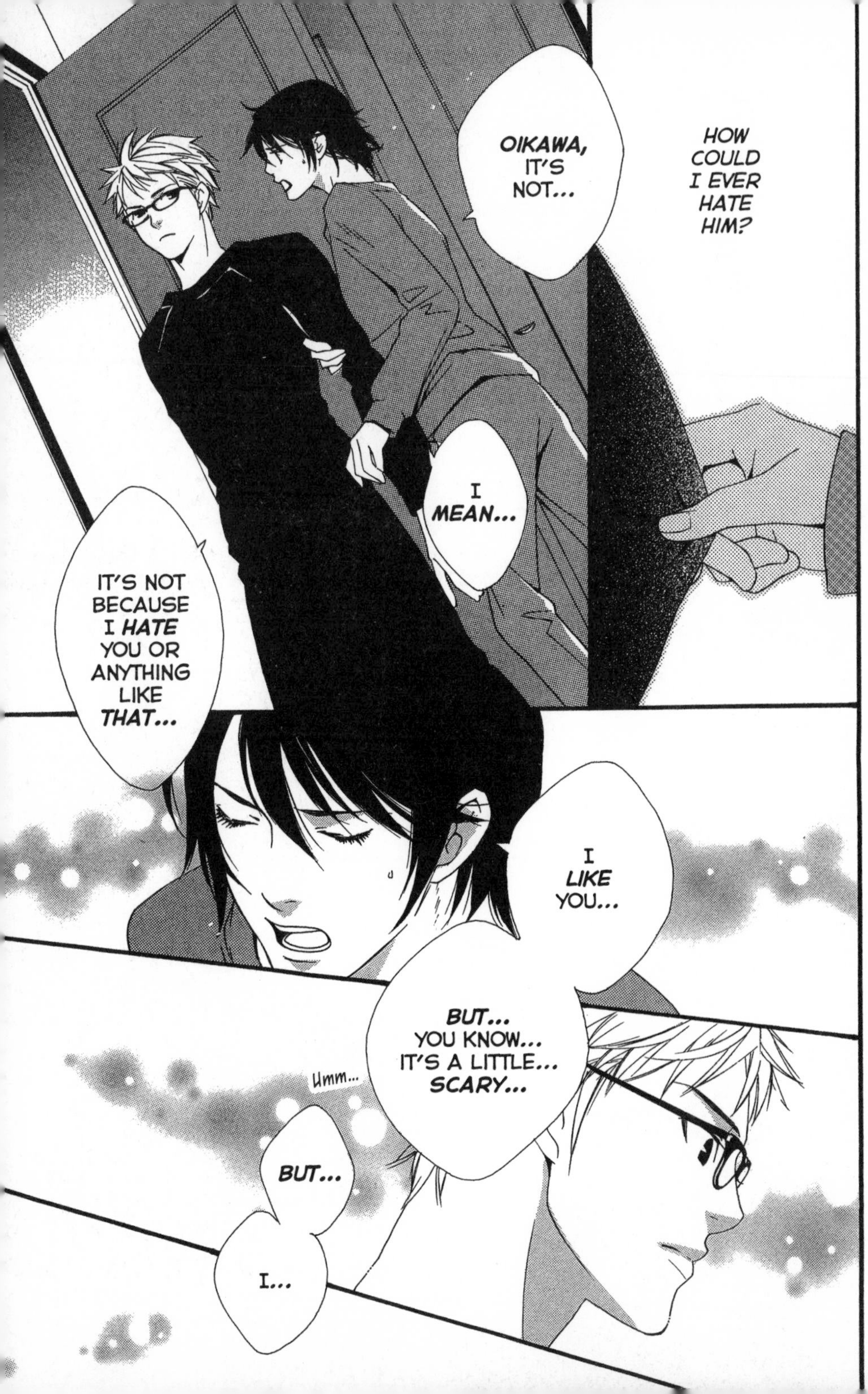
HOW COULD I EVER HATE HIM?
OIKAWA, IT'S NOT...
I MEAN...
IT'S NOT BECAUSE I HATE YOU OR ANYTHING LIKE THAT...
I LIKE YOU...
BUT... YOU KNOW... IT'S A LITTLE... SCARY...
Umm...
BUT...
I...

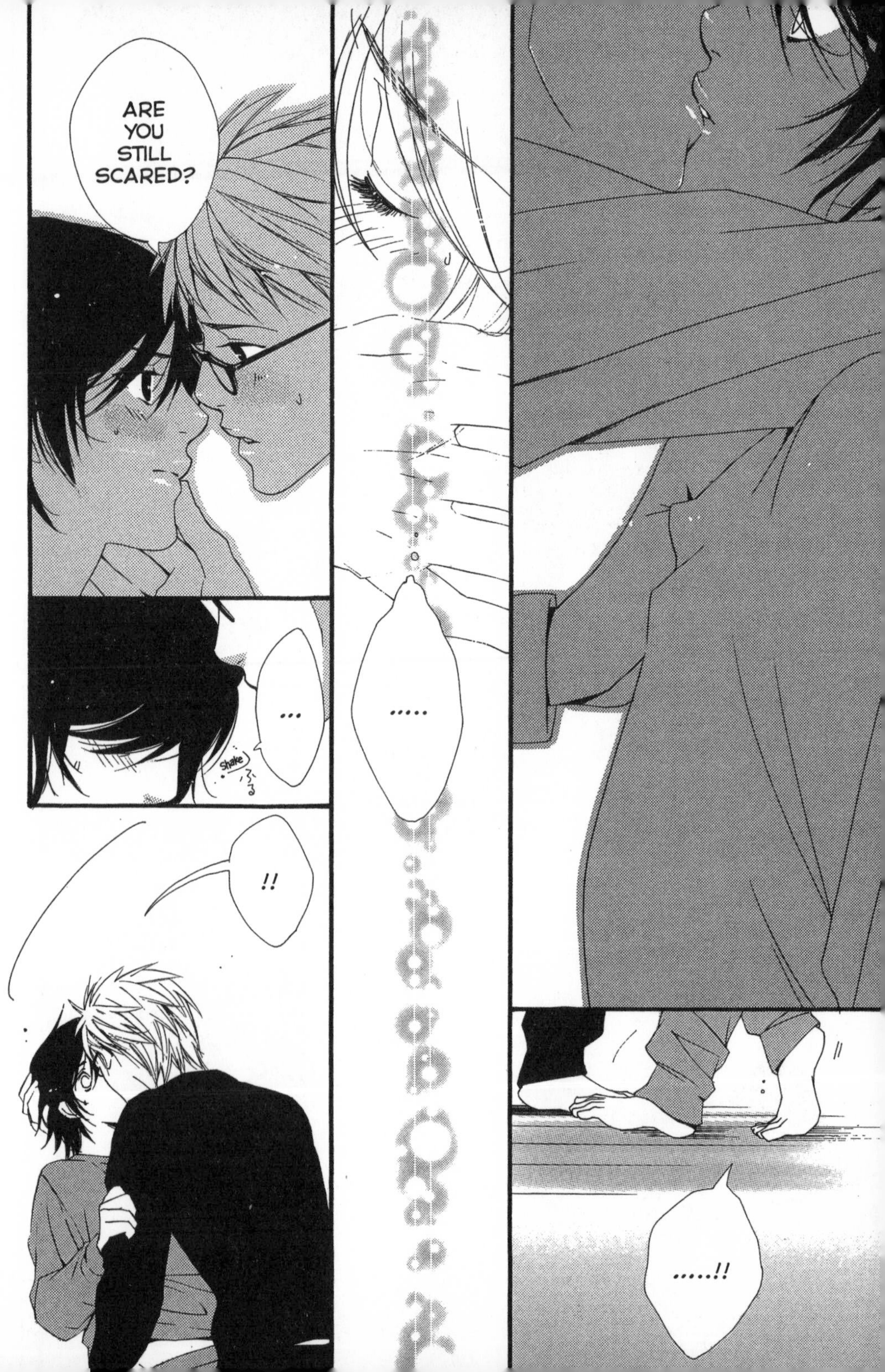
!!
.....!!
.....
ARE YOU STILL SCARED?
...
Shake
ふる
!!

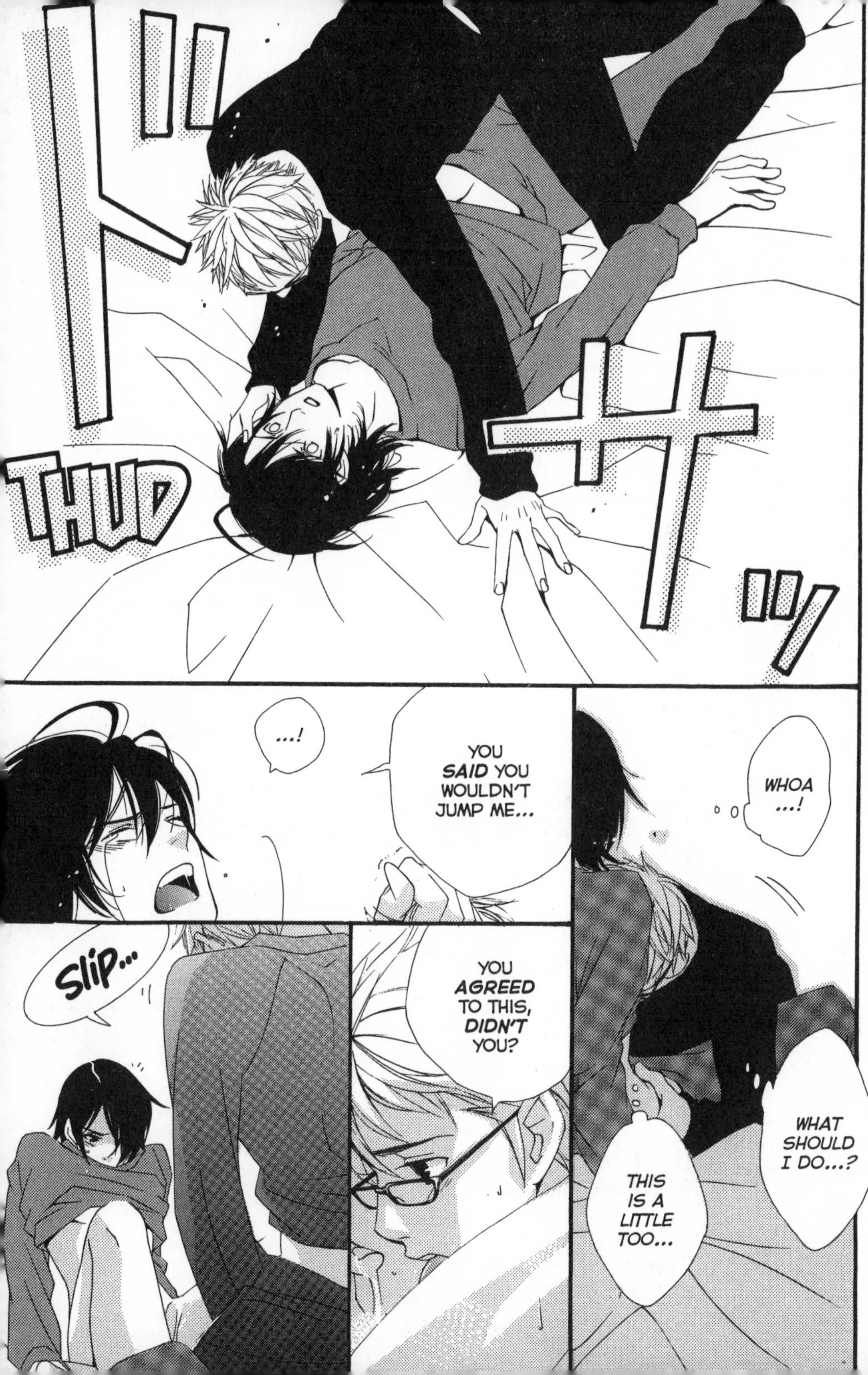
ドサッ
THUD
WHOA ...!
WHAT SHOULD I DO...?
THIS IS A LITTLE TOO...
YOU SAID YOU WOULDN'T JUMP ME...
...!
YOU AGREED TO THIS, DIDN'T YOU?
Slip...

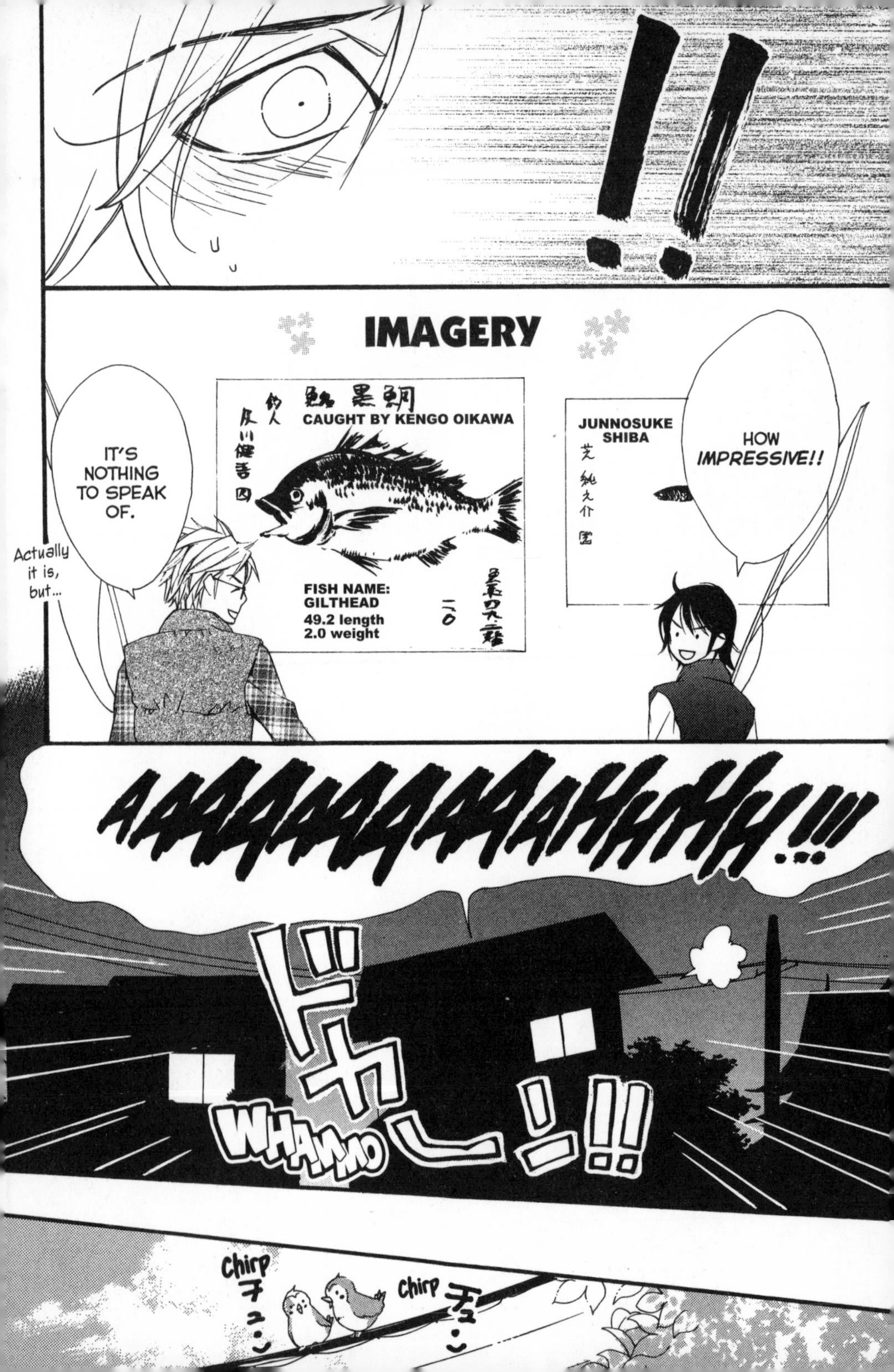
!!
IMAGERY
JUNNOSUKE SHIBA
HOW IMPRESSIVE!!
CAUGHT BY KENGO OIKAWA
FISH NAME: GILTHEAD
49.2 length
2.0 weight
IT'S NOTHING TO SPEAK OF.
Actually it is, but...
AAAAAAAAAAAAAHHHHH!!!
ドカ――ン!!
WHAMMO
Chirp
チュン
Chirp
チュン

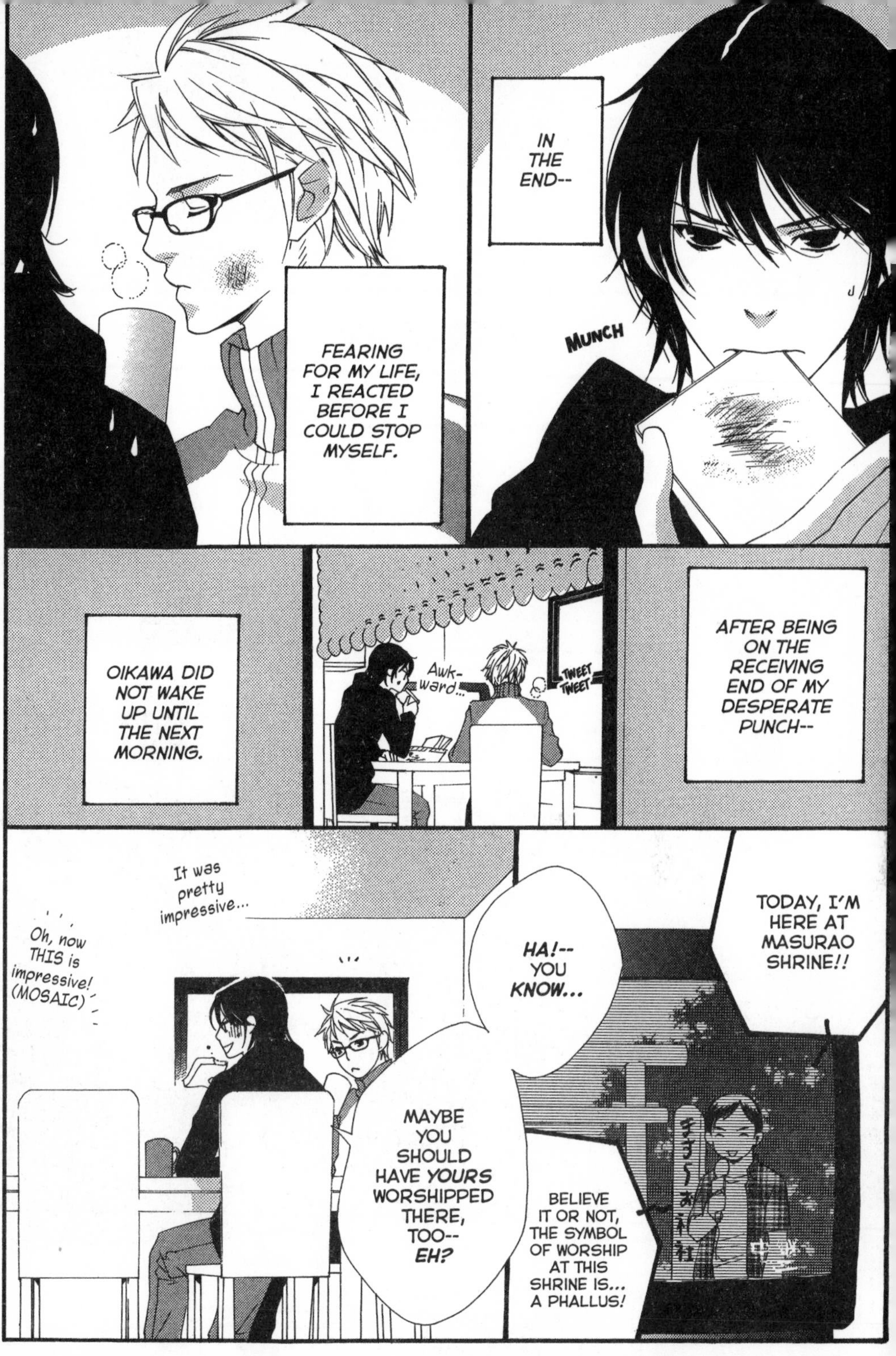
IN THE END--
MUNCH
FEARING FOR MY LIFE, I REACTED BEFORE I COULD STOP MYSELF.
AFTER BEING ON THE RECEIVING END OF MY DESPERATE PUNCH--
TWEET TWEET
Awk-ward...
OIKAWA DID NOT WAKE UP UNTIL THE NEXT MORNING.
TODAY, I'M HERE AT MASURAO SHRINE!!
BELIEVE IT OR NOT, THE SYMBOL OF WORSHIP AT THIS SHRINE IS... A PHALLUS!
HA!-- YOU KNOW...
MAYBE YOU SHOULD HAVE YOURS WORSHIPPED THERE, TOO-- EH?
It was pretty impressive...
Oh, now THIS is impressive! (MOSAIC)

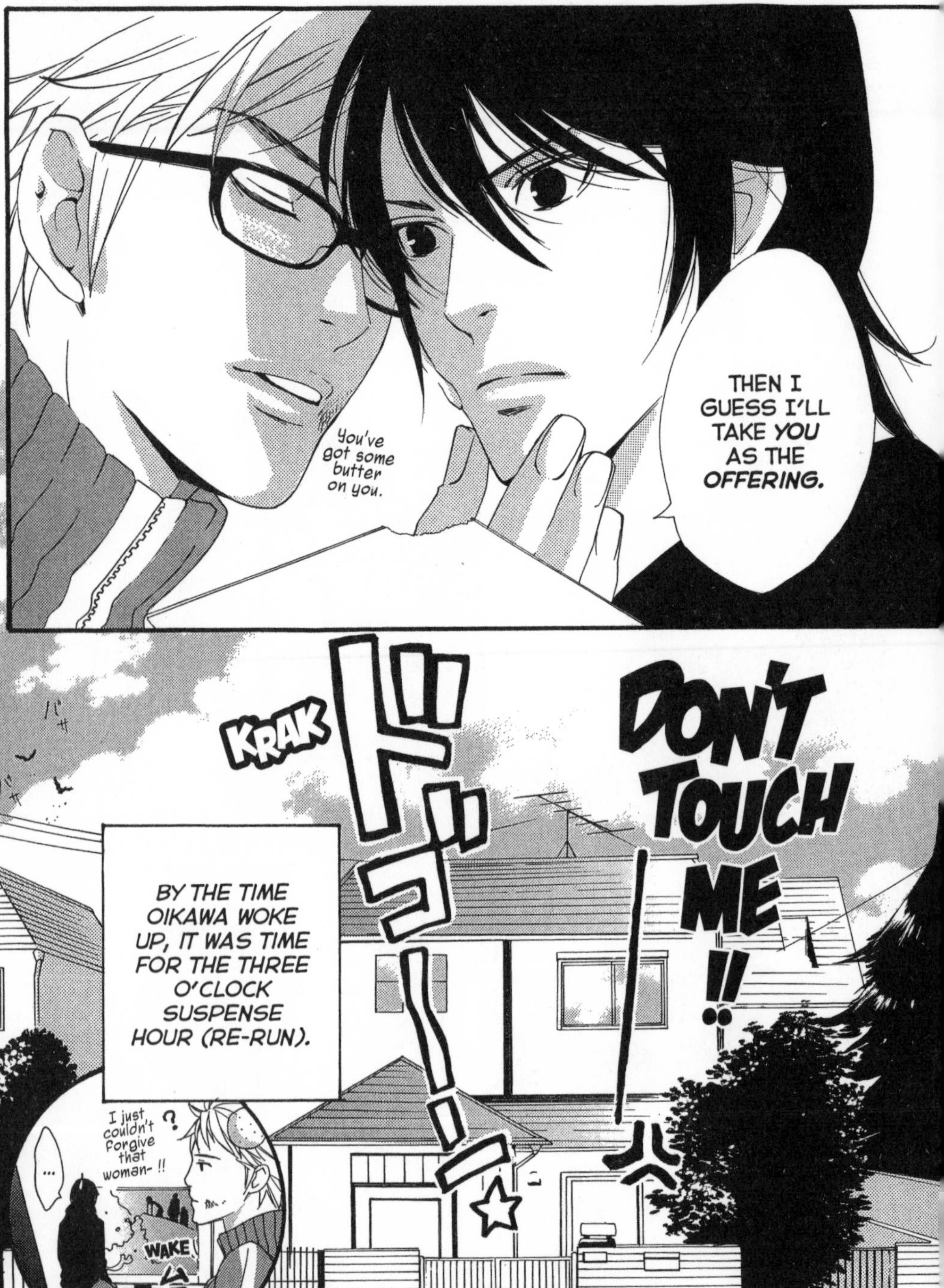
THEN I GUESS I'LL TAKE *YOU* AS THE *OFFERING.*
You've got some butter on you.
DON'T TOUCH ME!!
KRAK
BY THE TIME OIKAWA WOKE UP, IT WAS TIME FOR THE THREE O'CLOCK SUSPENSE HOUR (RE-RUN).
I just couldn't forgive that woman- !!
...
WAKE

GOING TO OIKAWA-KUN'S HOUSE / END

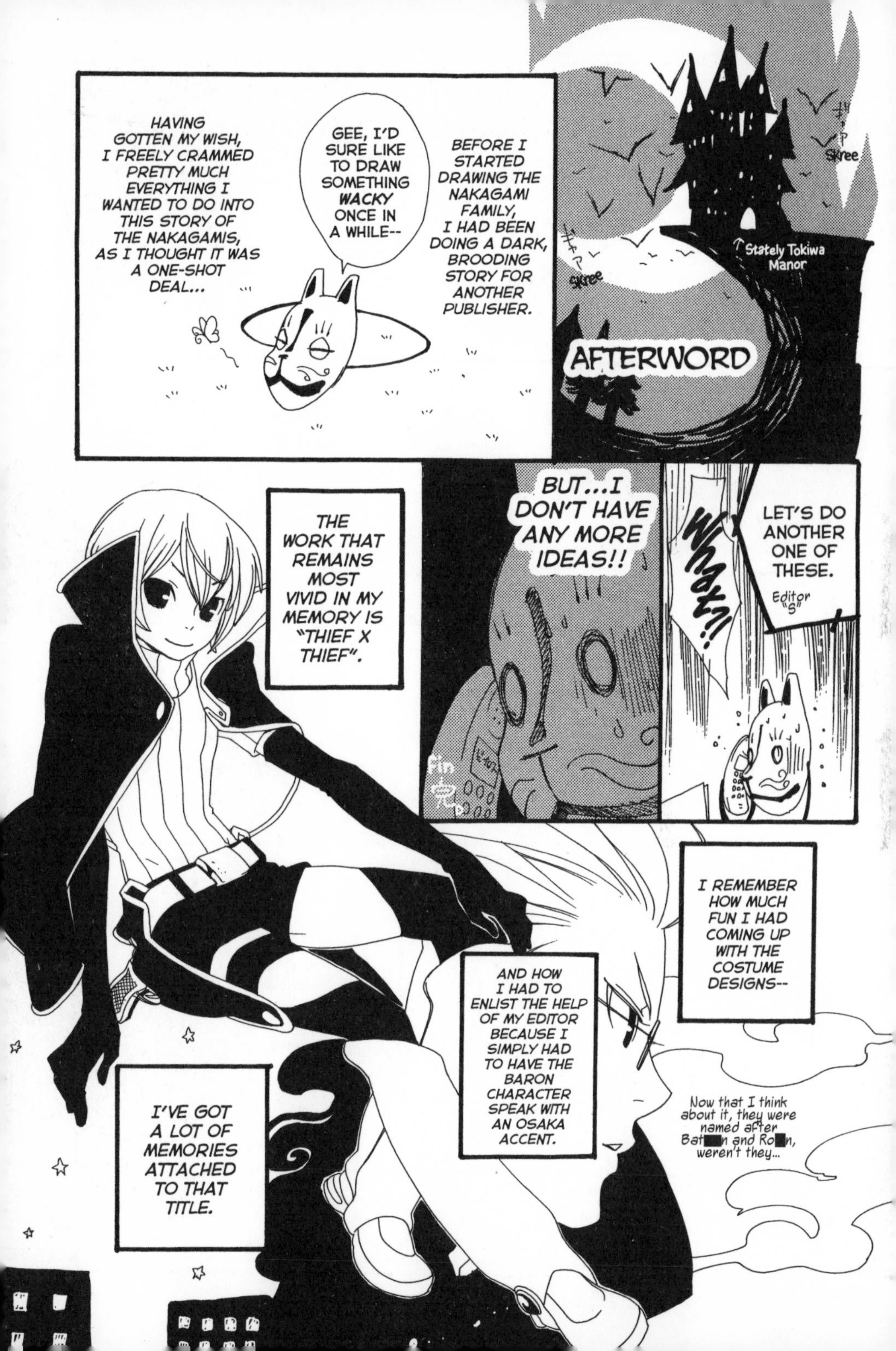

AFTERWORD
Skree
Stately Tokiwa Manor
Skree
BEFORE I STARTED DRAWING THE NAKAGAMI FAMILY, I HAD BEEN DOING A DARK, BROODING STORY FOR ANOTHER PUBLISHER.
GEE, I'D SURE LIKE TO DRAW SOMETHING WACKY ONCE IN A WHILE--
HAVING GOTTEN MY WISH, I FREELY CRAMMED PRETTY MUCH EVERYTHING I WANTED TO DO INTO THIS STORY OF THE NAKAGAMIS, AS I THOUGHT IT WAS A ONE-SHOT DEAL...
LET'S DO ANOTHER ONE OF THESE.
Editor "S"
WHAT?!!
BUT...I DON'T HAVE ANY MORE IDEAS!!
Fin
THE WORK THAT REMAINS MOST VIVID IN MY MEMORY IS "THIEF X THIEF".
I REMEMBER HOW MUCH FUN I HAD COMING UP WITH THE COSTUME DESIGNS--
AND HOW I HAD TO ENLIST THE HELP OF MY EDITOR BECAUSE I SIMPLY HAD TO HAVE THE BARON CHARACTER SPEAK WITH AN OSAKA ACCENT.
Now that I think about it, they were named after Bat[redacted]n and Ro[redacted]n, weren't they...
I'VE GOT A LOT OF MEMORIES ATTACHED TO THAT TITLE.

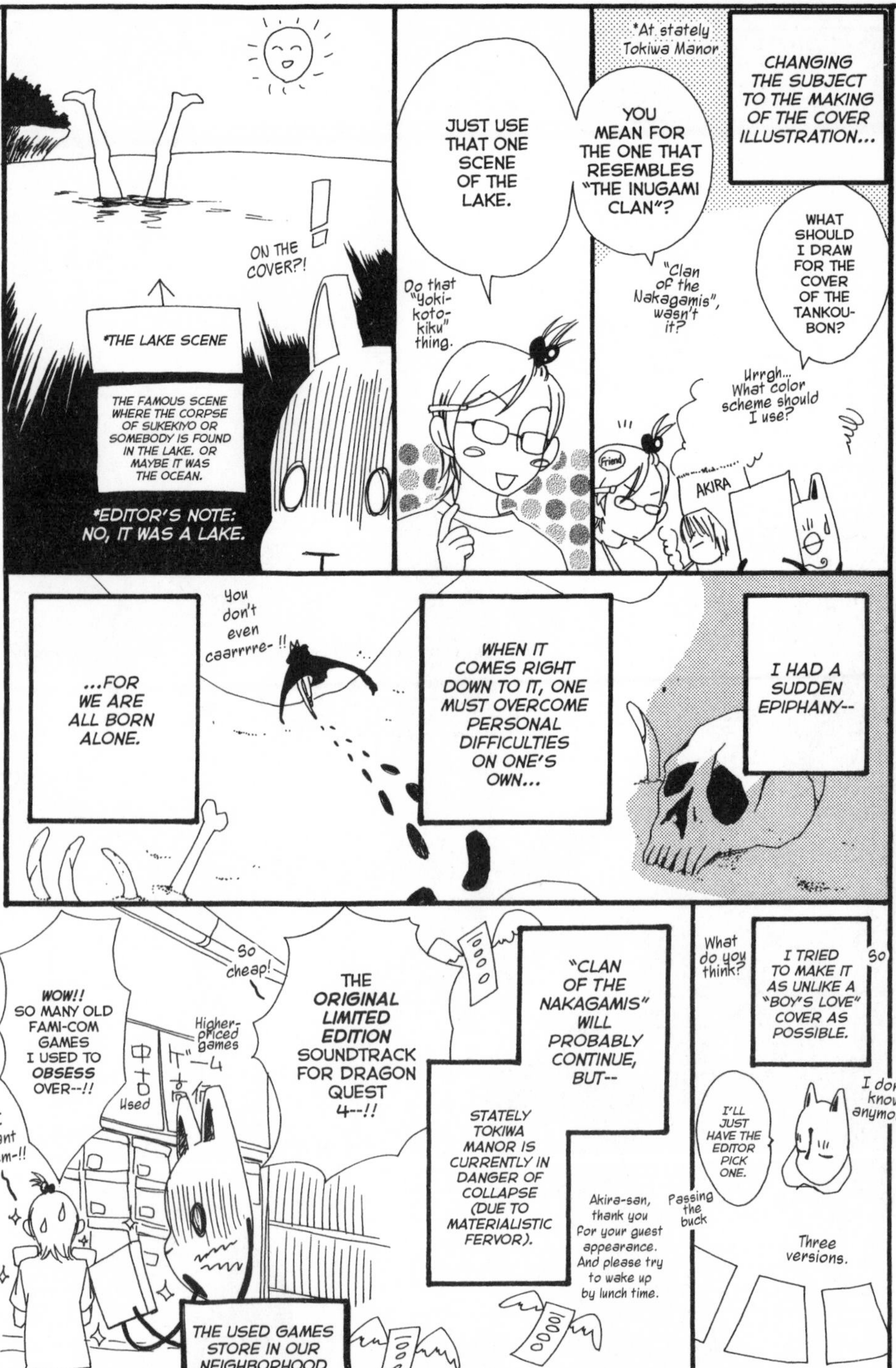

CHANGING THE SUBJECT TO THE MAKING OF THE COVER ILLUSTRATION...
*At stately Tokiwa Manor
WHAT SHOULD I DRAW FOR THE COVER OF THE TANKOUBON?
YOU MEAN FOR THE ONE THAT RESEMBLES "THE INUGAMI CLAN"?
"Clan of the Nakagamis", wasn't it?
Urrgh... What color scheme should I use?
Friend
AKIRA
JUST USE THAT ONE SCENE OF THE LAKE.
Do that "Yoki-koto-kiku" thing.
!
ON THE COVER?!
*THE LAKE SCENE
THE FAMOUS SCENE WHERE THE CORPSE OF SUKEKIYO OR SOMEBODY IS FOUND IN THE LAKE. OR MAYBE IT WAS THE OCEAN.
*EDITOR'S NOTE: NO, IT WAS A LAKE.
I HAD A SUDDEN EPIPHANY--
WHEN IT COMES RIGHT DOWN TO IT, ONE MUST OVERCOME PERSONAL DIFFICULTIES ON ONE'S OWN...
You don't even caarrrre-!!
...FOR WE ARE ALL BORN ALONE.
So
I TRIED TO MAKE IT AS UNLIKE A "BOY'S LOVE" COVER AS POSSIBLE.
What do you think?
I don't know anymore.
I'LL JUST HAVE THE EDITOR PICK ONE.
Passing the buck
Three versions.
"CLAN OF THE NAKAGAMIS" WILL PROBABLY CONTINUE, BUT--
STATELY TOKIWA MANOR IS CURRENTLY IN DANGER OF COLLAPSE (DUE TO MATERIALISTIC FERVOR).
Akira-san, thank you for your guest appearance. And please try to wake up by lunch time.
THE ORIGINAL LIMITED EDITION SOUNDTRACK FOR DRAGON QUEST 4--!!
So cheap!
WOW!! SO MANY OLD FAMI-COM GAMES I USED TO OBSESS OVER--!!
Higher-priced games
Used
I want them-!!
THE USED GAMES STORE IN OUR NEIGHBORHOOD

*WHAT IS STATELY TOKIWA MANOR?!...THE RESIDENCE OF HOMERUN KEN SENSEI AND OLDER SISTER NORIKAZU AKIRA SENSEI, A PLACE WHERE BIG LEAGUE MANGA ARTISTS ARE NURTURED.

Nakagami
Gokurakuchohta

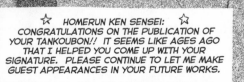

☆ HOMERUN KEN SENSEI: ☆
CONGRATULATIONS ON THE PUBLICATION OF
YOUR TANKOUBON!! IT SEEMS LIKE AGES AGO
THAT I HELPED YOU COME UP WITH YOUR
SIGNATURE. PLEASE CONTINUE TO LET ME MAKE
GUEST APPEARANCES IN YOUR FUTURE WORKS.

YOUR ACTUAL OLDER SISTER, NORIKAZU AKIRA

Hybrid Child

by Shungiki Nakamura

Half machine...
Half human...

What can your Hybrid Child do for you?

ISBN# 1-56970-902-5 $12.95

Hybrid Child © Shungiku Nakamura 2005.
Originally published in Japan in 2005 by BIBLOS Co. Ltd

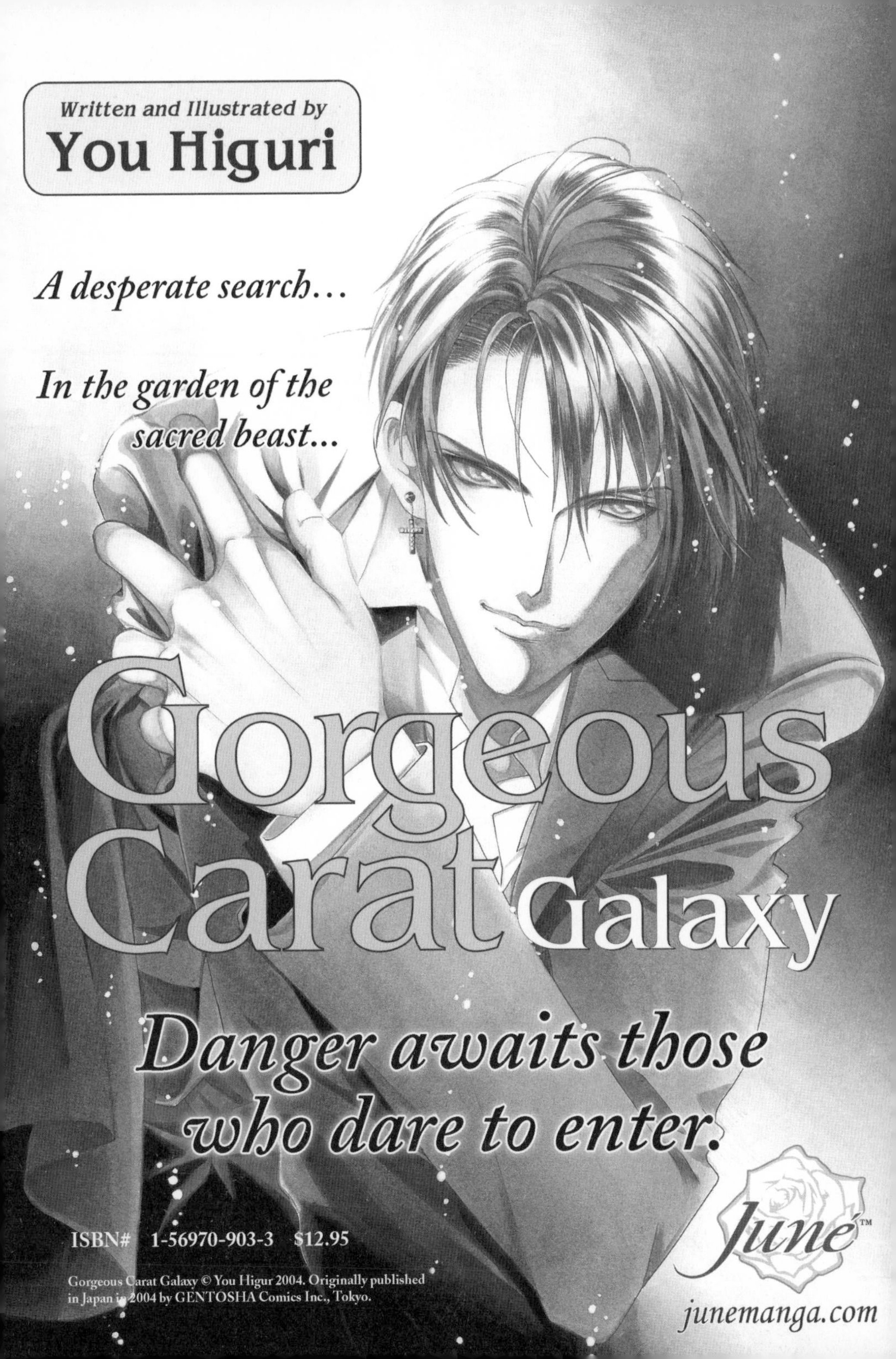
Written and Illustrated by
You Higuri
A desperate search…
In the garden of the sacred beast…
Gorgeous Carat Galaxy
Danger awaits those who dare to enter.
ISBN# 1-56970-903-3 $12.95
Gorgeous Carat Galaxy © You Higur 2004. Originally published in Japan in 2004 by GENTOSHA Comics Inc., Tokyo.
Juné™
junemanga.com

THE DAY OF REVOLUTION

MIKIYO TSUDA

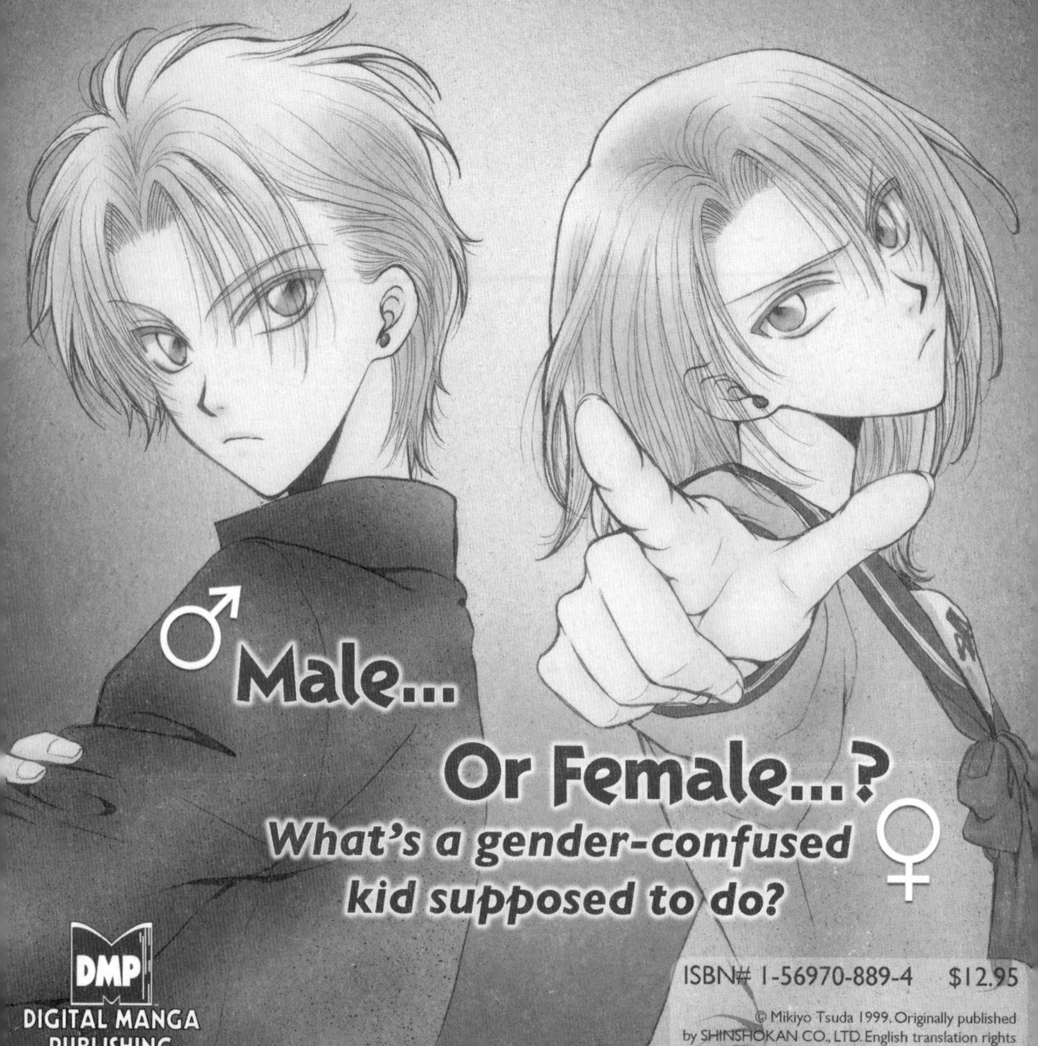

♂ Male...

Or Female...? ♀

What's a gender-confused kid supposed to do?

DMP
DIGITAL MANGA PUBLISHING

ISBN# 1-56970-889-4 $12.95

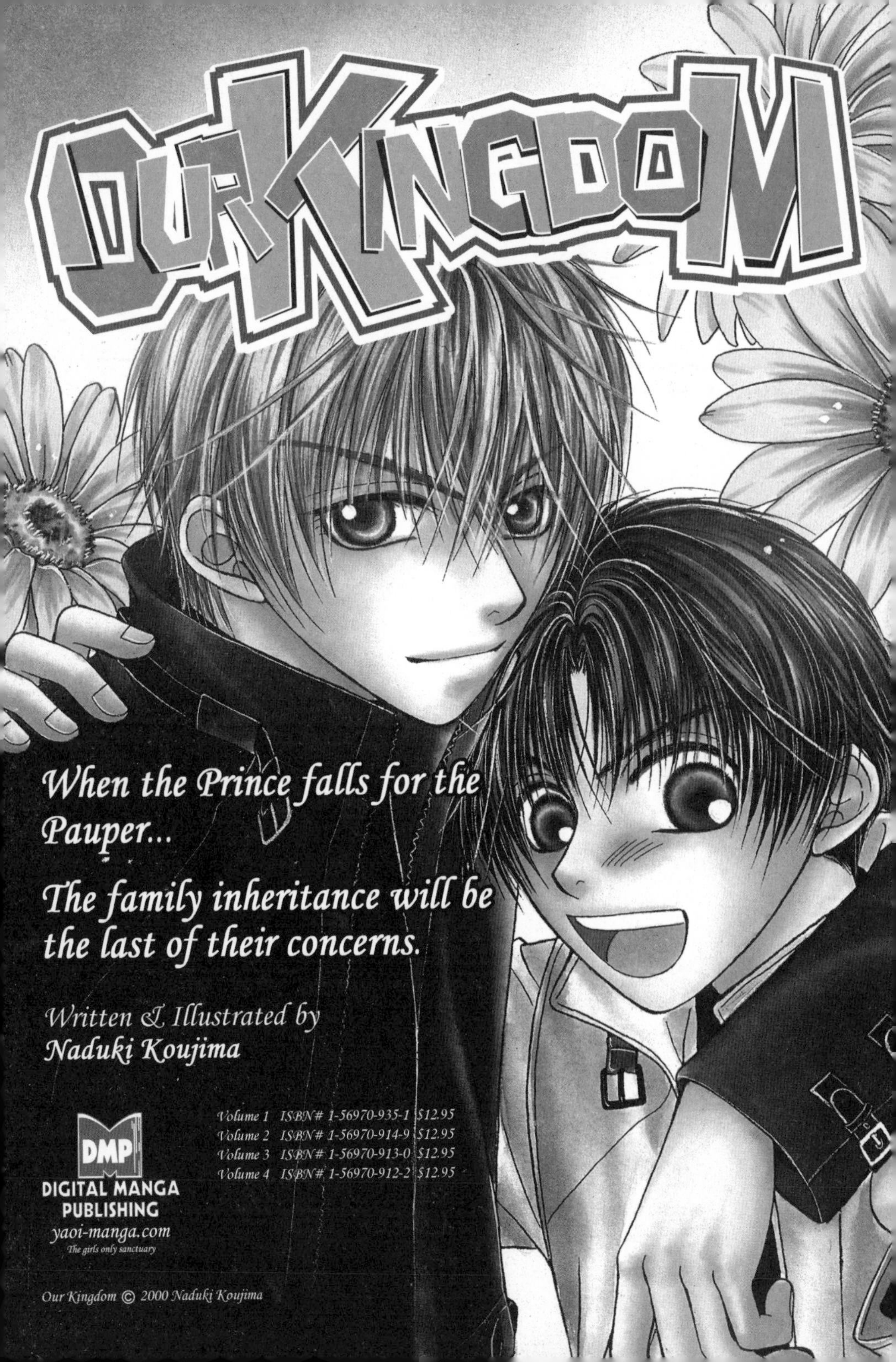
OUR KINGDOM
When the Prince falls for the Pauper...
The family inheritance will be the last of their concerns.
Written & Illustrated by
Naduki Koujima
Volume 1 ISBN# 1-56970-935-1 $12.95
Volume 2 ISBN# 1-56970-914-9 $12.95
Volume 3 ISBN# 1-56970-913-0 $12.95
Volume 4 ISBN# 1-56970-912-2 $12.95
DMP
DIGITAL MANGA PUBLISHING
yaoi-manga.com
The girls only sanctuary
Our Kingdom © 2000 Naduki Koujima

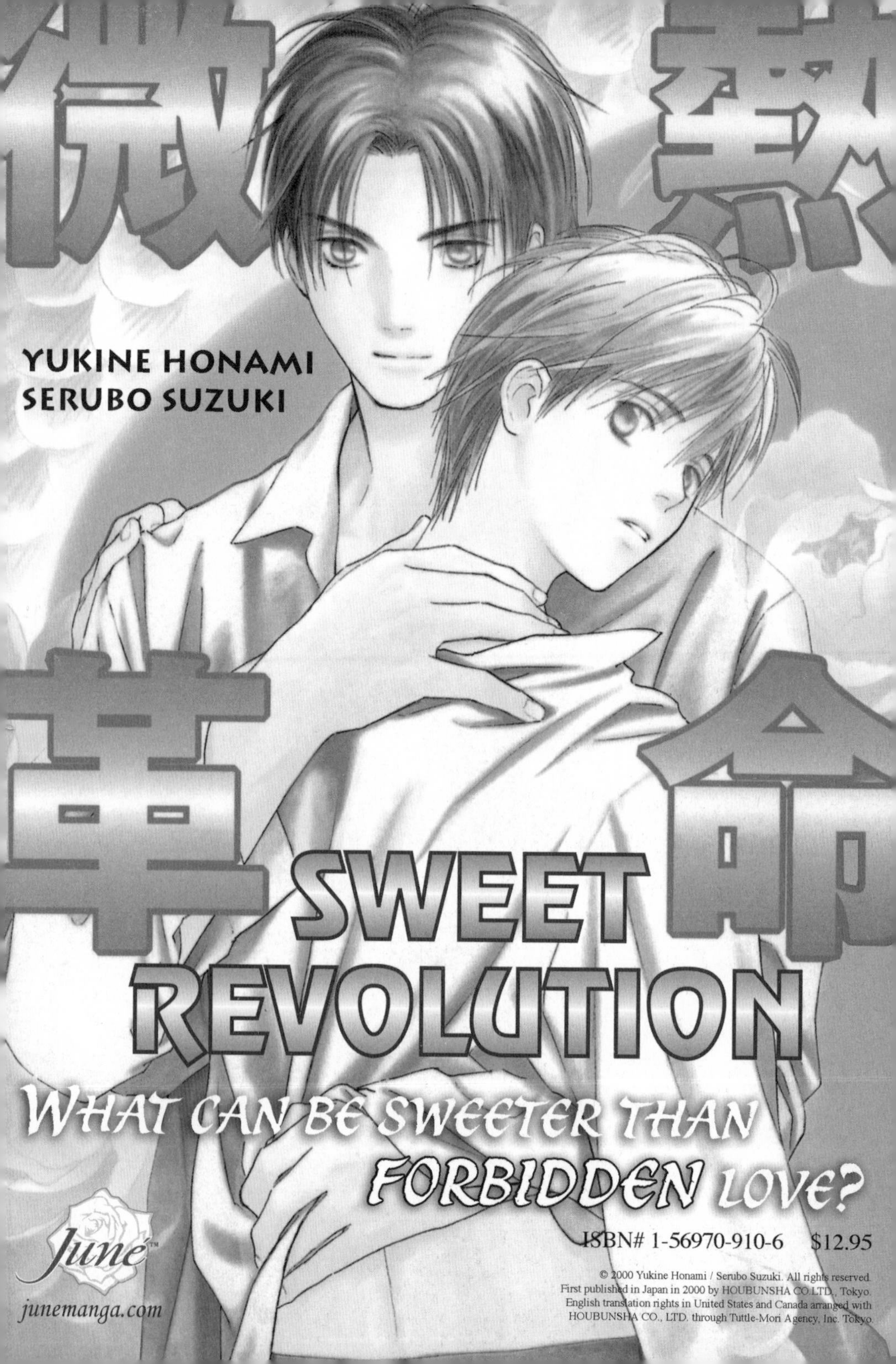
微熱
YUKINE HONAMI
SERUBO SUZUKI
革命
SWEET REVOLUTION
WHAT CAN BE SWEETER THAN FORBIDDEN LOVE?
June™
junemanga.com
ISBN# 1-56970-910-6 $12.95
© 2000 Yukine Honami / Serubo Suzuki. All rights reserved.
First published in Japan in 2000 by HOUBUNSHA CO.LTD., Tokyo.
English translation rights in United States and Canada arranged with
HOUBUNSHA CO., LTD. through Tuttle-Mori Agency, Inc. Tokyo.

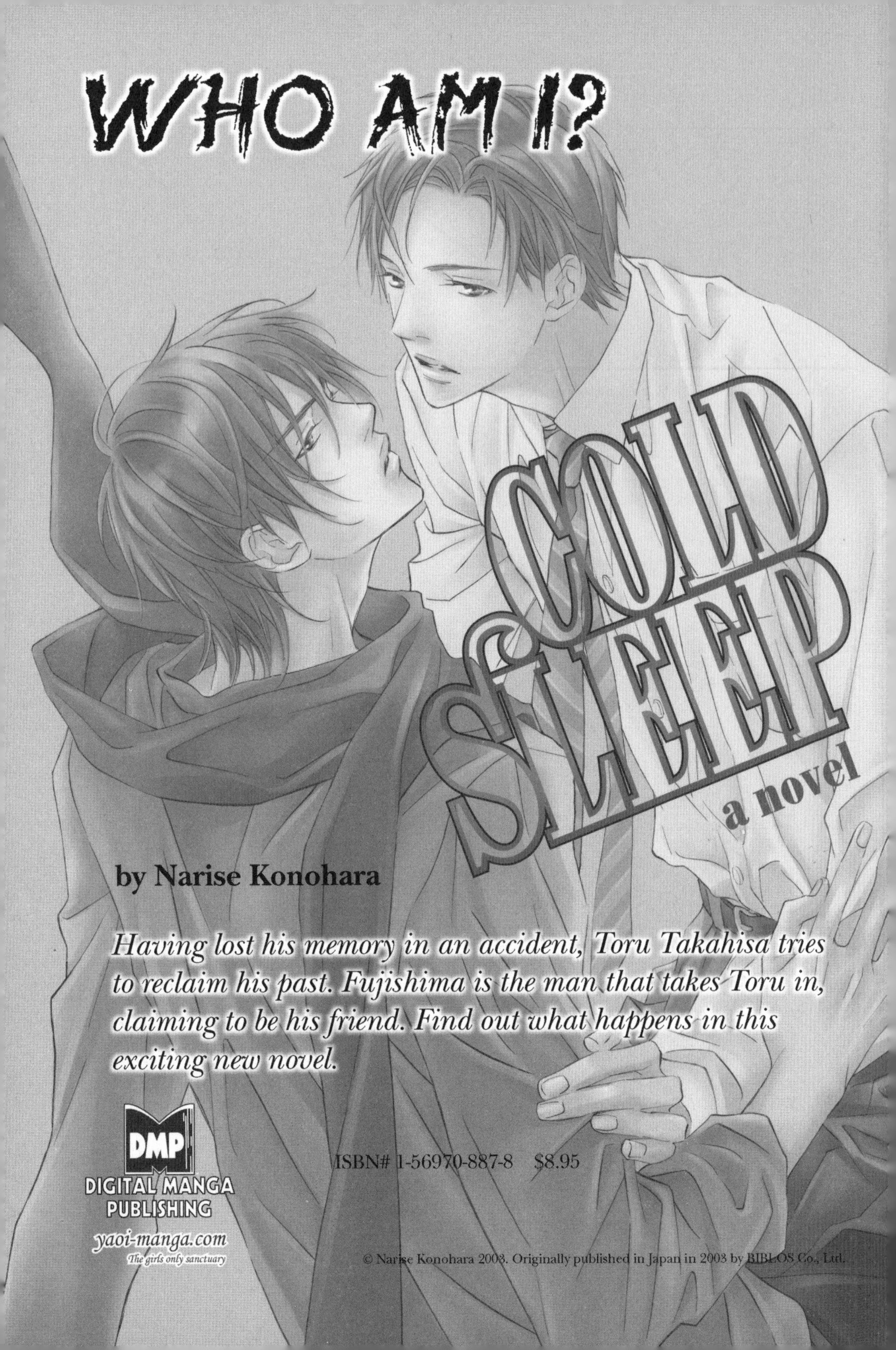
WHO AM I?
COLD SLEEP
a novel
by Narise Konohara
Having lost his memory in an accident, Toru Takahisa tries to reclaim his past. Fujishima is the man that takes Toru in, claiming to be his friend. Find out what happens in this exciting new novel.
DMP
DIGITAL MANGA PUBLISHING
yaoi-manga.com
The girls only sanctuary
ISBN# 1-56970-887-8 $8.95
© Narise Konohara 2003. Originally published in Japan in 2003 by BIBLOS Co., Ltd.

STOP

This is the back of the book! Start from the other side.

NATIVE MANGA readers read manga from *right to left*.

1
2
1
3
2
3
5
4
4
6
5
7
8
6

*If you run into our **Native Manga** logo on any of our books... you'll know that this manga is published in it's true original native Japanese right to left reading format, as it was intended. Turn to the other side of the book and start reading from right to left, top to bottom.*

Follow the diagram to see how its done.
Surf's Up!

NATIVE MANGA
READ RIGHT TO LEFT

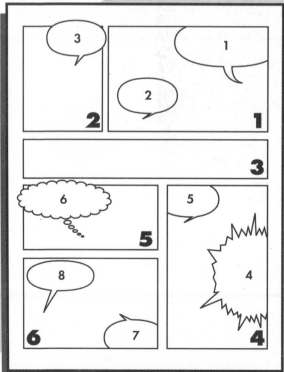

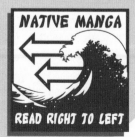